For Reference

Not to be taken from this room

ASIAN AMERICANS

OTHER RECENT VOLUMES IN THE
SAGE FOCUS EDITIONS

ASIAN AMERICANS

Contemporary Trends and Issues

Pyong Gap Min
editor

SAGE Publications
International Educational and Professional Publisher
Thousand Oaks   London   New Delhi

S

Copyright © 1995 by Sage Publications, Inc.

For information address:

SAGE Publications, Inc.
2455 Teller Road
Thousand Oaks, California 91320

SAGE Publications Ltd.
6 Bonhill Street
London EC2A 4PU
United Kingdom

SAGE Publications India Pvt. Ltd.
M-32 Market
Greater Kailash I
New Delhi 110 048 India

Printed in the United States of America

Library of Congress Cataloging-in-Publication Data

Min, Pyong Gap, 1942-
    Asian Americans: Contemporary trends and issues / Pyong Gap Min.
      p. cm. — (Sage focus editions: 174)
    Includes bibliographical references and index.
    ISBN 0-8039-4335-0 (cloth). — ISBN 0-8039-4336-9 (pbk.)
      1. Asian Americans.   2. Title.
  E184.06M56   1995
  973'.0495—dc20   94-37827

95 96 97 98 99 10 9 8 7 6 5 4 3 2 1

Sage Production Editor: Diane S. Foster

Contents

Acknowledgments

I would like to acknowledge several people who have assisted me in completing this book project over the last 4 years. First of all, I wish to thank Lisamarie Stermann and Erica Klusner, two graduate students, for editing several versions of the manuscript to make the writing styles less scholarly and more lively for student readers. Second, Yo Han Choi, a Queens College undergraduate student, has helped me with library research using 1990 census reports. Critical comments by several anonymous reviewers and by Mitch Allen, the editor at Sage, have guided me in organizing the book in its current form. Finally, I wish to thank Frances Borghi, Tricia Bennett, Diane Foster, and Jacqueline Tasch from Sage Publications for quickly processing and editing the manuscript.

1

Introduction

PYONG GAP MIN

After the California Gold Rush in 1848, a large number of Chinese workers were brought to California to be used as cheap labor for mining and railroad construction. The Chinese Exclusion Act of 1882 and the ensuing rampant racial violence against Chinese workers pushed most Chinese workers away from California. After the Chinese were legally barred from entry into the United States, plantation and farm owners in Hawaii and California began to bring in Japanese, Filipino, Korean, and Indian workers. But laws passed in the early 1920s barred Asian nationals from entering the United States for about 40 years. Many Japanese and Korean women came to the United States as wives of American servicemen after World War II and the Korean War. Nevertheless, until 1970, the Asian American population had been kept to a relatively small number.

The liberalization of the U.S. immigration law in 1965 made the mass migration of people from Asian countries to the United States possible. More than 200,000 Asian immigrants have been admitted to the United States annually over the last 2 decades, accounting for about 45% of total immigrants to this country. As a result, the Asian American population increased from 1.5 million in 1970 to about 7.3 million in 1990. Heavily concentrated in Los Angeles, New York, and several other large cities, Asian Americans in general and several Asian ethnic groups in particular have emerged as significant minority groups, making American race and ethnic relations far more complicated than before.

Asians' trans-Pacific migration to major American cities has significantly changed their lives in terms of traditional customs, values, and other

1

elements of lifestyle. However, Asian immigrants also affect the cities where they settle. The presence of Asian immigrants in large numbers has a significant impact on the economy, politics, education, culture, social services, and, most important, intergroup relations in cities. In 1993, Michael Woo, a long-time Chinese American city councilman in Los Angeles, won the Democratic Party primary for mayor of Los Angeles. Although he was defeated in the general election by the Republican candidate, his selection as a candidate for mayor in the second-largest city in the United States says much about the impact of post-1965 Asian immigration on politics in many California cities. The 1990 black boycott of two Korean retail produce stores in Brooklyn received national media headlines. The Brooklyn boycott and the victimization of Korean merchants during the 1992 Los Angeles riots symbolize the repercussions of the new Asian immigration on intergroup conflicts in large American cities.

The impact of the massive migration of Asians is most keenly felt in major American universities. Their higher socioeconomic status and emphasis on children's education have enabled post-1965 Asian immigrants to send their children to prestigious universities in a much higher proportion than their share of the population. Although Asian Americans account for only 3% of the U.S. population, they constitute over 30% of the students at several University of California campuses, including UC Berkeley, UCLA, and UC Irvine, and over 15% in many prestigious state and private universities, including Columbia, Cornell, and Harvard. As long as the current influx of Asian immigrants continues, the proportion of Asian American students at elite universities will increase at a faster rate than the overall population.

The dramatic increase in the number and proportion of Asian American students over the last 2 decades has in turn influenced curriculums and academic programs in many colleges and universities. Under pressure from Asian American students, many universities in the University of California system and other major American universities have established Asian American studies programs and offer many Asian American courses. Other colleges and universities lack an Asian American studies program but offer Asian American courses to meet the growing needs of the Asian American student population. As the number and proportion of Asian American students continue to increase on many campuses, more and more colleges and universities are expected to offer Asian American courses.

To meet the growing demands, several books have recently been published for use as textbooks in Asian American courses at colleges and universities. Three popular examples are: *Strangers from a Different*

Shore: A History of Asian Americans, by Ronald Takaki (1989), *Asian Americans: An Interpretive History,* by Suchen Chan (1991), and *Asian Americans: Emerging Minorities* by Harry Kitano and Roger Daniels (1988). Although all three books, particularly those by Takaki and Chan, are well-written, they lack information on issues and variables important to sociology. The first two books were written by historians, and the third was the collaboration of a historian and a scholar in the field of social work. This explains why all three books take a largely historical approach. It is not surprising that the three books, particularly those by Takaki and Chan, effectively detail the history of immigration and adjustment for each Asian ethnic group. The books are less effective in providing sociological data and discussing issues such as labor force participation and economic status, intermarriage patterns, and women's gender role changes.

This book intends to fill that gap. Although it adequately covers history, its main value lies in providing data on sociologically important variables and presenting discussions on sociological issues for Asian Americans as a whole and for each Asian group individually. Most of the authors are sociologists familiar with their field's issues and theories. Although individual contributors place different degrees of emphasis on the sociological approach, all contributors have made every effort to cover topics such as occupational and economic adjustment, assimilation and ethnicity, intermarriage, intergroup relations, and settlement patterns.

Chapter 3, which summarizes major contemporary issues concerning the experiences of Asian Americans as a whole, has selected sociologically important issues. Moreover, Chapter 2 and the six chapters on the six major Asian ethnic groups include tables that provide sociologically important data not available in the historically oriented textbooks.

Traditionally, journalists and scholars have emphasized Asian Americans' successful socioeconomic adjustment and their cultural mechanisms for success: work ethic, family ties, and emphasis on children's education. Since the early 1970s, an increasing number of Asian American scholars have disputed various cultural explanations and attacked the success image of Asian Americans (also known as the "model minority" thesis). Instead, they have stressed structural factors such as racism, institutional barriers, and discrimination, which Asian Americans have historically encountered. This structural approach and the critique of the model minority thesis currently dominate Asian American studies. Following that dominant pattern of scholarship, this book largely takes the structural approach, focusing on adjustment difficulties due to discrimination and other forms of social barriers rather than on Asian American success stories. Even when discussing families and cultures of particular Asian groups, this book has considered the effects of Asian Americans' adaptation on them.

We could organize a book on Asian Americans in three different ways. First, we could organize it by ethnic groups. The book by Kitano and Daniels (1988) is a good example of this approach, with each chapter covering one ethnic group. Second, we could organize it chronologically, starting with Chinese immigration in 1850. Two of the three above-mentioned works on Asian Americans, one by Takaki (1988) and the other by Chan (1991), present Asian American history largely in chronological order. Third, we can organize the book by various topics and issues. *Counterpoint: Perspectives on Asian America,* edited by Emma Gee (1976), was organized by topic.

This book has taken the first approach; Chapters 4 to 9 cover the six major Asian ethnic groups individually. Each of the six chapters focuses on a particular group, providing a comprehensive overview of that group. Although the six chapters differ somewhat in focus and content, all cover most of the following topics: immigration history, historical cases of discrimination, settlement patterns, socioeconomic adjustment, ethnicity and assimilation, intermarriage patterns, and marital and family adjustment. With the exception of Rubén Rumbaut, the authors wrote about their own ethnic groups and were therefore able to provide insider's knowledge about the cultures and family systems.

A book organized by ethnic groups is quite effective in providing undergraduate students, social workers, and others studying Asian Americans with descriptive information on each Asian ethnic group. However, it is limited in introducing advanced readers to the theoretical and practical issues pertaining to Asian Americans as a whole. To ameliorate this problem, this book devotes the next two chapters to Asian Americans as a whole. I hope these two chapters provide general information on Asian Americans and some of the important issues and theories concerning their collective experiences.

Let me summarize the focus and content of each chapter. Chapter 2, prepared by this editor, provides an overview of Asian Americans. The topics covered in this chapter are: the influx of Asian immigrants and the expansion of the Asian American population in the last two decades, the urban middle-class characteristics of the new Asian immigrants, settlement patterns of Asian Americans, their diversity, and Pan Asian unity. This chapter includes tables based on the 1990 census. It should be a good guide to students, social workers, policy makers, and lay people who want general information and statistics on the Asian American population.

Chapter 3, also written by the editor, offers a brief summary of major issues concerning the Asian American experience and, if available, relevant theoretical perspectives helpful in understanding these issues. I used two criteria in selecting major issues. First, as already indicated, I tried to include sociologically important issues relating to contemporary Asian American communities. Second, I selected issues and theories related to racism, structural barriers, and adjustment difficulties, issues that critics of the model minority thesis consider important to understand Asian American experiences. Using theories emphasizing structural barriers, the so-called "revisionist scholars" recently tried to reinterpret Asian Americans' socioeconomic adjustment, education, and family and marital life. Chapter 3 devotes much space to clarifying revisionist interpretations and issues and theories revisionist scholars consider important. Whereas Chapter 2 provides readers with a general, descriptive overview of Asian Americans as a group, Chapter 3 is intended to help readers understand different aspects of contemporary Asian American experiences from a critical outlook.

The next six chapters cover each major Asian ethnic group individually. Chapter 4 by Morrison G. Wong is devoted to Chinese Americans, the largest Asian ethnic group with the longest history in the United States. Wong's chapter reflects the structural approach more clearly than any other chapter in this book. His section on Chinese immigration history focuses on discriminatory policies and restrictive measures. The "institutional" or structural approach to Chinese American families is currently popular in reaction to various cultural explanations (see Chapter 3). Using the same institutional framework, Wong describes four different periods of change for Chinese families. His analysis of Chinese Americans' occupational and economic adjustments is structural: He interprets their adjustments as reactions to occupational discrimination and the opportunity structure in three different periods. He emphasizes the bipolar occupational distribution in the current Chinese community, discussed in Chapter 3 as one of the major issues concerning the socioeconomic adjustments of Asian Americans, particularly Chinese Americans. Wong's discussion of the other three major topics concerning Chinese Americans' experiences—education, Chinatowns, and modes of adaptation—also reflects his structural approach. Therefore, people who like the structural approach should particularly enjoy this chapter.

Chapter 5, by Setsuko Matsunaga Nishi, covers Japanese Americans, the group with the second-longest history of immigration and settlement in the United States, next to the Chinese. Due to the high standard of living in Japan, few Japanese immigrated to the United States in the post-1965 era.

Thus the vast majority of Japanese Americans are American born, whereas the opposite is true of other Asian groups. Because recent immigrants constitute a small proportion of Japanese Americans, Nishi devotes more space to their historical experiences than their current status. She focuses in particular on the Japanese American internment during World War II, its effects on the Japanese community and family life during the postwar era, and the redress movement. As a victim of the internment herself, Nishi testified before the Commission on Wartime Relocation and Internment of Civilians and conducted research on social and psychological effects of the internment. Because of her personal involvement, her analysis of the internment is very revealing.

Chapter 6, by Pauline Agbayani-Siewert and Linda Revilla, covers Filipino Americans, the second-largest Asian ethnic group, next to Chinese Americans. Among Asian countries during the last two decades, the Philippines has annually sent the largest number of immigrants, approximately 45,000 per year. The Philippines is a culturally heterogeneous country with many languages. This cultural diversity, combined with a long history of colonization, contributes to the factionalism and disunity that characterize the Filipino American community. Filipino Americans' adjustment significantly differs from other Asian groups, and the authors delineate the adjustment patterns unique to them. For example, recent Filipino immigrants consist mainly of highly educated professionals with good English skills, perhaps partially explaining why they have not established ethnic enclaves comparable to Chinatown or Koreatown. The authors also discuss Filipino Americans' unique socioeconomic adjustment patterns, characterized by a lower college enrollment rate and a lower self-employment rate but by a higher female labor force participation rate than other Asian groups. A social worker (Agbayani-Siewert) and social psychologist (Revilla), the authors include such topics as mail-order brides, the traditional Filipino family structure, and Filipino immigrants' marital and generational conflicts. As discussed in Chapter 3, a new trend in research on Asian immigrant families emphasizes marital and generational conflicts rather than family ties. This chapter reflects this new trend.

Chapter 7, by Manju Sheth, focuses on Indian Americans, another new Asian ethnic group to emerge in the post-1965 era. Indian immigrants, like Filipino immigrants, generally have strong educational and professional backgrounds. In contrast to other Asian groups highly concentrated in California, the largest group of Indian Americans live in the New York-New Jersey metropolitan area. Consistent with the structural approach of this book, Sheth focuses on racism, discriminatory measures, prejudice, and anti-Indian violence that earlier and contemporary Indian immigrants encountered in the United States. She also provides a historical analysis of Indian political movements to protect their civil rights and interests. Sheth points out that Indian immigrants identify themselves with particular regional-linguistic subgroups, not with the Indian national origin group. She indicates that religious places and organizations, Indian and ethnic newspapers, television, videotapes, and visits to their homeland all facilitate Indians' ethnic identity.

Chapter 8, by the editor, deals with Korean Americans. Along with the Indians and Vietnamese, they make up one of the new Asian ethnic groups that have grown rapidly since the liberalization of the immigration law in 1965. Because the vast majority of Korean Americans are post-1965 immigrants, this chapter focuses on new immigrants' adjustment and devotes little space to historical analyses of the pre-1965 immigrants and their descendants. Concentration in small business is a unique aspect of Korean immigrants' economic adjustment. This chapter therefore devotes much space to immigrants' small-business activities and their business-related intergroup conflicts, particularly conflicts with blacks. The section on "Ethnicity and Assimilation" discusses Korean immigrants' advantages in maintaining ethnic ties and their disadvantages in assimilating. Korean immigrants' cultural homogeneity and economic segregation enhance their ethnic ties but hinder their assimilation. Business-related intergroup conflicts have enhanced ethnic solidarity. This section provides an extended discussion on how the victimization of Korean merchants during the Los Angeles riots affected ethnic solidarity. Affiliation of Korean immigrant families with ethnic churches also facilitates their ethnicity. Like the chapter on Filipino Americans, this chapter pays great attention to marital and generational conflicts.

Chapter 9, by Rubén G. Rumbaut, covers Indochinese refugees, with a focus on Vietnamese refugees. Rumbaut has conducted more research on Indochinese refugees than any other social scientist. Because most Indochinese Americans came as refugees after the fall of South Vietnam in 1975, their experience fundamentally differs from other Asian immigrant groups. Rumbaut emphasizes that, although refugees of the Indochinese war share a common history and experiences, the various Indochinese subgroups—Vietnamese, Cambodians, Laotians, and ethnic Chinese from all three countries—have different social backgrounds, languages, cultures, and often adversarial histories. He contends that these differences in preimmigrant background contribute to different patterns of settlement and adaptation in the United States. The federal government funded a series of surveys on representative national samples of the Indochinese population. Rumbaut uses the results of these national sample surveys to analyze patterns of occupational and economic adaptation by ethnic groups and cohorts of arrival. Social scientists conducted many community surveys, ethnographic studies, and epidemiological and clinical studies on Indochinese refugee experiences. Using these studies, the author summarizes the socioeconomic backgrounds, exit experiences, health status, employment and labor force participation status, and other related adaptation characteristics of Indochinese refugees settled in particular cities.

Chapter 10, by the editor, speculates on future prospects of Asian Americans. The chapter focuses on changes in four areas. First, the phenomenal growth in the Asian American population and its concentration in several cities will enable Asian Americans to have a greater impact on social institutions in the cities of their concentration. Second, Americans will accept Asian Americans and their subcultures more positively in the future than they do now. Third, native-born Asian American adults, whose number will increase in the future at a faster rate than the total Asian American population, are likely to experience fewer problems in socioeconomic adjustment: unequal rewards from human capital investments, underrepresentation in managerial and executive positions, and class polarization. Fourth, descendants of post-1965 Asian immigrants will achieve a high level of cultural assimilation, but will maintain strong ethnic identity and social interactions with co-ethnics. In addition, they will maintain a stronger Pan-Asian identity and solidarity than their immigrant parents.

This book is prepared mainly for undergraduate and graduate Asian American courses. Each chapter provides a comprehensive reference list to help readers locate articles and books on particular issues or groups. In addition, Chapter 3, as well as the reference lists, are expected to be of great help to those who conduct research on Asian Americans. Although this book is directed mainly at Asian American courses, I believe it can be of great use to anyone—social worker, school teacher, or lay person—who wants to learn about Asian ethnic groups. All chapters focusing on particular ethnic groups, with the exception of the chapter on Indochinese refugees, discuss the marital and family adjustment of each group. This information on marital and family adjustment is likely to be very useful, particularly for social workers and school teachers who work with Asian American clientele and students.

References

Chan, S. (1991). *Asian Americans: An interpretive history.* Boston: Twayne.

Gee, E. (Ed.). (1976). *Counterpoint: Perspectives on Asian America.* Los Angeles: Asian American Studies Center, UCLA.

Kitano, H., & Daniels, R. (1988). *Asian Americans: Emerging minorities.* Englewood Cliffs, NJ: Prentice Hall.

Takaki, R. (1989). *Strangers from a different shore: A history of Asian Americans.* Boston: Little, Brown.

2

An Overview of Asian Americans

PYONG GAP MIN

This chapter provides an overview of Asian Americans, who comprise various groups diverse in culture, socioeconomic status, and generation. There are many significant topics and issues relevant to Asian American experiences. Therefore, it is almost impossible to provide an overall picture of Asian Americans in such a short chapter. This chapter presents data and introduces topics most useful for understanding current Asian American communities and their personal and collective experiences. The first section discusses how the Immigration Act of 1965 resulted in the influx of the new Asian immigrants. The urban, middle-class background of these new immigrants is the focus of the second section. The third section gives information on Asian American settlement patterns. Many American educators, social workers, and the general public tend to assume that Asian Americans are a homogeneous group. On the contrary, Asian Americans are quite diverse. The fourth section focuses on the diversity of Asian Americans and challenges the commonly held assumptions. The last section discusses the common threads that link all Asian Americans and that can be the bases for Pan-Asian ethnicity.

The 1965 Immigration Act and the Influx of Asian Immigrants

Asian immigration started in the mid-19th century when large numbers of Chinese laborers came to California to work in mining and railroad construction. However, in the late 19th and early 20th centuries, the U.S.

government took several discriminatory steps to prevent Asians from immigrating to the United States (see Chapters 4, 5, 6, and 7 for restrictive measures taken against the early Chinese, Japanese, Filipino, and Indian immigrants). As a result, the Asian American population was insignificant in size until the late 1960s. U.S. census data show that in 1960 Asian Americans numbered less than 900,000 (Xenos, Gardner, Barringer, & Levin, 1987). In the 1960s, Asian Americans were invisible to the American general public, except in several cities in Hawaii, California, Washington, and New York.

The Influx of Asian Immigrants

In 1965 the U.S. Congress passed the most liberal immigration law to date, known as the Immigration Act of 1965. The law came into full effect in 1968, opening the door to immigration from all countries by abolishing discrimination based on national origin. Asiatic exclusion had eliminated Asians from quota immigration for nearly 40 years. The new immigration law abolished Asiatic exclusion and allowed aliens to be admitted as immigrants using three criteria:

1. Their possession of occupational skills needed in the U.S. labor market (occupational immigration)
2. Their close relationships to those already here (family reunification)
3. Their vulnerability to political and religious persecution

An immigration quota of 20,000 was set for each country. Under the new immigration law, unmarried children under 21 years of age, spouses, fiancees, and parents of U.S. citizens could be admitted as "special immigrants," exempt from the quota limitation. Pastors and longtime overseas employees of the U.S. government could also be admitted as special immigrants, not restricted by the national quota. Therefore, each country could actually send more than 20,000 immigrants to the United States per year.

One major effect of the new immigration law was a shift in the major source of immigrants from European to non-European countries. Under the old immigration law, Asians and other non-European aliens were almost eliminated from quota immigration.[1] Therefore, European countries sent the vast majority of immigrants. By abolishing discrimination based on national origin, however, the 1965 Immigration Act opened the door to accelerated immigration from Asia, South America, and the Caribbean Islands. In 1960, Europeans constituted approximately 80% of total immigrants, and 8 of the 10 largest immigrant source countries were European (Arnold, Minocha, & Fawcett, 1987). Since 1965, the proportion of European immigrants has steadily decreased. In 1984, immigrants from European countries were only 18% of the total, and all 10 major source countries were non-European (Arnold et al., 1987).

The proportion of Asian immigrants increased from 9% in 1960 to 25% in 1970 and 44% in 1980 (see Table 2.1). Between 1980 and 1988, Asians made up 40% to 47% of the total U.S. immigrants. After Mexico, the Philippines and South Korea were the second- and third-largest source countries of immigrants. Three other Asian countries—China, India, and Vietnam—were among the 10 major source countries of U.S. immigrants in the 1980s. The share of Asian immigrants decreased between 1989 and 1992, mainly because a large number of Mexican and other Hispanic aliens legalized their status through the Immigration Reform and Control Act of 1986.[2] Due to the legalization, the total number of annual immigrants to the United States exceeded over 1 million during the period.

U.S. policy makers in the late 1960s and early 1970s never expected this phenomenal increase in immigration from Asian countries. At that time, because only a small number of Asian Americans were U.S. citizens, a relatively small number of Asians immigrated as relatives of U.S. citizens. However, many Asian immigrants have become naturalized citizens since the mid-1970s and have invited their spouses, children, parents, and brothers/sisters with their own families to join them in the United States.

The economic recession in the early 1970s forced the federal government to revise the 1965 Immigration Act in 1976, severely curtailing the entry of occupational immigrants. In the 1980s, as a result of this revision, more than 90% of nonrefugee immigrant visas were annually given to aliens with relatives in the United States. The 1976 revision restricted the immigration of Asian professionals, particularly Asian medical professionals (Yochum & Agarwal, 1988). However, the drastic reduction of occupational immigrants and the concomitant increase in family reunification immigrants helped new immigrant groups, including Asian groups, to bring more immigrants here. Using different family reunification categories, Asian immigrant groups brought increasing numbers of relatives to the United States in the 1980s.

The Immigration Act of 1990, which further revised the 1965 Immigration Act, intends to significantly increase the number of employment-based immigrants and temporary foreign workers. This new law is thus expected to increase the number of immigrants from European countries by bringing more occupational immigrants. Yet it is unlikely to reduce the immigration

Table 2.1 Annual Asian Immigrants by Country of Birth, 1960, 1965-1992

Year	All Countries (A)	All Asian Countries (B)	B as % of A	China[a]	Japan	The Philippines	Korea	India	Vietnam
1960	265,398	23,864	9.0	3,681	5,471	2,954	1,507	391	—
1965	296,697	19,788	6.7	4,057	3,180	3,130	2,165	582	—
1966	323,040	39,878	12.3	13,736	3,394	6,093	2,492	2,458	275
1967	361,972	59,233	16.4	19,741	3,946	10,865	3,956	4,642	490
1968	454,448	57,229	12.6	12,738	3,613	16,731	3,811	4,682	590
1969	358,579	73,621	20.5	15,440	3,957	20,744	6,045	5,963	983
1970	373,326	92,816	24.9	14,093	4,485	31,203	9,314	10,114	1,450
1971	370,478	103,461	27.9	14,417	4,357	28,471	14,297	14,310	2,038
1972	384,685	121,058	31.5	17,339	4,757	29,376	18,876	16,926	3,412
1973	400,063	124,160	31.0	17,297	5,461	30,799	22,930	13,124	4,569
1974	394,861	130,662	33.1	18,056	4,860	32,857	28,028	12,779	3,192
1975	386,194	132,469	34.3	18,536	4,274	31,751	28,362	15,733	3,039
1976	398,613	149,881	37.6	18,823	4,285	37,281	30,803	17,487	3,048
1977	462,315	157,759	34.1	19,764	4,178	39,111	30,917	18,613	4,629
1978	601,442	249,776	41.5	21,315	4,010	37,216	29,288	20,753	88,543
1979	460,348	189,293	41.1	24,264	4,048	41,300	29,248	19,708	22,546
1980	530,639	236,097	44.5	27,651	4,225	42,316	32,320	22,607	43,483
1981	596,600	264,343	44.3	25,803	3,896	43,772	32,663	21,522	55,631
1982	594,131	313,291	52.7	36,984	3,903	45,102	31,724	21,738	72,553
1983	559,763	277,701	49.6	25,777	4,092	41,546	33,339	25,451	37,560
1984	543,903	256,273	47.1	23,363	4,043	42,768	33,042	24,964	37,236
1985	570,009	264,691	46.4	24,789	4,086	47,978	35,253	26,026	31,895
1986	601,708	268,248	44.6	25,106	3,959	52,558	35,776	26,227	29,993
1987	601,516	257,684	42.8	25,841	4,174	50,060	35,849	27,803	24,231
1988	643,025	264,465	41.1	28,717	4,512	50,697	34,703	26,268	25,789
1989	1,090,924	312,149	28.6	32,272	4,849	57,034	34,222	31,175	37,739
1990	1,536,438	338,581	22.0	31,815	5,734	63,756	32,301	30,667	48,792
1991	1,827,167	358,533	19.6	33,025	5,049	63,596	26,518	45,064	55,307
1992	973,977	356,955	36.6	38,907	11,028	61,022	19,359	36,755	77,735

SOURCE: Immigration and Naturalization Service, 1960-1978, 1979-1992.
a. Up to 1981 immigrants from China included both immigrants from mainland China and those from Taiwan. Since 1982, immigrants from mainland China have been tabulated separately from those from Taiwan.

flow from Asian countries, because the number of immigrants based on family reunification was not reduced. Therefore, Asian immigration is likely to continue on the current scale in the near future. Korea's improved economic conditions during recent years have contributed to a significant reduction of Korean immigration since 1988.

Table 2.2 Comparison of the United States With Asian Countries in Per Capita Income

Country	Per Capita Income ($)
United States (1988)	$13,123
Japan (1989)	$15,030
South Korea (1988)	$2,180
Taiwan (1988)	$6,200
The Philippines (1986)	$667
India (1988)	$300
China (1986)	$258

SOURCE: World Almanac and Imprint of Pharos Books (1991, pp. 698, 718, 723, 726, 743, 756).

Motives and Causes of Mass Exodus

Most post-1965 Asian immigrants are economic migrants who crossed the Pacific mainly to seek a higher standard of living in the United States. The great disparities in economic development between the United States and major Asian source countries support the economic nature of Asian immigration. The standard of living in the United States in 1987, as measured by per capita income, was 10 times higher than the Philippines, 12 times higher than India, and 3 times higher than South Korea (see Table 2.2). Japan is the only Asian country to achieve a level of economic development comparable to the United States. Thus only a very small number of Japanese have immigrated to the United States over the last 20 years.

Although economic motives are the determining factor for most recent Asian immigrants, structural factors—political, military, economic, and cultural connections between the United States and various Asian countries—also influence Asians' propensity to immigrate to the United States, explaining why some countries send more immigrants than others. Among Asian countries, the Philippines have annually sent the largest number of immigrants over the last two decades. Cultural dependency resulting from U.S. colonization and a sizable U.S. military presence in the Philippines are mainly responsible for the mass migration. Moreover, the U.S. military presence in the Philippines has contributed to interracial marriages, providing the basis for subsequent kin-centered immigration. South Korea was the second-largest source country of U.S. immigrants from Asia during recent years. Similar structural linkages between the United States and

South Korea have contributed to that exodus. It is also important to note that the normalization of relations between the United States and China in 1979 opened the door to immigration for people from China.

The United States was deeply involved in the Vietnam War from the early 1960s until the fall of South Vietnam in April 1975. Some 18,000 Vietnamese came to the United States as immigrants between 1960 and 1974, most of them wives of U.S. servicemen who served in South Vietnam (Gordon, 1987). Since the fall of South Vietnam in 1975, nearly 1 million people from Vietnam and other Indochinese countries have come to the United States. Most were admitted to the United States under refugee status, but others have come as family members (spouses and children) of U.S. citizens or long-term overseas employees of the U.S. government. Thus, the U.S. political connection with South Vietnam and military involvement in the Vietnam War were mainly responsible for the influx of Indochinese refugees and immigrants, who make up a significant proportion of post-1965 Asian immigrants.

The Radical Increase in the Asian American Population

As expected, the influx of Asian immigrants over the last quarter century has led to a radical increase in the Asian American population in the United States. Table 2.3 shows the population changes for total Asian and Pacific Islander Americans and major Asian ethnic groups between 1970 and 1990. The Asian American population in 1970 was less than 1.5 million. It increased to 3.5 million in 1980, a growth rate of more than 200%, and to 7.3 million in 1990, when it represented 2.9% of the U.S. population.

The Japanese made up the largest Asian ethnic group in 1970. However, due to a large influx of immigrants, the Chinese and Filipinos, respectively, emerged as the first- and second-largest Asian ethnic groups in 1980. Although in the 1980s the Philippines sent more immigrants to the United States than mainland China, the Chinese experienced a greater population increase because many immigrants of Chinese ancestry came from Hong Kong, Taiwan, and Indochinese countries, as well as from mainland China. As indicated in Chapter 9, approximately 225,000 of the more than 1 million Indochinese refugees are ethnic Chinese and are most likely to have reported themselves as Chinese rather than Vietnamese or Cambodian in the 1990 census. Although the 1990 census reported the number of Vietnamese Americans as a little more than 600,000, the total number, including those of Chinese origin, may have been over 800,000.

Table 2.3 Changes in Asian and Pacific Islander American Population, 1970-1990

	1970[a]	1980	% Increase From 1970 to 1980	1990	% Increase From 1980 to 1990
Total U.S. population	203,211,926	226,545,805	11.4	248,709,873	9.8
Asian Pacific Islander population	1,439,562	3,550,439	164.6	7,273,662	107.8
Asian Pacific Americans as % of total population	0.7	1.5		2.9	
Chinese	436,062	806,040	84.8	1,645,472	104.1
Japanese	591,290	700,974	18.5	847,562	20.9
Filipino	343,060	774,652	125.8	1,460,770	88.6
Korean	69,1550	354,593	412.9	798,849	125.3
Indian		361,531		815,447	125.6
Vietnamese		261,729		614,547	134.8

SOURCE: U.S. Bureau of the Census (1973, Table 140; 1983, Table 62; 1993a, Table 3).
a. In the 1970 census, Asian Indians were classified into a white category and Vietnamese Americans were not tabulated separately. Since 1980 the census has classified Asian and Pacific Islander Americans into one racial category.

The Urban and Middle-Class Backgrounds of the New Asian Immigrants

Asian and white European immigration to the United States in the 19th century usually involved a move from rural areas to American cities, so that it was an integral part of the urbanization process. For this reason, some sociologists (Handlin, 1959; Sowell, 1975) consider black migration from rural areas of the South to northern industrial cities in the first half of the 20th century comparable to the intercontinental migration of Europeans to the United States. Consistent with their rural background, earlier immigrants were characterized by low levels of education and preimmigrant occupations. In the 19th century, Japanese, Chinese, Italian, Irish, and Polish immigrants were mainly farmers and unskilled workers, and they were mostly illiterate (Fallows, 1979; Handlin, 1951; Thomas & Znaniecki, 1927).

In sharp contrast, most post-1965 Asian immigrants have come from urban areas, particularly large metropolitan cities. For example, a predeparture survey conducted in 1986 shows that 52% of the 1986 Filipino immigrants lived in Manila and its neighboring provinces at the time of

Table 2.4 Percentages of College Graduates From Asian Immigrant Groups by Year of Entry

Country of Origin	(A) 1970-1980	Year of Entry (B) 1980-1984	(C) 1985-1990
All countries	22.2	20.5	26.9
All Asian countries	37.4	33.6	40.7
India	63.1	67.8	42.2
The Philippines	47.9	45.0	46.1
China	27.6	22.6	38.6
Korea	31.6	29.5	36.0
Vietnam	11.9	11.8	6.8

SOURCE: Figures for (A) adjusted from U.S. Bureau of the Census (1984, Table 255). Figures for (B) and (C) adjusted from U.S. Bureau of the Census (1993b, Table 3).

departure (Carino, Fawcett, Gardner, & Arnold, 1990, p. 26). The same predeparture survey reveals that 70% of the 1986 Korean immigrants lived in metropolitan areas and that another 21% lived in cities (Park, Fawcett, Arnold, & Gardner, 1990). Because of this urban background, their immigration may not involve some of the problems that European peasant immigrants to American cities once encountered. Lifestyles in American cities and Asian metropolitan cities are quite similar, although there are some significant cultural differences. Most Asian immigrants are generally familiar with American urban lifestyles before they arrive. They may not feel the sense of crisis, isolation, and alienation that the earlier peasant immigrants experienced.

Consistent with their urban background, post-1965 Asian immigrants are generally highly educated and have had white-collar and professional occupations in their countries of origin. Based on 1980 and 1990 census reports, Table 2.4 shows educational levels of Asian immigrants admitted in the 1970s and the 1980s in comparison to other groups. These new Asian arrivals have a much higher educational level than both the U.S. general population and all other new immigrants. In the percentage of college graduates, Asian immigrants surpass the U.S. general population by a large margin. Indian and Filipino immigrants admitted in the 1970s show exceptionally high proportions of college graduates. A large number of Indian and Filipino professional immigrants were admitted in the early 1970s, and a significant proportion were medical professionals (Yochum & Agarwal, 1988).

Several factors explain the middle-class background of recent Asian immigrants. First, middle-class Asians are more motivated to immigrate to the United States than lower-class Asians because they feel a greater gap between life aspirations and local realities. Thus relative deprivation is more important than absolute deprivation in understanding immigration motives (Portes & Rumbaut, 1990, pp. 12-13). Second, middle-class Asians have the resources for legal immigration to the United States, including information usually unavailable to lower-class Asians(Yoon, 1993). Third, and most important, the 1965 Immigration Act allowed alien professionals to be admitted as legal immigrants to meet labor shortages in some professional occupations. Highly educated Asian professionals, particularly those educated in the United States, took advantage of the third preference category of the 1965 Immigration Act (the professional category) in immigrating to the United States or changing their status to permanent residents.

When the unemployment rate rose with the economic recession in the mid-1970s, the federal government severely restricted the admission of occupational immigrants. The government discouraged alien professionals from immigrating by passing the Eilberg Act and the Health Professions Educational Assistance Act in 1976 (Yochum & Agarwal, 1988). The former required alien professionals to have job offers from U.S. employers before they could gain admission as legal immigrants. The latter, in effect, removed physicians and surgeons from eligible categories of labor certification. Since the late 1970s, the U.S. Department of Labor has discouraged other types of occupational immigration by not issuing labor permits to many qualified prospective immigrants.

As a result, the proportion of occupational immigrants, including professional immigrants, has decreased drastically since the late 1970s. During the last 10 years, most Asian immigrants (more than 85%) have been granted permanent status based on family reunification. This change in Asian immigration patterns has led to a change in the immigrants' socioeconomic background. More recent Asian immigrants are less select and more diverse in their socioeconomic status than the Asian immigrants admitted in the 1970s (Carino et al., 1990; Min, 1989; Park et al., 1990). As shown in Table 2.4, Asian immigrants admitted in the early 1980s had slightly lower levels of education than those admitted in the 1970s, although between 1980 and 1990 there were great improvements in education in both the United States and the respective Asian countries. The proportion of college graduates in the U.S. general population increased from only 16.2% in 1980 to 20.2% in 1990. Although Asian immigrants admitted in the 1980s still surpass the general population in the college graduation rate, the educational gap between Asian immigrants and the U.S. general population is much narrower now than it was 20 years ago.

Settlement Patterns

Regions, States, and Counties With Asian Concentration

In the past, Asian immigrants were heavily concentrated in Hawaii, California, and other West Coast states. Recent Asian immigrants have also settled on the West Coast in large numbers. However, available data indicate that recent Asian immigrants have slightly altered the tendency to concentrate in the West. In 1970, 70.4% of Asian Americans lived in the West, compared to 17.1% of the U.S. general population (U.S. Bureau of the Census, 1973, Table 140). In 1980, the proportion of Asian Americans in the West decreased to 63.6% (U.S. Bureau of the Census, 1983, Table 62) and then to 55.7% in 1990. By contrast, the proportion of Asians residing in the Northeast increased from 14.0% in 1970 to 18.4% in 1990.

Table 2.5 shows the three highest-ranking states of intended residence for five major Asian immigrant groups in four different time periods, 1974, 1979, 1986, and 1992. For all five major Asian immigrant groups, California is the most common destination. Filipino and Vietnamese immigrants in particular are heavily concentrated in California. Los Angeles, San Francisco, San Jose, and San Diego are common destinations.

New York state is the second most common settlement area for three of the five major Asian immigrant groups. The proportions of Chinese, Indian, and Korean immigrants who settled there have also gradually increased over the years. For Chinese and Indian immigrants, New York is as popular as California. Most New York-bound Asian immigrants settle in New York City, whereas California-bound Asian immigrants scatter in several cities. New York City, therefore, has received more Indian and Chinese immigrants than any other American city. In 1992 the state of New York was the second most common destination, even for Filipino immigrants. In 1979 Illinois was the third most common destination for Chinese, Filipino, Korean, and Indian immigrants. However, most recently (in 1992) New Jersey attracted more Asian immigrants than Illinois. This reflects the recent tendency of Asian immigrants to consolidate in the New York-New Jersey area, as well as in California.

Table 2.6 shows the distribution of Asian and Pacific Islander Americans in seven states, based on the 1990 census. Seventy-four percent of Asian

Table 2.5 Major States of Destination for Asian Immigrant Groups
in Selected Years

Ethnic Group	Year	Most Common	%	Second Most Common	%	Third Most Common	%
Chinese	1974	California	30.2	New York	25.2	New Jersey	4.3
	1979	California	37.8	New York	23.7	Illinois	3.6
	1986	California	37.7	New York	30.5	Massachusetts	3.6
	1992	California	30.0	New York	28.2	Texas	4.7
Filipino	1974	California	30.5	Hawaii	10.4	Illinois	8.2
	1979	California	46.4	Hawaii	12.1	Illinois	5.6
	1986	California	51.0	Hawaii	8.6	Illinois	5.7
	1992	California	44.0	New York	9.0	New Jersey	6.7
Korean	1974	California	22.2	New York	9.1	Maryland	7.8
	1979	California	28.8	New York	9.0	Illinois	5.6
	1986	California	27.5	New York	11.0	Illinois	5.3
	1992	California	30.7	New York	12.0	New Jersey	6.8
Indian	1974	New York	25.2	Illinois	11.9	California	11.4
	1979	California	17.9	New York	15.4	Illinois	10.9
	1986	California	17.1	New York	16.0	New Jersey	12.2
	1992	California	22.5	New York	13.8	New Jersey	11.0
Vietnamese[a]	1986	California	44.0	Washington	12.2	Texas	9.4
	1992	California	43.1	Texas	8.6	Washington	4.1

SOURCE: Immigration and Naturalization Service, 1974, 1979, 1986, 1992.
a. Data for Vietnamese immigrants for the first 2 years are not available.

and Pacific Islander Americans reside in these states. Because approximately 93% of those classified as Asian and Pacific Islander Americans are Asian Americans, these seven states represent Asian American states. California is the largest, with nearly 3 million Asian and Pacific Islander Americans. Nearly 40% of all Asian and Pacific Islander Americans have settled in California, making up 9.6% of the state's residents. New York and Hawaii are the second- and third-largest Asian American states, with nearly 700,000 settled in each. Asian and Pacific Islander Americans make up 62% of the Hawaiian population. In addition to a quarter-million Japanese, large numbers of Filipinos, Chinese, Koreans, and Hawaiians live in Hawaii.

Table 2.7 shows counties with an Asian and Pacific Islander population of 150,000 or more. Los Angeles County has the largest number of Asian and Pacific Islander Americans, nearly 1 million, or 11% of the total county population. Los Angeles can be considered the capital of Japanese, Filipino, and Korean Americans. Honolulu County has the second-largest

Table 2.6 States With a Large Asian and Pacific Islander Population (200,000 or more)

State	Number	%
California	2,845,659	39.1
New York	693,760	9.5
Hawaii	685,236	9.4
Texas	319,459	4.4
Illinois	285,311	3.9
New Jersey	272,521	3.7
Washington	210,958	2.9
Other states	1,970,758	27.1
U.S. total	7,283,662	100.0

SOURCE: U.S. Bureau of the Census (1993a, Table 262).

Table 2.7 Counties With a Large Asian and Pacific Islander Population (150,000 or more)

County	Number of Asian and Pacific Islander Americans	Total County Population	Asian and Pacific Islander Americans as % of Total Population
Los Angeles	955,329	8,863,164	10.8
Honolulu	526,459	836,231	63.0
New York City[a]	512,719	7,322,564	7.0
Santa Clara (CA)	261,466	1,497,577	17.5
Orange (CA)	249,192	2,410,556	10.3
San Francisco	210,876	723,959	29.1
San Diego	198,311	2,498,016	7.9
Alameda (CA)	192,554	1,279,182	15.1
Cook (IL)	188,565	5,105,067	3.7

SOURCE: U.S. Bureau of the Census (1993a, Table 276).
a. New York City consists of five counties.

Asian and Pacific Islander population, with more than a half million. New York City, consisting of five counties, has the largest Asian and Pacific Islander concentration outside of the West Coast, with more than a half million. Nearly half of the New York City Asian and Pacific Islander Americans are Chinese. Since 1980, New York City's Chinatown has emerged as the largest overseas Chinatown in the world, surpassing San

Francisco's Chinatown. Indians, the second-largest Asian ethnic group in New York City, have a population of over 100,000. New York City is the largest Indian center in the United States.

With the exception of Cook County, Illinois, all other counties with a large Asian American population are in California. This shows California's importance as a place of settlement for recent as well as earlier Asian immigrants. Southern California, including Los Angeles and Orange counties and several adjacent counties, has the largest Asian concentration in the United States. Asian and Pacific Islander Americans represent a significant proportion of the population in several major cities in California. For example, they make up 29% of the San Francisco population and 20% of the San Jose population. Asians in these California cities can have significant effects on economy, education, politics, and even culture.

Levels of Segregation

Another important aspect of Asian American settlement patterns is their level of residential segregation. Earlier European white immigrants usually settled in ethnic ghettos located in transitional areas near the center of the city (Cressey, 1938; Park, Burgess, & McKenzie, 1967, chap. 2). As their economic condition and social standing improved, a significant proportion of immigrants moved to more desirable residential districts. Most second-generation natives dispersed to suburban areas, away from ethnic ghettos.

The earlier Chinese immigrants in San Francisco, New York City, Los Angeles, and other cities established segregated communities known as Chinatowns. Chinatowns were created somewhat involuntarily in response to racial oppression and violence against Chinese at the end of the 19th century (Yuan, 1970). Because of the conveniences of employment in ethnic businesses, ethnic food, and language, a large number of recent immigrants from Hong Kong and mainland China reside in Chinatowns (Kwong, 1987; Light & Wong, 1975). Consequently, a significant proportion of Chinese Americans in each major Chinese community still live in Chinatown. The 1990 census results indicate that approximately 50,000 Chinese reside in the Lower East Side of Manhattan—New York's Chinatown. They make up approximately 30% of Chinatown residents and one fifth of the Chinese Americans in New York City (New York City Department of Planning, 1992, p. 174).

Koreans in Los Angeles have also established an ethnic ghetto. About 3 miles west of downtown Los Angeles, Koreatown is the only officially recognized Korean enclave in the United States with a Koreatown sign on highway exits. Approximately 35% of the Koreans in the city of Los Angeles resided in Koreatown in 1980 (Min, 1993).

Indochinese refugees have established several ethnic enclaves in Orange County. About half of Orange County Indochinese refugees reside in Santa Ana, Garden Grove, and Westminster (Desbarats & Holland, 1983), their largest enclave. In 1988, the area along Bolsa Avenue from Magnolia to Bushard was officially designated "Little Saigon" by the City Council of Westminster (Takaki, 1989, p. 459).

By contrast, recent Filipino and Indian immigrants have not established ethnic ghettos. Instead they are widely scattered in suburban areas. Three factors explain why Indian and Filipino immigrants have not created ethnic ghettos. First, these two Asian immigrant groups lack cultural homogeneity; they consist of several linguistic-regional subgroups who significantly differ in language, customs, and ethnic identity. Subgroup differences and lack of national identity may make the need for a territorial community less urgent for Filipino or Indian immigrants than for Korean or Chinese immigrants. Second, as previously noted, Filipino and Indian immigrants are characterized by higher educational and occupational levels than other Asian immigrants. Immigrants from middle-class and professional backgrounds may not need an ethnic ghetto, historically a residential area for low-class immigrants. Filipino and Indian immigrants are also more fluent in English than other Asian immigrants, particularly because of their colonial experience with the United States and Britain, respectively. Most Filipino and Indian immigrants without serious language difficulties can stay away from ethnic ghettos, which provide new immigrants with ethnic employment, ethnic food, and other services that suit ethnic tastes.

Although Chinese and Korean immigrants are heavily concentrated in ethnic enclaves, Chinese and Korean Americans, as well as Filipino and Indian Americans, are also highly represented in suburban residential areas, compared to other minority groups. In fact, compared to the general population, Asian Americans are overrepresented in suburban areas. This is partly supported by census data. The 1990 census data enable us to compare Asian ethnic groups to other groups in the size of area of settlement. According to the census definition, "an urbanized area consists of a central city or cities surrounding closely settled contiguous territory that together have a minimum population of 50,000." As shown in Table 2.8, each Asian ethnic group shows a higher level of residence in census-defined "urbanized areas" than any non-Asian racial group. The table also reveals that each Asian group shows a higher level of residence in "urban fringes" than any non-Asian group. Because census-defined "urban fringes"

Table 2.8 Comparison of Asian Ethnic Groups With Other Groups in the Size of Area of Settlement (by percent)

| Ethnic Group | Total | Urban Areas | | | Outside Urbanized Areas | Rural Areas |
| | | Inside Urbanized Areas | | | | |
		Total	Central Cities	Urban Fringes		
White	72.0	59.8	26.1	33.7	12.2	28.0
Black	87.2	78.5	57.7	20.2	8.7	12.8
Hispanic	91.4	82.1	52.2	29.9	9.3	8.6
Chinese	97.6	94.6	53.6	41.0	3.0	2.4
Japanese	93.6	84.9	40.9	44.0	8.7	6.4
Filipino	95.0	88.2	44.8	43.4	6.8	5.0
Korean	94.5	90.0	41.7	48.3	4.5	5.5
Indian	95.3	90.6	40.1	50.5	4.7	4.7
Vietnamese	97.2	94.1	52.2	41.9	3.1	2.8

SOURCE: U.S. Bureau of the Census (1993a, Table 3).

outside of the central city are largely desirable suburban areas, the table indicates that Asian Americans are more highly represented in suburban residential areas than the general population. Most recent Asian immigrants, unlike those who came earlier, are not trapped in ethnic ghettos and can afford to reside in suburban areas by virtue of their high socioeconomic background.

Asian Americans, particularly new Asian immigrants who are not culturally assimilated, tend to live close to co-ethnics. Asian American residential segregation is especially high in California cities. Using data from the 1980 census and census tracts as a unit of analysis, Jiobu (1988, p. 114) measured segregation indices for blacks, Mexican Americans, and five Asian ethnic groups (Chinese, Japanese, Filipino, Korean, and Vietnamese) for 21 metropolitan cities in California. His study indicates that, with the exception of Japanese Americans, all Asian ethnic groups show segregation indices close to blacks for major California metropolitan cities. Vietnamese Americans are the most segregated Asian ethnic group. Their segregation index is higher than blacks for almost all California cities included in data analysis. Asian segregation levels are lower in states where Asian immigrants are not highly concentrated.

Asian American's Diversity

Many Americans—teachers, social workers, and the general public, as well as the mass media—assume that Asian Americans are a homogeneous group, physically and culturally distinguishable from other minority groups. But this assumption has little validity. Asian Americans are made up of physically and culturally diverse groups with different languages, customs, and values. Although people of Hispanic origin also consist of many different ethnic groups, as a whole they seem to have more cultural similarities than Asian ethnic groups. As a result of Spanish colonization, Hispanic ethnic groups have at least two important cultural commonalities: the Spanish language and Catholic religion. Asian Americans, however, have no common language or religion. Each major Asian ethnic group has its own language and dominant religion. Furthermore, as previously noted, some Asian ethnic groups have several languages and religions even among co-ethnics.

Cultural Diversity

Chinese, Koreans, and Japanese Americans are physically and culturally similar. All of Mongolian racial origin, they look so much alike that they often have trouble differentiating members of their own group from the other two Asian nationality groups. The three Asian ethnic groups have many cultural similarities that stem from Confucianism. Confucianism started in China in the second century B.C., spread to Korea, and then through Korea to Japan. China's cultural influence on Korea and Japan includes export of Chinese characters. Korea and Japan created their own written languages, but Chinese characters are still used in both countries. Probably because of their physical and cultural similarities, intermarriages between the three Asian groups are very common in Hawaii and California (Kitano, Yuang, Chai, & Hatanaka, 1984; Leon, 1975).

Despite their many physical and cultural similarities, Chinese and Korean communities have had little contact with the Japanese community, because Japan occupied Korea and Manchuria before World War II. Chinese and Korean community leaders in San Francisco, Los Angeles, and New York City maintain close relations to protect their common interests, but there are cultural barriers between them. For one thing, most Korean immigrants are Christians, compared to only a small proportion of Chinese Americans.

Vietnam was a Chinese colony for about 1,000 years, until the end of the 19th century. Colonization gave China a strong cultural influence on Vietnam. In accordance with Confucian values, the Vietnamese maintain strong family and kinship ties and emphasize children's education (Tran, 1988). In addition, they, along with the Chinese and Koreans, observe New Year's Day according to the lunar calendar. However, the Vietnamese, during nearly 100 years of French colonization, were influenced by French culture and religion. The French brought Catholicism to Vietnam; a significant proportion of Vietnamese refugees in the United States are Catholics. In addition, Vietnam, along with Cambodia and Thailand, is one of the major Buddhist countries in Asia. In survey studies, more Vietnamese refugees chose Buddhism as their religion than any other religion (Tran, 1988).

India and the Philippines are the two major Asian countries not influenced by Confucianism, making them different from other Asian ethnic groups. In India and Pakistan, Hinduism regulates many aspects of family and social life, as well as religious life. Other important religions in India, such as Islam, Sikhism, and Jainism, also affect Indian culture. Researchers indicate that all these religions affect Indian immigrants' adjustment to a new society, facilitating subethnic identity, but also hindering a Pan-Indian unity (Williams, 1988). Until gaining independence in 1947, India was under British colonial rule for about 100 years. British colonization had significant cultural effects on India, including the adoption of English as an official language. Mainly because of the linguistic diversity in India, English is still used in schools. Indian immigrants in the United States, therefore, have fewer language barriers than other Asian immigrant groups.

The Philippines has a long history of Western colonization. Only slightly influenced by major Asian religions and culture, the Philippines is probably the most Westernized country in Asia. The Philippines was a Spanish colony from the middle of the 16th century until the Spanish-American War in 1898. Spanish colonization had a strong cultural impact. Most important, the Philippines, like many Spanish colonies in South and Central America, became a major Catholic country well before the U.S. government was established in North America. At present, over three fourths of Filipinos are Roman Catholics (Pido, 1986, p. 18). The Philippines became a U.S. colony after the U.S. victory in the Spanish-American War of 1898, allowing the United States to exert a powerful cultural influence. Although the Philippines gained full independence in 1946, the American cultural impact can still be sharply felt in every aspect of life in the old colony. English is still used as an important language in public schools, which are modeled after the U.S. educational system. Therefore, Filipino immigrants, along with Indian immigrants, do not have a severe language barrier. Probably due to their cultural similarities, intermarriages between Filipino and Mexican or white Americans are much more common than marriages between Filipino and other Asian Americans (Burma, 1963; Catapusan, 1938; Jiobu, 1988, p. 162).

Diversity in Socioeconomic Status

As mentioned previously, recent Asian immigrants have high educational and preimmigrant occupational levels. This does not mean, however, that Asian immigrants are socioeconomically homogeneous. As reflected in Table 2.4, Vietnamese refugees and immigrants from mainland China are less educated than other Asian immigrants. Table 2.9 shows two indicators of economic conditions for Asian ethnic groups. Asian ethnic groups individually and as a whole fare well in terms of median family income when compared to white Americans. However, Asian and Pacific Islander Americans as a whole and three Asian groups—Vietnamese, Korean, and Chinese—in particular show higher proportions of families at the poverty level than white Americans. Many new Asian immigrant families are quite poor, whereas many old-timers have achieved economic mobility. As will be discussed in more detail in Chapter 4, the Chinese community is more severely polarized than others in socioeconomic status. Using all three indicators, Vietnamese Americans are socioeconomically far below white Americans and other Asian Americans.

Asian Americans' occupations are as diverse as their economic conditions. As will be shown in Chapters 6 and 7, a large proportion of Indian and Filipino immigrants are professionals, particularly medical professionals. By contrast, a significant proportion of Vietnamese and Chinese immigrants are low-level service and blue-collar workers. Korean immigrants are often self-employed in small businesses, as are Chinese Americans. However, Korean and Chinese Americans significantly differ in the types of businesses they operate. Korean immigrants are concentrated in the grocery business (including the green grocery), dry cleaning service, wholesale and retail sale of Korean-imported merchandise (wigs, handbags, jewelry, etc.), and American fast food service. In contrast, Chinese Americans have footholds in garment manufacturing, Chinese restaurants, and gift shops.

Asian women married to American servicemen represent a large portion of Asian immigrants since 1950. These women are not directly involved

Table 2.9 Indicators of Economic Status for Asian Ethnic Groups in Comparison to Other Groups

Group	Median Family Income	% of Families at the Poverty Level
White	$37,152	7.0
Black	$22,429	26.3
Hispanic	$25,064	22.3
Asian and Pacific Islander American	$41,251	11.6
Chinese	$41,316	11.1
Japanese	$51,550	3.4
Filipino	$46,698	5.2
Korean	$33,909	14.7
Indian	$49,309	7.2
Vietnamese	$30,550	23.8

SOURCE: U.S. Bureau of the Census (1993c, Table 5; 1994, Tables 48, 49).

in their respective Asian ethnic communities. However, because the vast majority invite family members to join them in the United States, they are inseparably connected to the ethnic community. More important, a large proportion of these women divorce their American spouses and find new partners in the ethnic community. Thus brides of U.S. servicemen add another dimension to the diversity of Asian Americans. Asian women married to U.S. servicemen generally have less education and more language difficulties than other Asian immigrants (Kim, 1977). They therefore need more social services to adjust successfully. Social work researchers pay great attention to interracially married Asian women.

Diversity in Generations

Finally, generational differences provide another dimension to Asian American diversity. The large influx of immigrants over the last 20 years is mainly responsible for a dramatic increase in the Asian American population: The majority of Asian Americans are Asian-born immigrants. The 1990 census shows that approximately 37% of Asian Americans are native-born Americans, compared to 92% of the U.S. general population (see Table 2.10). Because a relatively small number of Japanese immigrated to this country in the last 20 years, the vast majority of Japanese Americans are native-born second-, third-, or fourth-generation citizens.

Table 2.10   The Native (U.S.) Born as Percentage of the Total Population for Asian Ethnic Groups

Ethnic Group	%
Japanese	67.7
Filipino	35.6
Chinese	30.7
Korean	27.3
Indian	24.6
Vietnamese	20.1
Asian and Pacific Islander American	36.9
U.S. total	92.1

SOURCE: U.S. Bureau of the Census (1993c, Table 1).

For all the other Asian ethnic groups, however, most of the population is foreign born.

The Japanese American community has had little contact with other Asian American communities during recent years. There are two important factors contributing to the lack of interaction and communication between Japanese and other Asian American communities. First, as previously indicated, anti-Japanese feelings are common among Asian immigrants who experienced Japanese colonization. Second, in their values and positions on many social issues, recent Asian immigrants differ from Japanese Americans, who consist mainly of well-assimilated, native-born citizens.[3] A smaller proportion of the Chinese or the Filipino American population is native born than the Japanese. Yet some native-born Chinese and Filipino Americans are involved in community services and community politics, very often clashing with the immigrant generation (Kwong, 1987). Because most second-generation Koreans and Vietnamese are school-age children, their generational conflicts are largely limited to families (Kitano & Daniels, 1988, chap. 11; Min & Min, 1992). However, as discussed in Chapter 8, second-generation Koreans are beginning to participate in community activities, extending generational conflicts into the community.

Generational conflicts among Asian ethnic groups are observable on many high school and college campuses in California, New York, and other major Asian states. For example, many universities have two Korean clubs, one representing Korean immigrant students and the other representing second-generation Korean students. Korean immigrant students often complain that American-born Korean students do not know how to speak

Korean and are not polite to older Koreans. On the other hand, second-generation Korean students complain that Korean immigrant students are too authoritarian and too conservative and that they discriminate against female students.

Common Experiences and Pan-Asian Unity

As noted above, Asian ethnic groups differ in religion, language, and other cultural aspects. In addition, some Asian ethnic groups, such as Indians and Filipinos, have significant subcultural differences. Despite these interethnic and intraethnic differences, Asian Americans as a group have common life experiences favoring the development of Pan-Asian identity and unity. This section will discuss three of the several factors that contribute to the development of Pan-Asian identity (Espiritu, 1992; Lopez & Espiritu, 1990): (a) commonalities in values; (b) similar treatment from both government agencies and the general public; and (c) the internal need for collective strategies to protect their economic, political, and other interests.

Common Values

Cultural commonalities become an important basis for ethnicity (Gordon, 1964; Greeley, 1974; Issacs, 1975; Nash, 1989). That is, ethnicity develops and persists when members of a group share common languages, religions, values, and other cultural characteristics. We noted in the previous section that Asian Americans consist of culturally diverse groups. However, despite significant cultural differences, Asians tend to hold some common values that differ from dominant American values. Asian Americans are more or less group-oriented, in sharp contrast to the individualism that characterizes American values (Chung, 1991; Hall, 1981; Hirayama & Hirayama, 1984). Other Asian values include filial piety, respect for authority, self-control and restraint in emotional expression, emphasis on educational achievement, shame as a behavioral influence, middle position virtue, high regard for the elderly, and the centrality of family relationships and responsibilities (Chung, 1991; Ross-Sheriff, 1991). These values are common threads that tie all Asian groups together.

Perceived as a Homogeneous Group

Asian Americans share common experiences partly because they are treated as one group by governments and the general public alike. The U.S. Census Bureau classifies all Asian and Pacific Islander Americans as one group for statistical purposes. Following census classification, local and federal government agencies and school districts lump all Asian and Pacific Islander Americans together when compiling data for policy and resource allocation purposes. Therefore, all Asian and Pacific Islander ethnic groups need to make concerted efforts to protect their interests in welfare, health, education, business, and so forth. Mainly because governments and school systems allocate resources for Asian Americans as one group, several Pan-Asian organizations, such as the Asian American Mental Health Center, were established in Los Angeles, New York City, and other major Asian American centers to provide services for Asian Americans. Local and federal governments have designated May as Asian and Pacific Islander American month and promote ethnic festivals and other cultural activities. These government-sponsored cultural activities enhance Pan-Asian identity and interethnic interactions among all Asian Americans.

Moreover, most Americans have difficulty distinguishing members of various Asian ethnic groups, despite some observable physical differences. Thus Americans often refer to Koreans, Japanese, and even Cambodians as "Chinese." Asian Americans have been physically attacked by white or black Americans who mistook them for members of other Asian ethnic groups. In 1982, for example, Vincent Chin, a Chinese American, was murdered with a baseball bat by two white men who mistook him for Japanese. In 1990, a Vietnamese immigrant was severely beaten by black gangs in Brooklyn, New York, because they thought he was Korean. Each incident led Asian Americans to realize sadly that they could be targets of attack by non-Asian Americans simply because they share Asian-American physical characteristics. This in turn enhances Pan-Asian unity.

Practical Needs to Protect Group Interests

The mobilization approach to ethnicity emphasizes that ethnic unity should be understood in terms of group efforts to use ethnic symbols to obtain access to social, political, and material resources (Horowitz, 1977; Nagel, 1986; Olzak & Nagel, 1986; Yancy, Ericksen, & Juliani, 1976). Each Asian ethnic group is relatively small in number and thus not strong enough to influence politics and education, even on the local level. Therefore Asian ethnic groups need to form a Pan-Asian alliance to protect their common interests. This practical need for a Pan-Asian alliance is another thread that ties Asian Americans together (Espiritu, 1992). Although Asian Americans are concentrated on the West Coast and in New York City, no Asian ethnic group, with the exception of Japanese Americans in Hawaii, has a population large enough to elect its candidate, even as a city council member, using ethnic-based politics. Yet, the Asian American population in many West Coast cities is large enough to influence city politics with a Pan-Asian coalition. For example, the Asian and Pacific Islander population in Monterey Park, California, greatly increased in the 1980s, reaching 58% of the population in 1990 (U.S. Bureau of the Census, 1993a, Table 276). Japanese Americans in Monterey Park, mainly native born, made a coalition with Chinese immigrants to elect Asian American candidates for mayor and city council (Saito, 1989; Saito & Horton, 1993).

Pan-Asian Consciousness and Movements on College Campuses

Pan-Asian movements are more active on college campuses than in Asian American communities. The history of Pan-Asian movements on college campuses dates back to the late 1960s, before the large influx of new Asian immigrants. Two of the three factors discussed above, similar treatment and practical needs, contributed to Pan-Asian consciousness and movements on college campuses. Colleges and universities usually lump all Asian American students together by classifying them into one racial category for administrative purposes. Moreover professors and non-Asian students very often identify all Asian American students as the same racial group. The common experience of being identified in the same racial group, along with anti-Asian prejudice and discrimination on college campuses, facilitates the development of Pan-Asian consciousness. Asian American college students, like black and Hispanic students, have established ethnic clubs and have engaged in protest movements to protect their common interests.

Asian American students consistently demand that an Asian/Asian American studies program be established and that Asian/Asian American courses be taught. Pressures by Asian American students at San Francisco State University and the University of California, Berkeley in 1968-1969 resulted in the creation of Asian American courses at many University of California campuses (Endo & Wei, 1988). Recently, Asian American students at several campuses of the University of California system pressured administrators to establish Asian American programs or to enhance existing programs. Asian American students in several Ivy League schools on the East Coast made similar requests, contributing to the creation of courses, studies, and programs relevant to Asian American experiences (Kiang, 1988). Asian American students have also participated in community activism to protect the interests of Asian women workers (Kiang & Ng, 1988).

Conclusion

The Immigration Act of 1965 abolished discrimination based on national origin and thereby contributed to a large influx of Asians to the United States over the last 20 years. Since the early 1970s, the Philippines, South Korea, and several other Asian countries have annually sent large numbers of immigrants. As a result, the Asian American population increased five-fold from 1.5 million in 1970 to 7.3 million in 1990. The Asian American population will continue to increase in the next decade, unless there are dramatic changes in the current U.S. immigration laws. Asian Americans, heavily concentrated on the West Coast, have significant effects on politics, educational systems, welfare programs, and even culture in such cities as San Francisco, San Diego, San Jose, and Los Angeles.

Many Americans assume that Asian Americans are a homogeneous group. However, this assumption has little validity. Asian Americans consist of groups with diverse religions, languages, national origins, socioeconomic status, and even generations. There is no religion or language that ties all Asian ethnic groups together. Socioeconomic and generational differences within each Asian ethnic group further add to the diversity among Asian Americans.

Despite their diversity, Asian Americans have common life experiences fostering the development of Pan-Asian identity and unity. Three factors facilitate Pan-Asian unity. First, Asian American groups share a common set of values, such as group orientation, strong family ties, emphasis on education, and respect for the elderly. These shared values definitely strengthen Asian Americans' ties. Second, government agencies, including the U.S. Census Bureau, treat all Asian and Pacific Islander Americans as one group for statistical and policy purposes. More important, the general public does not distinguish among Asian ethnic groups when stereotyping or physically attacking Asian Americans. This effectively unites Asian Americans. Third, Asian ethnic groups need to form a broad Pan-Asian coalition to protect their common interests in politics, education, and other areas.

Notes

1. The McCarran-Walter Act of 1952 loosened the immigration restriction on Asians by assigning an immigration quota of 100 to each of the Asian countries and making Asian immigrants eligible for citizenship.

2. The U.S. Immigration Reform and Control Act of 1986 has two components: employer sanction and legalization of illegal residents. The employer sanction provision made it unlawful for employers to knowingly hire undocumented workers. The other provision allowed illegal residents admitted in 1982 and before to legalize their status as permanent residents. Through this legalization provision, more than 3 million illegal residents became permanent residents, the vast majority of them Mexicans, Haitians, and other South Americans.

3. Immigrants in general and Asian immigrants in particular tend to believe that through hard work and education they can achieve social mobility, and thus they underestimate the structural barriers encountered by all Asian Americans and other minority members in the United States. Native-born Asian Americans, whether of Japanese or Korean ancestry, are generally more sensitive to structural barriers encountered by Asian Americans than Asian immigrants.

References

Arnold, F., Minocha, U., & Fawcett, J. T. (1987). The changing face of Asian immigration to the United States. In J. Fawcett & B. Carino (Eds.), *Pacific bridges: The new immigration from Asia and the Pacific Islands* (pp. 105-152). Staten Island: Center for Migration Studies.

Burma, J. H. (1963). Interethnic marriage in Los Angeles, 1948-1959. *Social Forces, 42,* 156-165.

Carino, B. V., Fawcett, J. T., Gardner, R., & Arnold, F. (1990). *The new Filipino immigrants to the United States: Increasing diversity and change* (The East-West Population Institute Paper Series, No. 115). Honolulu: East-West Center.

Catapusan, B. T. (1938). Filipino intermarriage problem in the United States. *Sociology and Social Research, 22,* 265-272.

Chung, D. (1991). Asian cultural commonalities: A comparison with mainstream American culture. In S. Furuto, R. Biswas, D. Chung, & F. Ross-Sheriff (Eds.), *Social work practice with Asian Americans* (pp. 27-44). Newbury Park, CA: Sage.

Cressey, P. F. (1938). Population succession in Chicago, 1898-1930. *American Journal of Sociology, 64,* 364-374.

Desbarats, J., & Holland, L. (1983). Indochinese settlement patterns in Orange County. *Amerasia Journal, 10*(1), 23-46.

Endo, R., & Wei, W. (1988). On the development of Asian American studies programs. In G. Y. Okihiro, S. Hune, A. A. Hansen, & J. Liu (Eds.), *Reflections on shattered windows* (pp. 5-15). Pullman: Washington State University.

Espiritu, Y. L. (1992). *Asian American panethnicity.* Philadelphia: Temple University Press.

Fallows, M. R. (1979). *Irish Americans: Identity and assimilation.* Englewood Cliffs, NJ: Prentice Hall.

Gordon, L. W. (1987). Southeast refugee migration to the United States. In J. T. Fawcett & B. V. Carino (Eds.), *Pacific bridges: The new immigration from Asia and the Pacific Islands* (pp. 153-173). Staten Island: Center for Migration Studies.

Gordon, M. (1964). *Assimilation in American life: The role of race, religion, and national origin.* New York: Oxford University Press.

Greeley, A. (1974). *Ethnicity in the United States: A preliminary reconnaissance.* New York: John Wiley.

Hall, E. T. (1981). *Beyond culture.* Garden City, NY: Anchor.

Handlin, O. (1951). *The uprooted.* Boston: Atlantic Monthly Press.

Handlin, O. (1959). *The newcomers: Negroes and Puerto Ricans in a changing metropolis.* Cambridge: Harvard University Press.

Hirayama, H., & Hirayama, K. K. (1984). Individuality vs. group identity: A comparison between Japan and the United States. *Journal of International and Comparative Social Welfare, 2*(12), 11-20.

Horowitz, D. (1977). Cultural movements and ethnic change. *Annals of American Academy of Political and Social Science, 433,* 6-13.

Immigration and Naturalization Service. (1960-1978). *Annual reports.* Washington, DC: U.S. Government Printing Office.

Immigration and Naturalization Service. (1979-1992). *Statistical yearbook.* Washington, DC: U.S. Government Printing Office.

Issacs, H. (1975). *Idols of the tribe.* New York: Harper & Row.

Jiobu, R. M. (1988). *Ethnicity and assimilation: Blacks, Chinese, Filipinos, Japanese, Koreans, Mexicans, Vietnamese, and Whites.* Albany: State University of New York Press.

Kiang, P. N. (1988). The new wave: Developing Asian American studies on the East Coast. In G. Y. Okihiro, S. Hune, A. A. Hansen, & J. Liu (Eds.), *Reflections on shattered windows* (pp. 43-50). Pullman: Washington State University Press.

Kiang, P. N., & Ng, M. C. (1988). Through strength and struggle: Boston's Asian American student/community/labor solidarity. *Amerasia Journal, 15*(1), 285-293.

Kim, B. L. (1977). Asian wives of U.S. servicemen: Women in shadows. *Amerasia Journal, 4*(1), 91-115.

Kitano, H., & Daniels, R. (1988). *Asian Americans: Emerging minorities.* Englewood Cliffs, NJ: Prentice Hall.

Kitano, H., Yuang, W. T., Chai, L., & Hatanaka, H. (1984). Asian-American interracial marriage. *Journal of Marriage and the Family, 46,* 179-190.

Kwong, P. (1987). *The new Chinatown.* New York: Noonsday Press.

Leon, J. (1975). Sex-ethnic marriage in Hawaii: A non-metric multidimensional analysis. *Journal of Marriage and the Family, 37,* 775-781.

Light, I., & Wong, C. C. (1975). Protest or work: Dilemmas of the tourist industry in American Chinatowns. *American Journal of Sociology, 80,* 1342-1365.

Lopez, D., & Espiritu, Y. E. (1990). Panethnicity in the United States: A theoretical framework. *Ethnic and Racial Studies, 13,* 198-224.

Min, J., & Min, P. G. (1992). *The relationship between Korean immigrant parents and children.* Paper presented at the Annual Meeting of the American Sociological Association, Washington, DC.

Min, P. G. (1989). *Some positive functions of ethnic business for an immigrant community: Koreans in Los Angeles* (Final report submitted to National Science Foundation). New York: Department of Sociology, Queens College.

Min, P. G. (1993). Korean immigrants in Los Angeles. In I. Light & P. Bhachu (Eds.), *Immigration and entrepreneurship: Culture, capital, and ethnic networks* (pp. 185-204). New York: Transaction.

Nagel, B. (1986). Gypsies in the United States and Great Britain. In S. Olzak & J. Nagel (Eds.), *Competitive ethnic relations* (pp. 69-70). New York: Academic Press.

Nash, M. (1989). *The cauldron of ethnicity in the modern world.* Chicago: University of Chicago Press.

New York City Department of Planning. (1992). *Demographic profiles: A portrait of New York's community districts from the 1980 and 1990 censuses of population and housing.* New York: Author.

Olzak, S., & Nagel, J. (1986). *Competitive ethnic relations.* New York: Academic Press.

Park, I. H., Fawcett, J. T., Arnold, F., & Gardner, R. (1990). *Korean immigrants and U.S. immigration policy: A predeparture perspective* (The East-West Population Institute Paper Series, No. 114). Honolulu: East-West Center.

Park, R., Burgess, E., & McKenzie, R. (1967). *The city.* Chicago: University of Chicago Press.

Pido, A. J. A. (1986). *The Pilipinos in America: Macro/micro dimensions of immigration and integration.* Staten Island: Center for Migration Studies.

Portes, A., & Rumbaut, R. (1990). *Immigrant America: A portrait.* Berkeley: University of California Press.

Ross-Sheriff, F. (1991). Adaptation and integration into American society: Major issues affecting Asian Americans. In S. M. Furuto, R. Biswas, D. K. Chung, K. Murase, & F. Ross-Sheriff (Eds.), *Social work practice with Asian Americans* (pp. 45-64). Newbury Park, CA: Sage.

Saito, L. (1989). Japanese Americans and the new Chinese immigrants: The politics of adaptation. *California Sociologists, 12,* 195-211.

Saito, L., & Horton, J. (1993). The Chinese immigration and the rise of Asian American politics in Monterey Park, California. In E. Bonacich, P. Ong, & L. Cheng (Eds.), *Struggles for a place: The new Asian immigration in the restructuring political economy.* Philadelphia: Temple University Press.

Sowell, T. (1975). *Race and economics.* New York: David McKay.

Takaki, R. (1989). *Strangers from a different shore: A history of Asian Americans.* Boston: Little, Brown.

Thomas, W. I., & Znaniecki, F. (1927). *The Polish peasants in Europe and America.* New York: Knopf.

Tran, T. V. (1988). The Vietnamese American family. In C. H. Mindel, R. W. Habenstein, & R. Wright, Jr. (Eds.), *Ethnic families in America* (pp. 276-299). New York: Elsevier.

U.S. Bureau of the Census. (1973). *U.S. census of population: 1970, subject reports: Japanese, Chinese, and Filipinos in the U.S.* (PC[2]-1-C). Washington, DC: U.S. Government Printing Office.

U.S. Bureau of the Census. (1983). *1980 census of population, general population characteristics, United States summary* (PC80-1-B1). Washington, DC: U.S. Government Printing Office.

U.S. Bureau of the Census. (1984). *1980 census of population, detailed population characteristics, United States summary* (PC80-1-D1). Washington, DC: U.S. Government Printing Office.

U.S. Bureau of the Census. (1993a). *1990 census of population, general population characteristics, the United States* (CP-1-1). Washington, DC: U.S. Government Printing Office.

U.S. Bureau of the Census. (1993b). *1993 census of population, the foreign born population in the U.S.* (CP-3-1). Washington, DC: U.S. Government Printing Office.

U.S. Bureau of the Census. (1993c). *1990 census of population, Asians and Pacific Islanders in the United States* (CP-3-5). Washington, DC: U.S. Government Printing Office.

U.S. Bureau of the Census. (1994). *1990 census of population, general social and economic characteristics, the United States* (CP-2-1). Washington, DC: U.S. Government Printing Office.

Williams, R. B. (1988). *Religions of immigrants from India and Pakistan.* New York: Cambridge University Press.

World Almanac and Imprint of Pharos Books. (1991). *The world almanac and books of facts.* New York: Scripps Howard.

Xenos, P. S., Gardner, R. W., Barringer, H. R., & Levin, M. J. (1987). Asian Americans: Growth and change in the 1970's. In J. T. Fawcett & B. V. Carino (Eds.), *Pacific bridges: The new immigration from Asia and the Pacific Islands* (pp. 249-284). Staten Island: Center for Migration Studies.

Yancy, W., Ericksen, E., & Juliani, R. (1976). Emergent ethnicity: A review and reformulation. *American Sociological Review, 41,* 391-403.

Yochum, G., & Agarwal, V. (1988). Permanent labor certifications for alien professionals, *International Migration Review, 22,* 265-281.

Yoon, I. J. (1993). *The social origin of Korean immigration to the United States from 1965 to the present* (Papers of the Program on Population, No. 121). Honolulu: East-West Center.

Yuan, D. Y. (1970). Voluntary segregation: A study of New York Chinatown. In M. Kurokawa (Ed.), *Minority responses* (pp. 134-144). New York: Random House.

3

Major Issues Relating to
Asian American Experiences

PYONG GAP MIN

This chapter introduces major issues relating to Asian American experiences. Some are practical issues with policy implications, such as anti-Asian violence. Other issues concern Asian American experiences that have both theoretical and practical implications. For example, Asian Americans' degree of socioeconomic success is a question of interpretation, using a particular theoretical perspective, as much as a practical question concerning the economic well-being of Asian Americans. Therefore, whenever necessary, I will introduce a theoretical orientation useful for understanding the issue under consideration.

Depending on our ideological and/or theoretical position, we have different views about which issues are important to the experiences of Asian Americans. As stated in the introductory chapter, this book emphasizes structural factors such as institutional barriers, discrimination, and disadvantages facing Asian Americans, rather than the cultural mechanisms employed for their successful adjustment. This structural approach and the related theoretical perspectives have largely determined which issues concerning Asian Americans are presented in this chapter.

In the 1970s, the U.S. media and many scholars portrayed Asian Americans as successful minority groups that overcame disadvantages through hard work, family ties, and emphasis on children's education (Bell, 1985; Kitano, 1974; Kitano & Sue, 1973; Oxnam, 1986; Peterson, 1966; Ramirez, 1986). Largely in reaction to this "model minority" thesis, Asian American scholars began to emphasize the structural barriers facing Asian Americans. The revisionist critique of the model minority thesis currently has a powerful influence in Asian American scholarship (Chan, 1991, pp. 167-171; Chun, 1980; Crystal, 1989; Divoky, 1988; Endo, 1980; Furuto, Biswas, Chung, Murase, & Ross-Sheriff, 1990; Gould, 1988; Hurh & Kim, 1982, 1989; Kwong, 1987; Okihiro, 1988; Osajima, 1988; Suzuki, 1977; Takaki, 1989, pp. 474-484; Wong, 1985). The attack on the model minority thesis is not limited to academic research. Activists, social workers in Asian American communities, Asian American faculty members, and the U.S. Commission on Civil Rights have also expressed concerns about the negative consequences of the success image (Asian Pacific American Education Advisory Committee, California State University, 1990; U.S. Commission on Civil Rights, 1992; Yun, 1989). This chapter will introduce many issues that revisionist critics of the model minority thesis consider important.

Asian Americans' Underreward and Underemployment

Several topics discussed as major issues in this chapter concern socioeconomic adjustment. A question underlying all these issues is whether Asian Americans are socioeconomically successful. Traditionally, the U.S. media and many researchers have emphasized Asian American success stories. Those who considered Asian Americans successful focused on their high family incomes (relative to white family incomes) and their high educational levels.

However, revisionist critics claim that this traditional interpretation has little validity. They concede that Asian Americans excel in education and earn relatively high incomes. But they point out that to assess Asian American's success in socioeconomic adjustment, we must compare their incomes to their educational levels. Revisionist critics argue that Asian American workers do not receive economic rewards comparable to their education. To support this argument, many researchers have shown, using regression analysis, that Asian workers receive smaller economic rewards for their education than white workers (Cabezas & Kawaguchi, 1988; Cabezas, Shinagawa, & Kawaguchi, 1987; Hurh & Kim, 1989; Tsukada, 1988; U.S. Commission on Civil Rights, 1988; Wong, 1982). This means that Asian Americans need more education to maintain economic parity with white Americans.

Asian American workers' unequal rewards for their human capital investments suggest that they, like other racial minority members and women, encounter structural barriers in the labor market. Dual labor market theory is useful for understanding this social phenomenon. Dual labor market theory was created as an alternative to the human capital investment model to explain earnings. Dual labor market theorists distinguish between primary and secondary labor markets. The primary labor market is characterized by high wages, fringe benefits, job security, unionization, and opportunity for promotion; the secondary labor market has the opposite characteristics. The theory's central argument is that the kind of market a worker is located in is a more accurate predictor of his/her earnings than the worker's human capital investments (Edwards, Reigh, & Gordon, 1975; Gordon, 1972).

Using dual labor market theory, several sociologists (Bluestone, Murphy, & Stevenson, 1973; Doeringer & Piore, 1971; Piore, 1979) argue that a large proportion of minority members and new immigrants, regardless of their education, are trapped in the secondary labor market. Some revisionist scholars (Cabezas et al., 1987; Cabezas & Kawaguchi, 1988; Hurh & Kim, 1982; Lee, 1989; Toji & Johnson, 1992) use dual labor market theory as a frame of reference to discuss Asian Americans' unequal rewards for their education. Partly because of racial discrimination, a higher proportion of Asian Americans work in the secondary labor market than their education levels might indicate. Some scholars (Shin & Chang, 1988; Taylor & Kim, 1980) show that even Asian workers in the primary labor market, such as Korean immigrant physicians and Asian American government employees, are concentrated in periphery specialty areas or less influential positions.

Moreover, revisionist critics also point out that Asian Americans' high median family income compared to whites is not a good indicator of their socioeconomic position. Critics provide three reasons for not using family income to measure Asian American economic success. First, the relatively high median family income among Asian Americans is misleading because all Asian ethnic groups have more workers per family than whites. Asian Americans generally need more workers per family to maintain parity with white Americans. Second, Asian ethnic groups' median family incomes do not accurately reflect their standards of living, because Asian Americans are concentrated in San Francisco, Los Angeles, New York City, and Honolulu, where living expenses are much higher than in the United States as a whole. Finally, revisionist scholars argue that average family income is misleading because Asian ethnic groups are socioeconomically polarized. We will come back to this point in the next section.

Negative Effects of the Success Image on Welfare Benefits

Revisionist critics argue that the success image is not only invalid but also detrimental to the welfare of Asian Americans. They point out that because Asian Americans are assumed to be economically well-off, they are eliminated from affirmative action and other programs designed to help disadvantaged minorities. As Hurh and Kim (1989) forcefully argue, "Asian Americans are considered by the dominant group as 'successful' and 'problem free' and not in need of social programs designed to benefit disadvantaged minorities such as black and Mexican Americans" (p. 528). Nakanishi (1985-1986) points out that the alleged success of Asian Americans "disguises their lack of representation in the most significant national arenas and institutions" (p. 2). Several revisionist scholars also point out that the success stories of Asian Americans have stimulated anti-Asian sentiment and violence on college campuses and communities during recent years (Osajima, 1988; Takaki, 1989, p. 479; U.S. Commission on Civil Rights, 1986, 1992; Wong, 1991). In addition, Hurh and Kim claim that by defining Asian Americans as a model minority, the dominant group has led Asian Americans to develop "false consciousness." Many Asian Americans believe that they have attained middle-class status without realizing they are underemployed and overworked.

Revisionist scholars also point out that the positive stereotype of Asian Americans negatively affects other minority groups as well. By emphasizing the importance of cultural traits and values in Asians' successful adjustment, the success image in effect blames other less successful minority groups for their own failure. It thus legitimates the openness of American society. As one writer (Crystal, 1989) comments:

> The existence of a "model minority" supports the belief that democracy "works" and that the racism about which some ethnic groups complain is the product of their own shortcomings and is not inherent in society. To be able to make an assertion is, as one might imagine, extremely important to many persons in power. (p. 407)

The above criticism becomes significant because when politicians and journalists talk about the success stories of Asian Americans, they may intend to suggest that blacks and other minority groups have not succeeded because of their cultural deficiencies.[1]

Revisionist critics have made us aware that the positive stereotypes of Asian Americans can have negative consequences. However, one could argue that the revisionist critics fail to recognize the positive effects the model minority thesis has had on Asian Americans while overemphasizing its negative effects. Positive stereotypes are likely to lead policy makers to be less sensitive to the needs of Asian Americans and to stimulate anti-Asian sentiments among less successful whites and minorities. However, positive stereotypes are also likely to lead many Americans—managers, teachers, community leaders, and home owners—to hold more favorable views of Asian Americans and treat them more favorably. The connection between the positive stereotypes of Asian Americans and their favorable treatment in the classroom, job hiring, and housing is so obvious that we need not provide evidence to support this argument. Nevertheless, there is one empirical study that focused on the positive effects of these stereotypes. In her Westinghouse project, Choi (1988) showed that high school teachers expect Asian students to perform better in science and math and to be more motivated than white students. Based on the findings, she concluded that "the high expectation feedback the Asian students receive from their teachers might push them a little further than if teachers had a lower expectation of them" (Choi, 1988, pp. 17-18).

Underrepresentation in Executive and Managerial Positions

Another important issue regarding Asian Americans' socioeconomic adjustment is their underrepresentation in important administrative, executive, and managerial positions in corporate and public sectors. Asian Americans are well-represented in professional occupations mainly because they are highly educated and obtain professional certificates. However, they are severely underrepresented in high-ranking executive and administrative positions (Chan, 1989; Tang, 1993; Tom, 1988). For example, only two Asian Americans currently serve as presidents of major universities, although Asian American professors constitute a large proportion of the total faculty in American colleges and universities. Few Asian Americans hold important positions in local and federal governments.

Asian Americans may be at a disadvantage for these administrative positions because they lack communication and leadership skills, a result of the authoritarian child socialization techniques practiced in many Asian American families. However, it is also true that many well-qualified Asian Americans are not given these desirable positions because Asians are stereotyped as docile and lacking leadership skills. Compared to blacks, Asian Americans are severely underrepresented in leadership positions, particularly in higher education institutions and government, partly because affirmative action does not apply to them.

Closely related to the underrepresentation of Asian Americans in high-ranking executive and administrative positions is the so-called "glass ceiling." Glass ceiling refers to a situation in which people cannot advance beyond a certain level in their careers. The term can be applied to the mobility barrier facing women and minority members. However, the term is largely used to indicate the difficulty that highly educated Asian Americans encounter in reaching the top of the occupational ladder (Der, 1993; Duleep & Sanders, 1992; Rajagopal, 1990; Tang, 1993; U.S. Commission on Civil Rights, 1992, pp. 131-135). For example, analyzing the career histories of 12,200 Caucasian and Asian engineers, Tang (1993) showed that there was more racial disparity in managerial representation and upward mobility than in earnings. The glass ceiling has been the topic of many seminars and conferences on Asian Americans' occupational adjustment.

Class Homogeneity Versus Class Division

When people claim that Asian Americans are socioeconomically successful, they assume that Asian Americans are more or less homogeneous in socioeconomic status. However, as noted in the previous chapter, Asian Americans are not a socioeconomically homogeneous group. Indochinese refugees and immigrants from mainland China are far behind other Asian groups in socioeconomic status. There are also significant intraethnic differentials in socioeconomic status. Those who emphasize Asian American success in socioeconomic adjustment use statistical averages as the indicators. However, revisionist critics argue that averages are misleading because some Asian ethnic groups are socioeconomically polarized. Statistically speaking, Asian Americans have a bipolar distribution, with proportionally far more people both above and below the average. Occupationally, larger proportions of Asian Americans than white Americans occupy both the highest and the lowest tiers of the occupational hierarchy. Economically, a much larger proportion of Asian Americans than white Americans is at the poverty level, although proportionally more of them belong to the high-income brackets. As emphasized in Chapter 4, the Chinese American community is extremely polarized along class lines.

Asian American children's educational performance is also polarized. Using standardized test results as indicators, Asian American students as a group do much better than other minority students, even better than white students. Asian Americans stand well above white Americans in college enrollment.[2] However, as Hu (1989) indicates, Asian American students have the largest proportions of both the highest and the lowest Scholastic Achievement Test scores. Compared to whites, Asian American students include proportionally larger numbers of both super students and poor students. Revisionist scholars criticize the American media for focusing on

Asian American students' success stories, giving the impression that most Asian American students are super students.

Ethnic Solidarity Versus Class Conflict

The issue of class homogeneity versus class division is closely related to another issue: the issue of ethnic solidarity versus class conflict. Researchers traditionally emphasized each Asian community's strong ethnic ties based on common culture and national origin (Light, 1972; Miyamoto, 1939; Montero, 1975). For example, in his study of the Japanese community in Seattle, Miyamoto (1939) described ethnic solidarity as its most conspicuous characteristic. However, since the late 1970s, an increasing number of Asian American scholars have shown class conflicts in Asian ethnic communities. The Chinatown study by Light and Wong (1975) highlighted the class division between business owners and ethnic employees and their conflicts over economic interests. Based on his analysis of the Chinese community in Toronto, Thompson (1979) also indicated that class conflict affected the structure of a North American Chinese community. In another article (Thompson, 1980), he discussed major classes in Chinatowns in North America and suggested that a modified Marxian class model best describes the current structure of Chinese ethnic communities.

In the 1980s, several researchers showed the economic disadvantages of Chinese workers employed in ethnic businesses in Chinatowns in New York and San Francisco, jobs characterized by low wages and poor working conditions (Mar, 1984; Ong, 1984; Sanders & Nee, 1987). They suggested that Chinatown business owners achieve economic mobility largely by exploiting co-ethnic employees. The emphasis on economic exploitation is in sharp contrast with the enclave economy thesis, which emphasizes the economic benefits to both business owners and employees in an ethnic enclave (Portes & Bach, 1985; Wilson & Portes, 1980; Zhou, 1992). In his New York Chinatown study, Kwong (1987) stressed the Chinese community's polarization into the working and professional classes. Other scholars consider class division in the Chinese community important in understanding the differences, not only in their life chances, but also in lifestyles, including their family system (Glenn, 1983; Huang, 1981; Tasi, 1980; Wong, 1988).

Japanese Americans are culturally and socioeconomically more homogeneous than Chinese Americans and may therefore be less suitable for class analysis. Nevertheless, researchers have recently criticized the research tradition for overemphasizing the homogeneity and solidarity of

Japanese Americans (Okihiro, 1988). Researchers have increasingly emphasized the class conflict of the early Japanese community rather than its ethnic solidarity (Chan, 1991, p. 70; Ichioka, 1976, 1988). For example, in his study of first-generation Japanese, Ichioka (1988) highlighted the exploitative relationship between Japanese labor contractors and Japanese labor immigrants. Glenn (1980, 1986) analyzed the difficulty of Japanese American women engaged in domestic service, who were doubly exploited both as Asian Americans and as women.

Family Ties Versus Family Conflicts

Traditionally, the U.S. media and researchers depict Asian Americans as maintaining strong family ties, which facilitate their adjustment in American society. They emphasize that the harmony between husband and wife and parents and children in Asian American families, particularly Asian immigrant families, is based on traditional family values brought from Asian countries.

To what extent Asian Americans maintain family ties is an empirical question that can be determined by comparing Asian American families with white American families. However, our perception may be shaped by our particular approach or theoretical orientation. The traditional interpretation—that family ties facilitate Asian immigrants' adjustment—is the cultural approach, in that it tries to explain Asian Americans' adjustment in terms of their cultural mechanism, family ties. In reaction, more and more researchers now apply the structural approach, paying great attention to the effects of structural conditions on Asian American families. As Kibria (1993) states in her introduction to Vietnamese immigrant families:

> In contrast to such cultural explanations, I suggest that immigrant families must be analyzed in relation to the external structural conditions encountered by immigrants in the "host" society. These structural conditions provide the fundamental parameters—opportunities and conditions—within which immigrants must construct their family life. (p. 22)

Kibria (1993) indicates that the increase in Vietnamese women's control over economic and social resources and the concomitant decline in Vietnamese men's earning power and social status, contributed, along with other factors, to a shift in relative power from men to women. This shift in power, although desirable from the egalitarian point of view, brings about conflicts and tensions in marital relations as Vietnamese women challenge men's traditional patriarchal authority. The loss of parental social and economic resources and exposure to the American socioeconomic environment have also liberated Vietnamese children from parental control, increasing generational conflicts in Vietnamese immigrant families (see also Tran, 1988). Chapters 6 and 8 of this book discuss marital and generational conflicts in Filipino and Korean immigrant families (see also Min, 1993, for marital conflicts in Korean immigrant families).

Glenn's (1983) study of Chinese families was probably the first significant work to examine Asian American families using a structural approach. She emphasized the "changing structure of Chinese-American families resulting from the interplay between shifting institutional constraints and the efforts of the Chinese Americans to maintain family life in the face of these restrictions" (p. 35). Based on a historical analysis, she described three types of Chinese American families that emerged in three different periods: split household, small producer, and dual-wage worker. Similarly, in Chapter 4 of this book, Wong analyzes four types of Chinese families existing in four different periods. This structural approach to Chinese families is a good contrast to the cultural approach, which emphasized the effects of the Confucian ideology on Chinese American families (Hsu, 1971).

Asian Americans' Underutilization and the Myth of Their Mental Health

Another important issue with policy implications is the underuse of mental health services by Asian Americans and the myth of their mental well-being. Data show that, compared to white Americans, Asian Americans are underrepresented as mental health patients (Kitano, 1969; Snowden & Cheung, 1990; Sue & McKinney, 1980). Based on the data, policy makers and non-Asian social scientists assume that Asian Americans have lower rates of mental disturbance than the U.S. general population. They also assume that through strong family ties and informal ethnic networks, Asian Americans can adequately care for mental health patients informally without depending on formal service agencies.

Asian American social workers argue that both of the above assumptions are wrong. Asian American underrepresentation among mental health patients does not imply that they have lower rates of mental disturbance than the general population; it reflects their help-seeking behavior rather than their mental health status (Crystal, 1989). That is, moderately disturbed Asian Americans are reluctant to seek help from mental health services (Sue & Morishima, 1980). And their reluctance has much to do with cultural values emphasizing avoidance of shame and family integrity (Tsai, Teng, & Sue, 1975). Several studies reveal that Asian Americans, particularly Asian immigrants, have a high level of stress and other mental health problems, higher than white Americans (Hurh & Kim, 1990; Kuo, 1984; Loo, Tong, & True, 1989; Ying, 1988). Overall, recent Asian immigrants have more mental problems than native-born Asian Americans. Elderly Asian American immigrants, middle-aged immigrant women, and Southeast Asian refugees in particular have been identified as high risk (Crystal, 1989; Kim, 1988; Sue, 1993).

Asian Americans' mental disturbance is a serious issue. But Asian American social workers and community leaders consider their underuse of mental health services a more serious issue. Funding agencies and policy makers tend to allot funds for mental health services based on use and therefore underestimate Asian Americans' needs for mental health services. Asian American social workers argue that need, rather than demand, should determine funding targets and program policy. As Crystal (1989) states:

> Underutilization is an important issue for the Asian American community because it is still used by governmental agencies to buttress the belief that Asian Americans have low rates of mental disturbance. The criterion of use rather than need determines funding targets and program policy. What must be recognized is the distinction between needs and demands: Low demand as reflected in low utilization should not be misconstrued as an absence of need. (p. 408)

Asian American social workers recommend that mental health service agencies hire more bilingual and bicultural staff members to serve Asian American mental health patients with language difficulties and cultural differences. They also recommend that community education be given to Asian Americans so that they do not consider mental health problems shameful and private (Sue, 1993).

Lack of Political Representation

As previously discussed, Asian Americans have problems in their socioeconomic adjustment. Nevertheless, Asian Americans generally do well due to their success in education and their readiness to work long hours for economic mobility. Although Asian Americans are underrepresented in corporate businesses, they are well-represented in the small-business sector. Compared to blacks and Hispanics, Asian Americans are well-represented in professional occupations and small businesses. However, Asian Americans are greatly underrepresented in politics, far below blacks and Hispanics. As of 1992, there were only four U.S. Congress members of Asian ancestry: two in Hawaii and two in California. In contrast, there were 38 black and 20 Hispanic members of Congress. Outside of Hawaii, where Asians are numerically dominant, only five Asian Americans were elected to the state legislatures, all in Western states. There is only one Asian American on the city council in Los Angeles, the largest Asian American city on the U.S. mainland. Although New York City had nearly 550,000 Asian Americans in 1992, it has never had an Asian American on its city council.

Several factors contribute to Asian American underrepresentation in politics (see Espiritu, 1992, pp. 157-163; U.S. Commission on Civil Rights, 1992, pp. 157-163). First, because most Asian Americans are recent immigrants, most are not eligible to vote. Moreover, Asian Americans who can vote have lower voter participation rates than other populations (Nakanishi, 1985-1986). For example, a survey of California voters found that only 69% of Asian American citizens voted in 1984, compared to 80% of non-Hispanic white and black citizens (U.S. Commission on Civil Rights, 1992, p. 158). Their lack of interest in American politics and lack of knowledge about the American political system contribute to their relatively low voter participation rate.[3]

Even if eligible Asian Americans voted in a higher proportion than other populations, they would have difficulty getting Asian American candidates elected to Congress or state legislatures due to their small population size and low level of segregation. Although the Asian American population has radically increased over the last 20 years, it remains small compared to black and Hispanic populations. Outside of Hawaii, there is no congressional district where Asian Americans make up the majority of the population. Even in areas of California where Asian Americans compose a large proportion of residents, Asian American candidates have two additional disadvantages. As already discussed, the Asian American population is characterized by diverse ethnic groups, social classes, generations, and political ideologies. This diversity hinders Pan-Asian solidarity in electoral politics (Espiritu, 1992, p. 59). Furthermore, discriminatory apportionment schemes split Asian American voters in one area into several districts. For example, Koreatown, Chinatown, and Filipinotown in Los Angeles are each divided among several city council districts (U.S. Commission on Civil Rights, 1992, p. 159).

Discrimination in College Admission

Their cultural tradition stressing education and their higher professional socioeconomic status enable Asian immigrants to successfully educate their children, although there are big intergroup differences in terms of socioeconomic status and national origin (Wang, 1993). Although the United States is an achievement-oriented society, Asian societies put more emphasis on children's education. Many Asian immigrants made the trans-Pacific migration mainly in search of a better education for their children. A disproportionately large number of recent Asian immigrants were able to send their children to elite universities. Also, a large number of Asian students annually come to major universities for undergraduate and graduate study. As a result, Asian American enrollment at many prestigious American colleges and universities has increased dramatically. Several campuses of the University of California system have witnessed a phenomenal increase in the number of Asian American students since the mid-1970s. Over the last 20 years, the proportion of Asian American students has also significantly increased in several private universities with national reputations.

Administrators in prestigious universities, perhaps concerned about the radical increase in Asian American students, have taken measures to lessen the increase. Asian American students, faculty members, and community leaders charge that these elite universities used quotas to limit the enrollment of Asian American applicants (Takagi, 1990). Recent internal and external investigations suggest that these universities discriminated against Asian American students in granting admission. This is a controversial issue (Biemiller, 1986; Lindsey, 1987; Reynolds, 1988; Takagi, 1990, 1992; Takaki, 1982; Wang, 1988).[4]

The following are some of the major findings from several investigations (see Takagi, 1992):

1. A smaller proportion of Asian American applicants received admission than white applicants in several elite universities.
2. Both Asian applicants and Asian students admitted to Brown University had higher SAT averages than white counterparts.

3. A minimum score of 400 on the SAT verbal test was imposed at UC Berkeley to deny admissions to eligible Asian American immigrant applicants.
4. Asian American applicants to UC Berkeley who were eligible for the Educational Opportunity Program were automatically redirected to other University of California campuses.
5. The preferences given to children of alumni and to recruited athletic applicants largely explained the admission rate disparity between white and Asian applicants at Harvard.

Whether or not elite universities discriminated against Asian American students is a complicated issue that cannot be deciphered by statistical facts alone. As Takagi (1990) nicely analyzed, participants in the admissions controversy interpreted the same facts in different ways to justify their claims and counterclaims. In admissions policy, UC Berkeley and other universities combine strict academic criteria with supplemental criteria such as personal essays, extracurricular activities, and extra European foreign language courses. Asian American organizations argue that using supplemental criteria discriminates against Asian American students, who are generally disadvantaged in these areas. However, university officials justify the supplementary criteria in the name of student body *diversity*. That is, they claim that the supplemental criteria add diversity to the class by admitting students with more attributes than good grades and high test scores.

Conservative white politicians have used the Asian American student admissions controversy to attack affirmative action. They argue that elite universities use discriminatory quotas against Asian American students to create a floor for underrepresented black and Hispanic students. They suggest that abolishing affirmative action policies in admissions would eliminate discrimination against Asian American students. However, Asian American leaders object to the pairing of Asian American admissions with an attack on affirmative action. They argue that because Asian American students do not compete with black or Hispanic students, their admission is a separate issue from affirmative action.

When Jewish students in Ivy League schools increased in the first half of the 20th century, Jewish applicants encountered restrictive admission measures. Asian American students will continue to increase in major universities in the future. To lessen the increasing proportion of Asian American students, more restrictive measures may be taken in colleges and universities. However, any such restrictive measure is likely to meet a strong Pan-Asian opposition. If university officials attempt to use measures to curb the increase in Asian American students, it will be interesting to see what arguments they will use and how Asian American organizations will challenge their arguments.

Anti-Asian Violence

Minority members in the United States are often subject to "hate crimes" or "bias crimes"—crimes motivated by animosity toward victims because of their race, religion, sexual orientation, or national origin. In the 1980s, civil rights laws and ordinances were passed to protect minority citizens. Nevertheless, there is evidence that hate crimes against Asian Americans have increased since the early 1980s. The U.S. Commission on Civil Rights monitors and collects data on the violations of minority rights. It regularly releases reports on cases of discrimination and violence against minority members. The reports on anti-Asian discrimination and violence released by the agency in 1986 and 1992 both concluded that anti-Asian violence is on the rise (U.S. Commission on Civil Rights, 1986, 1992). Reports released by Los Angeles County in 1990 and 1991 also indicate that hate crimes against people of Asian ancestry have recently increased. Because the Hate Crimes Statistics Act enacted in 1990 requires the U.S. Attorney General to collect and report data on hate crimes, more accurate information on hate crimes against Asian Americans will be available in the future.

Several factors have contributed to the rise in hate crimes against Asian Americans. First of all, the great increase in the Asian American population has contributed to the rise in anti-Asian crimes. As previously noted, Asian Americans currently constitute a large proportion of the population in many cities. The increase in the Asian American population simply increases the likelihood that more Asian Americans will interact with members of non-Asian groups, and thus more of them will be targets of hate crimes. Moreover, the increase in Asian immigrants with language barriers and different customs is likely to increase the prejudice against Asian Americans.

Second, economic factors play an important role in the increase of anti-Asian violence. The economic recession that began in the mid-1970s coincided with the influx of Asian immigrants. Many Americans, both black and white, feel that new Asian immigrants took over their jobs and businesses, although research shows that this is not the case (Borjas, 1989; Simon, 1989). Many Korean immigrants established businesses in black inner-city neighborhoods as living conditions of the black underclass became increasingly worse. Korean merchants all over the country have been targets of black hostility in the form of physical assault, boycott, arson, murder, and press attack. Black hostility toward Korean merchants culminated during the Los Angeles race riots in the spring of 1992, when more than 2,000 Korean-owned stores were burned and/or looted. Undoubtedly, black people's perception that Korean immigrants economically exploit them is mainly responsible for black hostility toward Koreans.

Another economic factor influencing the recent rise in anti-Asian violence cases is the trade deficit between the United States and Japan and the general perception that Japanese imports cause economic problems in the United States. Vincent Chin, a Chinese American, was murdered in 1982 by two white auto workers who, mistaking him for a Japanese, sought a scapegoat for their economic problems (Wong, 1991). As the U.S. economic situation further deteriorated in 1991, U.S. media and high-ranking politicians blamed the Japanese for the trade imbalance. The high unemployment rate and the political controversy over trade deficits heightened anti-Japanese sentiments all over the country. Recent Japan bashing culminated in the murder of a Japanese businessman in his home in Ventura County, California, in February 1992. Two weeks before he was stabbed to death, he was threatened by two white young men, who blamed Japan for causing economic problems in the United States ("A Japanese," 1992).

Closely related to the economic factors in anti-Asian violence is the success image of Asian Americans. As previously discussed, both the U.S. media and scholars depict Asian Americans as "successful model minorities," which has negative effects on the interests of Asian Americans. The success image can heighten the resentment toward Asian American academic and economic success and in turn increase hate crimes against them. Many white Americans, particularly those in the lower tiers of the socioeconomic hierarchy, are jealous and resentful of Asian Americans' success. Out of their status anxiety, they believe that Asian Americans belong to an "inferior race." Asian Americans' success image only strengthens their status anxiety.

Notes

1. Since the late 1960s, various cultural explanations have been severely criticized in the field of race and ethnic relations in the United States mainly because of this conservative implication, the implication that they "blame the victims."

2. For example, the 1990 census indicates that 54.1% of Asian Americans 20 to 21 years old were enrolled in school in comparison to only 33.3% of their white counterparts (U.S. Bureau of the Census, 1993, pp. 1, 97, 98).

3. Survey studies have shown that Asian American immigrants are more interested in home country politics than politics in the United States.

4. Takagi's book (1992) most systematically analyzed the controversy.

References

Asian Pacific American Education Advisory Committee, California State University. (1990). *Enriching California's future: Asian Pacific Americans in the CSU.* Long Beach: Office of the Chancellor, California State University.

Bell, D. A. (1985, July 15). The triumph of Asian-Americans: America's greatest success story. *New Republic,* pp. 22, 24-31.

Biemiller, L. (1986, November 19). Asian students fear top colleges use quota systems. *The Chronicle of Higher Education,* p. 3

Bluestone, B., Murphy, W., & Stevenson, M. (1973). *Low wages and the working poor.* Ann Arbor: Institute of Labor and Industrial Relations, University of Michigan.

Borjas, G. (1989). *Friends or strangers: Impacts of immigrants on U.S. economy.* New York: Basic Books.

Cabezas, A., & Kawaguchi, G. (1988). Empirical evidence for continuing Asian American income inequality: The human capital model and labor market segmentation. In G. Y. Okihiro, S. Hune, A. A. Hansen, & J. M. Liu (Eds.), *Reflections on shattered windows: Promises and prospects for Asian American studies* (pp. 144-164). Pullman: Washington State University Press.

Cabezas, A., Shinagawa, L., & Kawaguchi, G. (1987). New inquiries into the socioeconomic status of Pilipino Americans in California. *Amerasia Journal, 13,* 1-22.

Chan, S. (1989, November/December). Beyond the affirmative action: Empowering Asian American faculty. *Change,* pp. 48-51.

Chan, S. (1991). *Asian Americans: An interpretive history.* Boston: Twayne.

Choi, M. (1988). *Race, gender and eyeglasses: Teachers' perceptions of Asian, Black and White students.* Paper submitted to Westinghouse Science Talent Search, Stuyvesant High School, New York City.

Chun, K. T. (1980). The myth of Asian American success and its educational ramifications. *IRCD Bulletin, 15,* 1-12.

Crystal, D. (1989). Asian Americans and the myth of the model minority. *Social Casework, 70,* 405-413.

Der, H. (1993). Asian Pacific Islanders and the "glass ceiling"—new era of civil rights activism. In LEAP Asian Pacific Islander Public Policy Institute and UCLA Asian American Studies Center (Eds.), *The state of Asian Pacific America: Policy issues to the year 2020* (pp. 215-232). Los Angeles: LEAP Asian Pacific Islander Public Policy Institute and UCLA Asian American Studies Center.

Divoky, D. (1988). The model minority goes to school. *Phi Delta Kappan, 70,* 219-222.

Doeringer, P. B., & Piore, M. (1971). *Internal labor market and manpower analysis.* Lexington, MA: D. C. Heath.

Duleep, H. O., & Sanders, S. (1992). Discrimination at the top: American-born Asian and white men. *Industrial Relations, 31,* 416-432.

Edwards, R., Reigh, M., & Gordon, D. (Eds). (1975). *Labor market segmentation.* Lexington, MA: D. C. Heath.

Endo, R. (1980). Asian Americans and higher education. *Phylon, 41,* 367-378.

Espiritu, Y. L. (1992). *Asian American panethnicity: Bridging institutions and identities.* Philadelphia: Temple University Press.

Furuto, S. M., Biswas, R., Chung, D. K., Murase, K., & Ross-Sheriff, F. (Eds.). (1990). *Social work practice with Asian Americans.* Newbury Park, CA: Sage.

Glenn, E. N. (1980). The dialectics of wage work: Japanese-American women and domestic service, 1905-1940. *Feminist Studies, 6,* 432-471.

Glenn, E. N. (1983). Split household, small producer and dual wage earner: An analysis of Chinese American family strategies. *Journal of Marriage and the Family, 45,* 35-46.

Glenn, E. N. (1986). *Issei, Nisei, war bride: Three generations of Japanese American women in domestic service.* Philadelphia: Temple University Press.

Gordon, D. M. (1972). *Theories of poverty and underemployment.* Lexington, MA: Lexington Books.

Gould, K. H. (1988). Asian and Pacific Islanders: Myth and reality. *National Association of Social Workers, 37,* 142-147.

Hsu, F. L. K. (1971). *The challenge of the American dream: The Chinese in the United States.* Belmont, CA: Wadsworth.

Hu, A. (1989). Asian Americans: Model or double minority? *Amerasia Journal, 15*(1), 243-257.

Huang, L. J. (1981). The Chinese American family. In C. H. Mindel & R. W. Habenstein (Eds.), *Ethnic families in America: Patterns and variations* (2nd ed., pp. 115-141). New York: Elsevier.

Hurh, W. M., & Kim, K. C. (1982). Race relations paradigm and Korean-American Research: A sociology of knowledge perspective. In Eui-Young Yu, E. Phillips, & Eun Sik Yang (Eds.), *Koreans in Los Angeles: Prospects and promises* (pp. 219-246). Los Angeles: Center for Korean and Korean-American Studies, California State University.

Hurh, W. M., & Kim, K. C. (1989). The "success" image of Asian Americans: Its validity and its practical implications. *Ethnic and Racial Studies, 12,* 512-538.

Hurh, W. M., & Kim, K. C. (1990). Correlates of Korean immigrants' mental health. *Journal of Nervous and Mental Disease, 178,* 703-711.

Ichioka, Y. (1976). Early Issei socialists and the Japanese community. In E. Gee (Ed.), *Counterpoint: Perspectives on Asian America* (pp. 47-62). Los Angeles: Asian American Studies Center, University of California at Los Angeles.

Ichioka, Y. (1988). *The Issei: The world of the first generation Japanese immigrants, 1885-1924.* New York: Free Press.

A Japanese businessman was stabbed to death. (1992, February 26). *Korea Times Los Angeles,* p. 2.

Kibria, N. (1993). *Family tightrope: The changing lives of Vietnamese Americans.* Princeton, NJ: Princeton University Press.

Kim, U. C. (1988). *Acculturation of Korean immigrants to Canada: Psychological, demographic and behavioral profiles of emigrating Koreans, non-emigrating Koreans, and Korean-Canadians.* Unpublished doctoral dissertation, Queens University at Kingston, Canada.

Kitano, H. (1969). Japanese-American mental illness. In S. C. Plog & R. B. Edgerton (Eds.), *Changing perspectives in mental illness* (pp. 256-284). New York: Holt, Rinehart & Winston.

Kitano, H. (1974). Japanese Americans: The development of a middleman minority. *Pacific Historical Review, 43*, 500-519.

Kitano, H., & Sue, S. (1973). The model minorities. *Journal of Social Issues, 29*, 1-9.

Kuo, W. H. (1984). Prevalence of depression among Asian Americans. *Journal of Nervous and Mental Disease, 172*, 449-457.

Kwong, P. (1987). *The new Chinatown*. New York: Noonsday.

Lee, S. (1989). Asian immigration and American race-relations: From exclusion to acceptance. *Ethnic and Racial Studies, 12*, 368-390.

Light, I. (1972). *Ethnic enterprise in North America: Business and welfare among Chinese, Japanese, and Blacks*. Berkeley: University of California Press.

Light, I., & Wong, C. C. (1975). Protest or work: Dilemmas of the tourist industry in American Chinatown. *American Journal of Sociology, 80*, 1342-1368.

Lindsey, R. (1987, January 19). Colleges accused of biases to stem Asians' gains. *The New York Times*, p. 6.

Loo, C., Tong, B., & True, R. (1989). A bitter bean: Mental health status and attitudes in Chinatown. *Journal of Community Psychology, 17*, 183-296.

Mar, D. (1984). Chinese immigrant women and the ethnic labor market. *Critical Perspectives of Third World America, 2*, 62-74.

Min, P. G. (1993). Korean immigrant wives' overwork. *Korea Journal of Population and Development, 21*, 23-36.

Miyamoto, S. F. (1939). *Social solidarity among the Japanese in Seattle* (Publications in the Social Sciences, Vol. 11, No. 2). Seattle: University of Washington.

Montero, D. M. (1975). *The Japanese American community: A study of generational changes in ethnic affiliation*. Doctoral dissertation, University of California, Los Angeles.

Nakanishi, D. T. (1985-1986). Asian American politics: An agenda for research. *Amerasia Journal, 12*(2), 1-27.

Okihiro, G. Y. (1988). The idea of community and a "particular type of history." In G. Y. Okihiro, S. Hune, A. A. Hansen, & J. M. Liu (Eds.), *Reflections on shattered windows* (pp. 175-183). Pullman: Washington State University Press.

Ong, P. (1984). Chinatown unemployment and the ethnic labor market. *Amerasia Journal, 11*, 35-54.

Osajima, K. (1988). Asian Americans as a model minority: An analysis of the popular press image in the 1960s and the 1980s. In G. Y. Okihiro, S. Hune, A. Hansen, & J. Liu (Eds.), *Reflections on shattered windows* (pp. 165-174). Pullman, WA: Washington University Press.

Oxnam, R. (1986, November 30). Why Asians succeed here. *New York Times Magazine*, pp. 89-90, 92.

Peterson, W. (1966, January 9). Success story, Japanese-American style. *New York Times Magazine*, pp. 20-21, 33, 36, 38, 40-41, 43.

Piore, M. (1979). *Birds of passage: Migrant labor and industrial societies*. London: Cambridge University Press.

Portes, A., & Bach, R. (1985). *Latin journey: Cuban and Mexican immigrants in the United States*. Berkeley: University of California Press.

Rajagopal, I. (1990). The glass ceiling in the vertical mosaic: Indian immigrants in Canada. *Canadian Ethnic Studies, 22*, 96-105.

Ramirez, A. (1986, November 24). America's super minority. *Fortune Magazine*, pp. 148-149, 152, 156, 160.

Reynolds, W. B. (1988). *Discrimination against Asian Americans in higher education: Evidence, causes, and cures*. Washington, DC: Civil Rights Division, Department of Justice.

Sanders, J., & Nee, V. (1987). The limits of ethnic solidarity in the enclave economy. *American Sociological Review, 52,* 745-767.

Shin, E. H., & Chang, K. S. (1988). Peripherization of immigrant professionals: Korean physicians in the United States. *International Migration Review, 22,* 609-626.

Simon, J. (1989). *The economic consequences of immigration.* Cambridge, MA: Basil Blackwell.

Snowden, L. R., & Cheung, F. K. (1990). Use of inpatient mental health services by members of ethnic minority groups. *American Psychologists, 45,* 347-355.

Sue, S. (1993). The changing Asian American population: Mental health policy. In LEAP Asian Pacific American Public Policy Institute and UCLA Asian American Studies Center (Eds.), *The state of Asian Pacific America: Policy issues to the year 2020* (pp. 79-93). Los Angeles: LEAP Asian Pacific American Public Policy Institute and UCLA Asian American Studies Center.

Sue, S., & McKinney, H. (1980). Asian Americans in the community mental health care system. In R. Endo, S. Sue, & N. Wagner (Eds.), *Asian Americans: Social and psychological perspectives* (Vol. 2, pp. 291-310). Palo Alto, CA: Science and Behavior Books.

Sue, S., & Morishima, J. (1980). *The mental health of Asian Americans.* San Francisco: Jossey Bass.

Suzuki, B. H. (1977). Education and the socialization of Asian Americans: A revisionist analysis of the "model minority" thesis. *Amerasia Journal, 4,* 23-51.

Takagi, D. Y. (1990). From discrimination to affirmative action: Facts in the Asian American admissions controversy. *Social Problems, 37,* 578-592.

Takagi, D. Y. (1992). *The retreat from race: Asian-American admissions and racial politics.* New Brunswick, NJ: Rutgers University Press.

Takaki, R. (1982). The myth of ethnicity: Scholarship of the anti-affirmative action backlash. *Journal of Ethnic Studies, 10,* 17-42.

Takaki, R. (1989). *Strangers from a different shore: A history of Asian Americans.* Boston: Little, Brown.

Tang, J. (1993). The career attainment of Caucasian and Asian engineers. *The Sociological Quarterly, 34,* 467-496.

Tasi, F. W. (1980). Diversity and conflict between old and new Chinese immigrants in the United States. In R. S. Bryce-Laporte (Ed.), *Source book on new immigration* (pp. 329-337). New Brunswick: Transaction.

Taylor, P. A., & Kim, S. S. (1980). Asian Americans in the federal civil service, 1977. *California Sociologist, 3,* 1-16.

Thompson, R. H. (1979). Ethnicity vs. class: An analysis of conflict in a North American Chinese community. *Ethnicity, 6,* 306-326.

Thompson, R. H. (1980). From kinship to class: A new model of urban overseas Chinese social organization. *Urban Anthropology, 9,* 265-293.

Toji, D. S., & Johnson, J. H. (1992). Asian and Pacific Islander American poverty: The working poor and the jobless poor. *Amerasia Journal, 18*(1), 83-91.

Tom, G. (1988). The bifurcated world of the Chinese American. *Asian Profile, 16,* 1-10.

Tran, T. V. (1988). The Vietnamese American family. In C. Mindel, R. Habenstein, & R. Wright, Jr. (Eds.), *Ethnic families in America: Patterns and variations* (3rd ed., pp. 276-302). New York: Elsevier.

Tsai, M., Teng, L. N., & Sue, S. (1975). Mental status of Chinese in the United States. *American Journal of Orthopsychiatry, 45,* 111-118.

Tsukada, M. (1988). Income parity through different paths: Chinese Americans, Japanese Americans, and Caucasians in Hawaii. *Amerasia Journal, 14*(2), 47-60.

U.S. Bureau of the Census. (1993). *1990 census of population, general population characteristics, the United States* (CP-1-1). Washington, DC: U.S. Government Printing Office.

U.S. Commission on Civil Rights. (1986). *Recent activities against citizens and residents of Asian descent.* Washington, DC: U.S. Government Printing Office.

U.S. Commission on Civil Rights. (1988). *The economic status of Americans of Asian descent: An exploratory investigation.* Washington, DC: U.S. Government Printing Office.

U.S. Commission on Civil Rights. (1992). *Civil rights issues facing Asian-Americans, 1990.* Washington, DC: U.S. Government Printing Office.

Wang, L. C. (1988). Meritocracy and diversity in higher education: Discrimination against Asian Americans in the post-bakke era. *Urban Review, 20,* 189-209.

Wang, L. C. (1993). Trends in admissions for Asian Americans in colleges and universities. In LEAP Asian Pacific American Policy Institute and UCLA Asian American Studies Center (Eds.), *The state of Asian Pacific America* (pp. 49-59). Los Angeles: LEAP Asian Pacific American Public Policy Institute and UCLA Asian American Studies Center.

Wilson, K., & Portes, A. (1980). Immigrant enclaves: An analysis of the labor market experiences of Cubans in Miami. *American Journal of Sociology, 86,* 305-319.

Wong, E. F. (1985). Asian American middleman minority theory: The framework of an American myth. *Journal of Ethnic Studies, 13,* 51-88.

Wong, M. (1982). The cost of being Chinese, Japanese, and Filipino in the United States, 1960, 1970, 1976. *Pacific Sociological Review, 5,* 59-78.

Wong, M. (1988). The Chinese American family. In C. H. Mindel, R. W. Habenstein, & R. Wright, Jr. (Eds.), *Ethnic families in America: Patterns and variations* (pp. 230-257). New York: Elsevier.

Wong, M. (1991). *Rise in hate crimes against Asians in the United States.* Paper presented at the Annual Meeting of the American Sociological Association in Cincinnati, OH.

Ying, Y. (1988). Depressive symptomatology among Chinese Americans as measured by the CES-D. *Journal of Clinical Psychology, 44,* 739-746.

Yun, G. (Ed.). (1989). *A look beyond the model minority image.* New York: Minority Rights Groups, Asian and Pacific American Project.

Zhou, M. (1992). *Chinatown: The socioeconomic potential of an urban enclave.* Philadelphia: Temple University Press.

4

Chinese Americans

MORRISON G. WONG

In 1990, the Chinese were the largest of more than 20 Asian groups residing in the United States. A diverse group, both culturally and on the basis of national origins the Chinese include those born in the United States, as well as those born abroad in China, Taiwan, Hong Kong, Vietnam, and in other countries. The history of the Chinese in the United States over the past 140 years is characterized by episodes of prejudice and discrimination, of racism, xenophobia, and exclusion, and more recently, of varying degrees of acceptance or tolerance. This chapter, divided into six distinct but interrelated sections, presents a sociohistory of the Chinese in the United States. First, the extent of Chinese immigration and the subsequent discriminatory policies and exclusionary measures are presented. Then the changing Chinese American family is discussed. The third section focuses on the economic and occupational adjustments of the Chinese in American society, followed by an analysis of their educational achievements. The unique social structure and problems of Chinatown are the topic of the fifth section. This chapter concludes by looking at the differing modes of adaptation of the Chinese in the United States.

Immigration and Discriminatory Measures

The Chinese were the first Asian group to immigrate in significant numbers to the United States. Although only 43 Chinese resided in the United States prior to 1850, the discovery of gold in California in 1848 initiated a dramatic and significant influx of Chinese immigrants. In the next 3 decades, over 225,000 Chinese immigrated to the United States. About 90% of the early Chinese immigrants were males coming from two southern provinces in China—Kwangtung and Fukien (Chinn, Lai, & Choy, 1969, pp. 2-4; Purcell, 1965). The poor economic and social conditions in China—overcrowding, drought, and warfare—encouraged many Chinese to immigrate to a distant country. The discovery of gold, tales that the streets of San Francisco were lined with gold, and the opening of job opportunities in the western part of the United States provided additional lures for many Chinese to seek their fortune in the United States (Chinn et al., 1969, p. 7; Dinnerstein & Reimers, 1988; Hirschman & Wong, 1981; Kitano, 1991; Lai & Choy, 1971, p. 22; Lyman, 1974; Wong, 1988, p. 234). One factor made all this possible—improved transoceanic travel. It was actually less expensive to travel to San Francisco from Hong Kong than from Chicago to San Francisco (Schaefer, 1991).

Era of Antagonism: 1850-1882

It is commonly believed that, unlike other immigrants, most Chinese came to California or "Gold Mountain" as sojourners, expecting to work for a time, accumulate their fortune, and then return home to China to live a life at a higher socioeconomic position than when they left. Hence their orientation toward the United States was not as immigrants, but as birds of passage, here today and gone tomorrow (Bonacich, 1973; Sung, 1971, chap. 3). Whether this was true or not, it should be noted that this sojourner pattern of migration was not unique to the Chinese, but was common among many European groups (Archdeacon, 1983; Kitano & Daniels, 1988). (See Chan, 1984, and E. Wong, 1985, for arguments suggesting that the Chinese were not sojourners.)

Chinese immigration increased dramatically during the decade of the 1850s and 1860s. Building upon an initial U.S. population of 43 before 1850, 41,397 Chinese immigrated to the United States in the 1850s and another 64,301 arrived in the 1860s (see Table 4.1 for immigration by decade through 1990). Chinese males outnumbered females by at least 15 to 1.

It did not take long before xenophobic and racist attitudes developed among the general population, prompting considerable institutional resistance to this Asian influx. The Chinese were accused of being dangerous, deceitful and vicious, criminal, cowardly, and "inferior from the mental and moral point of view" (Schrieke, 1936, p. 110). Racist legislation was passed in an attempt to restrict or exclude the Chinese from immigrating

Table 4.1 Chinese Immigrant Arrivals by Decade

Decade	Number of Chinese Immigrants
1820-1850	43
1851-1860	41,397
1861-1870	64,301
1871-1880	123,201
1881-1890	61,711
1891-1900	14,799
1901-1910	20,605
1911-1920	21,278
1921-1930	29,907
1931-1940	4,928
1941-1950	16,709
1951-1960	25,198
1961-1970	109,771
1971-1980	237,793
1981-1990	444,962

SOURCE: Immigration and Naturalization Service (1992).

to the United States. In 1852 California imposed a $50 head tax on each Chinese passenger who arrived by ship. This legislation was enforced for 20 years before it was declared unconstitutional. In 1855 a capitation tax of $50 was required of all passengers who were aliens ineligible for citizenship (i.e., Chinese), but this was declared unconstitutional 2 years later. In 1858 the California legislature passed an act that sought to prevent further Chinese immigration to the state. In his inaugural address of 1862, California Governor Leland Stanford pledged that "the settlement among us of an inferior race [meaning the Chinese] is to be discouraged" (Wu, 1972). The *New York Times* ("Growth," 1865) warned:

> We have four millions of degraded negroes in the South. We have political passion and religious prejudice everywhere. The strain upon the constitution is about as great as it can bear. And if, in addition to all the adverse elements we now have, there were to be a flood-tide of Chinese population—a population befouled with all the social vices, with no knowledge or appreciation of free institutions or constitutional liberty, with heathenish souls and heathenish propensities, whose character, and habits, and modes of thought are firmly fixed by the consolidating influence of ages upon ages—we should be prepared to bid farewell to republicanism and democracy. (p. 4)

Similarly, the California Senate's opposition to Chinese immigration rested on the argument that

> during their entire settlement in California, they have never adapted themselves to our habits, modes of dress, or our educational system, have never learned the sanctity of an oath, never desired to become citizens, or to perform the duties of citizenship, never discovered the difference between right and wrong, never ceased the worship of their idol gods, or advanced a step beyond the musty traditions of their native hive. Impregnable to all the influences of our Anglo-Saxon life, they remain the same stolid Asiatics that have floated on the rivers and slaved in the field of China for thirty centuries of time. (Sandmeyer, 1973, p. 39)

In partial response to this hostile atmosphere of Chinese restriction and exclusion, the Burlingame Treaty was signed in 1868. China granted tremendous economic incentives and advantages to American merchants and shippers hungry for the China market. In return, the United States was to guarantee the Chinese the right to freely immigrate to the United States (Chen, 1980).

During the 1870s, the Chinese population in the United States continued to increase dramatically. By 1880 over 105,000 Chinese resided in the United States, mainly in the far western states. Although most Chinese resided in California in every census period (see Table 4.2), their proportion of the state's population contracted drastically. In 1860 the Chinese made up 9.2% of California's population; in 1940, they constituted only 0.6% (Kitano & Daniels, 1988, p. 29).

The Chinese immigrant as coolie laborer or indentured contract slave laborer is another common misconception. For the most part, force and coercion were probably unnecessary, as many Chinese were more than happy to come to the United States to seek their "fortunes." Not having the means to finance their trip to the United States, the vast majority used an ingenious method called "the credit ticket system." They would borrow money for passage and expenses and obligate themselves to repay double the indebtedness. The persistence of this credit ticket system for almost a century is probably the best evidence that the Chinese were free immigrants (Melendy, 1984, p. 18).

In 1880 the Burlingame Treaty was amended, giving the United States the right to regulate, limit, or suspend Chinese immigration, but not to prohibit it absolutely. This amendment served as a harbinger of more extensive, exclusionary immigration policy.

Table 4.2 Geographical Distribution of the Chinese Population, 1870-1990

Year	Total	California	%	West	%	North-east	South Atlantic	North Central	South Central
1870	63,199	49,277	77	62,831	99	137	11	9	211
1880	105,465	75,132	71	102,102	99	1,628	74	813	848
1890	107,488	72,472	67	96,844	90	6,171	669	2,357	1,447
1900	89,863	45,753	51	67,729	75	14,693	1,791	3,668	1,982
1910	71,531	36,248	51	51,934	72	11,688	1,582	4,610	1,717
1920	61,639	28,812	50	38,604	60	12,414	1,824	8,078	2,076
1930	74,954	37,361	50	44,883	60	17,799	1,869	8,078	2,325
1940	77,504	39,556	51	48,840	60	19,646	2,047	6,092	2,879
1950	117,629	58,324	50	67,584	58	28,931	4,755	10,646	5,713
1960	237,292	95,600	40	148,386	63	53,654	8,555	18,413	8,284
1970	435,062	170,135	39	245,658	56	115,777	19,332	39,343	14,952
1980	812,178	325,832	40	428,195	53	217,624	50,730	74,944	40,685
1990	1,645,472	704,850	43	862,617	52	445,089	114,013	133,336	90,417

SOURCE: Melendy (1984, p. 185); U.S. Bureau of the Census (1983, Table 62; 1993a, Table 253).

Era of Exclusion: 1882-1943

Chinese immigration continued to increase dramatically, reaching its peak of 123,201 Chinese immigrants in the 1870s (see Table 4.1). Anti-Chinese agitation, inspired by real or imagined competition with white workers and perpetuated by racist propaganda, also continued throughout the 1870s (Sandmeyer, 1973; Saxton, 1971). Led by Denis Kearney, the Workingman's Party argued that: "The Chinese laborer is a curse to our land, is degrading to our morals, is a menace to our liberties, and should be restricted and forever abolished, and 'the Chinese must go,' " (Sandmeyer, 1973, p. 65).

Congress passed the Chinese Exclusion Act of 1882, the first and only immigration act to specifically designate an ethnic, racial, or nationality group for exclusion. This act prohibited all Chinese laborers, whether skilled or unskilled, from entering the United States for 10 years. All other Chinese entering the United States had to have identification certificates issued by the Chinese government. This act also explicitly denied naturalization rights to Chinese in the United States—making them "aliens ineligible for citizenship."

In 1888 the Scott Act was passed prohibiting Chinese from reentering the United States after a temporary departure. Passage of these acts resulted in a precipitous decline in Chinese immigration. About half of the 1870s' figure, or about 61,711 Chinese, immigrated to the United States in the 1880s. Chinese immigration was limited to a trickle in the 1890s, with just 14,799 Chinese entering the United States.

Faced with the expiration of the Chinese Exclusion Act, Congress enacted the Geary Act in 1892, continuing the exclusion of the Chinese from the United States for another 10 years and requiring that they carry a certificate of residency on penalty of deportation with no right of habeas corpus bail procedure (Chen, 1980; Tang, 1984). In 1902 Congress passed legislation making permanent the exclusionary immigration policies toward the Chinese (Kung, 1962). Although the legislation did not terminate all immigration from China, it substantially reduced it and checked any significant population growth of the Chinese in the United States (U.S. Bureau of the Census, 1975, p. 107; Wong & Hirschman, 1983).

For the next 6 decades, the Chinese population not only failed to grow, but actually declined. The restrictive immigration policy and subsequent Chinese emigration partially explain this decline. In 1882 there were perhaps 105,000 Chinese residing in the United States. By the 1920s the Chinese population in the United States had steadily declined by about 62,000 Chinese. Another factor that may account for the decline was the overwhelmingly male composition of the the mid-19th century Chinese immigration. In 1890 there were 26.8 Chinese males for every female (see Table 4.3). This sex ratio declined steadily and by 1940 there were 2.9 Chinese males to every female. The very low proportion of Chinese women in the United States meant a much delayed development of a sizable second-generation Chinese American population (Hirschman & Wong, 1986).

The infamous 1906 earthquake and fire destroyed much of San Francisco, as well as most municipal records, which included Chinese immigration and citizenship records. Hence a loophole was provided whereby the Chinese could immigrate to the United States. The "slot racket" or "paper son" form of immigration developed. American law provided that children of American-born fathers inherited their father's citizenship. Chinese residents would claim American birth and, because of the lack of records the authorities were powerless to disprove their contention. These American-born Chinese, actual or claimed, would then visit China, report the birth of a son, and thereby create an entry slot. Years later the slot could be used by a relative or the birth papers could be sold to someone wanting to immigrate. The purchaser, called a "paper son," simply assumed the name and identity of the alleged son. Under the terms of this type of

Table 4.3 Chinese Population in the United States, 1860-1990

Year	Total	Male	Female	Sex Ratio (males per 100 females)	% Foreign Born	% Under 14 Years Old
1860	34,933	33,149	1,784	1,858		
1870	63,199	58,633	4,566	1,284	99.8	
1880	105,465	100,686	4,779	2,106	99.0	
1890	107,475	103,607	3,868	2,679	99.3	
1900	87,863	85,341	4,522	1,887	90.7	3.4
1910	71,531	66,856	4,675	1,430	79.3	
1920	61,639	53,891	7,748	696	69.9	12.0
1930	74,954	59,802	15,152	395	58.8	20.4
1940	77,504	57,389	20,115	286	48.1	21.1
1950	117,140	76,725	40,415	190	47.0	23.3
1960	236,084	135,430	100,654	135	39.5	33.0
1970	431,538	226,733	204,850	111	46.9	26.6
1980	812,178	410,936	401,246	102	63.3	21.1
1990	1,645,472	818,542	827,154	99	69.3	19.3

SOURCE: Adapted from Glenn (1983, p. 8); Lyman (1974, pp. 79, 159); U.S. Bureau of the Census (1983, Table 58; 1993b, Table 1).

immigration, many Chinese in the United States developed a long-term pattern of sojourning (Glenn, 1983; Kung, 1962; Lee, 1960, pp. 300-307; Lyman, 1974; Sung, 1971, pp. 95-107; Wong, 1988; Yung, 1977).

In 1921 Congress enacted legislation denying to alien-born women their husband's citizenship. This restriction imposed especially tragic hardships for American-born Chinese males. Due to the unbalanced sex ratio and the enforcement of antimiscegenation laws, they were forced to seek wives in China. Later, when the Immigration Act of 1924 restricted aliens ineligible for citizenship from entering the United States, it made it impossible for Chinese American citizens to send for their wives. Interestingly, their children were admissible. Even Chinese merchants, who previously were allowed to bring their wives to the United States, were denied this immigration privilege. This law was changed in 1930 to allow wives of Chinese merchants, as well as those who were married to American citizens before 1924, to immigrate to the United States (Chen, 1984, p. 44; Chinn et al., 1969, p. 24; Sung, 1971, pp. 77-81).

Significant demographic changes in the Chinese population began in the 1920s and 1930s. The population decline that was triggered by the passage of the Chinese Exclusion Act had ended, and a small upturn due to natural increase and ingenuity in evading immigration regulations had set in. Between 1920 and 1940, the Chinese American population increased by 25%, from 62,000 to 78,000. Even more significant than the turnaround in numbers was that by 1940, American-born Chinese, for the first time, outnumbered the foreign-born segment of the community.

Token Immigration: 1943-1965

Pronounced demographic changes in the Chinese population were noted in the 1940s. Nearly 20,000 Chinese American babies were born during this decade, marking the first time in history that the most numerous 5-year cohort of Chinese Americans was persons under 5 years of age (Kitano & Daniels, 1988, p. 37).

The Magnuson Act of 1943 repealed the Chinese Exclusion Act of 1882, making Chinese immigrants, many of whom had been living in the United States for decades, finally eligible for citizenship. Moreover, to recognize China's position as a U.S. ally in World War II and to counteract Japan's propaganda campaign to discredit the United States in Asia (Chen, 1984), a token quota of 105 persons per year was set for Chinese immigration. Although small, the quota did open the door to further immigration and had an impact on the future formation of the Chinese family in the United States.

Passage of the War Brides Act in 1945 allowed approximately 6,000 Chinese women to enter the United States as brides of men in the U.S. armed forces. In 1946, an amendment to this act put Chinese wives and children of U.S. citizens on a nonquota basis. As a consequence, almost 10,000 Chinese females migrated to the United States in the next 8 years. This influx had a tremendous impact on the demographic structure of the Chinese American community.

The Displaced Persons Act of 1948 gave permanent resident status to 3,465 Chinese visitors, sailors, and students who were stranded in the United States because of the Chinese civil war. This same year saw the California antimiscegenation law declared unconstitutional.

In 1952 the Immigration and Naturalization Act, also known as the McCarran-Walter Act, was passed, eliminating race as a bar to immigration and giving preferences to relatives (Chen, 1980, pp. 211-213; Lee, 1956). However, this act was more of a rationalization of existing immigration policy than a reform. The quota system followed the national origins restrictions of the 1924 legislation with continued token quotas for Chinese—105 (Wong & Hirschman, 1983).

The Refugee Relief Act of 1953 allowed an additional 2,777 Chinese into the United States as refugees of the Chinese civil war. The Refugee Escape Act of 1957 protected the "paper sons," as the deportation requirement was waived under certain conditions. The San Francisco District Office of the Immigration and Naturalization Service received over 8,000 "confessions" of illegal entry during the 10-year amnesty period of 1959-1969 as paper sons sought to legitimate their entry (Melendy, 1984, p. 64).

In the mid-1950s, more than half of the Chinese population was native born. Along with the stranded college students from China, the Chinese were becoming increasingly middle class, disassociating themselves from the concerns of the Chinatowns and striving for acculturation into American society (Lyman, 1974, pp. 119-157). In 1962, a presidential directive was signed permitting refugees from the People's Republic of China to enter the United States as parolees (conditional status). By 1966 approximately 15,100 refugees had entered under this provision. Unlike previous immigration flows, Chinese immigration during the period from 1943 to the repeal of the quota law in 1965 was overwhelmingly female, with approximately nine females for every one male. Most of these women were wives of citizens admitted as nonquota immigrants (Chinn et al., 1969, p. 29; Melendy, 1984, p. 67; Simpson & Yinger, 1965, pp. 350-351; Yuan, 1966).

1965-Present: Open Chinese Immigration

By abolishing the national origins system, the Immigration Act of 1965 was probably the first immigration policy that practiced the principle of racial equality and the first real immigration reform in over a century. Perhaps the most significant consequence of this act for the Chinese was the dramatic increase in the number of Chinese immigrants to the United States (Boyd, 1971, 1974; Keeley, 1971, 1974, 1975a, 1975b; Wong & Hirschman, 1983). From the 1940s to the 1970s, the majority of the Chinese population had been native born. By 1980, however, this pattern changed. The majority of Chinese in the United States were foreign born, and this has become increasingly true.

A second consequence of the act was its influence on the changing nature of family life for Chinese in the United States. With its emphasis on family reunification, this act granted each country a quota of 20,000 immigrants per year. Since 1968, when the law went into full effect, approximately 22,000 Chinese have immigrated to the United States each year (M. Wong, 1985, 1986; Wong & Hirschman, 1983). Unlike the pre-1965 immigrants who came over as individuals, most of the new Chinese immigrants are

Table 4.4 Chinese Population in the United States by Major States, 1980 and 1990

State	1980		1990		% of Increase Between 1980 and 1990
	N	%	N	%	
California	325,882	40.1	704,850	42.8	116
New York	147,250	18.1	284,144	17.3	93
Hawaii	55,916	6.9	68,804	4.2	23
Texas	26,714	3.3	63,232	3.8	137
New Jersey	23,492	2.9	59,084	3.6	152
Massachusetts	24,882	3.1	53,792	3.3	116
Illinois	28,847	3.6	49,936	3.0	73
Washington	17,984	2.2	33,962	2.1	89
Rest of U.S.	161,211	19.8	327,668	19.9	103
Total	812,178	100.0	1,645,472	100.0	103

SOURCE: U.S. Bureau of the Census (1983, Table 62; 1993a, Table 253).

coming over as family groups—typically husband, wife, and unmarried children (Hong, 1976). A family chain pattern of migration has also developed (Glenn, 1983; P. Li, 1977; W. Li, 1977; Sung, 1977; Wong & Hirschman, 1983). During the 1970s, over 70% of Chinese immigrants were admitted under the preference system and the proportion of immigrants arriving under the "immediate relative of U.S. citizen" criterion had declined (Wong & Hirschman, 1983).

The Immigration Act of 1965 was amended in 1981, assigning the People's Republic of China, like the Republic of China (Taiwan), a quota of 20,000 immigrants. In 1987 the annual quota for Hong Kong was increased from 600 to 5,000 individuals. Currently, about 70% of the Chinese population is first-generation immigrants, the vast majority arriving after 1965 (U.S. Bureau of the Census, 1993a).

From 1980 to 1990 the Chinese population in the United States doubled from 812,000 to 1,645,000 (see Table 4.4). Much of the increase in population size is due to immigration. The relative concentration of Chinese in various states has not changed much. California still remains, by far, the major state of Chinese residence, with New York a distant second. Proportional population increases, as well as a doubling of the Chinese population since 1980, have been noted only for California, Texas, New Jersey, and Massachusetts.

The ebb and flow of Chinese immigration has greatly influenced the development and evolution of the Chinese American family. It is this topic to which we turn.

Family Patterns

Just as there is no typical American family, there is no typical Chinese family. The Chinese American family can best be viewed as a product of the complex interaction between structural factors (i.e., restrictive immigration policies and racism) and cultural factors (i.e., Confucian ethics). Because these factors are constantly undergoing change, the Chinese American family is not a static entity, but one that is also undergoing constant changes and adaptations to a changing society.

Traditional Chinese Family

The Chinese American family, both past and present, has its foundation in the traditional family structure of China, which was greatly influenced by Confucianism. Encompassing a much broader conception of the family than the nuclear unit of father, mother, and children, the traditional Chinese family included the extended kinship groups and clan members.

The traditional family in China was patriarchal. Roles were clearly defined, with the father and eldest son having the dominant role. Authority passed from father to the eldest son, and all were expected to obey them. Females were relegated to a subordinate position (Hsu, 1971).

The traditional Chinese family exhibited a patrilocal residential pattern. According to the ideal, grandparents, their unmarried children, and their married sons together with their wives and children all lived in one household. The more generations living under the same roof, the more prestigious the family. Married daughters lived in the household of their husbands' parents. This extended family provided additional laborers needed in an agriculturally based economy, as well as providing the members with some degree of economic security (Wolf, 1968).

The Chinese system of descent was patrilineal, with the household property and land to be divided equally among the sons. In exchange, however, the sons were to reciprocate by sharing equally in the responsibility for the care and support of their parents in their old age (Nee & Wong, 1985).

The Confucian practice of ancestor worship was greatly emphasized in the traditional Chinese family. It was believed that a Chinese male could achieve some sense of immortality only if his family line was continued (i.e., if he bore sons). In fact, it was believed that one of the greatest tragedies that a man could suffer was to die without having any sons to carry on the family name and perform the ancestor worship ritual of burning incense at his grave.

Filial piety, another Confucian value that was highly cherished, involved a set of moral principles taught at a very young age and reinforced throughout one's life. It consisted of mutual respect for those of equal status and of reverence and obedience toward one's elders. Duty, obligation, importance of the family name, service, and self-sacrifice to the elders are all elements of filial piety (Hsu, 1971; Kung, 1962, p. 206).

The Chinese American Family: 1850-1920

The structure of the traditional Chinese family, as well as Chinese customs and family norms, resulted in migration patterns in which the males left to seek economic opportunities, even in distant lands, for extended periods of time, while the wife and children remained in the home of the husband's parents in the village (Lyman, 1968; Nee & Wong, 1985). This practice had three major consequences. It guaranteed that the emigrating sons would continue to send back remittances to their parents to support them in old age (Glick, 1980). It instilled in the emigrating Chinese a sojourner, rather than immigrant, orientation (Barth, 1964, p. 157; Lyman, 1968; Siu, 1952). Last, it ensured a continual bond to the family and the village on the part of the emigrating men (Nee & Wong, 1985).

From the 1850s until the 1920s, the overwhelming majority of Chinese immigrants were men. More than half were single, and those who were not often were separated from their wives for long periods of time. In essence, many Chinese men in the United States were family men without their wives or family members. Hence not only did many of the early Chinese immigrants lead abnormal family lives, but one can hardly speak of Chinese family life during this period because there were so few Chinese women (Kingston, 1981; Lyman, 1968; Nee & Nee, 1972; Siu, 1952; Weiss, 1974; Wong, 1988, pp. 235-236). This bizarre family structure has been referred to as the "mutilated family" (Sung, 1967) or "split household" (Glenn, 1983).

The Chinese American Family: 1920-1943

Despite the numerous obstacles to family formation (i.e., imbalanced sex ratio and exclusionary immigration legislation) that resulted in the predominance of the mutilated family, a sizable second-generation Chinese population began to emerge by the 1920s and 1930s. Many of these early Chinese families consisted of small immigrant entrepreneurs or former laborers and their first-generation American-born children.

The small producer family functioned as a productive unit, with all family members, including the children, working in the small family business, usually within the ethnic economy. Because of their superior knowledge of English compared to their immigrant parents, American-born Chinese children often played a critical role in carrying out the daily business and domestic affairs of the family (Kingston, 1976; Lowe, 1943; Nee & Nee, 1972; Wong, 1950). The business was profitable only because it was labor intensive and family members put in extremely long hours (Glenn, 1983; Mark & Chih, 1982, p. 66).

The Transitional Chinese Family: 1943-1965

The liberalization of immigration policies after World War II slowly led to the normalization and formation of Chinese families in the United States. It enabled many mutilated families or split households to be reunited, and it encouraged Chinese men to return to Hong Kong in droves to find wives (Kitano, 1991, p. 199).

The stranded Chinese who were displaced by the Chinese civil war in 1948 had family backgrounds strikingly different from the other Chinese in the United States. Well-educated, usually with a college degree, they selected a spouse based more on individual preferences and love rather than relying on the traditional decision of elders or matchmakers. These former students settled in the suburbs near the universities and research facilities where they ultimately found employment (Ikels, 1985).

In those Chinese families where both spouses were native born, the family pattern approximated the American norm, consisting of the husband, wife, children, and occasionally elderly parents. The parent-child relationship was somewhere between the strict formality of the traditional Chinese family and the high degree of permissiveness of the white American family (Sung, 1967, pp. 162, 176).

The Modern Chinese American Family

The 1965 Immigration Act had a profound influence on the family life of the Chinese in America. Not only was there a dramatic increase in the

Chinese immigrant population, but most of the new Chinese immigrants were coming over as family units, typically a husband, wife, and unmarried children (Hong, 1976).

The modern Chinese American family can be classified into two major types. The first type, referred to as the "ghetto," "dual worker," or the "downtown" family (by Glenn, 1983; Huang, 1981; and Kwong, 1987, respectively), consists of the new immigrant Chinese family living in or near the Chinatown in the major metropolitan areas of this country. Both husband and wife are employed in the secondary labor market or enclave economy, in the labor-intensive, low capital service and small manufacturing sectors, such as the tourist shops, restaurants, and garment sweatshops (Light & Wong, 1975; M. Wong, 1980, 1983; Wong & Hirschman, 1983). Husbands and wives are, more or less, equal breadwinners in the family. Unlike the small-producer family, however, there tends to be a complete segregation of work and family life. Moreover, it is not uncommon for parents to spend very little time with each other or their children because of different jobs and schedules (Wong, 1988, p. 248).

The second type of Chinese family is the "uptown," middle class, white collar, or professional Chinese American family, which has moved away from Chinatown to the surrounding urban areas and suburbs (Kuo, 1970; Kwong, 1987; Yuan, 1966). These Chinese families are more modern and cosmopolitan in orientation and view themselves as more American than Chinese (Huang, 1981; Weiss, 1970, 1974). However, there is a tendency for these Chinese to be "semi-extended" or to reestablish a Chinese community in the suburbs (Huang, 1981, p. 123; Lyman, 1974, p. 149).

Although the Chinese and white population seem to exhibit similar general family characteristics, in 1990 they differed on specifics. For example, they both had about 98% of their respective populations in households as opposed to group quarters such as dormitories, institutions, or military quarters, but a greater proportion of members in the white households were nonfamily members and other relatives than in the Chinese households. In regards to family type, about 83% to 85% of both populations consisted of married couples, but a greater proportion of white families were headed by females with no husband present. About 58% to 60% of both the Chinese and white population were married; about one third of the Chinese, compared to one quarter of the white population, were never married. Moreover, whites were twice as likely to be separated, divorced, or widowed. Last, white households were much smaller than Chinese households. The majority of white households (59%) consisted of

Table 4.5 Family Characteristics of the Chinese and White Population in the United States, 1990 (in percent)

Characteristics	Chinese	White
Household type		
In household	97.6	97.5
Family householder	23.6	26.7
Nonfamily	7.3	11.7
Spouse	21.0	22.2
Child	31.2	29.3
Other relative	9.6	13.4
Nonrelative	4.9	4.0
Family type		
Married couple	84.8	83.0
Female head, no husband	9.4	12.7
Marital status		
Never married	31.6	24.3
Married	59.9	57.8
Separated, divorced, or widowed	8.3	17.9
Household size		
1 person	17.6	25.1
2 persons	23.9	33.8
3 persons	19.1	17.1
4 persons	20.0	14.7
5 persons	10.7	6.1
6 persons	4.9	2.0
7 or more persons	3.8	1.1

SOURCE: U.S. Bureau of the Census (1993a, Table 40; 1993b, Table 2).

one or two persons. A greater proportion of Chinese households had three, four, five, six, seven or more persons. See Table 4.5 for more details.

The modern Chinese family, whether ghetto or middle class, has more conservative sexual values, fewer out-of-wedlock births, and more conservative or traditional attitudes toward the role of women than the white population (Braun & Chao, 1978; Monahan, 1977). Divorce was once a rarity among the Chinese (Huang, 1981, p. 122). Although the incidence of divorce has increased among the younger generation, who were brought up to believe in the American ideal of romantic love and personal happiness in marriage (Wong, 1988, p. 249), the proportion of Chinese who are divorced remains significantly lower than the proportion of whites.

Economic and Occupational Adjustments

Since their arrival in the United States in the 1850s, the Chinese have undergone three main periods of wide-scale occupational adjustments. In the first period, a large number of Chinese worked in the mines, on the railroads, and in agriculture. During the second period of isolation, many of the Chinese became self-employed, serving their own ethnic community or specializing in occupations that were not competitive with whites. The last period is marked by tremendous socioeconomic advancement. This section will look more closely at these three periods of occupational adjustments.

Early Occupational Adjustments: 1850-1882

Before their arrival in the United States, the Chinese were perceived by the American public in negative stereotypes (Issacs, 1972).

> A Chinaman is cold, cunning and distrustful; always ready to take advantage of those he has to deal with; extremely covetous and deceitful; quarrelsome, vindictive, but timid and dastardly. A Chinaman in office is a strange compound of insolence and meanness. All ranks and conditions have a total disregard for truth. (Miller, 1969, p. 83)

In spite of these stereotypes, the Chinese were initially welcomed to the United States. Inflation as a result of the gold strikes, coupled with the shortage of women in the West, enabled the Chinese to find a temporary economic niche. Supplementing rather than competing with whites, they performed jobs such as washing clothes or cooking—jobs considered "women's work." However, once they began to compete with white workers, the flames of anti-Chinese agitation became widespread and grew in intensity.

In the early 1850s the Chinese began to head for the hills in search of gold, mining claims that other miners had abandoned. The meager profits that the Chinese were able to salvage from these abandoned claims created a sense of increased competition for scarce resources and jealousy among the white miners. Legal and extralegal means were sought to force the Chinese out of mining. A Foreign Miner's Tax was passed in 1852, and many mining districts passed resolutions or ordinances to expel the Chinese from their district (Chinn et al., 1969, pp. 30-32). During the last half of the 1850s, the Chinese were physically expelled from one mining camp after another. They were robbed and beaten, and some were murdered. These crimes were seldom punished because of the laxity of law enforcement, as well as a California Supreme Court ruling in 1854 that stated that no Chinese could testify against a white person. Their supposed threat to American labor became an early issue in the developing hostility (Cheng & Bonacich, 1984).

After the initial gold rush, many Chinese turned to service industries, such as the laundry or restaurant trade, or entered small-scale manufacturing of such items as brooms and sandals. Even in these occupations, however, the Chinese were not safe from violence. Notes one Chinese old-timer:

> Every Saturday night, we never knew whether we would live to see the light of day. We operated a laundry near a mining camp. Saturday was the night for the miners to get drunk. They would force their way into our shop, wrest the clean white bundles from the shelves and trample the shirts which we so laboriously finished. If the shirts were torn, we were forced to pay for the damages. One night, one of the miners hit his face against the flat side of an iron. He went away, but we knew that our lives were now in danger so we fled, leaving all of our possessions and money behind. The miner came back with a mob who ransacked our shop, robbed us of the $360 that was our combined savings and set fire to the laundry. We were lucky to escape with our lives. (Sung, 1971, pp. 44-45)

Some 12,000 Chinese laborers provided most of the labor force for the construction of the Central Pacific end of the transcontinental railroad during the 1860s (Sung, 1971, pp. 29-36). Oscar Lewis (1938) provides us with a glimpse into the lives of these Chinese railroad workers.

> Throughout the summer of 1866, "Crocker's pets," six thousand strong, swarmed over the upper canyon, pecking methodically at the broken rock of the cuts, trooping in long lines beneath their basket hats to pour wheelbarrow-loads of debris down the canyon-side, treading precarious paths with seventy bamboo poles, refreshing themselves at intervals with sips of tea kept near at hand in whiskey kegs emptied and abandoned by their white confreres. The Chinese were presently found to be adept at the backbreaking work of drilling and placing blasts, by then a major part of the work, for the upper ridges were scraped clear of soil by the winter deposits of ice.
>
> Track-layers followed close behind the graders, and locomotives pushed strings of flatcars loaded with construction iron, lumber, explosives, food, drink and

more men to the rail head. Cape Horn, a sheer granite buttress, proved the most formidable obstacle of the year; its lower sides dropped away in a thousand-foot vertical cliff that offered no vestige of a foothold. The indomitable Chinese were lowered from above on ropes, and there suspended between sky and earth, chipped away with hammer and chisel to form the first precarious ledge which was then laboriously deepened to a shelf wide enough to permit the passage of cars. Three years later, when overland trains crept cautiously along this ledge, passengers gazed straight down from their windows into thin air. (pp. 74-75)

With the driving of the golden spike at Promontory Point, Utah, marking the completion of the railroad in 1869, the Chinese turned to other railroad construction projects in the West. The Northern Pacific employed about 14,000 Chinese, and the Southern Pacific's lines, especially in California, were built almost entirely by Chinese labor (Kwong, 1979). During the next 9 years, they laid more than 1,800 miles of track in California (Chiu, 1963, p. 26) as well as in other states (Wong, 1994).

California farmers primarily relied on casual, seasonal harvest labor and not permanent workers, a pattern that has continued to the present. In the 1870s, the Chinese supplied much of this cheap, unattached labor. By 1880, seasonal farm work was the third-largest Chinese occupation in California, surpassed only by mining and domestic service (Melendy, 1984, p. 49).

In addition to the Chinese contribution to agriculture, tribute is due to them for their reclamation work. Thousands were employed in reclaiming the land upon which much of San Francisco rests (Sung, 1971, pp. 29-36). Moreover, the California Delta of the Sacramento and San Joaquin rivers was made productive by the levees, drainage ditches, and irrigation systems that were built by Chinese labor (Chiu, 1963, p. 72).

Although excluded from salmon fishing by restrictive legislation, by 1880 the Chinese were active in the fishing of sturgeon, shrimp, and abalone (Sung, 1971, pp. 42-57). By 1897, 26 Chinese shrimp camps dotted the shores of the San Francisco Bay (Kim, 1978, p. 3; Melendy, 1984, pp. 52-53; Spier, 1958, pp. 79-81, 128-36).

The Chinese were a dominant force in the cigar industry and played a significant role in the woolen mills. The shift in the clothing industry from home work to a routinized factory system enabled the Chinese to quickly dominate the manufacturing of ready-made clothes. They also provided the essential labor for the San Francisco boot, shoe, and slipper industries (Chinn et al., 1969, pp. 49-55; Chiu, 1963, pp. 89-108, 119-128).

Shifting Occupational Patterns: 1882-1945

The intense racial antagonism against the Chinese culminated in the passage of the Chinese Exclusion Act of 1882, forcing the Chinese to insulate themselves in Chinatowns, where they involved themselves in occupations that were either geared toward serving their own ethnic community or were rejected by or noncompetitive with whites. At this time a major shift in Chinese employment patterns occurred—from urban labor to self-employment in urban service occupations such as laundries, restaurants, and grocery stores (Chan, 1984, p. 67; C. Wong, 1980). The *New York Illustrated News,* on June 4, 1853, describes the unique adaptation the Chinese made to the laundry business.

> What a truly industrious people they are! At work, cheerfully and briskly at ten o'clock at night. Huge piles of linens and underclothing, disposed in baskets about the room, near the different ironers. Those at work dampening and ironing— peculiar processes both. A bowl of water is standing by the ironer's side, as in ordinary laundries, but used very differently. Instead of dipping the fingers in the water and then snapping them over dry clothes, the operator puts his head in the bowl, fills his mouth with water, and then blows so that water comes from his mouth in a mist, resembling the emission of steam from an escapepipe, at the same time so directing his head that this mist is scattered all over the place he is about to iron. He then seizes his flat iron. It is a vessel resembling a small deep metallic washbasin having a highly polished flat bottom and a fire kept burning continually in it. Thus they keep the iron hot without running to the fire every five minutes and spitting on the iron to ascertain whether it is still hot. (p. 359)

Besides laws excluding them from entering the country, various ordinances were passed to exclude those Chinese already residing in the United States from making a living. A laundry ordinance was passed in San Francisco whereby each laundry employing one horse-drawn wagon was required to pay a $2 per quarter fee; for those with two wagons, the fee was $4 per quarter, whereas those using no wagons paid $15 per quarter. The Chinese were the only laundry persons who picked up and delivered by foot. This ordinance was subsequently ruled unconstitutional (Melendy, 1984, p. 35). San Francisco prohibited the hiring of Chinese on municipal projects and banned the use of Chinese carrying poles for peddling vegetables (Chen, 1980, pp. 137-138). In 1880, San Francisco passed the Anti-Ironing Ordinance aimed at shutting down Chinese nighttime laundries (Chen, 1980, p. 138; Kitano & Daniels, 1988, p. 28; Ong, 1981; C. Wong, 1980).

In 1900 almost 7 out of every 10 Chinese were involved in agriculture or in domestic and personal services. At the turn of the century, a quarter of all Chinese men were employed in the stereotypical occupation of Chinese laundry workers. Over the next 3 decades, the proportion of Chinese in agriculture (mostly farm laborers), mining, and manufacturing declined sharply. At the same time, there were corresponding increases in trade and especially in domestic and personal services. Within this last category, the percentage of laundry workers remained at 25%, while the percentages of Chinese working as servants and waiters increased to 21% and 10%, respectively (Hirschman & Wong, 1986).

Bipolar Occupational Distribution

A glance at the occupational distribution of the Chinese in the United States suggests that they have been quite successful, perhaps even more successful than whites (see Table 4.6). For example, in 1990, a greater proportion of Chinese than whites was involved in white-collar occupations. Even more dramatic was the larger proportion of Chinese professionals compared to whites. However, closer analysis of the occupational distribution reveals two different patterns. The native-born Chinese are seemingly somewhat more occupationally advantaged, with 77% in white-collar occupations compared to 59% of the white population. Moreover, native-born Chinese were almost twice as likely to be involved in professional occupations as whites.

A different pattern is evident for foreign-born Chinese. They exhibit a bipolar occupational structure or the clustering of workers in both high-paying professional and managerial occupations and low-paying service jobs, with relatively few in between (Li, 1982, pp. 318-319; Sung, 1977, pp. 66-89; Wong, 1980). Hence foreign-born Chinese are not only more likely than whites to be involved in the professions, but they are also more likely to be involved in service occupations such as waiters, dishwashers, and other petty service roles in hotels, restaurants, and other entertainment activities (Hirschman & Wong, 1981; U.S. Bureau of the Census, 1993b, Table 4).

Another distinguishing characteristic of the Chinese in the United States is their much greater involvement in small businesses than other Americans (Kim, Hurh, & Fernandez, 1989; Hirschman & Wong, 1981). Most of these businesses are small, family-operated mom and pop grocery stores or restaurants that involve several or all members of the family, or small garment factories that subcontract from major manufacturers. Because

Table 4.6 Occupational Characteristics of the Chinese and White Populations, Ages 25-64, in the United States, 1990 (in percentages)

Occupations	Chinese Total	Native Born	Foreign Born	White Total
Professional	20.7	25.0	19.6	14.4
Managerial	15.1	18.2	14.3	12.8
Technical/sales	17.6	15.7	17.3	16.1
Administrative support	13.5	18.3	12.3	16.0
Service	16.5	8.6	18.5	12.0
Farm, forestry, and fishery	.4	.6	.3	2.5
Precision, production, and craft	5.6	5.0	5.8	11.9
Operatives and laborers	10.6	5.6	11.8	14.3
Class of workers				
Private	78.5	73.4	79.9	77.5
Government	13.9	20.3	12.3	14.3
Self-employed	6.7	5.8	7.0	7.7
Unpaid family labor	.8	.5	0.9	0.5
Number of workers in the family				
No workers	7.9	6.9	8.1	12.9
One worker	25.5	23.5	25.9	27.1
Two workers	47.6	55.2	46.2	47.3
Three or more	19.0	14.4	19.9	12.8

SOURCE: U.S. Bureau of the Census (1993b, Table 4; 1994, Tables 45, 47).

labor costs are minimal and relatively small amounts of capital are needed, many immigrants find readily available opportunities in small enterprises. Moreover, having a small business of one's own provides the immigrant with some sense of financial security, independence, and may be viewed as a channel of social mobility, especially if opportunities for advancement within the mainstream sector of the economy are difficult due to a lack of facility in the English language.

Despite the high proportion of Chinese in the professions, they are absent in executive, supervisory, or decision-making positions (Cabezas, Tam, Lowe, Wong, & Turner, 1988; Sue, Zane, & Sue, 1985). Moreover, when education and occupation are taken into account, Chinese Americans are actually receiving less than comparably qualified whites (Hirschman & Wong, 1984; Jiobu, 1976; U.S. Commission on Civil Rights, 1988; Wong, 1982). Charges of a glass ceiling continue. Although referring to Asian Americans in general, the following statements could easily apply specifically to the Chinese.

Table 4.7 Educational Characteristics of Chinese and White Populations in the United States, 1990 (in percentages)

Characteristics	Chinese	White
Less than 9th grade	16.8	8.9
9th to 12th grade	9.6	13.1
Not a high school graduate	26.4	22.0
High school graduate	14.5	31.0
Some college	18.3	25.4
College graduate	21.6	13.9
Postgraduate or professional degree	19.1	7.7

SOURCE: U.S. Bureau of the Census (1993b, Table 3; 1994, Table 40).

I am of the opinion that most Asian Americans are facing an insurmountable glass wall in the corporate world. As a matter of fact, most of us have given up hoping of advancing up the corporate ladder. The more we think about it, the more frustrated, discouraged, and depressed we become. . . .

Most of us have proved our technical capability. However, many major corporations tend to overlook the non-technical side of many Asian Americans. Corporations pick pigeon holes for us. And what is worse, they believe that we are quite content staying in those technologically airtight pigeon holes. (Liauh, 1989)

Discrimination against the Chinese persists. (See Chapters 2 and 3 for a more in-depth discussion on this issue.)

Education

Whether because of the influence of Confucian teaching that promoted family unity, respect for elders and those in authority, industry, a high value on education, and personal discipline (Hsu 1971; McGrath, 1983; Sung, 1967) or because of structural conditions that may have favored the educational progress of Chinese Americans in spite of considerable societal discrimination (i.e., selective immigration) (Hirschman & Wong, 1986), there is no question that the educational achievements of Chinese Americans have been spectacular, far surpassing the educational achievements of whites (see Table 4.7).

In 1990 a much greater proportion of whites than Chinese 25 years of age and older had completed high school and had some college education. At the higher levels of education, however, the Chinese population had greater educational achievements. The Chinese were twice as likely as whites to have one or more college degrees. About 41% of the Chinese population, compared to 22% of the white population, had completed 4 or more years of college. Even more dramatic is that the Chinese were about two and a half times more likely to have a postgraduate or professional degree—19.1% of Chinese compared to 7.7% of whites (U.S. Bureau of the Census, 1993b, Table 3; 1994, Table 40). In fact, the Chinese were much more likely to have a postgraduate or professional degree than whites were to have only a college degree. The extraordinary educational achievements of Asians have gained the attention of the American public and mass media (Bell, 1985; Brand, 1987; Butterfield, 1986; Divoky, 1988; Doerner, 1985; Lee & Rong, 1988; Shin, 1988; Lord & Linnon, 1988; Williams & McDonald, 1987).

Trends

The contemporary pattern of Chinese American educational success is not a recent phenomenon but has roots that extend back to the early 20th century. In 1910 the proportion of Chinese children attending school was significantly below the comparable enrollment figure for white children. By 1930, however, Chinese American children were more likely to be attending school than their white counterparts. Given the continued racism against Asians during this period, especially on the West Coast (Daniels, 1970; Nee & Nee, 1972), these educational achievements were remarkable. As Chinese Americans encountered a moderate amount of economic success in the postwar era, their educational attainments shot up to record levels. Regardless of the measure, Chinese had levels of education equal to or even higher than whites by 1960, and the advantage continues to widen (Hirschman & Wong, 1981, 1986; Wong, 1980, 1990).

However, there are two sides of this story. Despite their high educational attainment, a greater proportion of Chinese than whites were also at the lower end of the education spectrum. For example, in 1990, about 26% of the Chinese population compared to only 22.0% of the white population had not graduated from high school. Moreover, the Chinese (17%) were almost twice as likely as whites (9%) to have less than a 9th-grade education. The Chinese American community is increasingly becoming two separate communities: one educated, relatively affluent, and acculturated to American society; the other largely uneducated, distinctly nonaffluent, and still retaining much of its traditional culture.

Negative Factors in the Education of Chinese Students

The high educational achievements of Chinese students have not been without costs. The pressure to achieve educationally and to conform to the "model minority" stereotype has placed an inordinate amount of pressure on Chinese students. Those who fall short of superior academic performance sometimes feel guilty that they are personally failing or not living up to parental expectations. This pressure may lead to the use of drugs, mental problems, and/or suicide. Each year, colleges and universities on the West Coast report suicides or attempted suicides by Chinese students (Caudill, 1952; De Vos, 1960; Fischer, 1988; Kitano, 1991, pp. 200-201; Wong, 1990).

A related problem is the strategy for educational achievement used by many Chinese students, particularly the foreign born. Despite their lack of facility with the English language, many Chinese immigrant students are able to gain entrance to colleges, universities, and graduate or professional schools through a "risk aversive strategy" (Hsia, 1988). For Chinese high school students, this strategy usually entails an overconcentration on advanced courses in sciences and mathematics and a minimal concentration on English courses. The short-term benefit of this strategy is that their grade point averages go up; their scores on the quantitative section of college entrance examinations are, on the average, higher than white students. This allows them admission into colleges and universities. When in college, the same risk aversive strategy is employed. By concentrating in such fields as business, mathematics, science, and engineering, Chinese students are able to gain entrance to graduate or professional schools. Although such a strategy may allow many Chinese students to achieve short-term goals, their long-term goals may be severely curtailed. Their lack of facility with the English language, whether written and/or oral communication skills, may create an insurmountable barrier to their future socioeconomic and career placement (Wong, 1990).

Last, recent accusations of unequal treatment, insensitivity, racism, biases in the college entrance examinations, differential admission criteria, and quotas against the Chinese in higher education call into question the sacred belief in equality of educational opportunity (see Chapter 3 for a more in-depth discussion of the issues).

Chinatowns

Any discussion about the Chinese in the United States would be incomplete without some mention of Chinatowns. Chinatowns were formed in the later part of the 19th century—first in the major areas of Chinese concentration on the West Coast and then later on the East Coast. Protection from the discrimination and racism of the greater society was the major impetus for the Chinese segregating themselves in Chinatowns. This segregation was also maintained by the exclusion of the Chinese from the larger labor market and by housing discrimination (Yuan, 1963). To a certain degree, the caricature of Chinatown as a society unto itself, with its own system of government, organizational structure, and means of social control, is partly true.

Chinatown Social Structure

The organizational structure of Chinatown has its foundation in traditional China. Chief among such organizations or associations are the clans, the benevolent associations, and the secret societies.

The clans, or *tsu,* are organized along kinship lines and consist of families with common ancestors and those sharing a family name, even if a blood relationship is absent. In the past, the clans provided mutual assistance, a function increasingly taken on by government agencies.

The benevolent associations, or *hui kuan,* are based on the person's district of origin in China. Besides extending assistance to newcomers, the hui kuan used to provide loans and settle disputes among their members. They exercised considerable control over their members.

The associations were eventually governed by an umbrella group, the Chinese Consolidated Benevolent Association (CCBA), popularly known as the Chinese Six Companies in San Francisco. The Chinese Six Companies had benevolent and protective functions. Its agents met incoming ships, arranged for the initial housing and employment of migrants, organized medical treatment for the sick, arbitrated disputes between individual members, and performed other welfare functions.

> They gave me a lot of help. I celebrated festivals and all the Chinese holidays with my Tung Heung Hing Dai (brothers of the same village in China) in my family name association. Before my wife and children joined me here, my family name association was my family. Some of the members, in fact, assisted me when I started my own firm. (B. Wong, 1982, pp. 31-32)

Serving as the community's voice in the greater society, the Chinese Six Companies also came to exert a very high degree of social control over the lives of the early Chinese settlers.

A third form of social organization that developed in Chinatown was the secret societies or *tongs*. Some tong leaders gained respectability among the establishment, but others were involved in criminal or illegal services such as gambling, drugs, and prostitution, which were prevalent in any sizable Chinese American community. The infamous "tong wars" during the 1890s were a result of competition between tongs for scarce commodities—narcotics and Chinese women (Dillon, 1962; Light, 1977).

> The Chinese just fought each other on the streets. One group of Chinese Tong members on one side of the street fired their pistols at the rival Tong members on the other side of the street in broad daylight. All the pedestrians, Chinese or non-Chinese, had to seek shelter in the stores nearby. Ordinary Chinatown residents were fearful of the Tong Wars. They normally would close their shops and stay at home upon hearing any rumors about any possible outbreak of Tong Wars in Chinatown. Only the members of the rival Tongs were killing each other. It is a sad story. Chinese kill Chinese. What a shame! (B. Wong, 1982, p. 31)

All three types of Chinese organizations performed similar functions, providing mutual assistance and representing their members' interest to a sometimes hostile dominant group. As a consequence, conflicts among them were inevitable. Such conflicts were very violent in the 19th century, but in the 20th century, they were political in nature. Although the old associations have declined in significance, their power and influence within the Chinatown community, especially among the foreign born, is still considerable. Nonetheless, notes one observer:

> The CCBA is clearly not representative of the community, nor is it a mediating force among associations. It is a body created by the largest associations; it is arbitrary and nondemocratic, and it exists to enable a self-appointed elite to maintain control of Chinatown. (Kwong, 1987, p. 92)

Problems in Chinatown

Much of the economic survival of Chinatown is dependent on the tourist industry—a dependence that serves as a double-edged sword for Chinatown residents (Light & Wong, 1975). On the one hand, because slums and violence do not attract tourists, the economic leaders of Chinatown wish to present to the general public an image of Chinatown as a law-abiding and safe place. On the other hand, the maintenance of this image also forces the business leaders to keep the problems of Chinatown quiet and hidden and not seek outside assistance or social welfare. Hence, tourists or casual observers see Chinatown as an area of thriving businesses, a community of exotic sounds, sights, and smells, and a place where one can partake of "real" Chinese cuisine. They do not see that behind this glittering facade is another Chinatown with a wide range of social ills and economic problems associated with other ethnic ghettos. (For a contrasting view, see Zhou, 1992.)

Housing for many Chinese is old and substandard. Crime is on the increase, and the gang problem is becoming worse (Postner, 1988). Employment under sweatshop conditions is not unusual (Chin, 1965). Language insulates many Chinese from the rest of society.

A high proportion of men can find employment only in Chinese restaurants, and an even higher proportion of Chinese women can find work only in the garment industry. The garment shops are notorious for long hours and meager compensation (Light & Wong, 1975; Wong, 1983; Wong, 1987). There is a lack of sufficient recreational, social welfare, and therapeutic resources in Chinatown. These problems have grown more critical as Chinese immigration has dramatically increased.

The population density of San Francisco's Chinatown in the late 1980s was 10 times that of the city as a whole and was steadily increasing. Overcrowded Chinatowns are not conducive to good health. Tuberculosis, often equated with poverty, poor diet, and unsanitary, overcrowded facilities, was twice as common among the Chinese as among the white population in San Francisco (Wong, 1992).

The influx of thousands of new Chinese each year to the Chinatowns in major metropolitan areas has placed a tremendous strain on the community resources and services, leading to the surfacing of long-standing ghetto problems.

Modes of Adaptation

This last section deals with the various modes of adaptation of the Chinese into American society, a process that is continually being defined. Historically, the early Chinese did not easily assimilate, integrate, or participate in American society—nor were they allowed to. Racism kept them socially, economically, and politically apart. Jobs were largely limited to those who did not compete with the dominant group. Whatever opportunities existed for the Chinese were limited to their own communities. Their status as "aliens ineligible for citizenship" encouraged a sojourner rather than an assimilation orientation. More important, Chinese were identified by the dominant group as physically different, as foreigners, outsiders, and hence, unassimilable. They were not and, to some extent, are still not viewed as 100% Americans.

The demographics of the early Chinese also played a role in the slow rate of assimilation among Chinese Americans. Because almost all of the early Chinese were single males or married without wives and families, an American-born first generation was slow in developing—stable families that would move along an assimilation path.

Moreover, the Chinese in the United States have traditionally exhibited resistance to assimilation. Chinese ethnic communities seem to promote social and cultural exclusiveness and a low level of absorption into the larger society (Lyman, 1968, 1974; Purcell, 1980). Much of this self-imposed isolation is the product of not only of their personal views, but of the social control that the Chinese community organizations have had over their "citizens."

More recently, there have been some indications that American society is more willing to accept Chinese Americans as people, and not just as aliens. However, there will always be reminders that total social acceptance by the dominant group has not been obtained.

My parents run a Chinese restaurant. They were from the Old World 40 years ago and speak mostly Chinese at home and at the restaurant. Their lifestyle is Chinese-culture oriented. But I was born in the U.S. 27 years ago. I grew up with other white Americans and was educated in grade school, high school, college, and medical school in this country. I know more about the history, culture, and language of the U.S. and have thoughts that I am no different than other white Americans. Now that I am out of school practicing my profession as a physician, I definitely feel that people treat me like an ethnic and a member of another racial group. I am reminded that I am Chinese although my orientation and lifestyle are more American than Chinese. I have little knowledge about Chinese history, language, or culture. I am a U.S. citizen. Yet, I am treated as if I am not equal to other Americans. (B. Wong, 1982, p. 79)

Racial slurs, job tensions, and sporadic acts of violence all reinforce the idea that the Chinese are considered by their fellow citizens to be strangers from a different shore—not quite 100% or "real" Americans (Siao, 1990; Takaki, 1989; U.S. Commission on Civil Rights, 1986; Wong, 1989b, 1991; Zinmeister, 1987).

Acculturation or Pluralism?

Despite past patterns of insularity, several indicators suggest that Chinese Americans are now slowly moving in the direction of acculturation. One indicator is the geographic dispersion of the Chinese away from the Chinatown areas and into the metropolitan areas and the suburbs. As Chinese children attend suburban schools and develop friendships with white children, as they become more competent in English than in Chinese—in essence, as they become more acculturated—they will probably view themselves as more American than Chinese.

> We ABC (American-born Chinese) were ridiculed by the old immigrants as "Bamboo Stick" for not being able to speak Chinese and not being accepted as "white people." We are not here. We are not there. . . . We are different. Most of us are proud of the Chinese cultural heritage, but due to the pressure to assimilate and the lack of opportunity, we don't know much about the Chinese way. (B. Wong, 1982, p. 33)

Gradually drifting away from the older generation, the younger Chinese Americans will probably face a clash of generations, identity conflicts, and a lack of ethnic cohesion (Fong, 1965, 1968; Jiobu, 1988). One parent laments:

> Raising children does not do any good in this country. They leave when they are grown up. I seldom see them nowadays, with the exception of my youngest son who is running the factory in Chinatown. They are too independent in this country! They are selfish, too! (B. Wong, 1982, p. 32)

However, the suburbanization of the Chinese should not be viewed as total acceptance of the assimilation model. More often than not, the professional-status Chinese who have moved to suburbia have not "melted" into white, middle-class suburbanites. Instead, they have attempted to form a suburban Chinese community, suggesting cultural pluralism rather than assimilation orientation. Monterey Park provides such an example. In the early 1970s, it was a Los Angeles suburban town of mainly whites and Hispanics. Now the population is about 60% Asian, most of them middle class, and a majority of its businesses are Asian owned (Lemann, 1988). Moreover, although many Chinese Americans have escaped the ghetto (Chinatown), they still rely upon the ethnic enclave for special goods and services. As they seek to maintain their own cultural heritage, these Chinese communities remain important as custodians of tradition. Chinese families that have, in essence, become Americanized still retain some degree of cultural affiliation—food, a bilingual approach to language, Chinese organizations, and some pressure against mixed marriages (Lyman, 1977; Melendy, 1984, p. 81). In fact, the growth of Chinatowns throughout this country stands as a visible sign of the fallacy of the melting pot theory and reinforces the idea of the United States as a pluralistic society.

Another possible indicator of the acculturation of the Chinese family is the recent dramatic increase among the younger generation in the incidence of interracial marriages, particularly with whites (Barnett, 1963; Burma, 1952; Kitano & Yeung, 1982; Simpson & Yinger, 1965; Staples & Mirande, 1980; Weiss, 1970; Wong, 1989a; Yuan, 1980). Currently, approximately 22% of all marriages among the Chinese are with white partners (Wong, 1989a). Although this may be viewed as solid evidence of diminished social boundaries between the Chinese and the larger society—evidence that racial appearances, at least for the Chinese, do not seem to be a sufficient barrier—such a conclusion may be premature. There is some resistance on the part of the Chinese to intermarriage, and the prevalence of intermarriage among the Chinese is still considerably lower than among European groups, where outmarriage rates range from 50% to 80% (Alba & Golden, 1986). Hence the Chinese have a considerable way to go before being fully accepted as social equals. Whether the social boundaries between the Chinese and white population will continue to crumble, only time will tell.

In conclusion, because of their physical visibility, many Americans continue to see Chinese Americans as somehow not fully American, as "outsiders," even though their ancestors may have been in the United States for several generations. Although they may speak only English and have no ties to China, Chinese Americans are perceived as different, as "strangers from a different shore." No matter how Americanized they become, no matter how similar to whites in values, aspirations, mannerism, or actions, Chinese Americans will always be perceived as different. Ethnic identity and consciousness among Chinese Americans, therefore, regardless of the extent of their acculturation, are not likely to fully disappear.

Conclusions

The history of the Chinese in the United States is marked with episodes of individual and institutional prejudice, discrimination, and racism, and of isolation and exclusion from all that American society had to offer. They were discriminated against and excluded from the jobs that they undertook or pursued. They were isolated in Chinatowns and segregated from the greater society by various laws that prevented their participation in the political, judicial, social, economic, and educational institutions of American society. Finally, they were excluded from entering the United States in 1882—a policy that remained virtually in effect for about 80 years, until the passage of the 1965 Immigration Act. Despite this pervasive racism, the Chinese have continued to adapt to American society. As a group, their socioeconomic status has improved and on some indicators exceeds the achievements of whites, although there are great discrepancies between foreign-born and native-born Chinese. Moreover, despite such improvements, there is still a long way to go before full equality is achieved with the dominant group. Indicators, such as intermarriage rates, suggest that the acculturation of the Chinese to American society is slowly taking place, although it is still well below other European groups. Although the decade of the 1980s may be viewed as a decade of considerable progress on the part of the Chinese in American society, it will probably also be known as a decade when anti-Chinese antagonism and violence began to reemerge. Only time will tell what the 21st century holds for the Chinese in American society.

References

Alba, R. D., & Golden, R. M. (1986). Patterns of ethnic marriage in the United States. *Social Forces, 65,* 202-223.

Archdeacon, T. (1983). *Becoming an American: An ethnic history.* New York: Free Press.

Barnett, L. D. (1963). Interracial marriage in California. *Marriage and Family Living, 25,* 425-427.

Barth, G. (1964). *Bitter strength.* Cambridge: Harvard University Press.

Bell, D. A. (1985, July 14). The triumph of Asian-Americans. *The New Republic,* pp. 24-31.

Bonacich, E. (1973). A theory of middleman minorities. *American Sociological Review, 38,* 583-594.

Boyd, M. (1971). Oriental immigration: The experience of the Chinese, Japanese, and Filipino population in the United States. *International Migration Review, 5,* 48-60.

Boyd, M. (1974). The changing nature of the central and southeast Asian immigration to the United States: 1961-1972. *International Migration Review, 8,* 507-520.

Brand, D. (1987, August 31). The new whiz kids: Why Asians are doing so well and what it costs them. *Time,* pp. 42-51.

Braun, J., & Chao, H. (1978, Spring). Attitudes toward women: A comparison of Asian-born Chinese and American Caucasians. *Psychology of Women Quarterly, 2,* 195-201.

Burma, J. H. (1952). Research notes on the measurement of interracial marriage. *American Journal of Sociology, 57,* 587-589.

Butterfield, F. (1986, August 3). Why Asian students excel. *The New York Times,* pp. 22-25.

Cabezas, A., Tam, T. M., Lowe, B. M., Wong, A., & Turner, K. (1988). *Empirical study of barriers to upward mobility of Asian Americans in the San Francisco Bay area.* Unpublished manuscript.

Caudill, W. (1952). Japanese-American personality and acculturation. *Genetic Psychology Monographs, 45,* Part 1, 3-101.

Chan, S. (1984). The Chinese in California agriculture, 1860-1900. In G. Lim (Ed.), *The Chinese American experiences: Papers from the second national conference on Chinese American studies* (pp. 67-84). San Francisco: The Chinese Historical Society of America and The Chinese Culture Foundation of San Francisco.

Chen, H. (1984). Chinese immigration into the United States: An analysis of changes in immigration policies. In G. Lim (Ed.), *The Chinese American experiences: Papers from the second national conference on Chinese American studies* (pp. 44-47). San Francisco: The Chinese Historical Society of America and The Chinese Culture Foundation of San Francisco.

Chen, J. (1980). *The Chinese of America.* New York: Harper & Row.

Cheng, L., & Bonacich, E. (1984). *Labor migration under capitalism: Asian workers in the United States before World War II.* Los Angeles: University of California Press.

Chin, J. W. (1965). *Problems of assimilation and cultural pluralism among Chinese Americans in San Francisco: An exploratory study.* Master's thesis, University of the Pacific.

Chinn, T. W., Lai, H. M., & Choy, P. P. (Eds.). (1969). *A history of the Chinese in California: A syllabus.* San Francisco: Chinese Historical Society of America.

Chiu, P. (1963). *Chinese labor in California, 1850-1880.* Madison: State Historical Society of Wisconsin.

Daniels, R. (1970). *The politics of prejudice.* New York: Atheneum.

De Vos, G. (1960). The relation of guilt toward parents to achievement and arranged marriages among the Japanese. *Psychiatry, 23,* 287-301.

Dillon, R. H. (1962). *The hatchet men.* Sausalito, CA: Comstock.

Dinnerstein, L., & Reimers, D. M. (1988). *Ethnic Americans: A history of immigration.* New York: Harper & Row.

Divoky, D. (1988). The model minority goes to school. *Phi Delta Kappan, 70,* 219-222.

Doerner, W. R. (1985, July 8). Asians: To America with skills. *Time,* pp. 42-44.

Fischer, B. (1988). Whiz kid image masks problem of Asian Americans. *NEA Today, 6,* 14-15.

Fong, S. L. M. (1965). Assimilation of Chinese in America: Changes in orientation and social perception. *American Journal of Sociology, 71,* 265-273.

Fong, S. L. M. (1968). Identity conflict of Chinese adolescents in San Francisco. In E. B. Brody (Ed.), *Minority group adolescents in the United States* (pp. 111-132). Baltimore, MD: Williams & Wilkins.

Glenn, E. N. (1983). Split household, small producer and dual wage earner: An analysis of Chinese-American family strategies. *Journal of Marriage and the Family, 45,* 35-46.

Glick, C. E. (1980). *Sojourners and settlers: Chinese migrants in Hawaii.* Honolulu: University of Hawaii Press.

Growth of the United States through emigration—the Chinese. (1865, September 3). *New York Times,* p. 4.

Hirschman, C., & Wong, M. G. (1981). Trends in socioeconomic achievement among immigrant and native-born Asian-Americans, 1960-1976. *Sociological Quarterly, 22,* 495-513.

Hirschman, C., & Wong, M. G. (1984). Socioeconomic gains of Asian-Americans, Blacks, and Hispanics: 1960-1976. *American Journal of Sociology, 90,* 584-607.

Hirschman, C., & Wong, M. G. (1986). The extraordinary educational attainment of Asian-Americans: A search for historical evidence and explanations. *Social Forces, 65,* 1-27.

Hong, L. K. (1976). Recent immigrants in the Chinese-American community: Issues of adaptations and impacts. *International Migration Review, 10,* 509-514.

Hsia, J. (1988). *Asian Americans in higher education and at work.* Hillsdale, NJ: Lawrence Erlbaum.

Hsu, F. L. K. (1971). *The challenge of the American dream: The Chinese in the United States.* Belmont, CA: Wadsworth.

Huang, L. J. (1981). The Chinese American family. In C. Mindel & R. Habenstein (Eds.), *Ethnic families in America* (2nd ed., pp. 115-141). New York: Elsevier.

Ikels, C. (1985). Parental perspectives on the significance of marriage. *Journal of Marriage and the Family, 47,* 253-264.

Immigration and Naturalization Service. (1992). *Statistical yearbook of the Immigration and Naturalization Service.* Washington, DC: U.S. Government Printing Office.

Issacs, H. R. (1972). *Images of Asia: American views of China and India.* New York: Harper Torchbooks.

Jiobu, R. M. (1976). Earnings differentials between whites and ethnic minorities: The cases of Asian Americans, Blacks and Chicanos. *Sociology and Social Research, 61,* 24-39.

Jiobu, R. M. (1988). *Ethnicity and assimilation.* Albany: State University of New York Press.

Keeley, C. (1971, May). Effects of the Immigration Act of 1965 on selected population characteristics of immigrants to the U.S. *Demography, 8,* 157-169.

Keeley, C. (1974, April 3). The demographic effects of immigration legislation and procedures. *Interpreter Releases, 51,* 89-93.

Keeley, C. (1975a). Effects of U.S. immigration laws on manpower characteristics of immigrants. *Demography, 12*(May), 179-192.

Keeley, C. (1975b). Immigration composition and population policy. In P. Reining & I. Tinker (Eds.), *Population dynamics: Ethics and policy* (pp. 129-135). Washington, DC: American Association for the Advancement of Science.

Kim, B. L. C. (1978). *The Asian Americans: Changing patterns, changing needs.* Montclair, NJ: The Association of Korean Christian Scholars in North America.

Kim, K. C., Hurh, W. M., & Fernandez, M. (1989). Intra-group differences in business participation: Three Asian immigrant groups. *International Migration Review, 23,* 73-95.

Kingston, M. H. (1976). *Woman warrior.* New York: Knopf.

Kingston, M. H. (1981). *Chinamen.* New York: Ballantine.

Kitano, H. H. L. (1991). *Race relations.* Englewood Cliffs, NJ: Prentice Hall.

Kitano, H. H. L., & Daniels, R. (1988). *Asian Americans: Emerging minorities.* Englewood Cliffs, NJ: Prentice Hall.

Kitano, H. H. L., & Yeung, W. T. (1982). Chinese interracial marriage. *Marriage and Family Review, 5,* 35-48.

Kung, S. W. (1962). *Chinese in American life: Some aspects of their history, status, and contributions.* Seattle: University of Washington Press.

Kuo, C. L. (1970). The Chinese on Long Island—a pilot study. *Phylon, 31,* 280-289.

Kwong, P. (1979). *Chinatown, NY: Labor and politics, 1930-1950.* New York: Monthly Review Press.

Kwong, P. (1987). *The new Chinatown.* New York: Noonsday.

Lai, H. M., & Choy, P. P. (1971). *Outlines: History of the Chinese in America.* San Francisco: Chinese-American Studies Planning Group.

Lee, E. S., & Rong, X. L. (1988). The educational and economic achievement of Asian-Americans. *The Elementary School Journal, 88,* 545-560.

Lee, R. H. (1956, February). The recent immigrant Chinese families of the San Francisco-Oakland area. *Marriage and Family Living, 18,* 14-24.

Lee, R. H. (1960). *The Chinese in the United States.* Hong Kong: Hong Kong University Press.

Lemann, N. (1988, January). Growing pains. *Atlantic,* pp. 57-62.

Lewis, O. (1938). *The Big four.* New York: Knopf.

Li, P. S. (1977). Ethnic businesses among Chinese in the United States. *Journal of Ethnic Studies, 4*(3), 35-41.

Li, W. L. (1977). Occupational achievement and kinship assistance among Chinese immigrants in Chicago. *Sociological Quarterly, 18,* 478-489.

Li, W. L. (1982). Chinese Americans: Exclusion from the melting pot. In A. G. Dworkin & R. J. Dworkin (Eds.), *The minority report: An introduction to racial, ethnic, and gender relations* (pp. 303-328). New York: Holt, Rinehart & Winston.

Liauh, W. (1989, May 27). Statement at the U.S. Commission on Civil Rights Roundtable Conference on Asian American Civil Rights Issues for the 1990s, Houston, Texas.

Light, I. H. (1977). The ethnic vice industry, 1880-1944. *American Sociological Review, 42,* 464-478.

Light, I. H., & Wong, C. C. (1975). Protest or work: Dilemmas of the tourist industry in American Chinatowns. *American Journal of Sociology, 80,* 1342-1368.

Lord, L., & Linnon, N. (1988, March 14). What puts the whiz in whiz kids. *U.S. News and World Report,* pp. 48-53.

Lowe, P. (1943). *Father and glorious descent.* Boston: Little, Brown.

Lyman, S. M. (1968). Marriage and the family among Chinese immigrants to America, 1850-1960. *Phylon, 29,* 321-330.

Lyman, S. M. (1974). *Chinese Americans.* New York: Random House.

Lyman, S. M. (1977). *The Asians in North America.* Santa Barbara, CA: ABC-CLIO.

Mark, D. M. L., & Chih, G. (1982). *A place called Chinese America.* Washington, DC: Organization of Chinese Americans.

McGrath, E. (1983, March 28). Confucian work ethic. *Time,* p. 3.

Melendy, H. B. (1984). *Chinese and Japanese.* New York: Hippocrene.

Miller, S. C. (1969). *The unwelcome immigrant: The American image of the Chinese, 1785-1882.* Berkeley: University of California Press.

Monahan, T. (1977, January-June). Illegitimacy by race and mixture of race. *International Journal of Sociology of the Family, 7,* 45-54.

Nee, V., & Nee, B. (1972). *A longtime Californ': A documentary study of an American Chinatown.* New York: Pantheon.

Nee, V., & Wong, H. Y. (1985). Asian American socioeconomic achievement: The strength of the family bond. *Sociological Perspectives, 28,* 281-306.

Ong, P. (1981). An ethnic trade: The Chinese laundries in early California. *Journal of Ethnic Studies, 8,* 95-113.

Postner, G. L. (1988). *Warlords of crime.* New York: Penguin.

Purcell, V. (1965). *The Chinese in Southeast Asia.* London: Oxford University Press.

Purcell, V. (1980). *The Chinese in Southeast Asia.* Oxford: Oxford University Press.

Sandmeyer, E. C. (1973). *The Anti-Chinese movement in California.* Urbana: University of Illinois Press.

Saxton, A. (1971). *The indispensable enemy: Labor and the anti-Chinese movement in California.* Berkeley: University of California Press.

Schaefer, R. (1991). *Racial and ethnic groups.* Boston: Little, Brown.

Schrieke, B. (1936). *Alien Americans: A study of race relations.* New York: Viking.

Shin, F. H. (1988). Asian-American students on college campuses. *Education Digest, 54,* 59-62.

Siao, G. W. T. (1990, September 14). Steep rise in anti-Asian hate crimes in Los Angeles County. *Asian Week,* pp. 1, 5.

Simpson, G. E., & Yinger, J. M. (1965). *Racial and cultural minorities.* New York: Harper & Row.

Siu, P. (1952). The sojourner. *American Journal of Sociology, 50,* 34-44.

Spier, R. F. G. (1958). Food habits of the nineteenth century California Chinese. *California Historical Society Quarterly, 38,* 79-136.

Staples, R., & Mirande, A. (1980). Racial and cultural variations among American families: A decennial review of the literature on minority families. *Journal of Marriage and the Family, 42,* 887-903.

Sue, S., Zane, N. W. S., & Sue, D. (1985). Where are the Asian American leaders and top executives? *P/AAMHRC Research Review, 4*(1/2), 13-15.

Sung, B. L. (1967). *Mountain of gold.* New York: Macmillan.

Sung, B. L. (1971). *The story of the Chinese in America.* New York: Collier.

Sung, B. L. (1977). Changing Chinese. *Society, 14*(6), 44-99.

Takaki, R. (1989). *Strangers from a different shore: A history of Asian Americans.* Boston: Little, Brown.

Tang, V. (1984). Chinese women immigrants and the two-edged sword of habeas corpus. In G. Lim (Ed.), *The Chinese American experiences: Papers from the second national conference on Chinese American studies* (pp. 48-56). San Francisco: The Chinese Historical Society of America and The Chinese Culture Foundation of San Francisco.

U.S. Bureau of the Census. (1975). *Historical statistics of the United States.* Washington, DC: U.S. Government Printing Office.

U.S. Bureau of the Census. (1983). *1980 census of the population, general population characteristics, United States summary* (PC80-1-C1). Washington, DC: U.S. Government Printing Office.

U.S. Bureau of the Census. (1993a). *1990 census of population, general population characteristics, the United States* (CP-1-1). Washington, DC: U.S. Government Printing Office.

U.S. Bureau of the Census. (1993b). *1990 census of population, Asians and Pacific Islanders in the United States* (CP-3-5). Washington, DC: U.S. Government Printing Office.

U.S. Bureau of the Census. (1994). *1990 census of population, general social and economic characteristics, the United States* (CP-2-1). Washington, DC: U.S. Government Printing Office.

U.S. Commission on Civil Rights. (1986). *Recent activities against citizens and residents of Asian descent.* Washington, DC: Clearing House.

U.S. Commission on Civil Rights. (1988). *The economic status of Americans of Asian descent: An exploratory investigation.* Washington, DC: Clearing House.

Weiss, M. S. (1970). Selective acculturation and the dating process: The patterning of Chinese-Caucasian interracial dating. *Journal of Marriage and the Family, 32,* 273-278.

Weiss, M. S. (1974). *Valley city: A Chinese community in America.* Cambridge, MA: Schenkman.

Williams, D. A., & McDonald, D. H. (1987, April 23). A formula for success: Asian American students win academic honors—and cope with the mixed blessings of achievement. *Newsweek,* pp. 77-79.

Wolf, M. (1968). *The house of Lim.* New York: Appleton-Century-Crofts.

Wong, B. (1982). *Chinatown: Economic adaptation and ethnic identity of the Chinese.* New York: Holt, Rinehart & Winston.

Wong, B. (1987). The role of ethnicity in enclave enterprises: A study of the Chinese garment factories in New York City. *Human Organization, 46,* 120-130.

Wong, C. C. (1980). The continuity of Chinese grocers in Southern California. *Journal of Ethnic Studies, 8*(2), 63-82.

Wong, E. F. (1985). Asian American middleman minority theory: The framework of an American myth. *Journal of Ethinic Studies, 13,* 51-88.

Wong, J. S. (1950). *Fifth Chinese daughter.* New York: Harper.

Wong, M. G. (1980). Changes in socioeconomic achievement of the Chinese male population in the United States from 1960 to 1970. *International Migration Review, 14,* 511-524.

Wong, M. G. (1982). The cost of being Chinese, Japanese, and Filipino in the United States 1960, 1970, 1976. *Pacific Sociological Reivew, 25,* 59-78.

Wong, M. G. (1983). Chinese sweatshops in the United States: A look at garment industry. In I. H. Simpson & R. L. Simpson (Eds.), *Research in the sociology of work* (Vol. 2, pp. 37-79). Greenwich, CT: JAI Press.

Wong, M. G. (1985). Post-1965 immigrants: Demographic and socioeconomic profile. In L. A. Maldonado & J. W. Moore (Eds.), *Urban ethnicity: New immigrants and old minorities* (pp. 51-71). Beverly Hills, CA: Sage.

Wong, M. G. (1986). Post-1965 Asian immigrants: Where do they come from, where are they now, and where are they going? In R. J. Simon (Ed.), *The annals of the American Academy of Political and Social Science* (Vol. 487, pp. 150-168). Beverly Hills, CA: Sage.

Wong, M. G. (1988). The Chinese-American family. In C. H. Mindel, R. W. Haberstein, & R. Wright, Jr. (Eds.) *Ethnic families in America* (3rd ed., pp. 230-257). New York: Elsevier.

Wong, M. G. (1989a). A look at intermarriage among the Chinese in the United States. *Sociological Perspectives, 32,* 87-107.

Wong, M. G. (1989b, November). *The rise of anti-Chinese violence in the United States.* Paper presented to the Forth Worth chapter of the Organization of Chinese Americans, Arlington, TX.

Wong, M. G. (1990). The education of white, Chinese, Filipino, and Japanese students: A look at "high school and beyond." *Sociological Perspectives, 33,* 355-374.

Wong, M. G. (1991). *Rise in hate crimes against Asians in the United States.* Paper presented at the annual meeting of the American Sociological Association, Cincinnati, OH.

Wong, M. G. (1992, September). *Macro-social influences on the health of Asian Americans.* Paper presented at the National Conference on Behavioral and Sociocultural Perspectives on Ethnicity and Health, Washington, DC.

Wong, M. G. (1994, March). *The sociohistory of the Chinese in Texas.* Paper presented at the Southwestern Social Science Association Annual Meetings, San Antonio, TX.

Wong, M. G., & Hirschman, C. (1983). The new Asian immigrants. In W. McCready (Ed.), *Culture, ethnicity and identity: Current issues in research* (pp. 381-403). New York: Academic Press.

Wu, C. (Ed.). (1972). *CHINK!* New York: World.

Yuan, D. Y. (1963). Voluntary segregation: A study of new Chinatown. *Phylon, 24,* 255-265.

Yuan, D. Y. (1966). Chinatown and beyond: The Chinese population in metropolitan New York. *Phylon, 22,* 321-332.

Yuan, D. Y. (1980). Significant demographic characteristics of Chinese who intermarry in the United States. *California Sociologist, 3*(2), 184-197.

Yung, J. (1977). A bowlful of tears: Chinese women immigrants on Angel Island. *Frontiers,* 2(2), 52-55.

Zhou, M. (1992). *Chinatown: The socioeconomic potential of urban enclave.* Philadelphia: Temple University Press.

Zinmeister, K. (1987). Asians: Prejudice from top and bottom. *Public Opinion, 10,* 8-10, 59.

5

Japanese Americans

SETSUKO MATSUNAGA NISHI

In contrast to the dramatic doubling of the Asian population in the United States in each of the 2 decades between 1970 and 1990, Japanese Americans have increased relatively slowly and constitute a rapidly diminishing proportion of that population. With little "push" for emigration from modern Japan, two thirds of Japanese Americans now are native born, compared to only 40% or less of other Asian ethnic groups.

Well into the fourth and fifth generations in this country, Japanese Americans have more than a century of experience in American race relations—as contract labor recruited for Hawaii's plantations and the opening of the West in the later decades of the 19th century; through the travails of the Yellow Peril campaigns leading to the banning of further immigration in 1924; raising families and earning a living in a severely discriminatory economic system in the Depression years; the forced removal and incarceration during World War II; reentry into American society and the long effort for recovery from degradation; and, finally, to institutionalized discrimination and scapegoating in the current wave of Japan bashing. How did they cope and adapt?

This chapter provides an overview of Japanese Americans, identifying issues of significance to this group and to knowledge about them. The approach is essentially sociological, although the work of other disciplines will be tapped. As a population studied over the span of a century, the theoretical concerns, often embedded in heated public controversies, have changed with the course of social scientific development: from the rationalization of racist ideology and descriptions of immigrant institutions, to

95

analyses of indicators of assimilation and acculturation to the dominant group, stratification processes, cultural values and achievement, economic segmentation, and institutionalized discrimination.

Space constrains the desirable amount of detail in data and analysis. The broad coverage and the topics included are intended to allow for some comparability with groups discussed in other chapters. The following emphases are based on the author's research interests as a sociologically trained social psychologist:

1. Social structural/processual linkages between culture and individual behavior
2. Antecedents and life course consequences of their removal and incarceration on a racial basis during World War II
3. Institutionalized discrimination, the modern form of racism and sexism

Immigration History

Three distinct strands of immigration were drawn from Japan, marked by vastly differing circumstances of "push" and "pull" factors: first, the pre-1924 Exclusion Act immigration, beginning in 1884; second, the post-World War II coming of war brides, and, finally, the post-1965 arrivals from modern Japan.

Pre-1924 Immigration

Well over 100 years ago, in the last decades of the 19th century, significant migration from Japan began—relatedly—a few years after Chinese labor immigration was closed off with the passage of the Chinese Exclusion Act of 1882. Two earlier efforts, one to Hawaii and the other to California, were ill-fated. The 149 Japanese who went to work on plantations in Hawaii in 1869 were so mistreated that, by the end of the year, the Japanese government had brought some of them home and stopped further emigration.

Not until 1884, at the urging of representatives of the then Kingdom of Hawaii and under conditions of the Irwin Convention and supervision of the governments of both Hawaii and Japan, did labor immigration resume. Nearly 30,000 plantation workers came in the next decade, only about half of whom stayed (Chan, 1991, pp. 11-12; Conroy, 1953). Between 1894, when the Irwin Convention ended, and the 1908 Gentlemen's Agreement, 125,000 Japanese came to Hawaii under the auspices of emigration companies and another 17,000 on their own (Moriyama, 1985, pp. 13-24). Before long, they were the largest ethnic group on the islands, numbering 61,000 by 1900. This was of great portent to their not being incarcerated during World War II and to their social and political position when Hawaii achieved statehood in 1959 (Daniels, 1988, p. 101).

On the U.S. mainland, the first Japanese immigrants were a small group of political refugees from the Meiji Restoration. Arriving in 1869, they established the Wakamatsu Tea and Silk Colony in Gold Hill, El Dorado County, near Sacramento, but it was disbanded after 10 years for lack of funds (Chuman, 1976, pp. 3-9, Kitano, 1969, pp. 12-13). Believed to be the first marriage of a Japanese in California was the union between Masamizu Kuni of this colony and a "Negro girl," who had one child (Kitano, 1969, p. 13). Except for a small but influential number of students encouraged to obtain Western education to facilitate Japan's modernization, emigration ended until 1884.

Disgruntled with contractual failures and plantation regimentation, many Japanese left Hawaii for California, and more came directly from Japan to the mainland, primarily to the Western states: 2,270 between 1884 and 1890; 27,440 between 1891 and 1900 (Chuman, 1976, p. 11). The Californians who succeeded in getting passage of the 1882 Chinese Exclusion Act now turned their energy against the Japanese (Daniels, 1988, pp. 112-113). This resulted in a series of progressively more exclusionary "Gentlemen's Agreements" between Japan and the United States in 1900, 1905, and, finally, in 1908, prohibiting passports to laborers headed for Hawaii and the United States (Chuman, 1976, pp. 19-37).

In 1905 to 1906, the San Francisco Board of Education precipitated what President Theodore Roosevelt considered to be a major international incident with Japan by resolving to segregate Japanese children in the schools. The furor in Japan was immediate and intense; the action was regarded as a grave racial insult, indicating rising animosity against the Japanese, a campaign led by organized labor against their economic competitors. But to Roosevelt, the threat to U.S. foreign policy in the Far East was more grave; Japan had won the war against China in 1895 and against Russia in 1905 and was seen as a potential military competitor in the Pacific. Roosevelt actively intervened, inviting the school board to Washington, where he urged them to rescind their action. But it was clear that this was tied to the curtailment of immigration from Japan. The resulting Gentlemen's Agreement of 1908 accomplished a rapid reduction in Japanese labor immigration and, importantly, provided for the coming of family-arranged wives of laborers already here (Chuman, 1976, pp. 19-37).

Thus began the period of concentrated family establishment, which, in contrast to the Chinese, assured the continuation of generations of Japanese in the United States. Whereas male immigration took place mainly in the decades before and after the turn of the century, females were about 10 years younger and came primarily in the 6 years preceding the passage of the 1924 Oriental Exclusion Act. Thus, on average, Issei (literally, first generation) women were destined to have unusually early and long widowhoods. That the Nisei (second generation) were born in an extremely concentrated span of time had enormous consequences in the crisis of World War II. We shall come back to the long-term consequences later.

Figure 5.1, reproduced from a study by Dorothy Swaine Thomas, graphically depicts the dramatic fluctuations of immigration to and emigration from the continental United States in response to these events.

Between 1921 and World War II, Japanese who immigrated to the continental United States numbered substantially less than those who returned home from the United States, consisting primarily of a small number of students and clergy. The 1924 Oriental Exclusion Act effectively halted immigration from Japan for nearly 30 years. Japanese immigration resumed in 1952 with the passage of the McCarran-Walter Immigration Act. In addition to a tiny annual quota of 185 immigrants assigned to Japan, relatives of U.S. citizens could come as nonquota immigrants under the family reunification provisions of the act.

War Brides in the 1950s

The overwhelming majority (see Table 5.1) of immigrants from Japan in the decade of the 1950s were women, primarily wives of U.S. servicemen (Chan, 1991, p. 140; Daniels, 1988, p. 307; Glenn, 1986, pp. 58-66; Kim, 1977, p. 91). Despite prevalent stereotypes, war brides were of diverse socioeconomic backgrounds, but almost all had experienced the extreme deprivations of war-ravaged Japan and many were employed in jobs bringing them in contact with American GIs. Glenn (1986) and Spickard (1989, pp. 123-157), based on their interviews with war brides and a review of the literature, characterized these women as predominantly urban and relatively less bound by the traditional Japanese woman's role. The American men whom they married were disproportionately from rural, small-town, blue-collar backgrounds (Spickard, 1989, p. 129). Despite discouragement by the military, GIs did marry Japanese women, but they could not bring their wives and children to the United States under the 1945 War Brides Act, because Japanese were still barred under the 1924 Exclusion

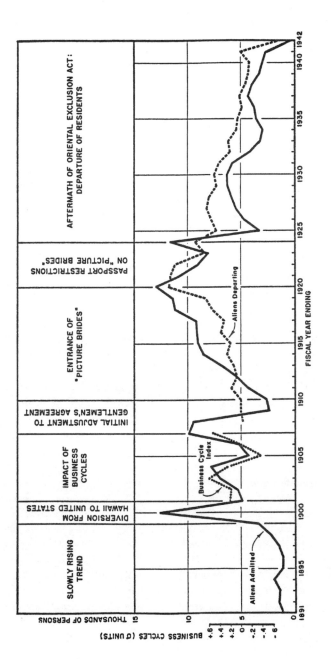

Figure 5.1. Japanese Immigration to and Emigration From Continental United States, by Fiscal Years, 1891-1942, and Index of U.S. Business Cycles, by Calendar Years, 1900-1906

SOURCE: From Thomas, Dorothy, et alia, *Salvage: Japanese-American evacuation and resettlement.* Copyright © 1952, The Regents of the University of California. Reprinted with permission.

Table 5.1 Immigration of the Japanese by Sex

Year	Male	Female	Total	Female Immigrants as % of Total
1950	16	29	45	64.4
1951	45	161	206	78.2
1952	153	4,581	4,734	96.8
1953	198	2,291	2,489	92.0
1954	685	3,377	4,062	83.1
1955	708	3,435	4,143	82.9
1956	1,342	4,280	5,622	76.1
1957	765	5,357	6,122	87.5
1958	868	5,559	6,427	86.5
1959	810	5,283	6,093	86.7
1960	824	4,812	5,636	85.4
Total	6,414	39,165	45,579	85.9

SOURCE: Immigration and Naturalization Service (1950-1960).

Act. Amendments in 1947 and 1948 to the War Brides Act and a period from August 1950 to February 1952 enabled a few servicemen to bring their Japanese wives to the United States. But it was not until the passage of the McCarran-Walter Act in late 1952 that a significant number of war brides came to the United States. As evident in Table 5.1, 86% of the more than 45,000 Japanese immigrants during the 1950s were female, and, according to Kim's (1977, p. 91) estimation, three fourths of these women were admitted as wives of American citizens.

The Post-1965 Immigration

The Immigration Act of 1965 brought a profound change in the presence of Asians in the United States, doubling their numbers in each of the subsequent decennial censuses. But the growth of the Japanese American population has been at a much slower rate: 27%, from 464,332 in 1960 to 591,290 in 1970; 19% in the next decade, to 700,974 in 1980, and 21% in the 1980s, to 847,562 in 1990 (see Table 2.3 in Chapter 2). After nearly 40 years of severely restricted immigration from Asia, the 1965 reforms provided for a quota of 20,000 per country and several categories of nonquota immigrants. Thus Asians soon constituted 45% of all immigrants to the United States. But the annual numbers from Japan remained about the same, ranging from 4,000 to 6,000 (see Table 2.1 in Chapter 2), a precipitously decreasing proportion of the total immigration from Asian countries. The immigrants from Japan between 1960 and 1964 made up 20.4% of total immigrants from all Asian countries, but those coming from Japan between 1985 and 1989 constituted only 1.6% (see Table 2.1 in Chapter 2). Thus the U.S. population of Japanese descent became increasingly American born, only 32% being foreign born in 1990, in striking contrast with other Asian background populations, all of whom were between 65% and 80% foreign born (see Table 2.10 in Chapter 2).

The immigration history of Japanese Americans, spanning more than a century of changes in the world economy, reflects these transformations in the sending and receiving countries. The dislocation of rural workers in the Meiji era push for modernization in Japan, combined with the need for primary industry workers in Hawaiian plantations and the development of the West in the United States, brought the first wave of mostly male Japanese immigrant workers. Before long, fierce opposition from American labor led to the closure of labor immigration from Japan in 1908, but brides of already settled Japanese male workers were allowed to come to the United States until 1924. With the enforcement of the National Origins Quota system in 1924, all Asian immigration, with the exception of Filipino immigration, effectively ceased for 30 years, until the McCarran-Walter Act of 1952 provided for a tiny annual quota based on a proportion of the resident population of that origin. The postwar years saw a virtually exclusively female immigration from Japan, almost all of them wives of U.S. servicemen.

By 1965, when discrimination based on national origin came to an end in the immigration law, Japan was a world economic power, that could employ all of its trained work force. The absence of a push factor is the major reason for the very small number of Japanese who have immigrated to the United States over the last quarter century. By contrast, the pressure for emigration to the United States was very high in other Asian countries, such as India and the Philippines, where modernization has not been fast enough to engage highly trained workers. At the same time, the United States faced shortages of such trained workers and thus permitted entry of aliens under the occupational preference provisions of the 1965 Immigration Act. The New York state health care industry is a notable example of how doctors, nurses, and technicians from the developing Asian countries came to fill the severe shortages in the least desirable sectors of the system. Their distribution in the health care system in the 1980s still manifested institutionalized patterns of socioeconomic disadvantages. By contrast, there was a conspicuous absence of foreign-born Japanese medical professionals relative to other Asians (Nishi, 1985).

Changing Patterns of Discrimination

Ineligibility for Citizenship and Its Castelike Consequences

Today's "model minority" stereotype of Asian Americans obscures a history of blatant 19th century racism, in which Japanese labor was recruited aggressively for the plantations of Hawaii and the building of railroads in the West—at least partially to be played off against Chinese labor. Although desirable as labor, the Japanese were a nonwhite racial group whose presence in American society was not welcomed, and numerous measures were taken to maintain a castelike separation.

Once they arrived in the United States, exclusion from citizenship was the basic barrier. In 1790, Congress acted to enable "any alien, being a free white person, to become a citizen" and, in 1870, modified it to include "persons of African nativity or descent." Despite numerous challenges, the courts, including the landmark 1922 *Ozawa vs. U.S.* decision, maintained that Japanese aliens, not being of the "white" race or of African background, were ineligible for citizenship. Not until the 1952 McCarran-Walter Act, by which all races became eligible, could Japanese become citizens (Chuman, 1976, pp. 65-71). Even the 1918 law, which made those who served in World War I eligible for citizenship, excluded Asians until the passage of special legislation 17 years later in 1935 (Chuman, 1976, p. 70).

Among the consequences of their ineligibility for citizenship were state laws prohibiting their buying land—California, 1913; Arizona, 1917; and Washington, 1921—and leasing land or being guardians of their American-born citizen children who owned land—California, 1920. But the record of their increasing concentration in agriculture until World War II suggests that these were not effective deterrents.

The 1924 Quota Immigration Act, better known as the Oriental Exclusion Act, prohibited entry to "aliens ineligible for citizenship." This policy effectively barred any significant Asian immigration, except for tiny quotas, until the 1952 McCarran-Walter Act, in which one provision removed the racial basis of eligibility for citizenship. With no replacement immigration, the foreign-born Japanese were a concentrated age cohort, as were their children, and thus they shared to an unusual degree a common context of historical discrimination. Succinctly characterized by Miyamoto (1984, p. x), the Issei, because of their ineligibility for citizenship, "were permanently restricted to an inferior status," which also profoundly affected the Nisei, citizens by birth, who identified with their alien parents. Aside from *de jure* discrimination, patterns of occupational and related residential segregation sustained their castelike relations in American society until World War II. These will be discussed in a later section.

Forced Removal and Incarceration During World War II

A central event in the history of Japanese Americans was their World War II evacuation, incarceration, and resettlement on a racial basis, deemed by the American Civil Liberties Union as "the greatest deprivation of civil liberties by government in this country since slavery" (Ennis, 1981, pp. 144-149). It was the epitome of a long history of discrimination, which had become less blatant and more embedded in patterns of occupational segregation for the Issei, who relied on their ethnic community to cope with a generally hostile economic and social environment. For the Nisei, most of whom were still in the relatively protected atmosphere of school, it was a shocking disillusion that their government did not trust them and that the Constitution did not protect them from forced removal and incarceration without charges or trial.

Some 112,000 persons of Japanese descent living in the three West Coast states and the southern half of Arizona—about 90% of the Japanese in the continental United States—were ordered removed to camps. Two thirds were American citizens, and the others were longtime legal residents. Ironically, despite serious debate in government, the 158,000 Japanese Americans in Hawaii, 37% of its population, were not considered a threat; on the contrary, they were viewed as essential to the islands' defense, and thus were not removed en masse (Culley, 1984; Weglyn, 1976, p. 50).

Elsewhere (Clausen & Nishi, 1983) we summarized our participant observation experience of evacuation and incarceration:

Pearl Harbor was no less stunning to Japanese Americans than to the American populace generally. But, in addition, they felt overwhelming uncertainty about their vulnerability to being identified with the enemy. The Issei, excluded from United States citizenship, were Japanese citizens by law. As enemy aliens they did not know what to expect for themselves. And, indeed, the Department of Justice arrested in an immediate sweep more than a thousand who had been under surveillance as leaders of Japanese American community activities. They were taken away with no notice, and their families did not know where they were taken nor for how long. News of these sudden arrests spread rapidly. With no communication from the interned Issei, rumors and apprehension spread; families packed a suitcase for father and waited.

For weeks after Pearl Harbor, fear and uncertainty prevailed. False rumors of Japanese American fifth column activity abounded. Then, just as Japanese Americans recovered some degree of normality in work and school activities, in late January, 1942, a campaign was launched calling for the mass evacuation of Japanese Americans. (pp. 9-12)

Contrary to the outcome for Hawaii, the controversy at the highest levels of government between the War Department and the Department of Justice was powerfully influenced by the West Coast congressional delegation. On February 19, 1942, President Franklin D. Roosevelt signed Executive Order 9066, which authorized the Secretary of War to designate "military areas" and remove "any or all persons" from these areas (Irons, 1983, pp. 3-74; tenBroek, Barnhart, & Matson, 1954, p. 112). Again, returning to our description of the events (Clausen & Nishi, 1983):

They were first ordered removed—with 24 hour notice—from certain restricted zones such as Terminal Island near Los Angeles. Then, on March 2, 1942, military zones were established from which Japanese Americans were to be excluded but from which they were permitted to relocate in other areas. On March 27, however, voluntary outmigration was prohibited, and removal to hastily prepared assembly centers began. (On March 24, a curfew had been imposed on enemy aliens and all persons of Japanese ancestry, ordering them to be in their homes between 8 p.m. and 6 a.m.). Every family was assigned a number which each member wore on a tag. They were permitted to bring only what they could carry.

If removal ended their uncertainty, incarceration was not merely disruptive; it was often catastrophic from the standpoint of losing almost everything they had striven so hard to acquire, along with treasured family heirlooms symbolizing the all-important continuity of the *ie,* or household.

The assembly centers, built mainly on racetracks and fairgrounds, were enclosed in barbed wire, guarded from towers with searchlights, and surrounded by armed soldiers. Former horse stables and flimsy tarpaper barracks housed families. Sheets were hung from ceilings for privacy. Latrines and showers were open. Mass-prepared meals of unfamiliar style were served after long waits in line in large Army-type messhalls. Rarely did families eat together.

Evacuees stayed in assembly centers for an average of 100 days before being moved by the Army to centers run by the War Relocation Authority, a civilian agency. The ten relocation centers were on public land, mostly desert tracts, all isolated. The barracks were partitioned so that a family of five or six lived in a room 20 by 25 feet without running water or cooking facilities. These facilities were shared in a central building by 250 to 300 persons in a block of about a dozen of barracks. Army cots and blankets and a small stove were provided.

In early 1943, the Army decided to establish a Nisei combat team of volunteers who passed a loyalty review. In this connection, all adult relocation center inmates were administered a questionnaire requiring a Yes or a No declaration of position regarding complete loyalty to the United States. Torn between anger at their government's unjust treatment and hope for their reacceptance in American society, Japanese Americans reacted strongly to the loyalty questionnaire. It touched off intense divisions, including violent outbreaks, in the camps and within families. The renunciants—the angry, disillusioned, and embittered—and their dependents were segregated in Tule Lake camp, from which some ultimately went to Japan.

The resettlement program was based on a legal ruling that citizens could not be detained without charge. Inevitably, Nisei of employable age and skills were the first to go. Resettlement was a period of family separation with efforts to reunite under great difficulties. The West Coast was reopened in September 1945, when, ironically, in some locales more anti-Japanese feeling was aroused on their return than by their removal. (pp. 10-12)

Three Japanese Americans—Gordon Hirabayashi, Minoru Yasui, and Fred Korematsu—who challenged the constitutionality of the military orders were convicted; these convictions were sustained by the U.S. Supreme Court in 1943 and 1944. Mitsuye Endo's *habeas corpus* case, decided by the Supreme Court in 1944, succeeded in finding that "loyal" citizens could not be detained but avoided dealing with the constitutional questions (Irons, 1983). Irons, a legal historian, has made a detailed analysis of the documentation in these four cases and concludes that this "record reveals a legal scandal without precedent in the history of American law. Never before has evidence emerged that shows a deliberate campaign to present tainted records to the Supreme Court" (Irons, 1983, p. viii). Although the three convictions were overturned in decisions from 1983 to 1987, the constitutional precedent of these wartime cases still stands, as Justice Robert Jackson stated in his dissent in the Korematsu case, as a "loaded weapon for the hand of any authority that can bring forward a plausible claim of an urgent need," a weapon that is "still aimed at the members of any racial or nationality minority held hostage to the acts of their county of origin" (Irons, 1983, p. 366).

Postwar Adaptation and Redress

Despite the policy of the War Relocation Authority in its resettlement program to discourage the reformation of Japanese American communities, their shared wartime incarceration seared in most of them a self-consciousness about their ethnic identity and great need for mutual help as they sought to reestablish their lives in cities such as Chicago, Cleveland, Saint Louis, Denver, New York, and so on. As in other migrations, resettlement proceeded via networks of kin and friends, who shared whatever they had of information and resources such as housing (Matsunaga, 1943, 1944; Nishi, 1963; Shibutani, 1944).

Later we will present data regarding their socioeconomic adaptation after the virtually total loss of their prewar economic resources, if any. For now, we note only that extreme labor shortages in the war years and a great economic expansion in the period after the war were fortuitous for the resettlers as they reentered the labor market.

As Japanese Americans moved toward recovery and the reestablishment of their complex network of social organizations, two important collective goals emerged. They became the bases around which Japanese American society, fractured by the strains of the war years, rallied together. One goal was the Japanese American Claims Act, passed by Congress in 1948, which provided for compensation for documented property losses. The amount paid has been estimated at $25 million, out of a total loss of $149 million to $370 million in 1948 dollars. Adjusted for inflation and investment expectations, losses in 1983 figures estimated for the fact-finding Commission on Wartime Relocation and Internment of Civilians were $1.2 to $6.4 billion (Arnold, Barth, & Langer, 1983).

The other goal was citizenship for the Issei. The 1952 McCarran-Walter Act was a significant turning point in immigration and naturalization policy. It removed, at last, the racial bar to immigration and naturalization, which was the basis for so many other restrictions upon the Issei, such as the alien land laws. Although the immigration quota established for Japan was only 185, the family reunification provision enabled a significant number of Japanese, particularly women, to enter in the years before the 1965 reforms.

The impetus for redress of wartime grievances came as much from the third generation, Sansei, particularly from those involved in the Third

World movements on college campuses in the 1960s and 1970s, as from those who were directly victimized. Our own research in Chicago in the early postwar years (Nishi, 1963) found that the Nisei were preoccupied with getting on with their lives after the lost fruits of their parents' long years of struggle in the West Coast prewar years and their own lost years in camp. Indeed one prevalent view among Japanese Americans was that speaking of these painful events in public would do no good and would only raise ill feelings. Many Sansei have reported that their parents did not speak of their wartime incarceration to their children (Nagata, 1993; Ng, 1984). Peter Irons (1992) tells the story of Karen Korematsu, who was in junior high in the early 1970s.

> One day in her civics class, a fellow student gave a report on the internment and mentioned the Supreme Court decision in the Korematsu case. When Karen got home that evening, she asked her father, "Dad, are we related to that Korematsu?" He paused for a while and then said, "Well, that was me." . . . Fred Korematsu had been . . . convicted of violating a military exclusion order in 1942. The Supreme Court upheld his conviction in 1944, and Fred felt personally responsible for the internment of all Japanese Americans. He carried that stigma and shame with him for forty years.

The dam of silence was at last broken in 1981, when the Commission on Wartime Relocation and Internment of Civilians heard testimony from 750 persons in the major cities throughout the country. The often emotional public expressions of grief and anger after 40 years of constrained silence were surprising for their depth as well as pervasiveness. The investigative Commission had been established by an act of Congress in 1980, following a decade-long development of a social movement for redress, including reparations for their forced removal and years of imprisonment. The National Council for Japanese American Redress, led by William Hohri, sued the United States for billions in damages, but failed. The Commission found that "race prejudice, war hysteria, and failure of political leadership," not "military necessity," were the causes of the "grave injustice done to Americans and resident aliens of Japanese ancestry who, without individual review or any probative evidence against them, were excluded, removed and detained by the United States during World War II" (Commission on Wartime Relocation and Internment of Civilians, 1982, p. 18). The Commission's recommendations were enacted into law in 1988, providing for an official apology, individual reparations of $20,000 for those still alive at the date of the bill's signing, and the establishment of a foundation for research and education about these and similar events.

With the still-standing constitutional precedents of the Japanese American wartime cases, could it happen again? In our own testimony to the Commission on Wartime Relocation and Internment of Civilians (Nishi, 1982), we analyzed the cumulative circumstances leading to our removal and incarceration:

1. The existence of stereotypes, or popularly held exaggerated, selective, and overgeneralized racial beliefs about the group
2. The presence of strong economic competitors
3. The occurrence of a disruptive social crisis
4. The spread of rumors and beliefs blaming the group
5. Transfer of authority from civilian rule to the military

Regrettably, the vigor of racist beliefs and economic competition among groups continues in American society, ready for a precipitating crisis to set into motion the other conditions leading to ouster and incarceration.

Fallout From Japan Bashing

As a racially visible minority group, Japanese Americans are also vulnerable to being identified as foreign and thus prey to the new nativism that has risen in the United States as its international economic position has declined. Japan is viewed as the primary competitor, and the rise and fall of trade tensions have their barometric indicators of violence against Japanese Americans—often generalized against other Asian Americans. The 50th anniversary of Pearl Harbor occurred as the American economy continued its recession, and anti-Japanese American hate incidents have risen significantly in recent years. However, the reporting of hate crimes is seriously flawed because of the reluctance of victims to come forward and the absence of uniformity in reporting criteria until the 1990 enactment by Congress of the Hate Crimes Statistics Act. The U.S. Commission on Civil Rights (1992, p. 22) reported, on the basis of fact finding in a series of Asian American roundtable conferences conducted in San Francisco, New York, and Houston, that bigotry and violence were among the major concerns expressed. Japanese Americans, together with other Asian Americans, are caught in the intersection of international and domestic tensions.

Table 5.2 Distribution of Japanese in the United States, 1900-1990

Year	U.S. Including Hawaii & Alaska	Continental U.S.	West Coast States	%	California	%	Hawaii	Alaska
1900	85,716	24,326	18,269	75.1	10,151	41.7	61,111	279
1910	152,745	72,157	57,703	80.0	41,356	57.3	79,675	913
1920	220,596	111,010	93,490	85.1	71,952	64.8	109,274	312
1930	278,743	138,834	120,251	86.6	97,456	70.2	139,631	278
1940	285,115	126,947	112,353	88.5	93,717	73.8	157,905	263
1950	326,384	141,773	98,310	69.3	84,956	59.9	184,611	N.A.
1960	464,368	260,195	178,985	68.8	157,317	60.5	203,355	818
1970	588,324	369,755	259,456	70.2	213,277	57.7	217,715	854
1980	700,974	459,631	323,351	70.4	261,822	57.0	239,748	1,595
1990	847,562	598,010	393,405	65.8	312,989	52.3	247,486	2,066

SOURCE: Adapted from Kitano (1969, pp. 162-164); Thomas (1952, p. 575); U.S. Bureau of the Census (1973, Table 1; 1983, Table 62; 1993, Table 253).

Settlement Patterns

Geographic Concentration in the Pacific Region

Despite a West Coast history of exclusionary efforts, culminating in their forced removal during the crisis of World War II, and a government resettlement policy to encourage geographic dispersal, Japanese Americans continue to this day to be heavily concentrated in the three Pacific states on the mainland and in Hawaii (see Table 5.2). A higher proportion than any other Asian American group, nearly 80%, live in the West. Contrary to the usual pattern of immigrants, who are originally concentrated in ethnic ghettos and then disperse from their initial settlement areas, Japanese Americans became increasingly concentrated in the West Coast states, from three fourths in 1900 to nearly 90% by 1940. This corresponds to their increasing occupational concentration in agriculture, which will be discussed in the next section.

Miyamoto's (1984) study of the prewar Seattle community and Modell's (1977) study of Los Angeles indicate the clustering of Japanese businesses and related residences in "Japan Towns," but also residential spread. Because of their small numbers and proportion in urban centers and more than half distributed in rural areas, most Japanese Americans were not ghettoized in their residential patterns. Even in Los Angeles County, where the largest numbers lived, Japanese Americans constituted only 1.3% of the total population, and the Little Tokyo of that city was not a residential community, but only a few blocks of stores, offices, and ethnic institutions.

Wartime Removal and Resettlement

After their wartime removal and incarceration, the West Coast states were closed to Japanese Americans until January 1945, several years after the resettlement program out of the camps had been under way in states outside the Western region. Chicago was the favorite destination, and our Chicago study (Caudill, 1950; Caudill & De Vos, 1956; Nishi, 1963) estimated that the Japanese population peaked at about 20,000 in 1946-1947 and had already dropped to a little over 11,000 by 1950. Many of our interviewees in 1947-1948 told us that they longed to go back "home," even though their families had nothing left there and would have to start over.

Indeed, by 1950, 69.3% of the Japanese in the mainland were back in the West Coast states (see Table 5.2). Their continuing heavy presence in Hawaii and the Pacific Coast states has been crucial to their rise in state and federal political participation.

Integration and Suburbanization

Still, their numbers in other regions—about 6.5% each in the Northeast, Midwest, and South in 1980 (U.S. Bureau of the Census, 1983)—are highly visible. In 1990, New York state had 35,281 Japanese, less than half of whom lived in New York City (U.S. Bureau of the Census, 1993a, p. 530). The Japanese Chamber of Commerce in New York conducts a biennial census of Japanese nationals employed by overseas Japanese firms and their families in the New York metropolitan area. According to the chamber, about two thirds of the Japanese counted in the U.S. Census Bureau in this area are high-level corporate managers and their dependents here on 3- to 5-year rotating assignments and are not permanent residents. Their unusually advantaged social and economic traits, therefore, tend to give a favorable, if distorted, tilt to the characterization of New York-area Japanese Americans.

Several studies of residential patterns (Denton & Massey, 1988; Massey & Denton, 1988) document the increasing integration and suburbanization of Asian Americans. Even in San Francisco, where their concentration is greatest in the United States, there is a greater probability of residential contact with Anglos than with other Asians (Massey & Denton, 1988, p. 608). Fugita and O'Brien (1991, pp. 82-84) found that the Sansei (third-generation Japanese Americans) grew up in California neighborhoods where Japanese Americans made up a smaller proportion of the residents than in the neighborhoods where the Nisei (second-generation Japanese Americans) grew up. There is no question that Japanese Americans are now highly structurally assimilated in their housing patterns, despite the persistence of regional concentration in the West.

Socioeconomic Adjustment

Pre-World War II: The Issei Era

We have already discussed the origins of Japanese immigration to fill labor needs on Hawaii's plantations as further Chinese arrivals were restricted and many left agriculture for other pursuits. In contrast, the Japanese became increasingly concentrated in farming and related occupations. As the Congressional Committee Investigating National Defense Migration (U.S. House of Representatives, 1942) reported in 1942, their increasing geographic concentration was largely a consequence of their exclusion from diverse economic opportunity:

> Limited occupational outlets have discouraged dispersion of the Japanese from their initial ports of entry on the West Coast. Indeed, concentration has become increasingly marked.... The newly arrived immigrants found a demand for their labor in railroad construction and maintenance and in sugar-beet work of the Mountain States. These sources of employment gradually disappeared as Mexicans and other groups gained preference. The Mountain States contained 21 percent of the Japanese population in 1900 and only 6.8 percent in 1940.... The withdrawal of the Japanese is strikingly evident in Montana, where the number declined from 2,441 in 1900 to 508 in 1940. (p. 92)

There is considerable documentation of the rise to competitive importance of the Issei (first-generation Japanese Americans) in a specialized sector of the growing agricultural economy of the West Coast (Iwata, 1962; Jiobu, 1988; Modell, 1977; Nishi, 1963, pp. 37-49). Despite numerous efforts by their competitors, including laws against land ownership, the Japanese did not withdraw from agriculture. Forty-five percent of the West Coast Japanese were in agricultural occupations in 1940, 46.7% in California.

The average size of Japanese farms in California shrank from 70.1 acres in 1920 to 44.4 acres in 1940, and the farms became increasingly located close to urban markets. Compared to the average California farm, Japanese cultivated a far higher proportion of their land with relatively more equipment and machinery.

> Although they operated only 0.7 percent of the state's land in farms and harvested 2.7 percent of all cropland harvest, they grew 42.0 percent of all acreage of commercial truck crops of the state. In value of truck crops, the Japanese produced about a third of the total for the state. (Nishi, 1963, p. 40)

In addition to control through crop specialization, they cooperatively organized control in the distribution system:

> Japanese growers and retail distributors have been closely linked through wholesale distributors; these latter have exercised considerable control over the production and distribution of fresh vegetables through various associations and credit mechanism. . . . Of the 167 fruit and vegetable merchants in the 3 Los Angeles wholesale markets, as of December 6, 1941, 29 were Japanese-owned. Of the 232 permanent stall operators in the open market yards, 134 were Japanese. (U.S. House of Representatives, 1942, p. 120)

From our analysis of these data, we concluded:

> The considerable achievement of the Japanese in agriculture, which surmounted a powerful effort for their exclusion, was accomplished by the efficient and concentrated use of what was accessible—that is, by technological adaptation . . . of the farming pattern in Japan of intensive cultivation of scarcely available land and by the culturally defined resources of the social organization of family solidarity and its extension in organized Japanese cooperative relationships. (Nishi, 1963, p. 43)

Thomas's (1952, pp. 596-597) compilation of California and Washington state census data (see Table 5.3) indicate that a fourth of employed Issei women, a fifth of Nisei women, and 13% to 16% of Nisei men worked as unpaid family labor on farms.

In addition to their extraordinary involvement in the labor intensive family business of truck farming, many Issei (15% of Issei males in California and 24% in Washington) were proprietors or managers. In the major nonfarm industries in which prewar Japanese Americans were employed—wholesale and retail trade and personal services—extremely high

Table 5.3 Labor Force Status and Occupational Distribution (%) of Japanese American Nativity and Sex in California and Washington, 1940

Labor Force Status and Occupations	California				Washington			
	Foreign Born		Native Born		Foreign Born		Native Born	
	Male	Female	Male	Female	Male	Female	Male	Female
Population 14 years and over	20,530	12,863	21,115	17,980	3,360	2,278	3,221	2,759
Not in labor force	1,780	7,777	8,732	12,417	282	1,126	1,589	1,828
On public emergency work	21	3	46	22	1	0	14	10
Seeking work	502	102	439	232	94	7	90	29
Employed	18,227	4,981	11,898	5,309	2,983	1,145	1,528	892
% of the employed								
Farmers and farm managers	21.4	4.7	13.3	1.5	18.6	4.5	14.5	2.1
Farm (wage) laborers and foremen	24.0	11.0	20.9	5.7	7.5	4.8	6.6	1.7
Farm laborers (unpaid, family)	1.2	24.9	12.9	18.1	0.9	21.3	15.6	21.0
Total employed: agricultural	46.6	40.5	47.2	25.2	27.0	30.6	36.7	24.8
Professional & semi-professional	2.9	3.3	2.3	3.7	2.7	2.7	2.1	3.6
Proprietors & managers	15.1	8.3	7.5	3.0	23.9	12.9	7.3	4.8
Clerical, sales, etc.	5.4	9.4	16.7	22.1	5.5	12.8	13.7	24.4
Service (excluding domestic)	5.6	12.1	2.8	8.9	12.6	17.9	8.8	10.1
Skilled laborers (craftsmen etc.)	2.0	0.6	2.3	0.5	4.3	1.0	2.4	1.0
Semi-skilled laborers (operatives etc.)	4.3	11.1	8.6	6.8	8.1	16.9	10.0	11.0
Unskilled labor	13.2	1.7	9.1	0.8	14.2	1.1	15.3	0.6
Domestic service	4.4	12.0	3.1	27.8	1.2	3.1	2.4	18.0
Total employed: nonagricultural	52.9	58.6	52.2	73.6	72.5	68.6	62.0	73.5
Occupations not reported	0.5	0.8	0.6	1.1	0.5	0.9	1.2	1.7

SOURCE: Adapted from Thomas (1952, pp. 596-597, Table 14).

proportions were employed by their co-ethnics. In the three major urban concentrations of Los Angeles, San Francisco, and Seattle in 1940, about half the Issei in these industries were self-employed and an additional 36% to 44% worked for other Japanese. Even the American-born and educated Nisei worked overwhelmingly for Japanese employers. In wholesale and retail trade and personal services in 1940, only 5.8% of the Nisei workers in Los Angeles, 7.6% in San Francisco, and 15.8% in Seattle were employed by Caucasians (Thomas, 1952, p. 603, Table 18).

For adaptive resources in a discriminatory economic system, the Issei drew on family labor and the support and cooperation of other Japanese in a network of obligatory mutual aid. As for the Nisei generation, most had not yet entered the labor force before World War II. But those who did found their options restricted to working mainly for other Japanese.

Coming of Age of the Nisei in the Workplace

The circumstances under which most Nisei entered the labor force were extraordinary indeed. Shaped by immigration policies, the age-sex pyramid of Japanese Americans (see Figure 5.2) exhibits very little overlap by age between the first and second generations and, significantly, an unusually age-concentrated cohort of Nisei—late adolescence and early adulthood at the beginning of the war. Thus many of the Nisei entered the labor market for the first time in resettlement out of the wartime concentration camps. Labor shortages were extreme during the war and in the postwar period, in the context of which employment opportunities became available. Furthermore outside the West Coast, there were fewer entrenched patterns of anti-Japanese discrimination. Thus by 1947, 2 years after the closing the wartime camps, Japanese Americans were considerably more diversified in both their workforce composition and occupational distribution (Bloom & Riemer, 1949; Nishi, 1963). In our 1947-1948 Chicago Survey (Bloom & Riemer, 1949, pp. 40-41; Caudill, 1950, pp. 82, 93-94; Nishi, 1963, pp. 58-60), we found that more than half of the Issei women were in the paid workforce, many for the first time, mainly as machine operators—42.6% in the garment trades. More than half of the Nisei first entered the paid workforce in Chicago resettlement, having been in school in the prewar West Coast and/or worked as unpaid family labor.

Thirty-seven percent of the Issei men of our Chicago sample and 64% of the Nisei men were working as craftsmen, foremen, or operatives. This is in striking contrast to the prewar occupational distribution on the West Coast, where there was a notable underparticipation of Japanese American males as craftsmen and operatives—8.1% in California (Nishi, 1963, p. 48, Table 5), although women in significant numbers worked as operatives.

The war and the forced removal, incarceration, and resettlement of Japanese Americans constituted a major turning point in their economic adaptation. Among the more significant changes in industry categories of Japanese Americans were:

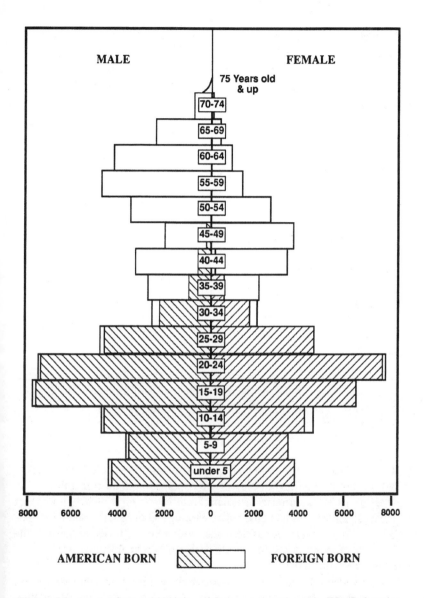

Figure 5.2. Age by Sex and Nativity of Japanese Americans in War Relocation Authority Centers, January 1, 1943 (Number)
SOURCE: War Relocation Authority, 1946, p. 93.

Table 5.4 Industrial Distribution (%) of Employed Persons in the Japanese American and the U.S. Total Populations in 1990

	Japanese Americans	*U.S. Population*
Total number of employed persons 16 and over	452,005	117,914,000
Agriculture, forestry, & fisheries	3.1	2.7
Mining	0.1	0.6
Construction	3.8	6.5
Manufacturing	13.7	18.0
Transportation, communication, & other public utilities	7.7	7.0
Wholesale trade	5.8	3.9
Retail trade	16.9	16.6
Finance, insurance, & real estate	7.9	6.8
Business and repair services	4.3	6.3
Personal, entertainment, & recreation services	5.6	5.3
Professional & related services	24.4	21.5
Public administration	6.6	4.8

SOURCE: U.S. Bureau of the Census (1993b, Table 4; 1993c, Table 647).

1. The reduction of employment in personal services—from 25% in 1940 to less than 5% by 1990—and the primary industries of agriculture, fishing, and forestry—from nearly 50% in 1940 to 3% by 1990

2. The increase in trade, finance, insurance, and real estate employment to more than 30%, and the increase in professional and related services to 24%

Their industrial distribution is similar to the majority population (see Table 5.4) except for their continuing underparticipation in manufacturing.

Using 1980 California census data, Jiobu (1988, pp. 179-209) found that Japanese Americans had attained an earnings level equal to that of whites. He also found Japanese Americans similar to white Americans in the weights of multiple factors such as hours worked, family status, and education as influencing earnings.

Nonetheless the residue of historic exclusion from the labor movement on the West Coast and inclusion in Hawaii was still visible in their strikingly different occupational distributions. In Hawaii the percentage of Japanese males in the craftsmen and foremen category (23.9% in 1980) is more like that of the U.S. total (20.9%) and double that of the Japanese in

California (12.4%). Underrepresented in the middle, Japanese Americans in California, as contrasted to those in Hawaii, consistently have had higher proportions in professional/technical occupations in the upper level and in lower categories of labor and service occupations. Elsewhere (Nishi, 1981), I have argued that this bimodality of occupational distribution of mainland Japanese Americans is a consequence of the early labor movement's exclusion of nonwhites and its leadership in the anti-Asian campaigns.

We also should note that despite their relatively high percentage in professional and managerial occupations (37%) compared to the total U.S. population (27%), Japanese Americans are proportionately much fewer in these high-level occupations than Asian Indians (44%) and Pakistani (45%) Americans (U.S. Bureau of the Census, 1993b, Table 4). Other economic indicators such as unemployment and poverty rates and median family income show that Japanese Americans fare better than the U.S. general population and much better than other Asian groups in these measures (see Table 2.9 in Chapter 2). However, these indicators should be interpreted with caution and considered in the context of several important factors. For example, 58% of Japanese American families have two or more workers, as contrasted to 47% of all American families (U.S. Bureau of the Census, 1993b, Table 4).

Another factor is the considerable variation that exists within the group. According to 1990 census data (see Table 5.5), 37% of Japanese Americans were in managerial and professional specialty occupations and 34% in technical, sales, and administrative support occupations. A third of the foreign-born males were in managerial occupations, in contrast to half that proportion (16%) of the native born males, indicating the large, although transitory, presence of employees of Japanese companies in the United States. Notable, also, are the striking differences between native-born and foreign-born women, a significant proportion of whom came to the United States as war brides in the post-World War era. Eighty-five percent of women born in the United States were in managerial (16%) and professional (21%) specialty occupations or technical, sales, and administrative support occupations (48%). Less than 60% of the foreign-born women were employed in these occupations, and considerably more were employed in service occupations (25%) and as operators, fabricators, and laborers (10%).

The Role of Education

A major component of the "model minority" ideology pertaining to Asian Americans came to popular attention in the late 1960s, the turbulent

Table 5.5 Occupational Distribution (%) of Japanese Americans by Nativity and Sex, 1990

Occupations	All Persons			Native Born			Foreign Born		
	Total	Male	Female	Total	Male	Female	Total	Male	Female
Managerial	17.6	20.7	14.5	16.0	16.3	15.7	21.3	32.3	10.0
Professional	19.4	19.6	19.3	20.1	19.0	21.3	17.8	21.0	14.5
Technical & sales	16.6	17.4	15.7	16.6	17.2	15.7	16.7	17.9	15.5
Administrative support	17.8	8.6	28.0	20.2	9.6	32.2	11.9	5.9	18.0
Service	11.1	8.7	13.8	8.6	8.3	9.0	17.5	9.9	25.2
Farming, forestry, & fishing	2.7	4.3	0.8	3.0	4.8	0.9	1.9	3.1	0.7
Precision production, craft, & repair	7.8	12.2	3.1	8.6	14.6	1.9	5.9	5.9	5.8
Operatives & laborers	6.9	8.4	5.3	6.9	10.1	3.3	7.1	4.0	10.2

SOURCE: U.S. Bureau of the Census (1993c, Table 4).

period of student revolts on college campuses(Peterson, 1966), when the age-concentrated second-generation Japanese American cohort attained occupational maturity in the thriving economy of postwar years. Their mobility as a racial minority subjected to a dramatic episode of American racism during World War II was conspicuous and attributed in exaggerated emphasis to diligence in educational achievement. Elsewhere (Nishi, 1981), we have elaborated on the sources of misunderstanding regarding the nature of Asian Americans' educational status.

Historically the sources of misunderstanding regarding the educational condition of Japanese Americans are multiple: the success myth, the overgeneralization of diverse characteristics, the inappropriateness of central tendency measures for a population with bimodal socioeconomic characteristics, not taking into account cost/benefit ratios for educational attainment relative to occupational attainment and income, and the failure to understand their unusual reliance on education for social mobility because of the historic closure of employment opportunity until World War II.

With these caveats against overgeneralizing about the educational attainment of Japanese Americans, we present 1990 data (see Table 5.6). Eighty-eight percent of Japanese Americans 25 years old and over were at least high school graduates in 1990, and 35% had completed 4 years of college or more. These figures were significantly higher than the U.S. population, of whom 75% had completed high school or more and 20% had completed

Table 5.6 Educational Attainment (%) of All Races, Asian and Pacific Islanders, and Japanese Americans by Nativity and Sex, 1990

Educational Attainment	All Races			Asian and Pacific Islander Americans		
	Total	Male	Female	Total	Male	Female
Completed 4 years of high school or more	75.2	75.7	74.8	77.5	81.5	71.0
Completed 4 years of college or more	20.3	23.3	17.7	36.6	41.9	31.8

Educational Attainment	Japanese Americans								
	All Persons			Native Born			Foreign Born		
	Total	Male	Female	Total	Male	Female	Total	Male	Female
Completed 4 years of high school or more	87.5	89.9	85.6	88.3	88.8	87.8	86.0	92.8	82.5
Completed 4 years of college or more	34.5	42.6	28.2	34.2	36.0	32.5	35.1	60.0	22.2

SOURCE: U.S. Bureau of the Census (1993b, Table 3).

college or more. The large sex difference in college completion (42% for males and 28% for females) among Japanese Americans is due largely to the striking sex difference among the foreign born (60% for males and 22% for females). The 60% college completion rate of foreign-born males is notable for its marked contrast with the 36% of native born Japanese Americans.

Assimilation and Ethnicity

Blocked Assimilation and the Ethnic Community— Pre-World War II Years

As we have seen, despite concerted efforts to exclude them and to bar their economic advance, the Issei managed to survive in a severely discriminatory society by increasing dependence on co-ethnics—both economically and socially. Careful accounts of early (Ichihashi, 1932; Ichioka, 1988) and prewar (Miyamoto, 1984; Modell, 1977; Thomas, 1952) Japanese American communities document the complex nature of the interlocking social organization of obligatory participation in which the immigrant generation helped, found expressive gratification and satisfaction, and maintained communication with each other. They insulated themselves from a hostile larger society and developed cooperative trade and business associations to negotiate favorable arrangements with the larger economy. Built on the principles of the often-described (Nakane, 1970; Reischauer, 1981; Yanagisako, 1985) reciprocal obligations among family members, people from the same prefectures or belonging to the same religious institution were interlocked in a social system of kinlike duties—claims and obligations—that extended to the economic and expressive cultural spheres as well.

The second-generation Nisei lived in two worlds—the Japanese community dominated by their parent's generation and the Caucasian-dominated world of school or, very marginally, of work. As Miyamoto (1984, pp. xii-xx) has described, the Nisei in prewar Seattle participated in the Japanese community through their parents at first, then through Japanese language schools conducted after regular school, through churches and their many regular activities for young people, athletic leagues, cultural clubs, the Japanese American Citizens League, and a few other civic and political organizations. Although their organizational goals differed, these ethnic activities all functioned to develop and maintain meaningful interpersonal ties with other Japanese Americans and an ethnic organizational relationship system beyond residential locality. Nisei felt excluded from, or uncomfortable with, the social world of their non-Japanese school peers. Thus the social solidarity experienced in friendships and joint activities with Japanese Americans was a crucial component to (a) reinforcing their ethnic identity, (b) socializing them into the values and practices of Japanese American society, (c) constituting them as a significant reference group to support and reinforce their ethnic identity and preferred values governing conduct, and (d) collectively coping with and protecting their group against hostility.

For the Nisei, the pressures to be "Americanized" and "assimilated" were great in the prewar years. It was not only the pervasive ideology of the times in American society, whereby diverse elements were to be absorbed in the great American "melting pot" (Zangwill, 1909). For the Nisei, it was also a way to assert one's legitimacy as an American. The dilemma posed was the harsh prospect of closure from opportunity in the larger economy and, thus, having to rely narrowly on family and co-ethnics in their petit bourgeois activities in farming, trade, and personal services such as gardening (Fugita & O'Brien, 1991, pp. 47-62; Miyamoto, 1984). Kikuchi's life histories of Nisei (Thomas, 1952, pp. 151-569) provide moving documentation of their entrapment in a narrow range of work opportunities, once out of school.

World War II and the Postwar Years

The wartime experience of forced removal and incarceration on a racial basis seared in the Nisei a self-consciousness of their being treated categorically by American society as Japanese. In their *de jure* exclusion from citizenship as well as in their *de facto* discrimination in life adaptations, the Issei had their own social world, which effectively insulated them from most external hostility. For the Nisei, as late adolescents and young adults in the process of establishing their identity, their jolting wartime treatment constituted a crucial turning point. It was not only that the United States had thrust them into isolated incarceration because they were of Japanese descent, all the inmates were there for the same reason. Whatever variations existed in their cultural and structural integration in American society, their treatment was absolutely categorical. Their shared trauma symbolized the meaning of their being Japanese in American society. In addition and as significantly, the years of banishment from American society (an average of 2½ years) were spent in intensely communal living arrangements, collectively coping with the many conflicts and crises (Leighton, 1945; Miyamoto, 1950; Thomas & Nishimoto, 1946) and constructing an elaborate array of social organizations for political, religious, artistic, athletic, and other social/recreational expressive activities. Thus the shared symbolic significance of being Japanese in American society was powerfully reinforced by their intense and virtually exclusive interaction with each other in collective actions to meet their needs. With the lack of privacy in the sections of barracks to which members of families were assigned, the communal feeding arrangements, the age-grading of activities, and, of course, the absence of family-based economic activity—the round of daily activities pushed members centrifugally away from the family. These strains on cohesiveness intensified the difficulties families were undergoing as the Issei father's roles—the economic provider and the representative of the family to the outside world—were destroyed by the circumstances of the war.

It was in resettlement, the movement to get Japanese Americans out of the camps, that the reciprocal obligations of family membership underwent their severest test. Seventy percent of those who had left the camps by the beginning of 1945 were between the ages of 15 and 35 years, whereas children under 5 and the elderly over 60 disproportionately constituted the "residue" (Thomas, 1952, pp. 115-116). Not unlike the age characteristics of the immigrants when they first came from Japan, the early "resettlers" (1942-1944) were mainly young adult Nisei. In this reentry into American society, the sex-ratio was more balanced, as women moved into the paid workforce in record numbers to fill the great labor demands in clerical and manufacturing work. With the recision of the military exclusion orders from the West Coast in December 1944 and the announced closing of the camps within 6 months to a year, the efforts of family members who were already out to assist their parents and younger siblings to relocate became a major preoccupation (Matsunaga, 1944; Nishi, 1963; Shibutani, 1944). The depth of the obligations toward parents and other kin experienced by the Nisei in the resettlement period is described and analyzed in several clinical studies that were a part of our Chicago Japanese American Personality and Acculturation Study (Babcock & Caudill, 1958, pp. 409-448; De Vos, 1960, pp. 287-301).

With the pending crisis of the closing of the camps, Japanese Americans individually were hard-pressed to find housing and employment in what were as yet largely unknown settings. Thus, the need for resettlement assistance far exceeded the resources of the War Relocation Authority offices established in major cities and voluntary agencies under religious auspices, such as the American Friends Service Committee and the Brethren Services Committee. Elsewhere (Nishi, 1963), we have provided a detailed account of the reemergence of an elaborate network of communication and social organizations among Japanese Americans in Chicago. Despite an explicit policy of the War Relocation Authority to accomplish both geographic and social dispersal, Japanese American society reemerged with much the same appearance as the prewar communities of the West Coast, but with important changes. The first major change was the generational transfer of responsibility as the Nisei came of age. Fortunately, it was a time when occupational opportunities opened, for the Nisei assumed unusually heavy obligations in assisting parents and younger siblings to readapt following the long war years in the abnormal confines of the guarded and isolated camps.

The second major difference was the permeability of the boundaries of the postwar Japanese American community, no longer either insular or geographically based. Japanese American society was identifiable by its network of communication among those whose shared wartime experience had welded an ethnic identity built on a strong sense of a common fate and the continuing familylike bonds of reciprocal claims and obligations. In addition to the expressive/gratificatory functions of religious and other ethnic cultural institutions, Japanese Americans, with their rights of citizenship, collectively sought to negotiate with a far less compactly closed larger society. The resources for meeting their employment and housing needs were now seen as being in the larger society. Nonetheless, Japanese Americans were expected to use their linkages in that society to facilitate the favorable positioning of their co-ethnics. In other words, Japanese American individuals used both "weak" and "strong" ties described by Granovetter (1973, 1982). They were obliged to use their weak or secondary relations at work, for example, to help their co-ethnics, with whom they were in a strong or kinlike relationship of reciprocal obligations.

The Post-1965 Era: Assimilation and the Persistence of Community

The significance of the post-1965 era for Japanese Americans is not so much the changes in immigration policy, so portentous for other Asians; rather it is the stirrings among the Sansei—third-generation Japanese Americans—as they were affected by the campus revolts by people of color and what Steinberg (1989, p. 3) has called an outbreak of "ethnic fever." The coming to maturity of the third generation—socialized in a far less overtly discriminatory context and increasingly assimilated in education, employment, housing, politics, friendships, and marriage—would, according to some theoretical perspectives, signal the decline of ethnicity. Yet, as Fugita and O'Brien (1991, pp. 95-117) have convincingly documented through their survey of Nisei and Sansei men in three California communities, Japanese Americans exhibit a remarkable continuity across generations in participation in ethnic voluntary associations. Especially noteworthy is that such participation was found to be higher in the areas where there were proportionately fewer co-ethnics, and it was compatible with belonging to nonethnic voluntary associations.

In the late 1960s the Sansei were among the key instigators of the movement for redress and reparations for the wartime treatment of Japanese Americans. Support for seeking reparations was far from unanimous at first; there were fears that talk of redress would stir resentment against them, that monetary reparations would trivialize the seriousness of the wartime violation of their civil rights, and that it was an impossible task. Nonetheless the movement eventually gained the backing and considerable involvement of most Japanese Americans in two major directions. In the 1970s the Japanese American Citizens League took on the redress issue as its top priority and in 1978 resolved that $25,000 in reparations should be given to all who had been incarcerated. In 1980 Congress established the

Commission on Wartime Relocation and Internment of Civilians, which compiled and studied documents and conducted hearings throughout the country, taking often moving testimony from 750 persons. The commission concluded in its widely publicized report (Commission on Wartime Relocation and Internment of Civilians, 1982) that "race prejudice, war hysteria, and failure of political leadership" and not military necessity were responsible for the relocation and internment and recommended an official apology and token reparations of $20,000 for each victim still living.

The other direction, led primarily through the National Council on Japanese American Redress (Hohri, 1988), was a class action lawsuit. *William Hohri et al. v. United States* (U.S. District Court for the District of Columbia, March 1983, CA-1750) sought to have the courts establish that the constitutional rights of Japanese Americans had been violated and asked for monetary damages of $210,000 per victim. Principles of sovereign immunity and the statute of limitations were invoked and prevented the case from actually being heard. Another concerted action through the courts challenged the legality of the convictions of Fred Korematsu, Gordon Hirabayashi, and Minoru Yasui for violating the exclusion and detention orders. Their convictions had been upheld by the U.S. Supreme Court in landmark cases in 1943, supporting the legal basis for the evacuation and incarceration. Led by a team of mostly Sansei lawyers, these *Coram Nobis* cases succeeded in having the convictions set aside, but they were frustrated in their attempt to have the constitutional issues reconsidered in the highest court (Irons, 1983, 1989; Minami, 1991).

Thus, although the indicators of structural assimilation provide solid documentation of the integration of Japanese Americans in American society, there is also strong evidence of the vitality of their linkages and remarkable continuing participation in ethnic community social organizations. The shared experiences of wartime internment and the social movement for redress and reparations—in which members of the third generation played a key role—reinforced both the shared identity and ethnic networks undergirding the contemporary Japanese American community.

Family Socialization: Values and Behavior

Our explication of the seeming contradiction between high assimilation and high ethnicity as characterizing many present-day Japanese Americans would be incomplete without considering the role of the family. The significance of family ties and kinlike reciprocal relations for Japanese

Americans already has been referred to in several contexts. Here we shall discuss very briefly how family interaction patterns created in the Nisei a receptivity for continuity in key Japanese cultural value preferences.

Significance of Family Relationships in Japanese Culture

The immigrant Issei brought with them a cultural system, which, at least in some respects, has remained less changed in the United States than in Japan, which underwent extremely rapid modernization. The family, not the individual, is the basic unit in Japanese society, responsible for the socialization and maintenance of social control of its members and accountable for their conduct (Miyamoto, 1984, pp. 5-8; Nakane, 1970; Reischauer, 1981). The all-important ethical basis of cultural values and the social relationships through which the values were manifest were incorporated in individual conduct through the family. As Miyamoto (1984) has neatly stated:

> Ethics for the Japanese is a practical social code applied to the regulation of daily social behavior . . . regulating the relationships of men. . . . Duty, or the conception of the social responsibility, is . . . the dynamic focus of the Japanese ethical system. . . . It is the ethical system of collective obligations . . . which gives the Japanese family a type of solidarity hardly to be conceived in the Western mind. (pp. 5-6)

Thus the reciprocal obligations learned in early years and reinforced in family relationships are extended as the obligatory mode of relating to other members of Japanese society.

Family Socialization of Japanese Values

In the late 1940s, in our study of Japanese Americans in Chicago, William Caudill (1950) and I (Nishi, 1963) stated what became known as the theory of value compatibility. It was our idea that the Japanese values brought by the Issei, although different from American middle-class values, contributed to their achievement and adaptation in American society. Caudill and De Vos (1956) were concerned with psychological adaptive mechanisms, whereas my own focus was on the social structural linkages between values and behavior.

I posited the following as constituting the preferred values of Japanese Americans in contrast to the emphases found in the dominant American culture (Nishi, 1963, pp. 72-78):

1. In the rank ordering of social objects, the successively more inclusive collectivities are higher than the less inclusive collectivities, the private individual being lowest. Lower-ranking units are obliged to subsume their own interest in enhancing those of the more inclusive group—*collectivity/individual.*
2. In status achievement, the emphasis is on training and performance in the duties and skills of the status role, which then earns status recognition and self-respect. This is in contrast to the legitimacy of role occupancy by chance or aleatory factors or ascription per se—*earned (by established criteria)/aleatory.*
3. In interunit relations, preference is for formality (correctness) in contrast to spontaneity or ad hoc behavior—*formal/spontaneous.*
4. In motivational appeal, the emphasis is on the moral requiredness of behavior rather than the voluntary expression of benevolence, compassion, gratitude, and so on—*law/grace.*
5. In motivational response, Japanese American society develops a high sensitivity to public regard and control of private feelings for expression in appropriate situations and ways—*public/internal.*

The work of Babcock (Babcock & Caudill, 1958), Caudill (1950, 1961, 1962), and De Vos (1954, 1955, 1960, 1975), both with our Chicago sample and subsequently in Japan, affirmed some distinctive features of family socialization, which made Japanese Americans receptive to the values described above (Nishi, 1963, pp. 367-409). Here, we briefly describe the connections.

1. The liberal and lengthy gratification of oral-tactile needs, the symbiotic physical closeness among family members, especially between mother and child, and the encouragement and acceptability of dependency create a strong affective solidarity in the family—*collectivity/individual.*
2. Although the self is emotionally bonded within the family, each role is highly specific. The differential expectations for behavior by age, sex, and sibling position are clearly seen and felt—including the inequalities of power and privilege inherent in such a hierarchical system. The responsible fulfillment of the exacting role requirements is prepared by the early socialization of affective interdependency in the family and necessary under the social reinforcement provided in the community in which the family is interdependent—*earned/aleatory.*
3. With these conditions, there is a need to constrain the potential for both positive and negative emotional overinvolvement. For, if given unchanneled vent, such overinvolvement would destroy the cohesiveness of the family in which the participants have a large investment. Thus personal reserve and constraint of emotional expression to appropriate circumstances—interper-

sonal skills—are learned very well and include: (a) the rules of conduct, (b) selective acknowledgment of disruptive attitudes and misconduct of others, and (c) empathetic alertness to cues coming from others—*formal/spontaneous.*

4. In seeking to understand the moral-obligatory or sacred quality attached to the fulfillment of role expectations, De Vos (1960, p. 290) posited a specifically Japanese pattern of guilt: "If a parent has instilled in a child an understanding of his capacity to hurt by failing to carry out an obligation expected of him as a member of a family, any such failure can make him feel extremely guilty"— *law/grace.*

5. Japanese child rearing often relied on shaming by ridicule and admonishments about damaging the family name by nonconformity to societal expectations— *public/internal.* Thus high sensitivity to the approval of others is inextricably involved with the potential for guilt.

These values and their incorporation as guides to conduct were adaptive for the Issei in developing an economic and social organization for their survival under the strictures of castelike status in prewar American society. For the Nisei, they functioned to require and sustain achieving behavior in the fortunately open educational system of the prewar West Coast and in their entry into the workforce as a fairly concentrated age cohort in the postwar period of unusual labor demand.

Family Bases of Japanese American Social Organizations

In our study (Nishi, 1963) of the re-creation of Japanese American society in Chicago in the period of resettlement out of the wartime camps, we examined the role of cultural values in the context of new internal and external circumstances. Through this network of meaningful and regularized relationships, behavioral norms were defined and maintained—as in fulfilling obligations to help family members and other co-ethnics in their reentry into American society and restoring the good name of Japanese Americans, particularly by their individual exemplary conduct for status achievement. Latently the ethnic subsociety, an extension of family relationship principles, constituted a personalized social support and reference group for individual striving in the larger society of newly opened opportunity.

We have already noted the remarkable continuity of participation of Japanese Americans in ethnic social organizations, despite high structural assimilation and the loss of such crucial manifestations of Japanese culture as language and religion.

Outmarriage and the Continuation of Japanese American Ethnicity

With antimiscegenation laws until 1948 and their wartime confinement as the Nisei approached the age of marriage, Issei (2%) and Nisei (4%) showed a very low outmarriage rate (Spickard, 1980, 1989). By the late 1970s, outmarriages by the then mostly Sansei Japanese in Los Angeles were 60% of the marriages—50% to non-Asians (Kitano, Yeung, Chai, & Hatanaka, 1984, p. 180). Nationally, the rate was 47.7% in 1980 (Sung, 1990, p. 18).

What are the implications of such high outmarriage rates for Japanese American ethnicity and community? There is some evidence that divorce rates, one indicator of family instability, are higher among the outmarried. The Fugita and O'Brien (1991, pp. 134-138) survey of Nisei and Sansei males in three California communities showed a divorce rate four times higher among the outmarried (22.2%) than among the inmarried (4.5%), regardless of generation. Significantly, those who participated in ethnic community organizations had lower divorce rates than those who did not. Not surprisingly, inmarried Japanese Americans showed a higher rate of affiliation with ethnic organizations (66.7%) than the outmarried (50.0%). Still, most relevant and notable is that half of the outmarried continued to maintain ethnic organizational memberships. This is remarkably high as compared to third-generation Euro-ethnics, less than 5% of whom belong to ethnic voluntary organizations (Goering, 1971; Roche, 1982).

The survey by Fugita and O'Brien (1991) included only men. As they acknowledge (p. 184), there very well may be even more active participation in the ethnic community by the intermarried. A higher proportion of the outmarried are women, and the maintenance of kin relationships in Japanese American communities is mostly by women (Yanagisako, 1977, 1985).

Conclusion

The more than 100-year course of Japanese in the United States has traversed a dramatically changing historical diorama. For the plantations of Hawaii in the 19th century, they were aggressively recruited as contract labor. In the frontierlike West, they were sought to perform cheap labor and were fiercely opposed by white labor and farm interests seeking to exclude them as competitors. With the closure of further labor immigration in the 1908 Gentlemen's Agreement and the admission of wives until the enforcement of the Oriental Exclusion Act of 1924, the immigrant generation adapted to a castelike social existence in an elaborately structured ethnic society. Such a community of kinlike obligatory involvement and accountability enabled the development of petit-bourgeois agriculture, trade, and personal service enterprises. Despite their exclusion from citizenship and laws to bar them from owning land, they succeeded in achieving a virtual monopoly in truck farming—the production and marketing of fresh produce.

The second generation, Nisei, grew up in the Depression and the dual worlds of schools in the larger society and of Japanese family and social organizations. The disillusioning disregard for their constitutional rights and banishment to isolated camps during the war years and their resettlement to urban centers outside the excluded West Coast marked a major turning point as the Nisei came of age. Fortuitous for their entry into the job market, it was a time of high labor demand. But there remained the duty to assist parents and younger siblings in their resettlement as the closing of the camps was announced. Japanese American society reemerged as a shared communication and organizational network to facilitate their recovery from degradation. Most evacuated Japanese Americans returned to the West Coast and reestablished themselves in the thriving economy of the postwar years. There they came to constitute a significant population base, regionally reinforced by the presence of Japanese Americans in Hawaiian politics.

In the last decade of the 20th century, the first-generation immigrants are nearly all gone. With little replenishment through immigration from modern Japan, two thirds of Japanese Americans are native born. The unusually age-concentrated second-generation are in their old age, as the third-generation are approaching their prime years. In their educational, occupational, and residential characteristics, they apparently have attained structural assimilation. Their outmarriage rate is over 50%. Politically their continuing heavy concentration in the Pacific states has enabled a strong presence in Congress and in state and local affairs. The United States has apologized and paid token reparations for their wartime incarceration.

Still Japanese Americans, along with other Asian Americans, continue to be the butt of the fallout from Japan bashing and antiforeignism. The model minority stereotype is a pervasive source of hostile, resentful attitudes and obscures attention to their needs as a racial minority in the United States, objects of direct, blatant hate as well as the subtle, sophisticated forms of modern racism—institutionalized discrimination. The extant constitutional precedents of the Japanese American wartime cases symbolize the fragility of constitutional safeguards of citizen rights in times of crisis. The residues of Japanese American stigmatization in wartime banishment have yet to be investigated systematically, although anecdotal accounts of the damage abound. Of great concern to Japanese Americans is that most Americans have little knowledge that their incarceration took place on a racial/ethnic basis, with no charge or trial.

Even more burdensome is that because most Americans do not understand the circumstances that led to the gross violation of their constitutionally protected rights, it could conceivably occur again—perhaps to victimize some other group identified by descent and race with an "enemy."

Thus both as a collective identity seared by wartime events and reinforced in the residues of stigma as well as by a network of communication and social organizations attending to their family-learned obligations to each other, Japanese American ethnicity retains a remarkable vitality—despite high structural assimilation and acculturation in American society.

References

Arnold, F. S., Barth, M. C., & Langer, G. (1983). Economic losses of ethnic Japanese as a result of exclusion and detention. In *Papers for The Commission on Wartime Relocation and Internment of Civilians.* Washington, DC: The Commission on Wartime Relocation and Internment of Civilians.

Babcock, C. G., & Caudill, W. (1958). Personal and cultural factors in the treatment of a Nisei. In G. Seward (Ed.), *Clinical studies in culture conflict* (pp. 409-448). New York: Ronald Press.

Bloom, L., & Riemer, R. (1949). *Removal and return: The socio-economic effects of the war on Japanese Americans.* Berkeley: University of California Press.

Caudill, W. A. (1950). *Japanese American acculturation and personality.* Doctoral dissertation, University of Chicago.

Caudill, W. A. (1961). Around the clock patient care in Japanese psychiatric hospitals: The role of the *tsukisoi. American Sociological Review, 26,* 204-214.

Caudill, W. A., & De Vos, G. (1956). Achievement, culture and personality. *American Anthropologist, 58,* 1102-1126.

Chan, S. (1991). *Asian Americans: An interpretive history.* Boston: Twayne.

Chuman, F. F. (1976). *The bamboo people: The law and Japanese Americans.* Chicago: Japanese American Citizens League.

Clausen, J. A., & Nishi, S. M. (1983). Preface to proceedings of research conference on social and psychological effects of exclusion and detention. In *Papers for the Commission on Wartime Relocation and Internment of Civilians* (pp. 1-40). Washington, DC: The Commission on Wartime Relocation and Internment of Civilians.

Commission on Wartime Relocation and Internment of Civilians. (1982). *Personal justice denied.* Washington, DC: The Commission on Wartime Relocation and Internment of Civilians.

Conroy, H. F. (1953). *The Japanese frontier in Hawaii: 1868-1898*. Berkeley: University of California Press.

Culley, J. H. (1984). Relocation of Japanese Americans: The Hawaiian experience. *Air Force Law Review, 24*, 176-183.

Daniels, R. (1988). *Asian America: Chinese and Japanese in the United States since 1850*. Seattle: University of Washington Press.

Denton, N. A., & Massey, D.S. (1988). Residential segregation of Blacks, Hispanics, and Asians by socioeconomic status. *Social Science Quarterly, 69*, 797-817.

De Vos, G. (1954). A comparison of the personality differences in two generations of Japanese Americans by means of the Rorschach test. *Nagoya Journal of Medical Science, 17*, 153-265.

De Vos, G. (1955). A quantitative Rorschach assessment of maladjustment and rigidity in acculturating Japanese Americans. *Genetic Psychology Monographs, 52*, 51-87.

De Vos, G. (1960). The relation of guilt toward parents to achievement and arranged marriage among the Japanese. *Psychiatry: Journal for the Study of International Process, 23*, 287-301.

De Vos, G. (1975). *Ethnicity: Cultural continuities and change*. Chicago: University of Chicago Press.

Ennis, J. (1981). Testimony before the Commission on Wartime Relocation and Internment of Civilians. In P. Irons (Ed.), *Justice at war: The story of the Japanese American internment cases* (p. 349). New York: Oxford University Press.

Fugita, S. S., & O'Brien, D. J. (1991). *Japanese American ethnicity: The persistence of community*. Seattle: University of Washington Press.

Glenn, E. N. (1986). *Issei, Nisei, warbride: Three generations of Japanese American women in domestic service*. Philadelphia: Temple University Press.

Goering, J. M. (1971). The emergence of ethnic interests: A case of serendipity. *Social Forces, 49*, 379-384.

Granovetter, M. S. (1973). The strength of weak ties. *American Journal of Sociology, 78*, 1360-1380.

Granovetter, M. S. (1982). The strength of weak ties: A theory revisited. In P. V. Marsden & N. Lin (Eds.), *Social structure and network analysis* (pp. 103-130). Beverly Hills, CA: Sage.

Hohri, W. (1988). *Repairing America: An account of the movement for Japanese American redress*. Pullman: Washington State University Press.

Hohri, William, et al. v. United States U.S. District Court for the District of Columbia, CA-1750 (March, 1983).

Ichihashi, Y. (1932). *Japanese in the United States: A critical study of the problems of the Japanese immigrants and their children*. Palo Alto, CA: Stanford University Press.

Ichioka, Y. (1988). *The Issei: The world of the first generation Japanese immigrants, 1885-1924*. New York: Free Press.

Immigration and Naturalization Service. (1950-1960). *Annual reports*. Washington, DC: U.S. Government Printing Office.

Irons, P. (1983). *Justice at war: The story of the Japanese American internment cases*. New York: Oxford University Press.

Irons, P. (1989). *Justice delayed: The record of the Japanese American cases*. Middletown, CT: Wesleyan University Press.

Irons, P. (1992). *Guilty by reason of race: The Constitution in wartime*. Paper presented at the Annual Ewen Lecture, Brooklyn College of CUNY, New York.

Iwata, M. (1962). The Japanese immigrants in California agriculture. *Agricultural History, 36,* 25-37.

Jiobu, R. W. (1988). *Ethnicity and assimilation.* Albany: State University of New York Press.

Kim, B. L. (1977). Asian wives of U.S. servicemen. *Amerasia Journal, 4,* 91-115.

Kitano, H. L. (1969). *Japanese Americans: The evolution of a subculture.* Englewood Cliffs, NJ: Prentice Hall.

Kitano, H. L., Yeung, W. T., Chai, L., & Hatanaka, H. (1984). Asian American interracial marriage. *Journal of Marriage and the Family, 46,* 179-190.

Leighton, A. (1945). *The governing of men: General principles and recommendations based on experience at a Japanese relocation camp.* Princeton: Princeton University Press.

Massey, D. S., & Denton, N. A. (1988). Suburbanization and segregation in U.S. metropolitan areas. *American Journal of Sociology, 94,* 592-626.

Matsunaga, S. (1943). *A survey of evacuee adjustment in the Saint Louis area.* Saint Louis: Washington University YMCA.

Matsunaga, S. (1944). *Resettlement of Japanese Americans in Saint Louis.* Unpublished master's thesis, Washington University.

Minami, D. (1991). Coram nobis and redress. In R. Daniels, S. C. Taylor, & H. L. Kitano (Eds.), *Japanese Americans: From relocation to redress* (pp. 200-202). Seattle: University of Washington Press.

Miyamoto, S. F. (1950). *The career of intergroup tensions: A study of the collective adjustments of evacuees to the crises at the Tule Lake relocation center.* Doctoral dissertation, University of Chicago.

Miyamoto, S. F. (1984). *Social solidarity among the Japanese in Seattle* (3rd ed.). Seattle: University of Washington Press.

Modell, J. (1977). *The economics and politics of racial accommodation: The Japanese of Los Angeles, 1900-1942.* Urbana: University of Illinois Press.

Moriyama, A. T. (1985). *Imingaisha: Japanese emigration companies and Hawaii.* Honolulu: University of Hawaii Press.

Nagata, K. (1993). *Legacy of injustice: Exploring the cross-generational impact of the Japanese American internment.* New York: Plenum.

Nakane, C. (1970). *Japanese society.* Berkeley: University of California Press.

Ng, W. L. (1984). *Collective memory and the Japanese American experience.* Paper presented at the Annual Meeting of the Association for Asian American Studies, New York, NY.

Nishi, S. M. (1963). *Japanese American achievement in Chicago: A cultural response to degradation.* Unpublished doctoral dissertation, University of Chicago.

Nishi, S. M. (1981). *The educational disadvantage of Asian and Pacific Americans: Its nature and policy implications.* Paper presented at the Annual Meeting of the American Educational Research Association, Los Angeles, CA.

Nishi, S. M. (1982). Testimony before the Commission on Wartime Relocation and Internment of Civilians, New York, NY.

Nishi, S. M. (1985). The status of Asian Americans in the health care delivery system in New York. *New York State Journal of Medicine, 85,* 153-156.

Peterson, W. (1966, January 6). Success story, Japanese American style. *The New York Times Magazine.*

Reischauer, E. O. (1981). *The Japanese.* Cambridge, MA: Belknap.

Roche, J. P. (1982). Suburban ethnicity: Ethnic attitudes and behavior among Italian Americans in two suburban communities. *Social Sciences Quarterly, 63,* 145-153.

Shibutani, T. (1944). *The first year of resettlement of Nisei in the Chicago area.* Unpublished manuscript of the Evacuation and Resettlement Study, University of California, Berkeley.

Spickard, P. R. (1980). *Japanese Americans and intermarriage: A historical survey.* Paper presented at the Annual Conference of the Association for Asian Pacific American Studies, Seattle.

Spickard, P. R. (1989). *Mixed blood: Intermarriage and ethnic identity in twentieth-century America.* Madison: University of Wisconsin Press.

Steinberg, S. (1989). *The ethnic myth: Race, ethnicity, and class in America.* Boston: Beacon.

Sung, B. L. (1990). *Chinese American intermarriage.* New York: Center for Migration Studies.

tenBroek, J., Barnhart, E. N., & Matson, F. W. (1954). *Prejudice, war, and the Constitution: Causes and consequences of the evacuation of the Japanese Americans in World War II.* Berkeley: University of California Press.

Thomas, D. S. (1952). *The salvage.* Berkeley: University of California Press.

Thomas, D. S., & Nishimoto, R. S. (1946). *The spoilage.* Berkeley: University of California Press.

U.S. Bureau of the Census. (1973). *1970 census of population, subject reports: Japanese, Chinese, and Pilipinos in the United States* (PC [2]-1G). Washington, DC: U.S. Government Printing Office.

U.S. Bureau of the Census. (1983). *1980 census of population, general population characteristics, United States summary* (PC80-1-B1). Washington, DC: U.S. Government Printing Office.

U.S. Bureau of the Census. (1993a). *1990 census of population, general population characteristics, United States* (CP-1-1). Washington, DC: U.S. Government Printing Office.

U.S. Bureau of the Census. (1993b). *1990 census of population, Asians and Pacific Islanders in the United States* (PC-3-5). Washington, DC: U.S. Government Printing Office.

U.S. Bureau of the Census. (1993c). *Population profile of the United States 1993.* Current population reports, Special studies series (P23-185). Washington, DC: U.S. Government Printing Office.

U.S. Bureau of the Census. (1993d). *Statistical Abstract of the United States: 1993, 113th ed.* Washington, DC: U.S. Government Printing Office.

U.S. Bureau of the Census. (1994). *1990 census of population, general social and economic characteristics, United States* (CP-2-1). Washington, DC: U.S. Government Printing Office.

U.S. Commission on Civil Rights. (1992). *Civil rights issues facing Asian Americans in the 1990.* Washington, DC: Author.

U.S. House of Representatives, Select Committee Investigating National Defense Migration. (1942). Findings and recommendations on evacuation of enemy aliens and others from prohibited military zones, 77 Congress, Second Session.

War Relocation Authority. (1946). *The evacuated people: A quantitative description.* Washington, DC: U.S. Government Printing Office.

Weglyn, M. (1976). *Years of infamy: The untold of America's concentration camps.* New York: William Morrow.

Yanagisako, S. J. (1977). Women-centered kin networks in urban bilateral kinship. *American Ethnologists, 4,* 207-266.

Yanagisako, S. J. (1985). *Transforming the past: Tradition and kinship among Japanese Americans.* Palo Alto, CA: Stanford University Press.

Zangwill, I. (1909). *The melting pot: Drama in four acts.* New York: Macmillan.

6

Filipino Americans

PAULINE AGBAYANI-SIEWERT
LINDA REVILLA

Filipino Americans are currently the second-largest Asian group in the United States, yet comparatively little is known about them. Although Filipinos have lived in the United States for over 200 years, it was not until the change in the immigration law in 1965 that their numbers started to increase dramatically. Filipino Americans in 1990 numbered over 1.4 million.

Because of the Philippines' history as a Spanish colony and an American colony, new Filipino immigrants are perhaps the most Westernized of all Asian immigrant groups. Most speak English and are familiar with American lifestyles. The majority are well-educated professionals. They stand in contrast with the American-born Filipinos, who have their own distinctive characteristics, among them less education and less income. Filipino Americans comprise persons of varying regional, linguistic, educational, social class, and generational backgrounds. The few studies on Filipino Americans point to the need for more information on this fast-growing and interesting Asian American group.

Cultural and Political History of the Philippines

The Philippines is an archipelago composed of about 7,000 islands, surrounded by the North and South China Seas and the Pacific Ocean. The population is considered to be Malay stock, with some foreign influences such as Chinese, Spanish, American, and Indian. There are eight major

134

ethnolinguistic groups, consisting of about 200 dialects; Filipino, the national language based mostly on the Tagalog dialect, is the most politically prominent. Language and the region of origin are two main differentiators among Filipinos in the Philippines and abroad (Alcantra, 1975; Pido, 1986).

Spanish Colonial Influences

The Philippines was a Spanish colony for more than 3 centuries following Ferdinand Magellan's landing on the island of Cebu in 1521. Spanish colonists controlled vast tracts of land and the political and economic systems of the islands. The Catholic Church, which succeeded in converting the majority of the population, also owned vast tracts of land and controlled the educational system. Manila became an important port for the Spanish galleon trade between Asia and the New World. Under Spanish rule, the majority of native people were reduced to being landless peasant sharecroppers (Karnow, 1989). Today over 80% of Filipinos are Catholic. Other cultural influences from Spain can be found in Filipino food, songs, and dances.

The Philippine-American War

The call for change was promoted by men like the martyred Jose Rizal in the late 19th century. Filipino rebels, led by Emiliano Aguinaldo, helped the United States defeat the Spanish in the Philippines during the Spanish American War. With the departure of the Spanish, Aguinaldo and his followers declared the Philippines an independent nation. Americans, who had been given the Philippines in the Treaty of Paris, heeded the cry of manifest destiny and replied by sending troops to the Philippines. The result was the Philippine-American War, known in the United States as the Philippines Insurrection, which began in 1899 and ended in 1902. It cost the lives of 200,000 to 1 million Filipinos. The Philippines became an American colony, beginning an American presence in the Philippines that continues today.

American Colonization and Colonial Influences

Under U.S. rule, an American democratic style of government was introduced to the Philippines, as was an American educational system. Filipino children were taught about American heroes like George Washington and Abraham Lincoln, learned about American ideals, and were required to speak English in school. Despite the changes in the Philippines brought about by the American colonizers, little was done to alleviate the land problem. This was to have consequences for Filipino migration to the United States. During the period of U.S. colonial rule, Filipinos were legally considered American nationals and as such were able to enter the United States freely. The Philippines became formally independent from the United States in 1946. However, the United States has continued to exercise a powerful military, economic, and cultural influence on its former colony. The trade relationship between the two countries has followed the colonial pattern, with the Philippines providing raw materials for, and importing manufactured goods from, the United States. The United States had kept large military and naval bases in the Philippines from the end of World War II until very recently. Moreover, English is still used as an important language in public schools and the overall U.S. cultural influence is still powerful.

Immigration History

Patterns of Filipino immigration to the United States reflect American economic and political policies. With the passage of the 1965 Immigration and Naturalization Act, Filipino immigration rapidly increased. Over the last 20 years, the Philippines has provided the United States with the largest group of immigrants next to Mexico. Since 1976 over 40,000 Filipino immigrants have entered the United States annually.

Louisiana Manilamen

Significantly, the first permanent Filipino settlements in the United States began in the late 18th century, long before American involvement in the Philippines. "Manilamen," forced to build and crew Spanish galleons, jumped ship in Mexico and Louisiana and made their way to the bayous. They established villages outside New Orleans as early as 1763. These early settlers made their livelihood in the fishing and shrimping industries; their descendants are currently in their eighth generation as Americans (Cordova, 1983; Espina, 1982).

The First Wave: *Pensionados*

Filipinos did not immigrate to the United States in large numbers until the beginning of the 20th century. Although some Filipino women immigrated to the United States as war brides of Spanish-American War veterans, the first large wave of Filipinos began arriving in 1903. The Pensionado Act, passed by the U.S. Congress, provided support to send young Filipinos to the United States for education on American life. The *pensionados,* as they were called, matriculated in such institutions as Harvard, Stanford, Cornell, and the University of California, Berkeley. They founded Filipino student organizations, some of which are still in existence, produced Filipino newsletters, and sent glowing reports back home of the educational opportunities to be found in the United States (Cordova, 1983; Melendy, 1977). Following completion of their studies, the pensionados returned to the Philippines to be social, political, and economic leaders. However, their pioneering efforts were continued as thousands of young Filipinos, inspired by the success stories of the pensionados, came to the United States in search of education.

The Second Wave: Laborers

Many would-be students found the cost of education prohibitive and thus turned instead to jobs. Along with other young men who had come to the United States seeking employment, they made up the bulk of the second wave of Filipino immigrants. Until 1935, when the Philippines became semi-independent, immigration of Filipinos to the United States was unlimited because as U.S. nationals Filipinos could travel here without obtaining visas. The second-wave Filipino immigrants were mostly men, both the would-be students and laborers recruited to fill the growing cheap labor demands in Hawaii, Alaska, and the western United States. Previously, the Chinese and the Japanese had been used to fill those labor demands. The Chinese Exclusion Act of 1882 put an end to Chinese immigration, and the 1907-1908 Gentlemen's Agreement with Japan severely restricted Japanese immigration. These restrictive measures against other Asian immigrant groups created the need for a new cheap labor source. During this time the Philippines was experiencing growing poverty. Many peasants turned to foreign employment as a way to regain economic control over their lives.

Early Immigration to Hawaii

One large organization that recruited laborers from the Philippines was the Hawaii Sugar Planters' Association (HSPA). Plantation and mill workers were given 3-year contracts that provided transportation to Hawaii,

Table 6.1 Life Expectancy at Birth of Whites, Japanese, Chinese, Filipinos: Hawaii, 1920-1980 (combined sexes)

Year	White	Japanese	Chinese	Filipino
1920	56.5	50.5	53.8	28.1
1930	61.9	60.1	60.1	46.1
1940	64.0	66.3	65.3	56.9
1950	69.2	72.6	69.7	69.1
1960	72.8	75.7	74.1	71.5
1970	73.2	77.4	76.1	72.6
1980	76.4	79.7	80.2	78.8

SOURCE: Adapted from Gardner, Robey, and Smith (1985, Table 7).

housing, food, fuel, and medical care. The first group of Filipino workers in Hawaii arrived in 1906. Between 1906 and 1934, 119,470 Filipinos came to work in the sugar fields and mills. The high point of such immigration occurred in 1925, when 11,621 Filipinos disembarked in Honolulu. After that year, the HSPA did not need to recruit workers; enough Filipinos were volunteering to make the trip to Hawaii (Cordova, 1983; Griffiths, 1978; Kitano & Daniels, 1988; Melendy, 1977; Pido, 1986; Sharma, 1980; Takaki, 1989).

Life on the Hawaii sugar cane plantations was difficult. Field hands worked 10 hours a day, 26 days a month, and earned about $20 a month. Women earned $14 a month. Filipino workers were on the lowest rungs of the ethnic ladder; they got paid less for doing the same jobs as Chinese and Japanese, and they had the poorest housing. Table 6.1 shows life expectancy at birth for whites, Japanese, Chinese, and Filipinos in Hawaii from 1920 to 1980. The life expectancy for Filipino Americans was much lower than for whites and the other two Asian immigrant groups in the first 3 decades.

Like other Asian immigrants at the turn of the century, the early Filipino immigrants consisted largely of male laborers, and thus the early Filipino community was characterized by a severe gender imbalance. In 1910 the ratio of Filipino men to women was 10 to 1; by 1920, it had worsened, 20 to 1. Only after 1940 was the ratio reduced to 3.5 to 1. This gender imbalance was the impetus for many of the problems experienced in the labor camps. Lacking a normal family life, Filipino male laborers had little to do in terms of recreation but to play sports, gamble, and spend money on taxi dancers and prostitutes. Eventually the HSPA realized that family men made better employees than bachelors and began encouraging the immigration of women and families. Thus Filipinos in Hawaii were able to form a stable community and start a second generation, beginning in the 1920s.

The early Filipino immigrants were instrumental in the unionization of plantation workers in Hawaii. As early as 1910, Filipinos in Hawaii were organizing themselves into unions. They were involved in several strikes during the 1920s and 1930s with other ethnic unions, most notably the Japanese. The first major success of multiethnic unions occurred in Kauai in 1940; by 1950 Hawaii plantation workers were the best paid in the world.

Early Immigration to the West Coast

During the 1920s, about 45,000 Filipinos arrived on the West Coast (Melendy, 1977). Most of them stayed on the West Coast, although some continued east to big cities such as Chicago, New York, and Philadelphia. In California, Washington, and Oregon, Filipinos were in the unenviable position of competing with white men for jobs and women. Discriminatory laws, coupled with language barriers and the Depression, made it virtually impossible for most Filipinos to get any work other than as migrant laborers or servants. Early Filipino immigrants on the West Coast, like those in Hawaii, were for the most part bachelors. In the 1930s about 25,000 Filipinos worked in the bread basket of California, the San Joaquin Valley. They traveled from season to season, from one farming community to another, following crops. Stereotyped as good for "stoop labor," Filipinos harvested crops such as asparagus, grapes, lettuce, carrots, and beets. They were used especially in the asparagus-growing industry, because it was believed that they were not bothered by the peat dust in which asparagus grew. In addition, because they were smaller than white men, it was believed that they could stoop more easily. The typical working schedule was 10 hours of work each day, for 26 days a month, with few Sundays or holidays off.

Organized by labor contractors who would negotiate contract terms with the farmers, Filipino laborers found it difficult to improve their abysmal working conditions. American labor unions provided no recourse. Against immigration, the labor unions worked instead to have Filipino laborers excluded from the United States. Growers often used "divide and control" techniques to keep wages down. Different ethnic groups were used for different types of farm labor and were used to break each other's strikes. Nevertheless Filipino laborers managed to organize themselves into unions and staged one of their strikes in Watsonville in 1930. Although the strike was not successful, it had a major impact on the fledgling Filipino unions, providing the impetus for the successful 1934 strike against the lettuce growers of Salinas (DeWitt, 1978). In the 1960s Filipinos would start the grape boycott that led to the formation of the United Farm Workers union.

Early Immigration to Alaska

Many of the Filipinos involved in organizing the agricultural unions were also active in organizing unions for Alaska cannery workers. Filipinos had been a presence in Alaska canneries since 1909 (Masson & Guimary, 1981). Recruited by contract laborers in the West Coast cities, thousands of young Filipino immigrant men made the journey north to work the short season of 3 months or the long season of 6 months. The contractor, who had negotiated with the cannery, was responsible for the workers' transportation to and from Alaska, their food, and wages. The canner was usually responsible only for housing the workers. Workers were often exploited by contractors. For example, in order to maximize profits for themselves, contractors often skimped on the food, feeding the workers poorly.

Despite many difficulties stemming from infighting and lack of support from American unions, in 1937 Filipino cannery workers were able to organize themselves into a union that successfully bargained with canners to improve wages and abolish the labor contractor system (Masson & Guimary, 1981).

Early Anti-Filipino Sentiment

Anti-Filipino sentiment was rampant on the West Coast during this period. Resentment over Filipino laborers' competition for jobs and white women grew as the region's economic situation worsened with the Depression. Because they were not eligible to become citizens, Filipinos could not own or lease land and could not obtain professional licenses in many states. In 1943, Filipinos were able to lease land in California, especially land vacated by interned Japanese Americans, but they were still unable to own land. Filipinos faced discrimination in a number of venues, including housing, hotels, restaurants, barber shops, pools, cinemas, tennis courts, and even churches (Melendy, 1977). Filipinos recall being spat upon, shoved off of sidewalks, and called racial slurs, among them "goo-goo" and "monkey." In 1928 Filipinos were run out of the Yakima Valley in Washington. The violence culminated in the 1930 riots in Watsonville,

California. A mob of white vigilantes raided a dance hall leased by Filipinos and harassed Filipinos in farm labor camps. Fermin Tobera, a 22-year-old laborer, was shot and killed in his bunk.

Legislation Affecting Filipinos

With the passage of the Tydings-McDuffie Act in 1934, the Philippines was granted commonwealth status and the immigration of Filipinos to the United States was restricted to 50 persons a year. The former American nationals suddenly became "aliens" ineligible for federal assistance and many jobs (Manzon, 1938). The Filipino Repatriation Act, passed in 1935, provided Filipino immigrants with free transportation back to the Philippines (Manzon, 1938). However, once there, the returnee could only return to the United States under the 50 per year quota. It is estimated that about 2,200 Filipinos returned to the Philippines under the terms of this act (Melendy, 1977). During World War II immigration was suspended for all but the Filipinos serving in the U.S. armed forces.

Thousands of Filipino immigrants and Filipino American men served in the United States during World War II. They were especially numerous in the Navy and in the Army, which had its own segregated First and Second Filipino Infantry Regiments (Cordova, 1983). Their valor, along with the heroism of men of the Philipine Army in the Philippines, helped change American attitudes toward Filipinos. Filipinos who served in the U.S. Armed Forces were able to become citizens in 1943.

When the Philippines gained independence in 1946, the immigration quota was doubled to allow 100 persons a year to immigrate, and Filipinos in the United States were allowed to become naturalized citizens. After the war the Filipino community in the United States was revitalized by the arrival of 16,000 women, war brides of Filipino and American veterans. Finally, with the passage of the Immigration and Naturalization Act in 1965, Filipino immigration accelerated to more than 20,000 per year. Besides descendants of the Louisiana settlers, there are four sizable generational groups of Filipinos in the United States: the first generation of early immigrants, the second and third generations, and the new wave of post-1965 immigrants.

The New Filipino Immigrants (1965-Present)

The liberalization of the immigration laws in 1965 has facilitated the immigration of people from Asian countries. The changes in U.S. immigration policy had a particularly great impact on the immigration patterns of Filipinos. As shown in Table 2.1 in Chapter 2, Filipino immigration reached the 30,000 level in 1973, only 5 years after the 1965 Immigration and Naturalization Act came into full effect. The annual number of Filipino immigrants continued to increase in the late 1970s and the 1980s. Since the late 1980s more than 50,000 Filipinos a year have been admitted to the United States as formal immigrants. The Philippines has sent more immigrants to the United States than any other Asian country over the last 2 decades and has been the second-largest source country of U.S. immigrants next to Mexico.

As a result of the large influx, the Filipino American population has experienced a dramatic growth over the last 2 decades. In 1979 Filipino Americans constituted the third-largest Asian ethnic group, with a population of approximately 340,000 (see Table 2.3 in Chapter 2). By 1980, the Filipino population had increased to over 770,000, emerging as the second-largest Asian group after the Chinese. In 1990, Filipino Americans nearly reached the 1.5 million mark, an increase of almost 90% in the 1980s. Considering Filipinos not counted in the 1990 census and the Filipino immigrants and students admitted between 1990 and 1994, the current number of Filipino Americans may be close to 2 million.

As noted in Chapter 2, the new Asian immigrants consist largely of the urban middle class. This background may be most conspicuous among Filipino immigrants. The 1980 census indicates that 48% of Filipino immigrants admitted to the United States between 1970 and 1980 completed 4 years of college (see Table 2.4 in Chapter 2), which compares with a college graduate rate of 16% for the U.S. population. Only Indian immigrants had a higher educational level than Filipino immigrants. The high socioeconomic background of the Filipino immigrants in the 1970s can be explained by the fact that most of them were professionals, particularly medical professionals such as nurses, physicians, surgeons, and pharmacists. More than 25% of Filipino immigrants admitted between 1968 and 1975 were occupational immigrants, and the vast majority of them were professionals. For example, Filipino immigrants classified as professional, technical, and kindred workers constituted 22.5% of total Filipino immigrants admitted to the United States in 1975 (Pido, 1986 , p. 74). The Philippines, along with India, sent more professional immigrants to the United States in the late 1960s and the early 1970s than any other country in the world. The departure of well-educated Filipino professionals was a brain drain from the Philippines, which was a concern for researchers and policy makers (Minocha, 1987).

As noted in Chapter 2, revisions of the 1965 Immigration and Naturalization Act in 1976 made it difficult for alien professionals to be admitted as formal immigrants; the vast majority of post-1976 immigrants have come to the United States under provisions allowing family reunification. Filipino immigrants admitted under family reunification are socioeconomically less select than the earlier occupational immigrants. Yet even more recent Filipino family immigrants are also characterized by relatively high educational levels. As shown in Table 2.4 in Chapter 2, 45% of the 1980-1984 Filipino immigrants and 46% of the 1985-1990 Filipino immigrants completed 4 years of college education. Clearly Filipinos with high educational qualifications have responded to the opportunity for immigration.

What has made the Philippines a major source country of the new immigrants? Why have such a large number of Filipinos responded to changes in U.S. immigration policy? To answer this question, it must be emphasized first of all that Filipinos are attracted by life in the United States because of the Americanization of Filipino culture through U.S. colonization (Carino, 1987). Filipinos are similar to most Americans in terms of language, customs, and values, and thus they are highly motivated to immigrate to the United States. Another important contributing factor to the mass exodus of Filipinos is the U.S. military presence in the Philippines. Since 1970, from 5,000 to 11,000 Filipino women a year have immigrated to the United States as wives of U.S. citizens (Liu, Ong, & Rosenstein, 1991), and most are wives of U.S. servicemen stationed in the Philippines. Since the U.S. air and naval bases in the Philippines were closed in January 1992, immigration through intermarriage is likely to have declined greatly.

Settlement Patterns

Concentration in the West Coast States

Like other Asian groups, Filipino Americans have shown a preference to settle in the West. This concentration has been consistent since the arrival of the first wave of Filipino immigrants at the turn of the century. As shown in Table 6.2, 71% of Filipino Americans resided in the West in 1990. Most U.S. Filipinos live in California. Interestingly, the proportion of Filipino Americans in California increased from 46% in 1980 to 52% in 1990, reflecting the tendency of Filipino Americans to consolidate in one state. Traditionally, California has been the magnet for Asian immigrants.

Table 6.2 Distribution of Filipinos in the U.S., 1980 and 1990

	1980		1990		Increase Between 1980 and 1990	
	N	%	N	%	N	%
Northeast	81,894	10.6	1,406,770	10.2	614,876	80.8
New York	35,630	4.6	62,259	4.4	26,629	74.7
New Jersey	24,470	3.1	53,146	3.8	28,676	117.0
Midwest	66,913	8.6	113,354	8.1	46,441	66.4
Illinois	44,317	5.7	64,224	4.6	19,907	44.9
Michigan	11,132	1.4	13,768	0.1	2,636	23.7
South	52,073	6.7	159,378	11.3	107,305	206.1
Virginia	19,111	2.4	35,067	2.5	15,956	83.5
Texas	15,952	2.0	34,350	2.4	18,398	115.3
Florida	14,218	1.8	31,945	2.3	17,727	124.7
West	520,179	66.5	991,080	70.5	470,901	90.5
California	358,378	45.8	731,685	52.0	373,307	104.0
Hawaii	132,075	16.9	168,682	12.0	36,607	27.7
Washington	25,662	3.3	43,799	3.1	18,137	70.7

SOURCE: U.S. Bureau of the Census (1983, Table 62; 1993a, Table 277).

But Filipino Americans currently show a higher level of concentration in California than any other Asian group. This may be explained by the fact that California has received two chains of Filipino immigrants (Liu et al., 1991). Chain 1 consists of Filipino old-timers admitted before 1965 and the family reunification immigrants they sponsored. California, along with Hawaii, had a large number of Filipino immigrants before 1965, and thus a large number of family reunification immigrants have settled in California. Chain 2 consists of the Filipino occupational immigrants admitted between 1965 and 1975 and the relatives they subsequently sponsored. California also attracted a large number of these immigrants. The warm climate in California may be another factor that has attracted a large number of post-1965 Filipino immigrants.

Hawaii, along with California, was an important ethnic enclave for early Filipino immigrants. However, Hawaii has received only a small proportion of post-1965 immigrants and thus has the lowest rate of growth in the Filipino population. In 1970 some 22% of Filipino Americans were settled in Hawaii, a proportion that decreased from 17% in 1980 to 12% in 1990. The steady decline in the growth of the Filipino American population relative to other states is attributable to the fact that Hawaii did not attract many Filipino professional immigrants immediately after the enforcement of the 1965 Immigration and Naturalization Act, immigrants who then started a new chain of migration (Liu et al., 1991). Instead of Hawaii, several non-Western states such as Illinois, New York, New Jersey, and Texas have received a substantial proportion of post-1965 Filipino immigrants because of greater professional opportunities there (Liu et al., 1991; Mangiafico, 1988).

Filipino Ethnic Enclaves

Although Filipino Americans are highly concentrated in the West, particularly in California, they have not established many easily recognized ethnic enclaves comparable to Chinatowns. Many Manilatowns in the West declined with the passing of the first Filipino immigrants. Although Los Angeles has officially proclaimed a Manilatown, it is nothing but "a sign on the Hollywood freeway, leading to a dozen shopfronts in a run-down area in downtown Los Angeles" ("American Survey," 1986). In regard to residential concentration, no consistent pattern has emerged that would characterize Filipino Americans in the United States. Filipino immigrants in Hawaii and Los Angeles tend to cluster in ethnic neighborhoods (Agbayani-Siewert, 1991; White, 1986), whereas those in Chicago do not have a concentrated business or neighborhood community (Kim, 1978). Lack of development of a Filipino territorial community by the early immigrants might be explained by both historical circumstances and sociocultural characteristics unique to Filipinos.

The first wave of Filipino immigrants were recruited by agricultural corporations, first in Hawaii and later in California. In California, the migratory existence of these workers made it difficult to establish any one area as a permanent business or residential community. Shops specializing in Filipino goods were usually owned and operated by other Asians, especially by Chinese (Yu, 1980). It has also been suggested that disunity among Filipinos based on regional loyalties, dialects, and kinship patterns was not conducive to building the cooperation needed to establish a visible and cohesive Filipino American community (Almirol, 1978; Min, 1986-1987; Yu, 1980). Moreover, because the earlier immigration laws did not contain provisions for Filipino women to migrate and racist antimiscegenation laws prevented intermarriage, permanent communities housing families were not initially established in California.

Recent Filipino immigrants are characterized by high educational and professional backgrounds with a good command of the English language.

These middle-class and professional characteristics seem to work against the establishment of Filipino ethnic enclaves. Filipino immigrants' prior familiarity with American culture through the U.S. influence on the Philippines and their ability to speak and read English make it easier for them to adapt to American life. Compared to other Asian immigrants, Filipino immigrants may not need to congregate with others outside of their kin group for mutual aid and support. The professional backgrounds and needs of recent Filipino immigrants also seem to discourage the establishment of ethnic neighborhoods. Kim (1978) found that educated professional Filipinos in the Chicago area preferred to settle near their places of employment and not in any identifiable ethnic enclave.

Despite the factors that seem to prevent the formation of Filipino ethnic enclaves, they do, nevertheless, exist. New Filipino immigrants have revitalized some old neighborhoods, such as Kalihi and Waipahu, in Hawaii. New immigrants have also formed their own enclaves, such as Daly City and Pinole near San Francisco.

Socioeconomic Adjustment

Education

The 1990 census indicates that Filipino Americans as a group are characterized by high educational levels. As shown in Table 6.3, using the percentage of college graduates as an indicator, foreign-born Filipinos are much more highly educated than the white population and more highly educated than the other three major Asian ethnic groups. As previously noted, Filipino immigrants who entered the United States in the early 1970s generally represented well-educated professionals, which inflated the educational level of Filipino Americans as a whole.

Native-born Filipino Americans do a little better in education than white Americans but are behind other Asian groups. The figures in the last row, the percentages of people 20 to 24 years old enrolled in schools, roughly reflect the percentages of Asian American college students who were born or raised in America. Filipino Americans are slightly higher than white Americans in the rate of college enrollment, but significantly lower than other Asian groups.

In addition to having low college enrollment rates, once in college Filipino Americans tend to drop out at a high rate. Data from the University of California, Los Angeles (the Office of Budget, Institutional Planning,

Table 6.3 Educational Characteristics of Filipino American and Other Groups, 1990

| | Filipino | | Chinese | | Japanese | | Korean | | White |
	F	N	F	N	F	N	F	N	Total
% of people 25 and over who graduated from high school	82.0	85.1	70.1	91.1	86.0	88.3	80.9	87.7	78.0
% of people 25 and over who completed 4 years of college	42.3	22.3	37.6	51.0	35.1	34.2	33.0	36.5	21.6
% of people 20 to 24 enrolled in schools	50.0	44.2	69.3	71.1	78.5	55.9	66.8	63.2	34.8

SOURCE: Adapted from U.S. Bureau of the Census (1993b, Table 2; 1994, Tables 40, 42).
NOTE: F = Foreign Born, N = Native Born.

and Analysis, 1987) show that Filipino Americans have a graduation rate of only 40%, much lower than the rates of other Asian groups. The University of California system admits disadvantaged minority students using affirmative action criteria. The UC affirmative action program partly requires that the ethnic composition of recent California freshman classes reflect that of the recent public high school graduates in the state. In 1988 Filipino Americans were no longer considered eligible for affirmative action for UCLA admissions because they were considered to have reached parity, using this narrow definition of affirmative action. Virata (1989) argues that a high dropout rate of Filipino college students and a large number of Filipino students enrolled in parochial high schools should be considered in the definition of affirmative action in college admission. Almirol (1988) extends the discussion on barriers in the UC system that prevent Filipino Americans from obtaining access to higher education. He notes that in fall 1985 only 0.6% of the master's students in the UC system were Filipino Americans.

Relatively few studies focusing on second-generation Filipinos have been conducted, and thus it is difficult to explain why native-born Filipinos are not doing as well as other Asian Americans in education. However, some educated speculations can be offered. Using a conflict perspective, Tamayo-Lott (1980) suggests that the low educational and socioeconomic achievements of Filipino Americans are due to a colonial mentality assumed from their immigrant parents. She further argues that, in addition to a colonial mentality imposed by parents, second-generation Filipinos tend to contend with exploitation and oppression in a white power structure as members of a subordinate group.

Another possible explanation for Filipino Americans' relatively low educational achievements is that Filipino American youth expect low rewards for their educational investments. As will be discussed later in this section, Filipino immigrants are much more highly educated than white Americans but tend to earn less. The perception that educational investments do not necessarily guarantee economic rewards may not give Filipino American children the motivation to work hard.

A final possible explanation may be that native-born Filipinos have lost much of their traditional cultural values stressing education. Filipinos in the Philippines tend to believe that education is the key to success in the world (Almirol, 1988). Kitano (1980) notes that second-generation Filipinos have minimal or no ties with the Philippines, generally do not speak their parents' dialects, and tend to acculturate into American life. This lessening of cultural ties by the children of Filipino immigrants may include a lessening of the high value placed on education held by their parents.

High Female Labor Force Participation Rate

One thing noteworthy in regard to Filipino Americans' socioeconomic characteristics is the exceptionally high labor force participation rate of Filipino American women. Filipino American women's active economic role is well-reflected in the 1980 U.S. census. It shows that 68% of Filipino women 16 years old and over participated in the labor force in 1979, much higher than the labor force participation rate of U.S. women in general (49%) and other Asian Americans. Both native-born and foreign-born Filipino women are similarly active in their economic role. Only native-born Japanese American women show a higher labor force participation rate than their Filipino American counterparts. Filipino American married women in particular show a much higher labor force participation rate than other Asian wives, as reflected by the figures in the first three columns of Table 6.4.

The high labor force participation rate of Filipino American women can be explained by several factors. First of all, many Filipino American women may have to work out of economic necessity (Gardner, Robey, & Smith, 1985). The 1980 census data show that Filipino households make a median family income well above that of U.S households in general. However, as will be discussed in more detail in the next subsection, Filipino American workers individually earn less than whites and most other Asian

Table 6.4 Filipino Women's Labor Force Participation Rate in Comparison With Other Asian Groups, 1979 (in percent)

	Filipino	Chinese	Japanese	Korean	Asian Indian	Vietnamese
Female family householders	79.0	70.3	72.5	71.1	58.2	56.0
Female spouses of householders	71.9	61.2	55.9	56.2	51.9	52.7
Female householders with no husband present	78.5	69.8	72.7	72.9	57.3	57.6
Native-born women	64.5	65.0	68.3	59.1	29.4	56.1
Foreign-born women	68.8	56.0	42.7	54.8	53.6	48.7

SOURCE: Adapted from Gardner, Robey, and Smith (1985, Table 12).

Americans. It also must be pointed out that Filipino families, in spite of their high family incomes, generally maintain a lower standard of living than whites and other Asians due to their large family size (see Table 7.5 in Chapter 7). Thus most Filipino families may need an extra worker to raise their standard of living.

The high labor force participation rate of Filipino immigrant women in particular may be partly related to their relatively high level of education and U.S. immigration policies. An exceptionally high proportion of Filipino immigrant women relative to other immigrant women entered the United States as professional and technical workers in the 1970s. At least until the revision in 1976, the occupational preference categories for admission favored aliens with high educational levels and professional occupations. A large number of well-educated Filipino women, particularly Filipino nurses, took advantage of occupational categories in the early 1970s. Almost all of these women held jobs in the Philippines, too.

Finally, an important contributing factor to the high labor force participation rate of Filipino American women has something to do with the Filipino cultural tradition. Agbayani-Siewert and Jones (in press) report that Filipino American women are more likely to work for income and cultural values. In their view, traditional Filipino cultural values and beliefs not only encourage but also expect women to work outside of the home. In the traditional Filipino culture, marital relations are based on egalitarian principles, radically different from the patriarchal principles held in other

Asian countries. Filipino women share more equal status with males than women in other Asian countries. Pido (1986) notes that Filipinos give recognition, deference, and opportunities to any family member, regardless of sex, who shows potential to increase the family's status and position. Cultural values emphasizing gender equality most likely influence the economic participation of Filipino women. These cultural values are reflected in public policies in the Philippines. Working married women are guaranteed 40 days of maternity leave with job security. Most recently, paternity leave has also been established in the Philippines.

Occupational and Economic Adjustment

Recently, Filipino Americans have been described as having attained occupational and economic parity with the white population (Mangiafico, 1988). Overall, Filipino Americans tend to be well-represented in higher occupational positions. However, a closer examination of census data suggests that the overall optimistic picture is misleading. The top occupational categories are generally held by foreign-born and not by native-born Filipinos. In fact, native-born Filipinos are underrepresented in the top occupational categories. For example, analysis of the 1990 census data shows that only 21.5% of native-born Filipino workers held managerial and professional occupations, compared to 27.2% of whites (see Table 6.5). Foreign-born Filipinos hold high occupations mainly because of their high educational levels. In fact, given their education, Filipino immigrants are underrepresented in professional and managerial occupations. This means that they have experienced downward mobility in occupational adjustment since their immigration. Carino and his colleagues (Carino, Fawcett, Gardner, & Arnold, 1990) compared the occupations held by Filipino immigrants prior to their departure from the Philippines with the occupations they held in the United States. They found that a smaller proportion of immigrants held professional and technical occupations in the United States than they did in the Philippines.

The 1990 census data showed that Filipino Americans earned a higher median family income ($46,698) than white families ($37,152) and that among Asian ethnic groups they earned the third-highest median family income next to the Japanese and Indians (see Table 2.9 in Chapter 2). However, once again this should not be interpreted as an indication of Filipino Americans' economic success. The high family income of the Filipino group is largely attributable to a larger number of workers per household. When income per person and not per household income is analyzed using the 1980 census, Filipino Americans earned less annually

Table 6.5 Occupational Characteristics of Filipino and White Americans 25
Years Old and Over, 1990

| | *Filipino* | | | *White* |
	Total	*Native Born*	*Foreign Born*	*Total*
Occupations				
Professional	15.0	10.8	17.8	14.4
Managerial	10.3	10.7	10.2	12.8
Technical/sales	15.6	18.2	15.0	16.1
Administrative support	21.0	22.5	20.7	16.0
Service	16.8	15.6	17.1	12.0
Farm	1.5	1.4	1.5	2.5
Precision, production, and craft	7.4	9.3	7.0	11.9
Operatives and laborers	11.0	11.6	10.9	14.3

SOURCE: U.S. Bureau of the Census (1993b, Table 3; 1994, Table 45).

($13,690) than white Americans ($15,572) and all other Asian groups, with
the exception of the Vietnamese.

As discussed in Chapter 3, Asian ethnic groups generally earn less than
white Americans of comparable educational levels. However, this problem of
underreward seems to be more severe for Filipino Americans—U.S.-born and
foreign-born Filipinos alike—than other Asian groups. For example, Woo's
analysis of the 1980 census data showed that among those who completed 4
years of college or more, only 20.5% of native-born Filipino Americans earned
$21,200 or more, compared to 51% of whites and about 45% of Japanese
(Woo, 1985). The same study also showed that foreign-born Filipinos received
similarly low returns from their educational investments compared to other
Asian immigrant groups. For this reason, some scholars argue that the labor
market segmentation approach is more useful for understanding Filipino
Americans' occupational and economic adjustment than the human capital
investment approach (Cabezas, Shinagawa, & Kawaguchi, 1986-1987).

Acculturation and Ethnic Identification

Acculturation

In the traditional model (Gordon, 1964), *cultural assimilation* or *acculturation* is the first stage of assimilation. However, new models of cultural

contact do not conceptualize acculturation as a unidimensional process dependent mostly upon length of time or the immigrant generation in the United States. Padilla (1980) and others (Keefe, 1980; Szapocznik & Kurtines, 1980) characterize acculturation as a complex process that includes elements of cultural awareness, ethnic loyalty, and ethnic identification. Related to this concept of acculturation is the concept of symbolic ethnicity, which suggests that well-assimilated third- and fourth-generation Americans maintain ethnicity mainly through symbols such as love of ethnic food and participation in ethnic festivals (Gans, 1979). Kitano and Daniels indicate that many third-generation Japanese Americans prefer to maintain their cultural heritage and ethnic ties while participating in mainstream America (Kitano, 1980; Kitano & Daniels, 1988).

Based on his analysis of 1980 census data, Jiobu (1988, p. 100) notes that foreign-born Filipinos recorded a 45% naturalization rate, which is higher than other Asian groups. Most Filipinos reported speaking English well, but language is a questionable indicator of Filipino immigrants' acculturation, because most Filipino immigrants entered the United States with the ability to speak English. Jiobu (1988, pp. 101, 103) indicates that 71% of Filipinos speak a language other than English at home, although 91% of them reported being able to speak English "well" or "very well." This suggests that most Filipinos who have become naturalized citizens and who can speak English well still prefer to speak their native language at home.

Recently Filipinos have been making headlines by challenging "English only" policies at the workplace ("Racism and English," 1989). For example, in January 1990, Harborview Medical Center in Seattle, Washington, implemented a policy dictating that English should be the only language used for business purposes with the General Accounting Department. Disciplinary actions for violating the policy included possible job termination. The policy was aimed primarily at seven Filipino workers in the accounting department. The Filipino workers filed a grievance supported by union representatives and the local community. Eventually the policy was rescinded (Akamine, 1990). Unfortunately, however, many more "English only" policies at the workplace remain intact.

Ethnicity

It is difficult to discuss Filipino ethnicity, given the complexity of language and regional divisions within the Filipino community. Furthermore there is a division between native-born and immigrant Filipinos, at least in Hawaii (Enriquez, 1991). The lack of strong ethnic identity has been associated with a myriad of problems besetting the Filipino community, including youth gangs and low educational achievement (Enriquez, 1991; the University of Hawaii Task Force on Filipinos, 1988). Thus the few studies that have examined Filipino ethnic identity warrant some attention.

The isolated and segregated living conditions of plantation life in Hawaii and farm labor camps in California enabled early immigrants to maintain strong ethnic identity. In a study of Filipino history in Hawaii, Sharma (1980) indicates that "active adaptation" to their constrained plantation situation enabled earlier Filipino immigrants to maintain a separate identity. In order to support her claim, she emphasizes how Filipinos modified their cultural tradition to accommodate the prevailing conditions. For example, multiple sponsors as godparents, sometimes as many as 200, were a part of almost every religious ceremony, from baptism to marriage. This facilitated continued contacts with friends and relatives and enabled the vast majority of single men to continue participating in community affairs. The celebration of these significant "rites of passage" continues to be important in the Filipino community in Hawaii, ensuring the maintenance of Filipino culture.

The importance of Filipino culture and history was stressed during the Filipino American "identity movement" of the 1960s (Bello and Reyes, 1986-1987). Part of this movement included the debate on whether to use the label Pilipino American rather than Filipino American. Morales (1974) notes that the pre-Hispanic alphabet in the Philippines did not have the letter *F* and that therefore the usage of Filipino is a product of the Philippines' Spanish colonial history. He argues that using Pilipino and not Filipino is symbolic of a break with the Spanish colonial legacy and thus represents a positive sense of ethnic identity. Another side of the issue is the argument that there is an *F* sound in some indigenous dialects. Furthermore, some members of the second and later generations have always called themselves Filipino; they feel that the "P" label emphasizes post-1965 immigrants, not reflecting their situation as American-born Filipinos. However, the debate on this issue is far from being over. Others argue that the words "Filipino" and "Philipino" are still derived from "Philippines," which is named after Philip of Spain, and therefore both terms reflect Spanish colonialism.

Filipino American ethnic identity has been associated with the level of acculturation and political orientation. In Revilla's (1993) study of first- and second-generation Filipino American students, those who identified themselves as "mostly Filipino" also tended to have political orientations affirming Filipino culture. They were also found to socialize mostly with Filipino and other Asian students. Those who identified themselves as "very Americanized" tended to have political orientations that were more assimilationist in nature. They consistently reported socializing more with Caucasian students. Interestingly, regardless of how the respondents identified themselves or what generation they belonged to, most of the respondents adhered to traditional Filipino values, especially those related to family togetherness and respect for elders.

Participation in Ethnic Organizations

Filipino Americans are a very diverse group with strong regional divisions and loyalties. Unlike the Chinese and Japanese Americans, who have generally been able to unify around political causes (Saito, 1993), Filipino Americans have been characterized as lacking a strong unity. In 1986 there were over 300 Filipino fraternal organizations in the Los Angeles area ("American Survey," 1986). Most Filipino ethnic associations perform social functions and are often based on place of origin, a common dialect, and kinship rather than on common economic and other class interests. Min (1986-1987) indicates that Filipino Americans have close family and kin networks, but that these ties do not necessarily tend to include cooperation with nonkin ethnic members. Pido (1986) argues that interfactional and interorganizational conflicts are part of the Filipino way of life.

Although Filipinos are not characterized as having a visible or territorial community, a sense of community does exist in the form of Filipino identity. Alegado (1991) indicates that the continuous social reproduction of the Filipino community in Hawaii results from the continuing influx of new Filipino immigrants and the experience of antiimmigrant prejudice and discrimination. He looks at the social and political contexts in which the Filipinos in Hawaii find themselves as variables influencing how the Filipino community organizes itself. According to Alegado (1991), the main social networks and community institutions include family/kinship networks, mutual aid societies, regional associations, Filipino American residential districts, the community media, and the Philippine Consulate. Most second- and third-generation Filipino Americans have some general ties with the Filipino community and specific ties with particular ethnic organizations. These organizations have helped to perpetuate Filipino ethnic identity during the 8 decades that Filipinos have lived in Hawaii.

The need for political power and a sense of discrimination may be the key factors that foster unity and cooperation among Filipino Americans.

Recently Filipino Americans in major Filipino centers such as Honolulu, Los Angeles, San Francisco, and Seattle have successfully united to elect Filipino Americans to political offices. Organizations based on professional ties have been formed to lobby for less restrictive legislation aimed at immigrants who practice medicine and law. In addition to possible changes within the Filipino population, more attention from business, government, and academic researchers will influence the ways that Filipinos cooperate with one another to protect common interests. As their numbers grow and common issues emerge, the sense of a Filipino community will most likely increase.

Filipino Intermarriage

Antimiscegenation

Carlos Bulosan, a Filipino writer, depicts a scene in a restaurant where a Filipino man, his white American wife, and their child were refused service. When the Filipino man asked the owner if he could buy a bottle of milk for his hungry child, the owner responded by pushing him outside, shouting, "you goddam brown monkeys have your nerve, marrying our women. Now get out of town!" (Bulosan, 1943, pp. 144-145). Bulosan was illustrating life for young Filipino men in the 1920s and 1930s. Most Filipino men at that time were bachelors ranging in age from 16 to 30. In 1930 immigrant Filipino men outnumbered Filipino women by approximately 23 to 1 (Empeno, 1976). California was just one of many states prohibiting marriages between white Americans and "unassimilable aliens." California's antimiscegenation law had been in existence since 1901. "Negroes, mulattoes, and Mongolians" were not allowed to marry whites, according to the California Civil Codes. Interpretation of the law, however, was often up to the county clerk who issued marriage licenses. Generally, Filipinos were considered to be "Mongolians." In 1933 the court case of *Roldan vs. Los Angeles County* was heard before the California Supreme Court. The court ruled that immigrant and American-born Filipinos were members of the "Malay" race and were thus eligible to marry whites. However, the California legislature quickly changed the civil code to include persons of the Malay race in the list of groups whose members could not marry whites. Other states, including Nevada, Oregon, and Washington, followed suit. California's antimiscegenation laws were ruled unconstitutional in 1948 (Cordova, 1983; Empeno, 1976; Melendy, 1977).

It took another 2 decades before antimiscegenation laws in other states were ruled unconstitutional.

Intermarriage Patterns

Few studies focusing on Filipino American intermarriage have been conducted. This dearth of research may in part be due to methodological reasons; many studies on intermarriage involve statistical analyses of marriage certificates in particular regions. The Spanish surnames of many Filipino Americans make it difficult to distinguish between Filipino Americans and persons of Hispanic background.

The few available studies indicate that Filipino Americans intermarry at a high rate relative to other Asian groups. Based on 1980 census data, Jiobu (1988, chap. 6) assessed intermarriage rates of several ethnic groups, including four Asian groups, in California. His study shows that 20% of Filipino married men in California had non-Filipino spouses in comparison to 27% of Filipino married women (Jiobu, 1988, p. 161). Filipino men in California recorded the highest intermarriage rate among all Asian groups, whereas Filipino women had the second highest rate after Japanese women. Many intermarried Filipino women included in the 1980 census data were those who married U.S. servicemen in the Philippines and subsequently immigrated. Excluding these intermarried women, Filipino American men seem to intermarry as frequently as Filipino American women. This goes against the general trend that Asian American women tend to intermarry at a much higher rate than Asian American men. It has been speculated that Asian American men may have a much lower intermarriage rate than Asian American women because they are not attractive to, or not interested in, white women because of their strong male chauvinism. Filipino American men seem to have a high intermarriage rate mainly because they are more Americanized and have a more egalitarian gender role orientation than other Asian American men and thus can get along better with white women than other Asian American men.

Like other Asian American counterparts, Filipinos involved in intermarriage are more likely to choose white partners. However, Filipino Americans differ from other Asian groups in intermarriage patterns in two important ways. First, as previously indicated, nearly as many Filipino men as Filipino women seem to have married white partners, whereas for other Asian groups, only women have usually married white partners. Second, Filipino Americans have rarely intermarried members of other Asian groups, whereas there has been a high level of intermarriage among three

Asian groups: Japanese, Chinese, and Korean Americans (Kitano, Young, Chai, & Hatanaka, 1984). Instead, the second most common type of Filipino intermarriage is with Hispanics (Jiobu, 1988; Urban Associates, 1974). Japanese, Chinese, and Korean groups frequently intermarry among themselves mainly because of their similar physical and cultural characteristics. Filipino Americans also seem to intermarry with Hispanics due to cultural similarities associated with the Spanish colonial rule, including Catholicism.

Research has shown that many Filipino intermarriages fail. For example, Schwertfeger's (1982) study looked at first marriages that took place in 1968 in Hawaii and then reexamined them in 1976. In 1968 the Filipino intermarriage rate was 43%, using the marriage, not the individual, as the unit of analysis. By 1976, 17.6% of those Filipino marriages had ended in divorce. Filipino-Filipino unions had an 11% divorce rate, in comparison to a 22% divorce rate for intermarried couples. Filipino brides with Chinese, Japanese, and Caucasian spouses had the highest divorce rates, over 20%. Filipino brides had the lowest divorce rates when they were married to Filipino and Hawaiian or part-Hawaiian men, 11% and 14.9% respectively. Filipino grooms had the highest divorce rates, over 20%, when they were married to Caucasian, Japanese, and Hawaiian or part-Hawaiian women. Filipino grooms had the lowest divorce rates when they were married to Filipino and Chinese women, 11% and 12.5% respectively.

Research suggests that most Filipino young people tend to accept intermarriage as an option. For example, in a study by Revilla (1989), Filipino American college students in Los Angeles were asked whether they had any preference in terms of the ethnicity of their potential marital partners. Forty percent of the respondents said they had no preference. Only 31% said they would prefer a Filipino partner. An overwhelming majority of those who indicated marriage preference for "others" preferred to marry Caucasians. These findings suggest that Filipino Americans will probably continue to intermarry at high rates.

Filipino Mail-Order Brides

A unique and apparently growing category of intermarriages results from American men meeting and marrying Asian women through the use of correspondence catalogs. During recent years, so-called "mail-order brides" have received significant coverage in the mainstream media. Articles have appeared in such media ranging from *People* magazine (Small & Mathison, 1985) to the *Wall Street Journal* (Joseph, 1984). In this kind of union, men usually respond to advertisements like these published in the March 9, 1989 issue of *Rolling Stone*: "Asian women desire romance!" and "Attractive Oriental ladies seeking friendship, correspondence." For a fee, responding men receive a catalog of pictures and descriptions of Asian women with whom they may correspond. Often, these pen pals become spouses.

Although there are no hard data on this phenomenon, the *Wall Street Journal* (Joseph, 1984) reported that the number of K-1 visas, which are for fiancees of American citizens, issued to Asians increased from 34 in 1970 to 3,428 in 1983. Of course, nearly all of the visas were issued to Asian women. One correspondence service reported that it introduced about 2,000 American grooms to Asian brides between 1980 and 1985 (Small & Mathison, 1985). Many of these mail-order brides are Filipino, as many as 75% according to one source (Mochizuki, 1987). Another source estimated that in 1984 alone some 7,000 Filipino women married Australians, Europeans, and Americans through this mechanism (Villapando, 1989). These women are most likely to turn to a correspondence marriage as a way to escape the poverty and lack of economic opportunity in the Philippines (Japanese American Citizens League, 1985).

The whole practice of having mail-order bride catalogs is fraught with controversy. The Japanese American Citizens League (1985) highlighted some of the legal and ethical issues surrounding mail-order brides, including the perpetuation of negative racial and sexual stereotypes of Asian women and their possible exploitation. Indeed, there are reports of mail-order brides being abused by their husbands, in addition to a few sensationalized accounts of these brides being murdered by their husbands (Villapando, 1989). Many Filipino mail-order brides who sought counseling at the Asian Counseling and Referral Service in Seattle were found to be from "isolated rural areas of the Philippines and could not speak English" (Mochizuki, 1987).

Lin (1991) recently compared intermarried Asian women who had met and married American husbands through correspondence catalogs (89% of whom were Filipino women) and intermarried Asian women who had met and married American husbands through conventional means. The two types of couples reported similar levels of marital satisfaction. However, the mail-order brides reported more physical abuse by husbands (17%) than the conventionally married women (7%). Furthermore, 15% of the mail-order brides reported receiving psychological abuse from their husbands, compared to none of the conventionally married women. Finally, 53% of the mail-order brides reported psychological distress, in comparison to

47% of the conventionally married women. It seems that this type of intermarriage is much more susceptible to marital conflict than conventional marriages.

Filipino American Cultural Values and Family Structure

Cultural Values and Beliefs

The Filipino family structure is built on cultural values that reflect a system of cooperation; it provides a supportive and protective system that members can depend on for a sense of belonging and help when needed. The Filipino family's value of smooth interpersonal relationships discourages outward displays of behavior that might lead to conflict and instead encourages passive nonconfrontation. Filipinos will rarely criticize or complain to others (Affonso, 1978; Guthrie & Jacobs, 1966; Lynch, 1981).

For Filipino families, dependence on, loyalty to, and solidarity of the family and kin group are of the highest priority. The interests or desires of the individual must be sacrificed for the good of the family. Cooperation among family members is stressed over individualism (Bulato, 1981; Tagaki & Ishisaka, 1982). Underlying this strong sense of family is the dominant cultural value of smooth interpersonal relationships (SIR), which permeates and guides the everyday lives and behaviors of Filipinos. Lynch (1981) describes SIR as the way to get along with others without creating open signs of conflict. Open displays of anger or aggression are discouraged, whereas displays of passive cooperative behavior are encouraged. SIR serve to bind the family and create a system of support and cooperation among its members. SIR are primarily maintained through four means: reciprocal obligation (*utang ng loob*), shame (*hiya*), going along with (*Pakikisama*), and protection of self-esteem (*amor proprio*).

Binding relationships are created through reciprocal obligations, where the moral principle dictates that when a favor or some service has been received, it must be returned (Almirol, 1982). It is within the family unit that *utang ng loob* manifests its greatest strength and obligation. Because reciprocal obligation is generally conducted through the exchange of services rather than material goods, there is never any way of knowing whether or not a debt has been paid. Duff and Arthur (1980) reported that the failure to meet obligations brings the feeling of guilt, which can threaten the individual's psychological well-being. *Utang ng loob* is a form of social control that assures the individual of help and protection. If the individual expects support from others, he or she must in turn be prepared to return it or suffer *hiya*.

Loosely translated, *hiya* means shame; it is experienced when the individual has failed at an intended goal or done something that results in disapproval by the family or others (Almirol, 1982). The desire to avoid *hiya* is attributed to the social norm of conformity. *Hiya* serves to maintain the importance of the group over the individual.

Related to *hiya* is *amor proprio*, which refers to one's self-esteem. Filipinos are very sensitive to criticism and are easily humiliated (Lynch, 1981). Being criticized can be taken as a personal insult. Affronts to *amor proprio* may require an aggressive action to protect the self. However, the value of *hiya* also functions to repress aggressive behavior and to protect the self against the shaming of others. Filipinos are careful not to criticize, complain about, or directly question others.

The final value to maintain SIR is *Pakikisama*, which means going along with others, even if one must contradict one's own desires. *Pakikisama* assures that good feelings are maintained and cooperation is practiced. It is through this value that the individual will sacrifice himself or herself for the family—regardless of personal interests, desires, and others outside the family unit.

Family Structure

The Filipino family is structured differently from other Asian groups in the distribution of authority and power. This difference is partly rooted in the indigenous Filipino culture prior to the Spanish cultural influence. Age is important in the family hierarchy, but it does not automatically translate into authority. Filipino elders are respected and viewed as wise, but do not maintain an ascribed authority over younger family members, as is characteristic of most other Asian groups. If possible, the elderly will contribute to the educational expenses of grandchildren and assist in household chores and caring for young children. Most children feel responsible for taking care of their elderly parents (Peterson, 1978).

Unlike other Asian groups, family authority is not patriarchal, but more egalitarian, where husband and wife share almost equally in financial and family decisions (Andres & Illada-Andres, 1987; Tayuzpay & Hillman-Guerro, 1969; Yu & Liu, 1980). Unlike Judeo-Christian explanations of Eve being created from the rib of Adam, a Filipino legend has both man and woman emerging simultaneously from a large bamboo tube (Andres & Illada-Andres, 1987). Filipino descendants are traced bilaterally through both parents.

Kinship Relationships

Kinship relationships are highly valued and are regarded as familial relationships whether by blood, marriage, or ritual kinship (Almirol, 1982; Guthrie, 1968; Holinstiener, 1981; Lynch, 1981; Peterson, 1978). Family membership is traced as far as to third cousins, but rarely beyond. The 1990 U.S. census shows that one Filipino American family has an average of 0.59 nonnuclear family members residing with them, the second-highest figure next to the Vietnamese among the six major Asian groups (U.S. Bureau of the Census, 1993a, p. 125). This indicates the great importance placed on kin ties by Filipino Americans. For Filipinos the kin group takes precedence over persons outside the group, the community, and laws. When a kin member is threatened, the family will rally around the individual to provide protection and support. Through cultural values such as reciprocal obligation and the structure of nuclear, extended, and fictive family relationships brought with them from the Philippines, recent Filipino immigrants provide support to one another in their early stage of adjustment to American society.

Fictive relatives are brought into the family through the *compadre* (co-parent) system. Fictive relatives are incorporated into the kinship network through religious rites of passage: baptism, confirmation, and marriage (Affonso, 1978). The *compadre* system is a legacy of Spanish colonial Catholicism, which complemented Filipino cultural values of family and community. This system is characterized by reciprocal obligations and increases the number of people in the support network the individual can draw upon. Godparents are sometimes expected to contribute to the child's education, provide financial assistance, and be attentive. The *compadre* system extends and binds familial ties, loyalties, and interdependence among people in the community. The early Filipino immigrants to the United States, between 1920 and 1936, made functional use of this practice. The absence of Filipino women and antimiscegenation laws prevented the early Filipino immigrants from establishing normal families. Coming from a society that placed a high value on familial relationships, the *compadre* system helped many single men to become incorporated into a family system.

Marital and Family Adjustment

Immigration to a new country entails a multitude of life changes for the individual. The immigrant must adjust to new values, norms, and patterns of interaction that may conflict with previous patterns of socialization. He or she must also cope with loss of familial and interpersonal supports and structural adjustment, such as problems with language, employment, and housing (Warheit, Vega, Auth, & Meinhardt, 1985).

In addition to the normal expected life transitions and stresses arising from daily life in technological society, the life changes associated with the immigrant experience represent potentially new psychological stressors that the immigrant must confront. Regardless of the impetus for immigration, the immigrant is vulnerable to extreme stress as a consequence of the immigration experience. Studies of immigrant stress have shown that there is a strong correlation between immigration and psychopathology (Suana, 1970; Warheit et al., 1985) and between the acculturative process and stress (Padilla, 1986). For Filipino families, the acculturation process creates familial conflict within the conjugal relationship and between parents and children.

Marital Relationships

The acculturation process, first of all, contributes to stress between spouses. Traditional Filipino values of smooth interpersonal relationships and spousal norms tend to discourage confrontive and open verbal communications. However, once in the United States, the pressure of being a new immigrant may place new demands on traditional styles of communication. The acculturative process introduces new values and roles that may conflict with the old ones and strain marital relationships. In his study of Filipino immigrant couples, Card (1985) reports that verbal communication between spouses is not as frequent as it was in the Philippines. Moreover, communication skills of the more personal type are not highly developed among Filipino immigrant couples. Spouses are hesitant to confront one another with problems that involve just themselves, although they discuss personal problems involving their children. Verbal communication that is deemphasized may become dysfunctional in a new situation that requires more direct and confrontive negotiation, understanding, or clarification (Agbayani-Siewert, 1986). In a survey of social service agencies serving Asian Americans in Los Angeles County, changes in child-rearing practices and spousal sex role expectations were found to be a major source of marital role strain and domestic violence among Filipino immigrant women (Agbayani-Siewert, 1991).

Filipino Children and Adjustment

Traditionally, Filipino children are perceived as a valuable gift and are expected to be obedient to and dependent on the family (Guthrie & Jacobs, 1966). As with most immigrant groups, Filipino children acculturate at a faster rate than their parents, whereas their parents continue to function using more traditional values brought with them from the Philippines. The young want to try out the new values and system, which may lead to conflict with their parents and among young people themselves. Kieth and Barranda (1969) report that Filipino young people are less autonomous and more dependent on the primary group than their American counterparts. The study shows that Filipino adolescents have later age norms for independent behavior than American young people. For example, they tend to stay out late, go steady, become engaged, and marry 3 to 7 years later than American youth. The Filipino family must cope with not only a generational gap, but also a cultural one.

Research on Filipino Americans suggests that generational conflict most often arises when parents rely on their traditional hierarchical authority and demand respect and obedience from their children (Morales, 1974; Tamayo-Lott, 1980). At the same time, their children—who have simultaneously been raised with the competing American values of independence, individualism, and assertiveness—tend to challenge their parents' roles (Forman, 1980; Morales, 1974). Parents then intensify their traditional hierarchical stance and demand more compliance from their children. This rigidity leads to the disruption of family communication (Santos, 1983).

In a study of cultural adaptation by Filipino families, Heras and Revilla (in press) found that mothers of less acculturated students had higher levels of family satisfaction than those of more acculturated students. They speculated that because Filipino mothers acculturate at a slower pace than their children, when their children behave in a more traditional manner the family structure is less likely to experience tension. Conversely, when their children behave in a more Americanized manner, the Filipino mothers experience less satisfaction with family life.

The need for economic survival has also created problems for the Filipino family. The majority of Filipino households with children have both parents working full-time. Most Filipino immigrants, like other Asian immigrants, tend to depend on strong family support to make economic adjustments, and working parents spend little time with children. Filipino community leaders and social service workers in Los Angeles have reported a growing practice of sending problematic adolescents back to the Philippines to live with extended family members. The lack of parental supervision, the need for economic survival, and the stress deriving from acculturation gaps compel some parents to seek a solution that removes the adolescent from the home and draws upon the family support system back in the Philippines (Agbayani-Siewert, 1990). The problems faced by Filipino Americans are exacerbated by lack of understanding and of culturally relevant services.

Conclusion

Filipino Americans are one of the fastest-growing minority groups and one of the largest Asian ethnic groups in the United States today. Yet they remain one of least understood and researched minority populations. One possible explanation for this lack of attention is that recent Filipino immigrants are often characterized as a highly professional and educated group on economic parity with whites. They are viewed as having relatively few problems and seem to fit the "model minority" stereotype. Second, Filipinos do not generally engage in political, social, and economic activities that would draw attention to themselves as a group. Overall, Filipino Americans do not organize as a cohesive population around political, economic, or ethnic issues as do other Asian groups. Instead, they belong to numerous competing organizations based on dialects, regional origins, and kinship ties. In addition, there are few Filipino scholars in academia, which has also contributed to lack of knowledge and understanding of Filipino Americans. In California, where the majority of Filipino Americans are settled, only a few Filipino scholars are working at colleges and universities. Most recently, there seems to have been an increase in research on Filipinos, but they are often treated as a comparison group with the focus on another Asian group.

Although the literature depicts the new Filipino immigrants as success-ful, there is evidence that native-born Filipinos and Filipino immigrants raised in the United States are not faring as well. More research that focuses on Filipino Americans as a population with unique experiences, issues, and problems is badly needed.

References

Affonso, D. (1978). The Filipino American. In A. L. Clark (Ed.), *Culture in childbearing health professionals* (pp. 128-153). Philadelphia: F. A. Davis.

Agbayani-Siewert, P. (1986). *Social service utilization of Filipino Americans in Los Angeles.* Unpublished Manuscript, the School of Social Welfare, University of California, Los Angeles.

Agbayani-Siewert, P. (1990). *Filipino American families: Practice guidelines for the social work practitioners.* Paper presented at the 36th Annual Meeting of the Council of Social Work Education, New Orleans.

Agbayani-Siewert, P. (1991). *Filipino American social role strain, self-esteem, locus of control, social networks, coping, stress and mental health outcome.* Doctoral dissertation, University of California, Los Angeles.

Agbayani-Siewert, P., & Jones, I. (in press). Filipino American women: Family and work. *Journal of Economics and Family.*

Akamine, M. (1990, April). English-only policy at Harborview withdrawn. *International Examiner,* p. 1.

Alcantra, R. R. (1975). *A guided study course—American subcultures: Filipino Americans.* Honolulu: University of Hawaii.

Alegado, D. T. (1991). *The social reproduction of the Filipino community in Hawaii.* Paper presented at the 8th National Conference of the Association for Asian American Studies, May, Honolulu.

Almirol, E. B. (1978). Filipino voluntary associations: Balancing social pressures and ethnic images. *Ethnic Groups, 2,* 65-92.

Almirol, E. B. (1982). Rights and obligations in Filipino American families. *Journal of Comparative Family Studies, 13*(3), 291-306.

Almirol, E. B. (1988). Exclusion and institutional barriers in the university system: The Filipino experience. In G. Okihiro, S. Hune, A. Hansen, & J. Liu (Eds.), *Reflections on shattered windows: Promises and prospects for Asian American studies* (pp. 59-67). Pullman: Washington State University Press.

American survey: The million who are there, but have not quite arrived. (1986, January 25). *The Economist.*

Andres, T., & Illada-Andres, P. (1987). *Understanding the Filipino.* Quezon City, the Philippines: New Day Publishers.

Bello, M., & Reyes, V. (1986-1987). Filipino Americans and the Marcos overthrow: The transformation of political consciousness. *Amerasia Journal, 13,* 73-84.

Bulato, J. (1981). The Manileno mainsprings. In F. Lynch & A. de Guzman, III (Eds.), *Four readings in Filipino values* (pp. 70-118). Quezon City, the Philippines: Ateneo de Manila University Press.

Bulosan, C. (1943). *America is in the heart.* Seattle: University of Washington Press.

Cabezas, A., Shinagawa, L., & Kawaguchi, G. (1986-1987). New inquiries into the socioeconomic status of Pilipino Americans in California. *Amerasia Journal, 13,* 1-22.

Card, J. (1985). Correspondence of data gathered from husband and wife: Implications for family planning studies. *Social Biology, 25*(3), 196-204.

Carino, B. (1987). Impacts of emigration on sending countries. In J. Fawcett & B. Carino (Eds.), *Pacific bridges: The new immigration from Asia and Pacific Islands* (pp. 305-326). Staten Island, NY: Center for Migration Studies.

Carino, B., Fawcett, J., Gardner, R., & Arnold, F. (1990). *The New Filipino immigrants to the United States: Increasing diversity and change* (The East-West Population Institute Paper Series No. 115). Honolulu: East-West Center Population Institute.

Cordova, F. (1983). *Filipinos: Forgotten Asian Americans.* Dubuque, IA: Kendall/Hunt.

DeWitt, H. (1978). The Filipino labor union: The Salinas lettuce strike of 1934. *Amerasia Journal, 5,* 1-21.

Duff, D., & Arthur, R. J. (1980). Between two worlds: Filipinos in the U.S. Navy. In S. Sue & N. Wagner (Eds.), *Asian Americans: Psychological perspectives* (pp. 202-211). Palo Alto, CA: Science and Behavior Books.

Empeno, H. (1976). Anti-miscegenation laws and the Pilipino. In J. Quinsaat (Ed.), *Letters in exile: An introductory reader on the history of Pilipinos in America* (pp. 3-71). Los Angeles: UCLA Asian American Studies Center.

Enriquez, V. (1991). Youth gangs: A submerged level of discourse. In Filipino Association of University Women (Ed.), *From Mabuhay to Aloha: The Filipinos in Hawaii* (pp. 174-183). Manila: Benipayo Press.

Espina, M. (1982). *Readings on Filipinos in Louisiana.* Privately printed.

Forman, S. (1980). Hawaii's immigrants from the Philippines. In J. McDermott, T. Tseng, & T. Maretzki (Eds.), *People and cultures of Hawaii* (pp. 155-183). Honolulu: University of Hawaii Press.

Gans, H. (1979). Symbolic ethnicity: The future of ethnic groups and cultures in America. *Ethnic and Racial Studies, 2,* 1-20.

Gardner, R. W., Robey, B., & Smith, P. G. (1985). Asian Americans: Growth, change, and diversity. *Population Bulletin, 40*(4), 1-43.

Gordon, M. (1964). *Assimilation in American life.* New York: Oxford University Press.

Griffiths, S. (1978). Emigrant and returned migrant investment in a Philippine village. *Amerasia Journal, 5,* 45-67.

Guthrie, G. M. (1968). The Philippine temperament. In G. Guthrie (Ed.), *Six perspectives on the Philippines* (pp. 49-83). Manila: Bookmark.

Guthrie, G. M., & Jacobs, P. (1966). *Childbearing and personality development in the Philippines.* University Park: Pennsylvania State University.

Heras, P., & Revilla, L. (in press). Acculturation, generational status, and family environment of Pilipino Americans: A study of cultural adaptation. *Family Therapy.*

Holinstiener, M. R. (1981). Reciprocity in the lowland Philippines. In F. Lynch & A. de Guzman, III (Eds.), *Four readings on Philippine values* (4th ed., pp. 69-92). Quezon City, the Philippines: Ateneo de Manila University Press.

Japanese American Citizens League. (1985, February 22). JACL report on Asian bride catalogs. *Pacific Citizen,* pp. 18-19.

Jiobu, R. (1988). *Ethnicity and assimilation.* Albany: State University of New York Press.

Joseph, R. (1984, January 24). American men find Asian brides fit their unliberated bill. *Wall Street Journal,* pp. 1, 22.

Karnow, S. (1989). *In our image: America's empire in the Philippines.* New York: Random House.

Keefe, S. (1980). Acculturation and the extended family among urban Mexican Americans. In A. M. Padilla (Ed.), *Acculturation: Theory, models, and some new findings* (pp. 85-110). Boulder, CO: Westview.

Kieth, R., & Barranda, E. (1969). Age independence norms in American and Filipino adolescents. *The Journal of Social Psychology, 78,* 285-286.

Kim, B. L. (1978). *The Asian Americans: Changing patterns, changing needs.* New Jersey: The Association of Korean Christian Scholars in North America.

Kitano, H. (1980). *Race relations.* Englewood Cliffs, NJ: Prentice Hall.

Kitano, H., & Daniels, R. (1988). *Asian Americans: Emerging minorities.* Englewood Cliffs, NJ: Prentice Hall.

Kitano, H., Young, W., Chai, L., & Hatanaka, H. (1984). Asian American intermarriage. *Journal of Marriage and the Family, 46*(1), 179-190.

Lin, J. (1991). Satisfaction and conflict in Asian American correspondence marriages. *Focus, 5,* 1-2.

Liu, J., Ong, P., & Rosenstein, C. (1991). Filipino immigration to the United States. *International Migration Review, 25,* 487-513.

Lynch, F. (1981). Social acceptance reconsidered. In F. Lynch & A. de Guzman, III (Eds.), *Four readings on Philippine values* (pp. 1-68). Quezon City, the Philippines: Ateneo de Manila University Press.

Mangiafico, L. (1988). *Contemporary American immigrants: Patterns of Filipino, Korean, and Chinese settlement in the United States.* New York: Praeger.

Manzon, M. (1938). *The strange case of the Filipinos in the United States.* New York: American Committee for Protection of the Foreign Born.

Masson, J., & Guimary, D. (1981). Pilipinos and unionization of the Alaskan canned salmon industry. *Amerasia Journal, 8,* 1-30.

Melendy, H. B. (1977). *Asians in America: Filipinos, Koreans, and East Indians.* Boston: Twayne.

Min, P. G. (1986-1987). Filipino and Korean immigrants in small business: A comparative analysis. *Amerasia Journal, 13,* 53-71.

Minocha, U. (1987). South Asian immigrants: Trends and impacts on the sending and receiving societies. In J. Fawcett & B. Carino (Eds.), *Pacific bridges: The new immigration from Asia and Pacific Islands* (pp. 347-376). Staten Island, NY: Center for Migration Studies.

Mochizuki, K. (1987, May 7). I think Oriental women are just great. *International Examiner,* p. 13.

Morales, R. (1974). *Makibaka, the Filipino-American struggle.* Darby, MT: Mountain View.

Office of Budget, Institutional Planning, and Analysis, UCLA. (1987, November 12). *Retention and graduation rates of entering cohorts.* Unpublished report.

Padilla, A. M. (1980). The role of cultural awareness and ethnic royalty. In A. M. Padilla (Ed.), *Acculturation: Theory, models, and some new findings* (pp. 49-84). Boulder, CO: Westview.

Padilla, A. M. (1986). Acculturation and stress among immigrants and later generation individuals. In D. Frick (Ed.), *The quality of urban life.* New York: Walter de Gruyter.

Peterson, R. (1978). *The elder Filipino.* San Diego, CA: Camponile.

Pido, L. L. L. (1986). *The Pilipinos in America: Macro/micro dimensions of immigration and integration.* Staten Island, NY: Center for Migration Studies.

Racism and English only in Ramona. (1989, November 19). *Pacific Ties,* p. 21.

Revilla, L. (1989). Dating and marriage preferences among Filipino Americans. *Journal of the Asian American Psychological Association, 13,* 72-79.

Revilla, L. (1993). Brown and proud: The ethnic identity of Pilipino American college students. In L. Revilla, G. Nomura, S. Wong, & S. Hune (Eds.), *Bearing dreams, shaping visions: Asian Pacific American perspectives* (pp. 107-124). Pullman: Washington State University Press.

Saito, L. (1993). Contrasting patterns of adaptation: Japanese Americans and Chinese immigrants in Monterey Park. In L. Revilla, G. Nomura, S. Wong, & S. Hune (Eds.), *Bearing dreams, shaping visions: Asian Pacific American perspectives* (pp. 33-43). Pullman: Washington State University Press.

Santos, R. (1983). The social and emotional development of Filipino American children. In G. Powell (Ed.), *The psychological development of minority group children* (pp. 131-146). New York: Brunner/Mazel.

Schwertfeger, M. (1982). Interethnic marriage and divorce in Hawaii: A panel study of 1968 first marriages. *Marriage and the Family Review, 5,* 45-59.

Sharma, M. (1980). Pinoy in paradise: Environment and adaptation of Pilipinos in Hawaii, 1906-1946. *Amerasia Journal, 7*(2), 91-118.

Small, M., & Mathison, D. (1985, September 16). For men who want old-fashioned girls... *People,* pp. 23, 127-129.

Suana, V. D. (1970). Immigration, migration, and mental illness: A review of the literature with special emphasis on schizophrenia. In E. B. Brady (Ed.), *Behavior in new environments* (pp. 291-352). Beverly Hill, CA: Sage.

Szapocznik, J., & Kurtines, W. (1980). Acculturation, biculturalism, and adjustment among Cuban children. In A. M. Padilla (Ed.), *Acculturation: Theory, models, and some new findings* (pp. 139-159). Boulder, CO: Westview.

Tagaki, C., & Ishisaka, T. (1982). Social work with Asian- and Pacific-Americans. In J. Green (Ed.), *Cultural awareness in the human services* (pp. 138-144). Englewood Hills, NJ: Prentice Hall.

Takaki, R. (1989). *Strangers from a different shore: A history of Asian Americans.* Boston: Little, Brown.

Tamayo-Lott, J. (1980). Migration of a mentality: The Pilipino community. In S. Sue, N. Wagner, & R. Endo (Eds.), *Asian-Americans: Social and psychological perspectives II* (pp. 132-140). Palo Alto, CA: Science and Behavior Books.

Tayuzpay, C., & Hillman-Guerro, G. S. (1969). The Filipino women: A study of multiple roles. *Journal of Asian and African Studies, 4*(1), 18-29.

The University of Hawaii Task Force on Filipinos. (1988). *Pamantasan.* Honolulu: University of Hawaii Task Force on Filipinos.

Urban Associates. (1974). *A study of selected socioeconomic characteristics of ethnic minorities based on the 1970 census: Vol. 2. Asian Americans.* Washington, DC: U.S. Government Printing Office.

U.S. Bureau of the Census. (1983). *1980 census of population, general population characteristics, the United States summary* (PC80-1-B1). Washington, DC: U.S. Government Printing Office.

U.S. Bureau of the Census. (1993a). *1990 census of population, general population characteristics, the United States (CP-1-1). Washington, DC: U.S. Government Printing Office.*

U.S. Bureau of the Census. (1993b). *1990 census of population, Asians and Pacific Islanders in the United States* (CP-3-5). Washington, DC: U.S. Government Printing Office.

U.S. Bureau of the Census. (1994). *1990 census of population, general social and economic characteristics, the United States* (CP-2-1). Washington, DC: U.S. Government Printing Office.

Villapando, V. (1989). The business of selling mail-order brides. In Asian Women United of California (Eds.), *Making waves* (pp. 318-326). Boston, MA: Beacon.

Virata, J. (1989, Summer/Fall). The cutting edge: Redefining affirmative action: A case study of Pilipinos. *Crosscurrents*, pp. 8-9.

Warheit, G., Vega, W., Auth, J., & Meinhardt, K. (1985). Mexican American immigration and mental health: A comparative analysis of psychosocial stress and dysfunction. In W. Vega & M. Miranda (Eds.), *Stress and Hispanic mental health: Relating research to service delivery* (pp. 76-109). Rockville, MD: National Institute of Mental Health.

White, C. (1986). Residential segregation among Asians in Long Beach: Japanese, Chinese, Filipino, Korean, Indian, Vietnamese, Hawaiian, Guamian, and Samoan. *Sociology and Social Research, 70,* 266-267.

Woo, D. (1985). The socioeconomic status of Asian American women in the labor force: An alternative view. *Sociological Perspectives, 28,* 307-338.

Yu, E. (1980). Filipino migration and community organization in the United States. *California Sociologist, 3,* 76-102.

Yu, E., & Liu, W. T. (1980). *Fertility and kinship in the Philippines.* Notre Dame, IN: University of Notre Dame Press.

7

Asian Indian Americans

MANJU SHETH

The 1990 census reported that there were 815,447 Asian Indians in the United States, making it the fourth-largest Asian American group. This figure represents a remarkable growth rate: The Indian population doubled in the 1980s and grew by 10 times between 1970 and 1990. Although a few thousand Indians, mostly farmers, first came to the United States in the early 20th century, most Indians in the United States have immigrated since the reformed 1965 Immigration Act took effect. The new Indian immigrants consist mainly of college-educated, urban, middle-class professional young men and women of religious, regional, and linguistic diversity.

Research on the Asian Indian immigrant experience in the United States is very limited. Neither American nor ethnic Indian scholars have given this group sufficient attention (Hess, 1976; Nandi, 1980). This chapter is based on public documents, previous studies, articles published in Indian ethnic media, organizational resources, and my own observations. It is organized around the following questions:

When and why did Asian Indians immigrate to the United States?

How were Indian nationals treated by the host society and what were their reactions?

What is the pattern of their residential distribution across the nation?

What was their socioeconomic profile upon arriving and how has it changed subsequently?

How did their ethnic identity change?

What contributions, if any, have Asian Indians made to American society and what are their future prospects?

History of Indian Immigration to the United States

India is home to almost 900 million people, representing 16% of the current world population. Although endowed with a rich history of civilization, Asian Indians have often had to seek work in other lands, partly as a result of internal political conflicts and partly due to the exploitation of natural resources and Indian people by foreign invaders, particularly by British colonialism, which lasted for 200 years (Minocha, 1987; Gupta, 1979).

The Indian diaspora has spread like a banyan tree from South Asia to all over the world for more than 2,000 years (Tinker, 1977). By 1981 about 13.5 million persons of Indian origin were living outside India (Madhavan, 1985). Any discussion of India before 1947 should include the entire Indian subcontinent, because Pakistan and Bangladesh were part of India until then, and all people of Indian origin were known as East Indians.

Throughout history diverse groups from India came to the United States for different purposes: students, scholars, diplomats, political activists, religious leaders, merchants, visitors, sojourners, immigrants, and refugees (Helweg & Helweg, 1990; Kritz, 1987). For the convenience of analysis, the history of Asian Indian immigration can be roughly divided into two phases: (a) the early immigrants from 1907 to 1924 and (b) the post-1965 immigration.

Early Immigration

Although Indians did not emigrate to the United States in large numbers until 1904, they arrived in North America as early as 1750. A man from Madras may have been the first Indian to travel to the United States. A group of approximately 200 Parsi (Zoroastrian faith) merchants designed a plan to emigrate from Bombay, perhaps inspired by the earlier emigration of Gujaratis to other British colonies. Also, isolated individuals such as sailors were brought to the United States as indentured servants by captains of merchant marine ships in New England; some of them were sold into slavery and moved to Salem, Massachusetts, as well as to other parts of the Atlantic seaboard and the South (Jensen, 1988, p. 12; Chandrasekhar, 1982a).

During the period between 1820 and 1870, 196 Indians, mainly from the state of Punjab, came to this country. Indian merchants were reported in Philadelphia in 1889 (Jensen, 1988). The number of Indians in the United States reached 5,000 by 1910, and a total of 8,000 more Indians had arrived by 1924. However, due to the enforcement of the Asiatic Exclusion provision of the national origins quota system, only a little more than 100

Indians came to the United States during the 1930s. More than three quarters of the East Indians in the United States in the early 20th century came from Punjab; others came from Gujarat, Oudh, and Bengal (Banerjee, 1969, p. 2). Most Indian immigrants came directly from India to the Pacific coast, and others came through East Asia.

The early Indian immigrants can be divided into two groups: (a) farmers and laborers and (b) middle-class students, elites, and political refugees. The middle-aged farmers and laborers from Punjab were mainly attracted to Canada. Two thirds of them were of the Sikh faith, and Muslims and Hindus constituted the other third. Nevertheless they were collectively labeled "Hindoos," because most (85%) of the Indian people were Hindus (Takaki, 1989, pp. 294-314). They were turned away from Canada several times (Kurian, 1991; Mazumdar, 1984b). Finally, their entry was legally barred in 1909. As a challenge, the Sikhs chartered a Japanese ship, the *Komagata Maru,* and sailed directly from India to Vancouver in 1914. Sadly, they were not allowed to disembark and were forced to return home after 2 months in port. From 1908 to 1920 a total of 5,391 Indians were admitted to the United States. More than 3,000 Indians were prohibited from entering, and nearly 1,700 went back to India (Das, 1923, pp. 10-14). The Indians who were admitted worked in lumber mills, on vegetable and fruit farms, and on railroads.

A small number of early middle-class entrants, mostly nonimmigrant Indians of various statuses, trickled in throughout the 19th and early 20th centuries (Mazumdar, 1984b; Melendy, 1977, p. 202). Most of them settled in major urban centers on the East Coast. Many returned to India, but some who remained practiced their professions and married white women. Because of their high socioeconomic status and English language skills, they enjoyed respect and power in the community.

During the 1920s more than 1,000 students arrived and settled, largely on the West Coast. As many as 37 Indian elite activist students and other leaders developed a movement for Indian freedom called Gadar. More students were seen on American campuses after India's independence in 1947. Their main goal was to help build their country by learning science and technology in the United States (Helweg & Helweg, 1990).

The trading *jatis* (endogamous hereditary social groups; *caste* is a misnomer) of India had been involved in trade with foreign countries since ancient times (Tinker, 1977, p. 3). By the turn of the 20th century, there were 500 Indian traders in the United States, including several Parsi merchants in the Northeast (Jensen, 1988) and other export-import businessmen in Los Angeles. Some of the well-known earlier Indian merchants were Jagjit Singh, Dalip Singh Saund (who was also the first and only Asia-born congressman), and the Watumal brothers (founders of a very successful business group in Hawaii that continues to thrive today). Most of these early merchants and Sikh agribusinessmen financially supported India's independence movement in this country. Although small, the early middle class played a significant role in the intellectual exchange and struggle for rights in India and the United States.

The Indians' decision to emigrate at the turn of the century was influenced by a variety of factors operating at individual, national, and international levels (Chan, 1991; Helweg & Helweg, 1990; Jensen, 1988). One important factor was the financial hardships caused by British colonial oppression in India. The British hampered the development of colonized nations, displacing people from their traditional economies and forcing them to emigrate (Gupta, 1979; Jensen, 1988; Mazumdar, 1984a, pp. 316-317). In addition, the opportunity to enhance the Indian independence movement was an important factor for the emigration of earlier Indians.

As their numbers increased beginning in 1907, a series of discriminatory measures were taken against Indians by the U.S. and Canadian governments. White workers, union officials, politicians, and the media became hostile and pressured the state and federal governments to pass exclusionary laws against Indians. The exclusionary policy of 1917 (the Barred Zone Act), which was followed by the Asian Exclusion Act of 1924, prohibited Indians from immigrating to the United States (Arnold, Minocha, & Fawcett, 1987, p. 105). Such restrictive measures ended in 1946 when Indians, after many court battles and lobbying activities, attained the right of naturalization by virtue of the Luce/Celler Bill (Chandrasekhar, 1982a; Melendy, 1977; U.S. Commission on Civil Rights, 1992).

Although a few thousand students and visitors came between 1948 and 1964, this interim period remained relatively quiet. Many women in Japan, South Korea, the Philippines, and South Vietnam married U.S. servicemen stationed in those countries and subsequently immigrated to the United States as spouses of U.S. citizens. They constituted the majority of Asian immigrants during the interim period. There was no military connection between India and the United States during the Cold War. This is the main reason why there was no substantial Indian immigration to the United States during that time.

Post-1965 Immigration

India has become one of the major beneficiaries of the 1965 Immigration Act. In 1965, 582 Indians came to the United States as formal immigrants.

Table 7.1 Immigrants From India and Other South Asian Countries, 1970-
1990

Year	Total	India N	India %	Pakistan N	Pakistan %	Bangladesh N	Bangladesh %	Sri Lanka N	Sri Lanka %
1970	11,884	10,114	85.1	1,528	12.9			226	1.9
1975	19,297	15,773	81.7	2,620	13.6	404	2.1	432	2.2
1980	27,912	22,608	81.0	4,265	15.3	532	1.9	397	1.4
1985	33,469	26,026	77.8	5,744	17.2	1,146	3.4	553	1.6
1989	42,112	31,175	74.0	8,000	19.0	2,180	5.2	757	1.8
1990	42,624	30,667	72.0	9,729	22.8	1,252	2.9	976	2.3

SOURCE: Immigration and Naturalization Service (1965-1977, 1978-1989; *Statistical Yearbook*, 1990).

The number gradually increased in the early 1970s. Since 1976, it has leveled off to an average of 20,000 per year (see Table 7.1). The Indian population in the United States increased to more than 800,000 in the 1990 census. Moreover, about 70,000 Indian refugees from business and professional classes, expelled by the Idi Amin regime in Uganda in the early 1970s, were admitted to this country under a special clause. Some of them have been invited back to Uganda to rebuild the collapsed economy. Many overseas Indians also immigrated from other countries, particularly the Caribbean Islands and the British Commonwealth countries. As shown in Table 7.1, Pakistan, Bangladesh, and Sri Lanka have also sent a large number of immigrants to the United States since1965.

India has been one of the major source countries of foreign students in the United States during recent years. Of the more than 400,000 foreign students who entered the United States during 1990-1991, about 7% were from India (Dodge, 1991), making India fourth among the 67 countries that sent students to the United States during that period. Because of the professional prestige of science-related occupations and their practical applications for India, engineering was the most popular field of study among Indian students until the 1970s. However, recently the fields of business and information science have replaced engineering. Unlike the patriotic motive for the freedom and economic development of their home country, post-1965 students have as their primary goal enhancing their own professional careers.

Many Indians who have come to the United States as nonimmigrants have adjusted their status after a brief stay. More than 50% of the Indians officially counted as immigrants were already physically present in the

United States and adjusted their status to permanent residents (Arnold et al., 1987, p. 118). Students have composed a large proportion of Indian status adjusters. For example, 80% of the 1,789 Indian status adjusters between 1966 and 1967 came to the United States as students (Immigration and Naturalization Service, 1966, 1967). More immigrants from India and China than from any other Asian country have entered as students and adjusted their status to permanent residents. Indians residing in the United States have a better opportunity to become citizens by transferring their status in person. One result of this situation is that it has severely restricted direct immigration from India.

This brings us to the issue of the unfairness of the current U.S. immigration policy for countries with a large population. The quota limitation of 20,000 persons annually permitted per country discriminates against India, which has nearly 900 million people, in comparison to small countries such as Jamaica.

Post-1965 Indian immigrants have generally come from large cities in all parts of India. They represent several religious and linguistic groups, although the majority are Hindus. The major religions of Indian immigrants include Hinduism, Islam, Sikhism, Christianity, and Jainism. India's educated emigrants to the United States originated primarily from three states: about 60% from Gujarat, 30% from Punjab, and 10% from Kerala (Helweg & Helweg, 1990, pp. 11-17). Another important characteristic of post-1965 Indian immigrants is that most of them are fluent in English. As a result of the British colonization, English is still spoken as one of the official languages in India.

Residential Patterns of Asian Indians

The early Indian immigrants, like other Asian immigrants, were concentrated in the West Coast, particularly in California. However, as discussed in Chapter 2, the post-1965 Asian immigrants have settled more widely throughout the United States, reducing their level of concentration on the West Coast. This tendency to stay away from the West seems to be most obvious in the residential pattern of Asian Indians. As shown in Table 7.2, nearly 20% of Indian Americans have settled in California, and only another 3% reside in other West Coast states. Thus only 23% of Indian Americans live in the West. Although California has a proportionally smaller number of Indians compared to other Asian groups, in the decade of the 1980s this state experienced a higher level of Indian population increase

Table 7.2 Distribution of Asian Indians by Regions and Major States in 1980 and 1990

	1980		1990		Increase	
	N	%	N	%	N	%
U.S. Total	361,531	100.0	815,447	100.0	453,916	125.6
West	71,992	19.9	188,608	23.1	116,616	162.0
California	57,901	16.0	159,973	19.6	102,072	176.3
Midwest	85,175	23.6	146,211	17.9	61,036	71.7
Illinois	35,749	9.9	64,200	7.8	28,452	79.6
Michigan	14,690	4.1	23,845	2.9	9,155	62.3
Ohio	13,106	3.6	20,848	2.6	7,742	59.1
Northeast	120,758	33.4	285,103	35.0	164,345	136.1
New York	60,505	16.7	140,985	17.3	80,480	133.0
Pennsylvania	15,212	4.2	28,386	3.5	13,184	86.7
New Jersey	29,510	8.2	79,440	9.7	49,930	169.2
South	83,606	23.1	195,525	24.0	111,919	133.9
Texas	22,231	6.1	55,795	6.8	33,564	151.0
Florida	9,144	2.5	31,457	3.9	22,313	244.0
Virginia	8,483	2.3	20,494	2.5	12,011	141.6
Maryland	13,705	3.8	28,330	3.5	14,625	106.7

SOURCE: U.S. Bureau of the Census (1983, Table 62; 1993a, Table 253).

than other states. This suggests that Asian Indians, following the pattern of other Asian groups, may also consolidate in California in the future.

By contrast, the largest proportion, 35%, of Indian Americans reside in the Northeast, and most are in two states: New York and New Jersey. The New York-New Jersey metropolitan area, home to more than 200,000 Indians, can be considered the capital of Asian Indians in the United States. In New York City alone, there are more than 140,00 Indian Americans, making them the second-largest Asian ethnic group following Chinese Americans. Some 17,000 Indians are also settled in Jersey City, New Jersey. The high concentration of Indian immigrants in New York and New Jersey can be explained by the fact that these two states absorbed a large number of Indian immigrant medical professionals in the late 1960s and the early 1970s; following the pattern of chain migration, many other Indian immigrants subsequently settled in the two states.

A large number of Indian Americans have also settled in such states as Illinois, Texas, and Florida. Most Indians in Illinois reside in Chicago. Until the 1965 Immigraion Act was revised in 1976, Chicago absorbed many Indian medical professionals. Whereas the Indian population in Illinois proportionally decreased between 1980 and 1990, it substantially increased in Texas and Florida in the same decade.

Indian grocery stores and other ethnically oriented businesses flourish in Flushing and Jackson Heights (in the Queens borough of New York City), in Edison and Iselin (in central New Jersey), and on Devon Street (in Chicago). However, Asian Indians have not established an Indian ethnic enclave in any city comparable to the Chinatowns in many cities or the Koreatown in Los Angeles. The subethnic diversity characterizing Indian immigrants is a disadvantage for establishing a territorial community. Moreover, because Indian immigrants, like Filipinos, are generally fluent in English, they may not need a territorial community.

Although post-1965 Asian Indians have not formed "Little India" eco-logical ghettos, they have created symbolic communities. They tend to settle around workplaces such as high technology firms, hospitals, univer-sities, and hotels/motels in or around metropolitan areas or along state highways (Helweg & Helweg, 1990; Hsia, 1988). Parallel to their popula-tion growth, Indians have developed places of worship, stores, and other services around their residences. Moreover, property ownership has a special meaning for Asian Indians. They buy hotels, motels, stores, and houses for both living and investment purposes.

A single house can accommodate members of an extended family, a custom continued from India. The Indian family modifies and decorates the interior of the house with images of gods/goddesses and artwork to suit Indian religious and cultural needs. A house also offers privacy and protection from Americans. It is a symbol of permanent residence for Indians living in the United States. Selection of the intended residence is based on pragmatic criteria such as access to work, proximity to the best schools and neighborhoods for their children's education, property values, and proximity to relatives and friends.

Despite friction with a few Americans, Asian Indians have started imprinting their culture on American schools, residential streets, and marketplaces by giving the names of Indian deities such as Laxmi and national leaders like Mahatma Gandhi to shopping centers, squares, and streets in the areas where they live or do business. This practice has been supported by local politicians. India's independence and other holidays are now recognized by local and state political offices. Indians have donated funds to American politicians, universities, and hospitals, which help to increase their clout. Thus the settlement patterns of the Indian community are influenced by and have an impact on American society.

Table 7.3 Percentages of Bachelor's and Master's Degree Holders for Indian and White Americans 25 Years Old and Over, 1990

	Indian Americans			Native Born	U.S. Population
	Immigrants Before 1979	Immigrants 1980-1984	Immigrants 1985-1990		
Bachelor's degree holders	71.1	67.8	42.2	44.0	20.3
Master's degree holders	44.9	27.5	21.7	20.7	7.2

SOURCE: U.S. Bureau of the Census (1993b, Table 3).

Socioeconomic Adjustment of Asian Indians

Education

Indian immigrants who are highly educated had an upper-middle or middle-class professional background prior to immigration. Table 7.3 shows percentages of Indian Americans who received bachelor and master degrees based on the 1990 census. All subgroups of Asian Indians have exceptionally high levels of education compared to the U.S. population. The Indian immigrants admitted to the United States before 1980 in particular are characterized by high educational levels; 71% completed 4 years of college and 45% completed a master's program. This high educational and occupational level of Indian immigrants in the 1970s was due to two factors. First, a large number of Indian physicians, pharmacists, nurses, and other medical professionals were allowed to immigrate to the United States during that time. Second, as previously noted, many Indians who came as foreign students and completed their master's and Ph.D. programs in the United States changed their status to permanent residents.

It is important to note that Indian immigrants admitted in the 1980s, although much more highly educated than the U.S. population, show lower levels of education than their counterparts in the 1970s. Indian immigrants admitted in the late 1980s in particular differ substantially from those admitted in the 1970s; only 22% of the 1985-1990 Indian immigrants earned a master's degree, compared to 45% of the 1970s' Indian immigrants. The substantial drop in Indian immigrants' educational level in recent years can be explained by the drastic decrease in the number of Indian professional immigrants due to 1976 revisions of the immigration law (see Chapter 2). For example, in 1992 only 6% of Indian immigrants

Table 7.4 Percentage Comparison of Indian Americans With White Americans in Occupations, 1990

| | Indian | | | White |
	Total	Native Born	Foreign Born	White
Professional	29.6	22.2	30.0	14.4
Managerial	14.0	10.8	14.1	12.8
Technical & sales	20.0	22.5	19.9	16.1
Administrative support	13.2	17.9	13.0	16.0
Service	8.1	12.1	7.9	12.0
Farm	0.6	0.8	0.6	2.5
Precision, production, & crafts	5.2	5.3	5.2	11.9
Operatives & laborers	9.4	8.5	9.4	14.3

SOURCE: U.S. Bureau of the Census (1993b, Table 4; 1994, Table 45).

were Third Preference professional immigrants and their family members, whereas 86% were admitted based on family reunification (Immigration and Naturalization Service, 1992). As discussed in Chapter 2, this change in immigrants' educational level and socioeconomic background is a trend common to all Asian immigrants.

Occupational Adjustment

The occupational profiles of current South Asian immigrants reflect their high educational attainments. As shown in Table 7.4, 30% of Indian workers were engaged in professional occupations in 1990, compared to only 14% of white workers. Indian Americans are more highly represented in professional occupations than any other immigrant/minority group. Medical professionals make up a large proportion. Health professionals, technologists, and technicians constituted 16.3% of the total Indian workers in 1980 (Barringer, Gardner, & Levin, 1993; U.S. Bureau of the Census, 1983, pp. 1-161). Indians represent the largest foreign health professional group in the United States. Indian professionals also include a large number of engineers and scientists who hold academic positions.

In addition to their education, two other factors contribute to Indians' high occupational levels relative to other Asian immigrants. First, most Indian immigrants do not have serious language barriers and thus have been more successful in maintaining their preimmigrant professional occupations than other highly educated Asian immigrants. Second, a large proportion of Indian immigrants have adjusted their status to permanent residents after completing their graduate programs in the United States. U.S.-educated Asians, whether they are Indian or Korean, are more successful in finding occupations in their major fields.

The majority of Asian Indians work in occupations similar to those they had in India before their emigration. However, when Indian immigrants are unable to continue employment in their own fields, they often become self-employed in professions and small businesses. Many types of consulting firms are listed in the Indian business directory. The consulting practice includes various fields, such as medicine, law, engineering, accounting, and business. At any given time, some Indian physicians, engineers, and scientists, including those with doctoral degrees, are also unemployed. Some of these Indians find opportunities in the hospitality industry (hotels and motels) and in careers involving small capital investments such as travel agencies, newsstands, real estate, and major insurance companies.

Newly arrived South Asians often enter new occupations to work independently and to escape discrimination from American employers. In the last 2 decades, a large number of Indians and Pakistanis have found career opportunities as taxi drivers and owners in the nation's large metropolitan centers. Indian and Pakistani taxi drivers are visible particularly in New York City, where, according to one knowledgeable Indian community leader, about 40% of taxi drivers are of Indian and Pakistani origin. Interestingly, some South Asian taxi drivers and owners have college and professional degrees in their home countries or the United States in fields such as engineering, science, and business administration (Pais, 1991).

Indian-owned businesses are concentrated in a few service and retail trade businesses. One such business is the motel/hotel business. The newsstand business is also a popular Indian ethnic business that is very visible in New York City. There are also a large number of Indian-owned gas stations and car repair shops. Gujarati Indians are overrepresented in small business (Kim, Hurh, & Fernandez, 1989). The media have publicized a Gujarati subcultural group called Patels and labeled them "Potels, Hotels and Motels" (Sterba, 1987). Patels owned farms and engaged in agriculture in India, which required close intragroup networking and mutual assistance. In the United States, they have established firm inroads in the hospitality industry by purchasing and running small motels, which requires the same support groups as the farms did.

Income

By virtue of their high educational level, Indian Americans generally hold good jobs and earn high incomes. As shown in Table 2.9 in Chapter 2, in 1989 Indian Americans as a group earned substantially higher family incomes than white Americans and had the second-highest incomes among all Asian ethnic groups. However, like other Asians, Indian Americans do not get equal rewards for their educational investments. Based on the results of regression analysis, Barringer and Kassebaum (1989) showed that Asian Indians were "paid well but less than their education and occupational concentration would produce if they were not a minority in the United States" (p. 517). Moreover, although Asian Indians are concentrated in professional occupations, 7% of Indian American families were living at the poverty level in 1990, which was as high as white families (see Table 2.9, Chapter 2). This indicates that even an affluent immigrant community can have many poverty-stricken families.

Discrimination Against Asian Indians

Historically, Asian Indians suffered prejudice and discrimination under British colonial rule in India and as a result of their immigrant status in other commonwealth countries (Gupta, 1979; Jensen, 1988). The British massacre of thousands of innocent, unarmed women and children at the Jaliawala Baag in Punjab, the treatment of East Indians with other "coloured" people as they were called, and the "Dot Buster" incidents in New Jersey and other states in the United States sadly reflect the Euro-American perception of race and culture that has penetrated deeply into the dominant mind-sets and institutions (Takaki, 1987). Historical, ethnographic, and statistical evidence attest to the fact that Asian Indians have suffered widespread prejudice, discrimination, and barriers to equal opportunity on various levels (Chandrasekhar, 1982b; Dutta, 1979, 1982; Hess, 1976; Jensen, 1988; Melendy, 1977; U.S. Commission on Civil Rights, 1992).

Racism Against Early Indian Immigrants

Discrimination against Indians in North America in the early 20th century was reflected in the federal policy on immigration and citizenship, as well as state legislative restrictions on marriage, landholding, and voting, particularly in California, where most Indians lived at that time.

The British in India and their representatives in this country, in cooperation with American and Canadian authorities, formulated racist policies and practices against the early East Indian immigrants (Jensen, 1988).

For example, a California congressman and a South Carolina senator introduced measures in 1914 to exclude "Hindu" laborers from the United States and were strongly supported by the governor general of immigration. Labor unions and white co-workers were invariably opposed to Asian immigrants and often harassed them. Although Chinese, Japanese, and Korean immigrants were not eligible for citizenship in the early 20th century, Asian Indians were awarded citizenship on the grounds that they were not "Mongolians." However, in 1923 the U.S. Supreme Court ruled that Asian Indians were not "free white persons" and therefore could not become American citizens (Takaki, 1989, p. 298). The Supreme Court also revoked the citizenship of those naturalized prior to the court ruling, arguing that their documents were obtained "fraudulently" (Chandrasekhar, 1982b; Gonzales, 1990; Jensen, 1988; Kitano & Daniels, 1988, pp. 89-104; Melendy, 1977).

Other forms of official harassment and discrimination against Asian Indians included thousands of cases of rejection, deportation, and "voluntary" return to India from 1907 to the 1940s (Chandrasekhar 1982a; Melendy, 1977, pp. 202-206). In September 1907, 200 white workers invaded the East Indian community in Bellingham, Washington, and drove about 700 Punjabis across the border into Canada, causing serious injuries (Hess, 1976; Takaki, 1989, p. 297). Immigration restrictions, combined with miscegenation laws in California, deprived Punjabi men of a reunion with their own families in Punjab. Intermarriages of necessity between Sikh men and Mexican women were the only means of circumventing the Alien Land Law of 1913. By creating a negative image of Indians as "the least desirable race of immigrants," "ragheads," "a tide of turbans," and "the Hindu menace," the nativists subjected them to the inhumane treatment. Nevertheless, upper jatis, members of the highly educated middle class, were treated better than laborers.

Discrimination Against the New Asian Indians

Indian and other East Asian immigrants continue to suffer from personal prejudice as well as institutional discrimination, even when they are highly educated and qualified (Chandrasekhar, 1982a; Dutta, 1979, 1982; Fisher, 1980; Hsia, 1988; U.S. Commission on Civil Rights, 1992). Despite their fluency in English and good academic qualifications, many young Indian Americans have been rejected by select universities, partly due to racial bias (D'Souza, 1991; Hsia, 1988). This rejection can be partially explained by the university administration's reaction to the visibility of Indian students in the physical sciences and partially by the "political correctness" issue, which argues that the admission of Asian students should be limited to make room for members of less advantaged minorities.

Indian immigrants also face much discrimination at the workplace. Reports of the government, Indian and Asian American professional organizations, the media, and research reflect the dissatisfaction of Indian Americans with employment (Bellinger, 1988; Chaddha, 1978; Datta, 1975; Edward, Nandi, & Lanier, 1985; Sheth, 1989-1993). A recent study of the career mobility of Asian American engineers, many of whom are Asian Indians, shows mixed results regarding their earnings, career status, promotion, and attrition (Tang, 1993). The earning gap between Asian immigrants and Caucasians disappeared in the 1980s, after an average 10 years in a career. However, a great deal of evidence points to stronger barriers against Asian immigrants in managerial and other positions of authority, a typical case of the "glass ceiling." Of all Asian engineers, only Asian Indians are well-represented in managerial positions, perhaps due to their facility with the English language and their preemigration experience with bureaucracy (Gordon, DiTamaso, & Farris, 1991).

The American Association of Indian Physicians from India (AAPI) claimed that Indians educated in foreign medical schools were denied opportunities for licensing, residencies, and staffing privileges (V. Kulkarni [AAPI president], personal communication, May 2, 1992). The myths and allegations involving negative stereotypes of foreign medical schools and their graduates were propagated by several elite medical journals in 1973-1974 newspaper advertisements recruiting physicians and on television shows such as *Dateline America* (Gupta, 1991; Varki, 1992).

Cases of discrimination against Indians at work include a radiographer named Johnson at the University of Illinois who was denied promotion on the basis of his national origin and color. This was done in retaliation when he filed a complaint with the Equal Employment Opportunity Commission (Soparawala, 1992). In another instance, a credit manager named R. Patel was dismissed from a Japanese corporation in California in 1987 because of his speech accent. This was the first time the EEOC sued an employer in an accent case ("A Community," 1992).

At the community level, there have been numerous "Dot Buster" incidents (the dot refers to the mark worn on a Hindu woman's forehead, which symbolizes Lord Shiva's third eye protecting her; it also indicates the woman's married status). Members of the Indian community are randomly harassed in central and north New Jersey, where there is a high concentration of Indians. Moreover, Navroze Mody, an Indian professional, was killed by a gang in 1987 in Jersey City.

Many other Indian residents in New Jersey and other cities continue to experience racial harassment, ranging from ethnic slurs to serious physical violence. For example, Dr. Saran, a physician, was severely beaten with a baseball bat by three young white men, one of whom was the son of a police commissioner, just for walking in Jersey Heights in 1987. B. Patel, also a physician, was attacked by two teenagers in Jersey City in 1992. He suffered serious knife cuts, chemical burns of his eyes and face, and head injuries; the assailants, shouting, "Hindu, go home," slashed the tires on his car while his family was inside (Pancholi, 1992). Recently, a new anti-Indian gang called the Lost Boys emerged in central New Jersey. Other incidents of discrimination and harassment include: the physical threats and beating of Indian university students and professionals in New Jersey; the painting of swastikas on a Jain temple and an Indian grocery store in South Jersey (DiStephano, 1991); bomb threats on a Hindu temple in Chicago; and the taunting and degrading of Indian children by American pupils and teachers.

In Elmont City, a predominantly white Long Island suburb, 200 Indian Christian families from Kerala suffered racial attacks on their houses and verbal abuse from the town's white teenagers for years ("A Community," 1992). In most situations, the Indian community complained about the insensitivity and laxity of the local criminal justice system in prosecuting the assailants. Despite a long struggle, some of the assailants were tried and sentenced only lightly or acquitted.

The contributing factors to this anti-Indian harassment and violence include Asian Indians' geographical concentration, their lack of communication skills, foreign speech accents, cultural differences, religious diversity, and the perception of Asian Indians as a model minority. The Indian community has established organizations in response to this anti-Indian harassment and violence. Indian political and professional organizations have been formed to reduce this problem, which will be discussed in the section on ethnicity. In addition, the Indian community has held protest rallies and candlelight vigils.

Ethnicity and Pluralism

Subethnicity and Cultural Pluralism

In the United States, ethnic identity involves the subjective identification of immigrants and minority members with their group's race, national origin, religion, language, values, symbols, food preferences, and the institutions that serve the group's sense of distinctiveness (Gordon 1964, pp. 26, 27; Thernstrom, 1980). Asian Indians are characterized by subethnicity: Indian immigrants identify themselves not with the Indian national origin group, but with a particular linguistic-regional subgroup. Several subcommunities of Indians, such as Gujaratis and Punjabis, do not form an ethnic group in the same sense as other American ethnic groups (Varma, 1985, p. 30). The self-concept of ethnic identity is very complex and varies among Indians, depending on region of origin, national language, diet, jati, religion, or sect. Ethnicity for Indian Americans should be viewed as a dynamic rather than a static phenomenon, reflecting the interaction among various groups (Lopez & Espiritu, 1990). It is also conceptualized in terms of layers of group identities, as is found in New York City (Fisher, 1980, p. 2; Leonard, 1992). Each person has a number of different identities.

The sources of Indian ethnicity are Indian religions, languages, families, and specific Indian values such as nonviolence. Asian Indians express pride in their history, civilization, and values, as well as their scientific, educational, and professional achievements. Individually and organizationally, diligent efforts have been made to socialize children into Indian culture and values. Indian versus American identity is important in dealing with issues of citizenship, divorce, passport, social security payments, and the like (Saran 1985, pp. 107-116). Indians maintain their ethnic identity by means of religious places and organizations, Indian and ethnic newspapers, television, videotapes, and visits to their homeland. The factors that most facilitate Indians' ethnic identity is their professional social class (which affords them visits to and from India), privacy for engaging in Indian lifestyles, and the like.

The Role of Indian Religions

Hinduism, Buddhism, Jainism, and Sikhism are religions that originated in India, whereas Islam, Christianity, Zoroastrianism, and Judaism were introduced in India (Mandelbaum, 1972; Williams, 1988, p. 4). In India the Hindus constitute about 83%; Muslims, the largest minority, 11%; Christians, 3%; and Sikhs, 2%. Hinduism was first introduced to the United States by Swami Vivekanand, a young intellectual religious leader who represented India to the World Parliament of Religions in Chicago in 1893. Later, many Vedanta centers were established in this country (Vidyatmananda-Swami, 1972). Swami Vivekanand's centenary was celebrated across the United States during 1992-1993. In addition, eminent Western figures such as Emerson, Thoreau, Einstein, Schweitzer, Whitman, Martin Luther King, Jr., and Sisters Nivedita and Mirabahen were influenced by Indian indigenous religions and values. Moreover, small groups of young Americans have adopted Hinduism, Islam, and Sikhism (Williams, 1988).

Post-1965 Indian immigrants as a group are more religious here than they were back in India because it is one effective way of maintaining ethnic identity for themselves and their children. In order to maintain their religion, Indian immigrants have established hundreds of Hindu and Jain temples and a few Sikh Gurudwaras (Fenton, 1988; Williams, 1988, p. 11). Muslims and Christians generally share their worship places with other nationalities of the same faith.

The Role of Native Languages

The 1980 census indicates that of all people of Indian ancestry who speak one of the 16 major Indian languages, the majority (55%) spoke Hindi, the official and national language that is spoken in North and Central India. Originating from Sanskrit, Hindi is associated with the elite Brahmins of North India, who met with conflict and violence in South India. Gujarati was the next most frequently spoken language and represented a majority from a single northwestern state. Punjabi, Bengali, Malayalam, and Tamil followed Gujarati (Fisher, 1980; Xenos, Barringer, & Levin, 1989).

Changes have been noted in the speech patterns of various South Asian languages with each successive generation of Indians, whether they have settled in the United States or in other parts of the world (Gambhir, 1988). In contrast to those settled in other countries, who have maintained their language and culture for generations, Indians in the United States are rapidly losing touch with their linguistic roots. However, many second-generation South Asians are attempting to learn regional Indian languages, indeed to the delight of their parents. At the community level, language classes for children, literary societies for adults, regional groups' national conventions, entertainers, and visitors from South Asia all help to keep Indian languages and identity alive.

The Role of Indian Organizations

Indian organizations have served various purposes for Indian people both in India and in the United States. Those organizations that serve to maintain the religion and culture of Indian immigrants have always met social and cultural needs at different times and places. In the early 20th century, East Indian nationals formed organizations to help two causes: India's independence from the British and the struggle for citizenship and other civil rights of Indian immigrants in the United States (Jensen, 1988, pp. 270-283). Led by middle-class professionals, these organizations attained the support of the American media and many eminent politicians, resulting in changes in government policy affecting the causes mentioned above. Some of these organizations were the Hindusthan Association of America and the Vedanta Society. One of the most prominent organizations, the Gadar Party, will be discussed later in this chapter.

Among the Indian activists, businessmen, and professionals who played an important role in the twin causes were Lala Lajpat Rai of Punjab and Sardar Jagjit Singh, a Westernized Sikh. Under their efficient leadership, the Luce/Celler Bill was passed by Congress in 1945. This bill granted token quotas to India and China. Mubarak Ali Khan, a successful farmer who arrived in 1913, founded the Indian Welfare Rights in America in 1937 and convinced the U.S. attorney general that granting Indians citizenship would provide links to Asia. Many Indian leaders and religious organizations worked in unity for the twin causes during most of this time. American religious and secular organizations did not support the Indian causes until the late 1930s. Other supporters at the time included *Time* magazine and some prominent diplomats and politicians. Although President Roosevelt was sympathetic to the Indian independence movement, he was pressured not to show his support by Winston Churchill of Great Britain and conservatives in Canada and the United States.

During the post-1965 period, two types of Indian organizations have played different roles for the Asian Indian community: (a) parochial organizations that function to bind their people together and (b) Pan-Indian organizations that strive to protect their rights in the United States. Parochial organizations are centered around shared religions, linguistic ties, and states of origin in India. Parochial organizations also cater to immigrants of the same religion, sect, profession, or educational institution, as the size of their population increases (Fisher, 1980; Mehta, 1984; Saran, 1985; Sheth, 1994; Williams, 1988).

Before the 1970s, Indian organizations in the United States were limited to those organized and operated by university students on local campuses. Membership and participation were extended to the growing community of transient Asian Indians. Indians celebrated religious and national holidays with Indian music, dances, and food, as well as lectures and discussions on Indian issues. They showed and cherished Indian movies, which incidentally were also very popular among the non-Indian communities throughout the non-Western world. Although these student-based Indian organizations were mainly concerned with providing a social life for sojourner Indians, they also have a historical significance. Since the mid-1970s, Indian institutions, organizations, and community centers have been formed around Asian Indian communities in cities and suburbs (Sheth, 1994).

Pan Indian organizations operating at the national and international levels include the Associations of Indians in America (AIA), the National Federation of Indian Associations (NFIA), Vishwa Hindu Parishad (VHP), and the Global Organization of People of Indian Origin (GOPIO). These Pan-Indian organizations were established to meet political, cultural, and civic needs of Asian Indians. The AIA originated in New Jersey in the early 1970s, moving into other states. A proliferation of organizations around the Indian communities in metropolitan Philadelphia and South Jersey, also known as the tri-state Delaware Valley, has occurred rapidly since the 1970s (Sheth, 1994). The Pan-Indian associations function to further Indians' economic and political status as a minority in the United States (Fisher, 1980).

Political Organizations and Movements

The leadership of Mahatma (the politician/saint) Gandhi, who was universally respected for his ideals and practice of nonviolence, and other Indian leaders helped India gain independence in 1947. Mahatma Gandhi became an inspiration for Dr. Martin Luther King, Jr., in the United States and for other oppressed people around the world. The independence movement in India was assisted by the Gadar political movement of Indians in the United States.

The Gadar Movement

The Gadar (revolution or mutiny in Arabic) was a militant movement of East Indians that emerged in San Francisco as a response to the oppression of British colonialism in India and to the discriminatory and exclusionary practices against Indian immigrants by Canada and the United States (Banerjee, 1969; Ganguly, 1980; Jensen, 1988; Juergensmeyer, 1982, pp. 48-49; Kitano & Daniels, 1988). The Gadar identity was a combination of nationalist and communal sentiments brought from India and the working-class consciousness and ethnicity immigrants discovered in America. The purpose of the Gadar was to inform, create anti-British propaganda, and thereby elicit international sympathy and support for the Indian freedom movement.

A series of newspapers in many Indian languages, also named Gadar, was the movement's main channel of communication. Many Indian students, political activists, and working-class Indians in the United States contributed to the movement. The Gadar leaders received financial aid and other help from Germany and also sympathy from Irish Americans, who held the British as a common enemy. Despite the appeals of revolutionaries to President Wilson for support of the Indian freedom struggle, the Gadar movement failed. The failure was due to several factors: surveillance of the revolutionaries by British, Canadian, and American authorities, particularly in California; individual feuds between leaders; problems in planning the organization; and communal conflict, including the murders of 25 Indians by fellow Indians commissioned by the British (Banerjee, 1969, p. 69; Jensen, 1988). Many revolutionaries were arrested, convicted, imprisoned, and even executed in the United States and India. The movement withered away with the legal reforms of 1946 in the United States and with India's independence in 1947. As a memorial, the Gadar Hall still stands in San Francisco.

Citizenship and the Reclassification Movement

In the early 20th century, the major political issue was U.S. citizenship; in the 1990s, it is dual or multinational citizenship. This contrast may indicate the expertise of the new Indians in making international demands and their need to maintain Indian citizenship and identity. The U.S. Supreme Court ruled in 1923 that Indians were not considered Caucasians and therefore not eligible for citizenship. Moreover, Indians who had been naturalized were deprived of their citizenship. The early Indian leaders decided to fight denationalization, or the creating of "stateless persons" (Das, 1923). Sakharam Ganesh Pandit, a lawyer, won his citizenship in 1927, and Bhagat Singh Thind, a U.S.-educated agribusinessman, received his citizenship later. Some who never received their U.S. citizenship committed suicide. In the 1990s, Indian expatriates, called nonresident Indians (NRIs), have raised the issue of dual citizenship of India and the United States in an increasingly global economy.

Early Asian Indian immigrants had been labeled incorrectly as "Hindoos." They were later classified as East Indians to distinguish Indian nationals from Native Americans (Chandrasekhar, 1982b). Since 1980, the U.S. census has classified Indians as Asian Indians, a subcategory of Asian and Pacific Islander Americans (Dutta, 1979, 1982). This decision was mainly a result of long and careful planning, consultations, a decade of hearings before Congress and the Census Bureau, and lobbying efforts by the AIA during the 1970s.

Contributions to American Politics

Although Asian Indians are relative newcomers to American politics, they have caught up via campaigns, delegates, contributions, and a few Indian candidates. Dalip Singh Saund was a successful example of an Indian who made contributions to American politics. He came to the United States in 1920 and received three professional degrees (including a doctorate) from UCLA and the University of California, Berkeley. Saund was involved in the twin causes of Indian independence and Indians' citizenship rights in the United States, and he was elected to the Congress in 1957, becoming the first Asian-born congressman. He was twice reelected (Kitano & Daniels, 1988, p. 98).

Indian Americans' political consciousness and political participation in the post-1965 era are well reflected in their support of American elections. In 1992 presidential and congressional races, as well as at the state and local levels, the Indian community supported the Democratic and Republican parties and contributed substantially, particularly to the latter. One Indian physician collected $600,000 from fellow physicians in one night alone, the largest contribution by individuals. However, the Indian community did not have a well- organized collective effort to support any party.

The only Indian American legislator is a Maryland Democrat. Some Indians ran for local elections, however. Teaneck, New Jersey, for example, elected an Asian Indian as its mayor in 1992. Moreover, Indian persons have been appointed as delegates for presidential candidates from various states. In addition, a few Indians were appointed in an advisory capacity to governmental and nongovernmental organizations during the Reagan and Bush administrations. In reciprocity, American politicians have become regular keynote speakers at Indian cultural programs and at the fund-raising events organized by Indians in major American cities.

Marriage and the Family

Since ancient times, traditional customs relating to marriage and the family have been the foundation of Indian social life. In Indian history, marriage was both monogamous and polygamous. The structure of the

Indian family was joint (extended), patriarchal, patrilineal, and patrilocal. Jati endogamy and village exogamy were the rules. Selection of a mate was with parents' supervision only. Presently, this ideal is only partly realized. Industrialization and urbanization in India have changed the family structure, functions, the gender division of labor, and authority structure in the home, favoring more egalitarian relations between husband and wife.

Early Punjabi Immigrant Families

Early Indians in the United States had almost no family. Approximately half of the Indian men who came in the early 1900s were married but could not bring wives and children due to their sojourner status, financial costs, and the Barred Zone Act of 1917. Many women waited until 1946 to be reunited with their husbands. Due to the extreme shortage of Indian women, many educated, professional Indians married white women, and many working-class Indians married Mexican and Japanese women (Mazumdar, 1983a, 1983b, p. 571).

Children raised in the Mexican culture and language did not relate well to their Indian fathers (Leonard, 1982, p. 72). However, a large number of step-siblings were close knit as was evident from their signatures as witnesses at the marriage or birth of one another. Like first-generation marriages, most of the second-generation marriages also ended in divorce. Many early immigrant men died without leaving descendants (LaBrack, 1982).

Recent Indian Families

Most post-1965 Indian immigrants were married in India and came to the United States with their spouses. Students sent for their wives or returned to India to bring back brides. Sometimes they married American women. Most couples were young and did not have children until the 1970s.

Table 7.5 compares Indian Americans with three other Asian American groups and the U.S. general population on important family characteristics based on the 1990 census. Indian Americans show the lowest divorce rate and the lowest proportion of female-headed families among all Asian ethnic groups. The high stability of Indian American families reflected in these data can be explained by traditional Indian attitudes and values placing a strong emphasis on marriage and family and putting a stigma on divorce, as well as by the high socioeconomic background of Indian Americans. The group has the highest fertility rate among the four Asian

Table 7.5 Family Characteristics of Indian Americans and Other Groups, 1990

	Indian	Chinese	Filipino	Korean	U.S. General Population
Persons per family	3.8	3.6	4.0	3.6	3.2
% of married-couple families	90.6	84.8	78.8	84.1	78.6
% of female-headed families	4.5	9.4	15.1	11.3	16.5
Number of divorces per 1,000 persons 15 years old and over					
Male	19.3	23.1	37.4	22.8	74.2
Female	21.5	33.3	50.9	54.0	95.0
Female labor force participation rate	72.3	58.1	72.3	63.3	65.3
Children ever born per 1,000 women 35-44 years old	2,034	1,703	1,919	1,776	1,960

SOURCE: U.S. Bureau of the Census (1993a; 1993b).

ethnic groups, which again reflects traditional family characteristics associated with Indian culture.

Recently, a study examined the life changes and life satisfaction of 50 Indian couples who emigrated from the state of Kerala in India to the Chicago area. It was found that they had integrated into the United States structurally but not culturally (Ramola, 1992). Although some change has occurred in the division of labor and decision-making power among husbands and wives, partners do not want to give up their traditional gender roles. Contrary to the findings from similar studies using white American couples, wives were found to be more satisfied with their marriages than their husbands. This may be due to freedom from the social control and authority of elders in the extended family (Ramola, 1992). Although the extended family is the traditional ideal, modern Indian brides prefer the lifestyle of the nuclear family.

Intermarriages

Lee and Yamanaka (1990) compared Asian groups in intermarriage patterns. A younger, urban, native-born female with high socioeconomic status is more likely to marry outside her group than is her immigrant counterpart. Asian Indians and Chinese have the lowest rate of intermarriage among the six major Asian groups examined. Another study of a sample of Asian Americans living in California showed that inmarriages were equally common among Indian males and females, whether they married in India or in the United States (Hwang & Saenz, 1990, pp. 563-575). Both studies seem to concur on the general inmarriage behavior of Asian Indians.

Mate Selection

Interestingly, a sizable number of Indian immigrants seek mates through advertisements, either in Indian newspapers during a short visit there or in Indian ethnic newspapers in the United States; they also use referrals from friends, relatives, and marriage brokers to find mates. Immigration status has been used as one of the qualifications for marriage. A study of a sample of 213 matrimonial advertisements from 1981 to 1983 in an Indian ethnic newspaper offers insight into immigration involving matrimonial alliance (Bhargava, 1988). Over 41% of male seekers, in contrast to 16% of their female counterparts, emphasized permanent residency as the sole condition of eligibility for a prospective mate.

Both matrimonial candidates have traditional expectations from one another. The matrimonial transaction is supervised by parents or other relatives, regardless of the age and education of the candidates, as a sign of modesty and respectability. However, no data are available regarding the outcome of the matrimonial process. The ethnic newspaper advertisement is also used by some second-generation Indian Americans born and raised in the United States.

Second Generation

The second-generation Indian Americans of both genders born or raised in the United States are in schools, universities, or just beginning professional careers and marrying Indians or Euro-Americans with similar qualifications. Although most of them are successful, many of them also suffer from pressures to succeed, failure, and other social problems. They have quickly realized some contradictions with their parents as well as with American society (Agarwal, 1991). In spite of generation and cultural conflicts, they have somewhat compromised with both. Several youth have decided to work with politicians and run for political offices as a means of increasing the clout and equality of Indian community within American society. Second-generation females have closed the gender gap almost completely in education and occupation than the immigration generation.

Young women experience the double standard in mating and marriage with the young Indian males and in freedom from their parents. Second-generation Indian Americans have more freedom in choice of education, occupation, and marriage than the immigrant generation.

Women

Although woman immigrants arrived late on the immigration scene in the early 1970s, their relative education, occupation, and income are much lower than those of the Indian men, who have been equal to or ahead of American women. Hardly any research is conducted on Asian Indian women. Some immigrant women are successful professionals and white collar workers, happy in their marriages, and the advancement of children. They enjoy the relative freedom from the extended family. The marital conflict and the subsequent divorce rate is slowly increasing. Since women are the preservers of culture and tradition for themselves and their children, juggling careers and family in a foreign country is not easy.

Conclusion

Early Indian immigrants in California, like other Asian immigrants on the West Coast at the turn of the century, suffered from prejudiced attitudes by white Americans and the exclusionary policy and various discriminatory measures of the U.S. government. However, they were active in protecting the citizenship and civil rights of Indian immigrants in the United States and fighting against British colonialism in India.

Indians constitute one of the major new Asian immigrant groups in the post-1965 era. Although all Asian immigrant groups are characterized by a highly educated, middle-class, professional background, Indian immigrants consist mainly of professional immigrants. A large proportion of post-1965 Indian immigrants are physicians, nurses, pharmacists, scientists, engineers, professors, and accountants. By virtue of their high educational levels, relative fluency in English, and educational experiences in the United States, Indian immigrants do very well occupationally and economically. However, highly educated contemporary Indian immigrants are also subject to personal prejudice, racial violence, and discrimination in college admission and promotion. Despite their seeming success, Indian immigrants currently encounter many barriers.

Immigrants from India consist of diverse regional, linguistic, and religious subgroups. Thus the region of origin, language, religion, jati, or a combination of two or more of these, along with traditional Indian values, can be the basis of their ethnic identity. In addition, "twice migrants" from other countries significantly differ from "direct migrants" from India in their ethnic identity and subculture. Various parochial Indian ethnic organizations based on the place of origin, language, and religion help Indians maintain their subcultures and social interactions with co-ethnics. Several Pan-Indian Associations try to protect their political interests in India, as well as the civil rights in the United States. As the native born descendants of post-1965 Indian immigrants emerge in the Indian community, they have joined these organizations to overcome subethnic parochialism and engage in Pan-Indian movements to protect the interests of the entire Indian community.

References

A community regains its pride. (1992, April). *India Times.*

Agarwal, P. (1991). *Passage from India: Post-1965 Indian immigrants and their children: Conflicts, concerns and solutions.* Palos Verdes, CA: Yuvati.

Arnold, F., Minocha, U., & Fawcett, J. (1987). The changing face of Asian immigration to the United States. In J. Fawcett & B. Carino (Eds.), *Pacific bridges, the new immigration from Asia and the Pacific Islands* (pp. 105-152). Staten Island, NY: Center for Migration Studies.

Banerjee, K. K. (1969). *Indian freedom movement in America.* Calcutta: Jignasa.

Barringer, H. R., Gardner, R. W., & Levin, M. J. (1993). *Asians and Pacific Islanders in the United States.* New York: Russell Sage.

Barringer, H. R., & Kassebaum, G. (1989). Asian Indians as a minority in the United States: The effects of education, occupations, and gender on income. *Sociological Perspectives, 32,* 501-520.

Bellinger, R. (1988, November/December). Indian electronic engineers: A growing presence in the USA. *Darshan,* pp. 16-17.

Bhargava, G. (1988). Seeking immigration through matrimonial alliance: A study of advertisements in an ethnic weekly. *Journal of Comparative Family Studies, 19,* 245-261.

Chaddha, R. L. (1978, August). *Problems and perspectives of career advancement: A cross-section of Asian Indians.* Paper presented at Stanford Workshop, Stanford University, Palo Alto, CA.

Chan, S. (1991). *Asian Americans: An interpretive history.* Boston: Twayne.

Chandrasekhar, S. (1982a). A history of United States legislation with respect to immigration from India: Some statistics on Asian Indian immigration to the United States of America. In S. Chandrasekhar (Ed.) *From India to America: A brief history of immigration, problems of discrimination, admission and assimilation* (pp. 11-29). La Jolla, CA: Population Review.

Chandrasekhar, S. (1982b). Some statistics on Asian Indian immigration to the United States of America. In S. Chandrasekhar (Ed.) *From India to America: A brief history of immigration, problems of discrimination, admission and assimilation* (pp. 86-93). La Jolla, CA: Population Review.

Das, R. K. (1923). *Hindustani workers on the Pacific Coast.* Berlin: DeGruyter.

Datta, R. K. (1975). Characteristics and attitudes of immigrant Indian scientists and engineers in the U.S.A. *Journal of Scientific and Industrial Research, 34,* 74-79.

DiStephano, J. N. (1991, October 19). Ugly signs in S. Jersey: Swastikas. *The Philadelphia Inquirer,* pp. 1-2B, 41A.

Dodge, S. (1991, October 23). Foreign students in the United States. *Chronicle of Higher Education,* pp. 1, 31.

D'Souza, D. (1991). *Illiberal education: The politics of race and sex on campus.* New York: Free Press.

Dutta, M. (1979). Asian and Pacific American employment profile. In U.S. Commission on Civil Rights, *Civil rights issues of Asian and Pacific Americans: Myths and realities.* Washington, DC: U.S. Government Printing Office.

Dutta, M. (1982). Asian Indian Americans: Search for an economic profile. In S. Chandrasekhar (Ed.), *From India to America: A brief history of immigration, problems of discrimination, admission and assimilation* (pp. 76-79). La Jolla, CA: Population Review.

Edward, A. W., Nandi, P. K., & Lanier, J. E. (1985). Ethnic minority faculty on a predominantly white campus: Variables influencing adjustment and satisfaction. *Journal of Social and Behavioral Sciences, 31*(4), 94-99.

Fenton, J. Y. (1988). *Transplanting religious traditions: Asian Indians in America.* New York: Praeger.

Fisher, M. P. (1980). *The Indians of New York City: A study of immigrants from India.* New Delhi: Heritage.

Gambhir, S. K. (1988). *The modern Indian diaspora and language.* Unpublished manuscript, Department of South Asian Studies, University of Pennsylvania.

Ganguly, A. B. (1980). *Ghadar movement in America.* New Delhi: Metropolitan.

Gonzales, J. L., Jr. (1990). *Racial and ethnic groups in America.* Dubuque, IA: Kendall/Hunt.

Gordon, G. G., DiTamaso, N., & Farris, G. F. (1991, January/February). Managing diversity in research and development group. *Research-Technology Management.*

Gordon, M. M. (1964). *Assimilation in American life.* New York: Oxford University Press.

Gupta, R. K. (1991). International physicians facing issues of discrimination. *Labor Law Journal, 42,* 747-756.

Gupta, S. N. (1979). *British, the magnificent exploiters of India.* New Delhi: Chand.

Helweg, A., & Helweg, U. (1990). *The immigrant success story: East Indians.* Philadelphia: University of Pennsylvania Press.

Hess, G. (1976). The forgotten Asian Americans: The East Indian community in the United States. In N. Hundley (Ed.), *Asians in America* (pp. 157-178). Santa Barbara, CA: ABC-CLIO.

Hsia, H. (1988). *Asian Americans in higher education and at work.* Hillsdale, NJ: Lawrence Erlbaum.

Hwang, S., & Saenz, R. (1990). The problem posed by immigrant married on intermarriage research: The case of Asian Americans. *International Migration Review, 24,* 563-575.

Immigration and Naturalization Service. (1965-1978). *Annual report.* Washington, DC: U.S. Government Printing Office.

Immigration and Naturalization Service. (1979-1992). *Statistical yearbook.* Washington, DC: U.S. Government Printing Office.

Jensen, J. M. (1988). *Passage from India: Asian Indian immigrants in North America.* New Haven, CT: Yale University Press.

Juergensmeyer, M. (1982). The Gadar syndrome: Ethnic anger and nationalist pride. In S. Chandrasekhar (Ed.), *From India to America: A brief history of immigration, problems of discrimination, admission and assimilation* (pp. 48-58). La Jolla, CA: Population Review.

Kim, K. C., Hurh, W. M., & Fernandez, M. (1989). Intragroup differences in business participation: Three Asian immigrant groups. *International Migration Review, 23,* 73-95.

Kitano H., & Daniels, R. (1988). *Asian Americans, emerging minorities.* Englewood Cliffs, NJ: Prentice Hall.

Kritz, M. M. (1987). The global picture of contemporary immigration patterns. In J. Fawcett & B. Carino (Eds.), *Pacific bridges: The new immigration from Asia and the Pacific Islands* (pp. 29-52). Staten Island, NY: Center for Migration Studies.

Kurian, G. (1991). South Asians in Canada. *International Migration, 29*(3), 421-434.

LaBrack, B. (1982). Immigration law and the revitalization process: The case of the California Sikhs. In S. Chandrasekhar (Ed.), *From India to America: A brief history of immigration, problems of discrimination, admission and assimilation* (pp. 59-66). La Jolla, CA: Population Review.

Lee, S. M., & Yamanaka, K. (1990). Patterns of Asian American intermarriage and marital assimilation. *Journal of Comparative Family Studies, 21,* 287-305.

Leonard, K. (1982). Marriage and family life among early Asian Indian immigrants. In S. Chandrasekhar (Ed.), *From India to America: A brief history of immigration, problems of discrimination, admission and assimilation* (pp. 67-274). La Jolla, CA: Population Review.

Leonard, K. (1992). *Making ethnic choices: California's Punjabi-Mexican Americans.* Philadelphia: Temple University Press.

Lopez, D., & Espiritu, Y. E. (1990). Panethnicity in the United States: A theoretical framework. *Ethnic and Racial Studies, 13,* 198-224.

Madhavan, M. C. (1985). Indian emigrants: Numbers, characteristics, and economic impact. *Population and Development Review, 11*(3), 457-481.

Mandelbaum, D. G. (1972). *Society in India: Vol. 2. Change and continuity.* Berkeley: University of California Press.

Mazumdar, S. (1983a). Colonial impact and Punjabi emigration to the United States. In L. Cheng & E. Bonacich (Eds.), *Labor immigration under capitalism: Asian workers in the United States before World War II* (pp. 316-336). Berkeley: University of California Press.

Mazumdar, S. (1983b). Punjabi agricultural people in California. In L. Cheng & E. Bonacich (Eds.), *Labor immigration under capitalism: Asian workers in the United States before World War II* (pp. 549-578). Berkeley: University of California Press.

Mehta, M. (1984, May). *The role of family.* Paper presented at the Conference on Family: Bicultural Socialization, Washington, DC.

Melendy, H. B. (1977). *Asians in America: Filipinos, Koreans, and East Indians.* Boston: Twayne.

Minocha, U. (1987). South Asian immigrants: Trends and impacts on the sending and receiving societies. In J. T. Fawcett & B. V. Carino (Eds.), *Pacific bridges: The new immigration from Asia and the Pacific Islands* (pp. 347-374). Staten Island, NY: Center for Migration Studies.

Nandi, P. K. (1980, Summer). The world of an invisible minority: Pakistanis in America. *California Sociologists, 3,* 143-165.

Pais, A. (1991, July 12). Lure of the taxi business. *India Abroad.*

Pancholi, A. (1992, April 17). Return of the dotbusters? *India Abroad.*

Ramola, J. (1992). *Perceived changes of immigrants in the United States: A study of Kerala (Asian Indian) immigrant couples in greater Chicago.* Doctoral dissertation, Loyola University.

Saran, P. (1985). *The Asian Indian experience in the U.S.* Cambridge, MA: Schenkman.

Sheth, M. (1989-1993). *A report of the tri-state (NJ-PA-DEL) Asian professionals.* Unpublished manuscript.

Sheth, M. (1994). Asian Indian organizations in Philadelphia and South Jersey. In J. B. Toll & M. S. Gillam (Eds.), *Invisible Philadelphia: Communities through voluntary organizations* (pp. 71-73). Philadelphia: Kent Atwater Museum.

Soparawala, R. (1992, May 29). A landmark ruling on bias. *India Abroad.*

Sterba, J. (1987, January 27). Immigrant saga. *The Wall Street Journal.*

Takaki, R. (Ed.). (1987). *From different shores.* New York, Oxford University Press.

Takaki, R. (1989). *Strangers from a different shore: A history of Asian Americans.* New York: Penguin.

Tang, J. (1993). The career attainment of Caucasians and Asian engineers. *The Sociological Quarterly, 34,* 467-496.

Thernstrom, S. (Ed.). (1980). *The Harvard Encyclopedia of American Ethnic Groups.* Cambridge, MA: Harvard University Press.

Tinker, H. (1977). *The banyan tree.* New York: Oxford University Press.

U.S. Bureau of the Census. (1983). *1980 census of population, general population characteristics, United States summary* (PC80-1-B1). Washington, DC: U.S. Government Printing Office.

U.S. Bureau of the Census. (1989). *Statistical abstracts of the United States: 1989.* Washington, DC: U.S. Government Printing Office.

U.S. Bureau of the Census. (1993a). *1990 census of population, general population characteristics, the United States* (CP-1-1). Washington, DC: U.S. Government Printing Office.

U.S. Bureau of the Census. (1993b). *1990 census of population, Asians and Pacific Islanders in the United States* (CP-3-5). Washington, DC: U.S. Government Printing Office.

U.S. Bureau of the Census. (1994). *1990 census of population, general social and economic characteristics, the United States* (CP-2-1). Washington, DC: U.S. Government Printing Office.

U.S. Commission on Civil Rights. (1992). *Civil rights issues facing Asian Americans in the 1990s.* Washington, DC: Author.

Varki, A. (1992). Of pride, prejudice, and discrimination: Why generalizations can be unfair to the individual. *Annals of Internal Medicine, 116,* 762-764.

Varma, V. N. (1985). Indians as new ethnics: A theoretical note. In P. Saran & E. Eames (Eds.), *The new ethnics: Asian Indians in the United States* (pp. 29-41). New York: Praeger.

Vidyatmananda-Swami. (1972). *What religion is in the words of Swami Vivekananda.* Calcutta: Advaita Ashrama.

Williams, R. B. (1988). *Religions of immigrants from India and Pakistan: New threads in the American tapestry.* Cambridge: Cambridge University Press.

Xenos, P., Barringer, H., & Levin, I. J. (1989). *Asian Indians in the U.S.: A 1980 census profile.* Honolulu: East-West Population Studies Center.

8

Korean Americans

PYONG GAP MIN

The current Korean American community is largely the by-product of the influx of Korean immigrants since the liberalization of the immigration law in 1965. The Korean population in the United States increased from less than 100,000 in 1970 to nearly 1 million in 1990. Recent Korean immigrants have received a great deal of attention from both the U.S. media and the general public, probably because of the visibility of their business activities.

Although little historical research has been conducted on Korean Americans mainly because of their short immigration history, sociologists and other social scientists have studied Korean immigrants over the last 15 years. Results from these recent studies on various aspects of Korean immigrant experiences such as assimilation, economic adjustment, and family life are discussed in this chapter.

Immigration History

Korean immigration history can be roughly classified into three major periods: (a) the period of old immigration, (b) the intermediate period, and (c) the period of new immigration. The period of old immigration covers approximately 50 years between 1903 and 1949. The intermediate period focuses on the 15 years of Korean immigration following the Korean War in 1950. The period of new immigration involves a new wave of Korean immigrants following the enforcement of the 1965 Immigration Act.

Old Immigration

Between 1903 and 1905, more than 7,200 Koreans came to Hawaii to work on sugar plantations, composing the first wave of Korean immigrants to the United States (although nearly 100 Koreans had come to the United States after diplomatic relations were established between Korea and the United States in 1882). At the turn of the 20th century, Japanese workers, who had immigrated since 1885, monopolized plantation labor in Hawaii. Between 1900 and 1905, Japanese workers conducted numerous strikes, and many left plantations for urban areas in Hawaii or moved to California. Plantation owners, in need of cheap labor, decided to recruit Korean laborers to meet the labor shortage and counteract the demands of Japanese workers (Choy, 1979, p. 73).

Economic hardship in Korea can be considered the push factor for the first wave of Korean immigration. A nationwide famine in 1901 and the ensuing starvation forced the Korean government to relax its traditionally tight restrictions on emigration, although public opinion in the old Korean dynasty strongly opposed the emigration of its people. Horace Allen, the American minister to Korea, played a key intermediary role between the Korean government and the Hawaiian Plantation Association in Honolulu. Mainly because of his successful maneuvers, the Korean government relaxed its restrictions on emigration.

As noted above, the traditional push-pull approach is helpful in understanding why the migration of 7,200 Koreans to Hawaii occurred between 1903 and 1905. But the world capitalist system approach sheds new light on the role of the earlier Korean immigrants, as well as other earlier Asian immigrants, in an expanding U.S. capitalist economy in the late 19th and early 20th centuries (Cheng & Bonacich, 1984). Like other Asian immigrants to Hawaii and California, the pioneering Korean immigrants were admitted mainly to serve the economic interests of plantation owners. In this connection, it is important to note that the immigrants in Hawaii were admitted through the contract labor system, a practice outlawed in the United States at that time; recruiting agencies made it look like they were free immigrants so they would not violate the law (Patterson, 1988, chap. 8). Contract labor was a system in which an immigrant was "indentured to an employer for a period of (usually seven) years at wages lower than those paid to American citizens" (Patterson, 1988, p. 23). As contract laborers, Korean immigrants were forced to accept low wages and working conditions set by plantation owners.

Early Korean immigration to Hawaii came to a sudden end in the summer of 1905, shortly after the Korean Foreign Ministry instructed the mayors of the port cities to stop issuing passports. The Korean government had been informed of the hardships suffered by its emigrants in Mexico. This information might have led the Korean government to suspect similar conditions in Hawaii (Yun, 1977).

However, pressure from the Japanese government to halt Korean emigration to Hawaii played a more important role in the government's decision. The ample Korean workforce eliminated the Japanese workers' monopoly of plantation labor on the islands. Competition with Korean workers in Hawaii did not serve the economic interests of Japanese workers. Dissatisfied with low wages and poor working conditions, many Japanese immigrants moved out of Hawaii to California. Japanese diplomats in the United States worried that the increase in the Japanese population in California would result in anti-Japanese sentiments comparable to the anti-Chinese movements 30 years before. The Japanese government felt that a halt of Korean emigration would not only protect Japanese workers in the Hawaiian islands from competition but would also prevent them from moving to California (Patterson, 1988, chap. 13). In 1905, Korea became Japan's protectorate as a result of the Japanese victory in the Russo-Japanese War, putting Japan in a position to strongly influence its policies.

Most pioneering Korean immigrants, like their Chinese and Japanese counterparts, were sojourners who planned to return to Korea as soon as they earned enough money. Most were young males who had lived in Seoul, Inchon, and other urban areas of Korea and worked as manual laborers. This urban background provides a good contrast to the earlier Chinese and Japanese immigrants, who were mostly from rural areas and primarily from one part of their native countries (Patterson, 1988, p. 103).

Forty percent of the early Korean immigrants were Christians in Korea, and the majority of them attended Korean Christian churches in the United States (Choy, 1979). Patterson (1988, pp. 108-109) suggests that exposure to American missionaries in Korean cities was one major factor that influenced Koreans' decision to immigrate to the United States at the turn of the century.

Ethnic churches became the most important ethnic organizations for the pioneer Korean immigrants, helping them maintain social interactions with fellow Koreans and their cultural tradition. In addition, Korean churches were centers of the independence movement against Japan at the time (Lyu, 1977).

Although the immigration of Korean workers to the United States ended in 1905, about 2,000 more Koreans came to Hawaii and California before

Asian immigration was completely banned in 1924. The Koreans who immigrated between 1906 and 1923 can be classified into two major groups. The spouses of Korean workers constituted one major group. Most pioneering immigrants were unmarried single males who were later allowed to bring their "picture brides" from Korea. Although most of these men were in their late twenties and early thirties, they brought young wives from Korea, resulting in significant age differences. One book based on interviews with several surviving wives (Min, 1986) indicates that the mean age difference between husbands and wives was 14 years.

Korean political refugees and/or students made up the other major group of Koreans who came to the United States during this period. As Korean agitation against Japanese rule intensified before and after the annexation of Korea by Japan in 1910, many Korean intellectuals were singled out by Japanese officials for close surveillance. Many of them succeeded in escaping to the United States via Shanghai (Choy, 1979). These Korean students and political refugees, numbering about 600 in the following decade, played a leading role in organizing the Korean community, directing its activities toward Korean independence and the anti-Japanese movement.

The Intermediate Period

The national origins quota system came into full effect in 1924, completely barring Asian immigration until the end of World War II. The close political, military, and economic connections between the United States and South Korea, beginning with the Korean War in 1950, helped Korean immigration resume. As Table 8.1 shows, the number of Koreans admitted to the United States as permanent residents increased steadily after 1950, reaching a total of 2,362 in 1964. During the period between 1950 and 1964, more than 15,000 Koreans were admitted to the United States as legal immigrants.

Most of the Korean immigrants admitted during this intermediate period were war brides. During the Korean War, more than half a million U.S. soldiers were sent to South Korea, and tens of thousands were stationed there each year after the war ended. Many of these servicemen brought Korean wives home (Lee, 1991; Shin, 1987). Annual reports by the Immigration and Naturalization Service provide information on the number of people annually admitted as wives of U.S. citizens. According to the data, only one Korean woman was admitted as the wife of a U.S. citizen in 1950, but the number steadily increased over the years, reaching 1,340 in 1964. The data also show that wives of U.S. citizens made up more than

Table 8.1 Koreans Admitted to the United States, 1950-1964

Year	Immigrants	Nonimmigrants
1950	10	335
1951	33	187
1952	127	808
1953	115	1,111
1954	254	1,270
1955	315	2,615
1956	703	3,552
1957	648	1,798
1958	1,604	1,995
1959	1,720	1,531
1960	1,507	1,504
1961	1,534	1,771
1962	1,538	2,111
1963	2,580	2,803
1964	2,362	4,068
Total	15,050	27,459

SOURCE: Immigration and Naturalization Service (1950-1964).

40% of all Koreans admitted as legal immigrants between 1950 and 1964. Almost all of them were wives of U.S. servicemen. As will be shown later in this chapter, the number of Korean women admitted as wives of U.S. citizens steadily increased over the years, reaching the 3,000 mark in 1971.

War orphans constituted another major Korean immigrant group admitted during the intermediate period. During the Korean War, hundreds of thousands of Korean children lost their parents. During and after the war, U.S. servicemen stationed in South Korea adopted many of these children and brought them home. Later, nonmilitary U.S. citizens began to adopt Korean orphans as well. This international adoption significantly increased over the years. In the 1970s and 1980s, more than 3,000 Korean children were adopted annually by U.S. citizens and admitted to the United States. They accounted for about 60% of all alien children adopted by U.S. citizens.

Between 1950 and 1964, more Koreans came to the United States as nonimmigrant visitors than as legal immigrants. A large proportion of these nonimmigrant visitors were students. Some Koreans who came to the United States in the early 1950s to study were helped and influenced by U.S. servicemen stationed in Korea. Others sought the educational, economic, and occupational opportunities publicized by U.S. military and economic aides to South Korea. Thus, the military, political, and economic connections between the United States and South Korea were largely responsible for the migration of Korean students to the United States at this time, as well as for the migration of interracially married women and orphans. Many Koreans who came to the United States as students between 1950 and 1964 currently have professional occupations in the United States, including teaching positions at colleges and universities.

The New Immigration (1965-Present)

As indicated in the previous chapters, the Immigration Act of 1965 led to a dramatic increase in Asian immigration. Korea, along with the Philippines, China, and Vietnam, is one of the major source countries for the new immigration. The annual number of Korean immigrants steadily increased in the 1960s and the early 1970s, exceeding 30,000 in 1976. Between 1976 and 1989, 30,000 to 35,000 Koreans a year were admitted to the United States as immigrants. Only Mexico and the Philippines sent more immigrants to the United States during that period.

According to the 1970 census, the Korean population in the United States was 69,130. About 600,000 Koreans immigrated between 1970 and 1990 (see Table 8.2), bringing the 1980 Korean American population to 350,000, a five-fold increase over the 10-year period (see Table 2.3 in Chapter 2). The official count of Korean Americans in the 1990 census was close to 800,000. However, the U.S. census generally underestimates minority populations to a greater extent than the general population (Fein, 1990). The Korean group is no exception, particularly because many Koreans who originally come to this country as visitors stay here illegally and tend not to report to the census. Therefore, the actual number of Koreans in the United States in 1990 may have been close to 1 million, a 10-fold increase over the last 20 years.

Economic, political, and social conditions have improved in South Korea, particularly over the last 7 years or so. Koreans experienced a growth in per capita income from $843 in 1977 to $1,710 in 1985 and to $4,312 in 1990 (National Bureau of Statistics, 1984, p. 451; The Korean Statistical Association, 1991, p. 467). Many middle-class householders in Seoul and other large cities now own their own cars. Moreover social and political insecurity, which pushed many Koreans to the United States in the past, has been substantially reduced. South Korea had a popular presidential election at the end of 1987, putting an end to the 16-year-old military dictatorship. In the 1992 election, Koreans elected Kim Young Sam president, paving the way for rule by a

Table 8.2 Immigrant and Naturalized Koreans, 1965-1992

Year	Total Korean Immigrants	% of Korean Occupational Immigrants	Koreans Naturalized
1965	2,165		1,027
1966	2,492	18.4	1,180
1967	3,356	38.1	1,353
1968	3,811	27.8	1,776
1969	6,045	30.0	1,646
1970	9,314	30.8	1,678
1971	14,297	41.9	2,083
1972	18,876	45.0	2,933
1973	22,930	32.2	3,562
1974	28,028	33.5	4,451
1975	28,362	22.2	6,007
1976	30,830	14.6	6,450
1977	30,917	8.6	10,446
1978	29,288	11.8	12,575
1979	29,248	5.2	13,406
1980	32,320	2.9	14,073
1981	32,663	8.3	13,258
1982	30,814	3.5	13,488
1983	33,339	8.3	12,808
1984	33,042	8.8	14,019
1985	35,253	7.8	16,824
1986	35,776	8.6	18,037
1987	35,849	3.4	14,233
1988	34,703	8.9	13,012
1989	34,222	9.0	11,302
1990	32,301	9.9	10,500
1991	26,518	11.9	12,266
1992	19,359		8,297
Total	676,118		242,690

SOURCE: Adapted from Immigration and Naturalization Service (1965-1978, 1979-1992).

civilian president for the first time since President Syngman Rhee was ousted by a student uprising in 1960.

At the same time that people in South Korea have significantly improved their living conditions, they are also well informed about the adjustment difficulties of Korean immigrants in the United States. Because of their language barrier and labor market disadvantages, most Korean immigrants earn their living through self-employment in small businesses. Although this provides decent incomes for many Korean immigrants, there are numerous problems, including long work hours, physical danger, hostility by minority customers, and low social status (Min, 1990). The adjustment difficulties facing Korean immigrants are widely publicized in South Korea through books and movies. The damage done to Korean stores during the Los Angeles race riots in April 1992 further changed the general perception of U.S.-bound emigration in Korea. Many people in Korea donated money to help fellow Koreans in Los Angeles who lost their businesses overnight.

The significant improvements in economic, social, and political conditions in South Korea and the increasing publicity about Korean immigrants' adjustment difficulties in the United States have slowed the influx of Korean immigrants during recent years. As shown in Table 8.2, the number of U.S.-bound Korean emigrants has slightly decreased since the Seoul Olympic year of 1988. In 1992 the number was below 20,000. Because of the Los Angeles race riots' impact on the U.S. image, the annual number of Korean immigrants will likely be further reduced in the 1990s.

Another recent change in Korean immigration patterns is the lower socioeconomic background of Korean immigrants. Korean immigrants who came here in the 1970s generally represented the middle-class and upper-middle class segments of the Korean population. However, case studies show that recent Korean immigrants are lower in socioeconomic status (Hurh & Kim, 1988; Min, 1989c). A survey conducted recently in Seoul also indicates that lower-class rather than middle-class Koreans show a strong preference for immigration to the United States (Yoon, 1993). The increase in the standard of living in South Korea has partly contributed to this change. Middle-class Koreans are not attracted to U.S.-bound emigration, whereas lower-class Koreans may think that they can improve their economic conditions substantially by immigrating. As noted in Chapter 2, the change in the U.S. immigration law in 1976 made professional immigration almost impossible, greatly contributing to the change in the socioeconomic background of Korean immigrants. Since then, more than 90% of Korean immigrants have been admitted each year based on family reunification. Naturally, recent Korean family reunification immigrants have a lower socioeconomic background than the earlier Korean professional immigrants.

Settlement Patterns

Historically, Asian Americans have been concentrated in the western region of the United States. The Korean group followed this general

Table 8.3 Distribution of Koreans by Region and Major States (1980,1990)

Region	State	1980 N	1980 %	1990 N	1990 %	Increase Between 1980 and 1990 N	Increase Between 1980 and 1990 %
U.S. Total		354,593	100.0	798,849	100.0	444,256	125.2
Northeast	Total	68,151	19.2	182,061	22.8	113,910	167.1
	New York	34,157	9.6	95,648	12.0	61,491	180
	New Jersey	12,845	3.6	38,540	4.8	25,695	200.0
	Pennsylvania	12,502	3.5	26,787	3.4	14,285	114.3
Midwest	Total	62,214	17.5	109,087	13.7	46,873	75.3
	Illinois	23,989	6.8	41,506	5.2	17,517	73.0
	Michigan	8,714	2.5	16,316	2.0	7,602	87.2
South	Total	70,381	19.9	153,163	19.2	82,782	117.6
	Maryland	15,089	4.3	30,320	3.8	15,231	100.9
	Virginia	12,550	3.5	30,164	3.8	17,614	136.6
	Texas	13,997	3.9	31,775	4.0	17,778	127.0
West	Total	153,847	43.4	354,538	44.4	200,691	130.4
	Washington	13,083	3.7	29,697	3.7	16,614	127.0
	California	103,845	29.3	259,951	32.5	156,096	150.3
	Hawaii	17,962	5.1	24,454	3.1	6,492	36.1

SOURCE: U.S. Bureau of the Census (1983a, Table 63; 1993, Table 277).

pattern. As Table 8.3 shows, 44% of Korean Americans were settled in West Coast states in 1990. Nevertheless, Korean Americans are more widely scattered than other Asian ethnic groups. For example, the 1990 census shows that 76% of Japanese Americans and 68% of Filipino Americans are settled in the West (U.S. Bureau of the Census, 1993, p. 287).

California is the largest Korean state with nearly 260,000 Korean Americans settled there in 1990. Approximately 200,000 Koreans, more than 20% of total Koreans in the United States, resided in the Los Angeles-Long Beach metropolitan area in 1990. The presence of Koreans in Los Angeles is more clearly discernible in Koreatown, a Korean territorial community located approximately three miles west of downtown Los Angeles. Covering about 25 square miles, Koreatown is the residential and commercial center for Los Angeles Koreans. About 3,000 Korean-owned businesses with Korean-language signs are located in Koreatown where co-ethnics may find Korean food, groceries, books/magazines, and other services with distinctive cultural tastes (Min, 1993a).

Table 8.3 reveals that the percentage of Korean Americans in California increased from 29% in 1980 to 33% in 1990. Los Angeles and Orange counties have witnessed a particularly dramatic increase in the Korean population. Both the establishment of Koreatown as a territorial community and the mild weather in Los Angeles seem to have attracted more Korean immigrants to Southern California since the late 1970s.

In 1990, 12% of all Korean Americans were settled in New York state, a substantial increase from 9.6% in 1980. About 80,000 Koreans were settled in New York City, some 70% of them in the borough of Queens. Nearly 20,000 Koreans were settled in Flushing, Queens, accounting for 25% of the New York City Korean population. Flushing has recently emerged as the Koreatown of New York. Most Korean residents live near downtown Flushing, where they have established a Korean business district, *Hanin Sangga.* Many Korean restaurants, bakeries, barber shops, beauty salons, and video shops with Korean-language signs have been established there. Although the Los Angeles Koreatown is much larger in scale, the Flushing Korean enclave also serves as an overseas Seoul.

The Korean population in New Jersey marked a 200% growth rate during the 1980s, higher than that in any other state. This seems to be due, in part, to the increased number of Korean immigrants who, attracted by reasonably low housing prices, low crime rates, and quality schools, migrated from New York City to New Jersey suburban areas. It is also partly due to the increasing number of nonimmigrant Koreans working for overseas branches of Korean firms located in New Jersey. Between 1980 and 1990, Southern California and New York-New Jersey experienced greater increases in Korean population than the United States as a whole. This indicates the tendency of Korean immigrants to consolidate in the two areas. Hawaii, the center of the pioneer Korean immigrants, is no longer an important Korean center. Only 3% of U.S. Koreans were settled in Hawaii in 1990.

Economic and Occupational Adjustment

High Self-Employment Rate

An overwhelming majority of post-1965 Korean immigrants, drawn from the middle-class, held professional and other white-collar occupations in Korea. However, most of them were severely handicapped in their knowledge of the English language. In addition, American firms did not

Table 8.4 Los Angeles Koreans' Economic Segregation

	Male Respondents		Female Respondents		Total Respondents		Total Respondents & Family Members	
	N	%	N	%	N	%	N	%
Self-employed	179	53.0	57	35.8	236	47.5	374	45.1
Employed in ethnic firms	88	26.0	49	30.8	137	27.6	248	29.9
Employed in nonethnic firms	71	21.0	53	33.3	124	24.9	207	25.0
Total	338	100.0	159	100.0	497	100.0	829	100.0

SOURCE: Min (1989c).

recognize professional certificates acquired in Korea. Therefore Korean immigrants had difficulty finding similar white-collar and professional occupations in this country. Instead, they initially found employment in low-paying, menial jobs as cooks, waiters/waitresses, gas station attendants, and other kinds of laborers. Many Korean immigrants have turned to small business as an alternative to these blue-collar occupations (Min, 1984, 1989a; Yoon, 1991).

Based on a 1986 survey, Table 8.4 shows the extent to which Korean immigrants in Los Angeles are concentrated in small business. Fifty-three percent of Korean male workers in Los Angeles and 36% of female workers are self-employed. Approximately 45% of Korean immigrant workers in Los Angeles are self-employed in small businesses, and another 30% find employment in the Korean ethnic market. This means that only one out of four Korean workers is employed in a non-Korean firm. Case studies (Kim, 1981; Kim & Hurh, 1985; Min, 1992a) indicate that other Korean communities have similarly high levels of self-employment.

The high self-employment rate of Korean immigrants and their economic segregation have far-reaching effects on many noneconomic aspects of their lives, such as assimilation, family life, children's education, and intergroup relations. Some of these effects will be discussed later in this chapter.

Business Types

The grocery/liquor retail store is the most common Korean business in the Los Angeles Korean community. According to the Korean-American

Grocers Association of Southern California, there were about 2,800 Korean-owned liquor/grocery stores in Southern California as of August 1990, constituting about 25% of the total liquor/grocery businesses in the area. Koreans in communities such as Atlanta, Philadelphia, and Seattle are also heavily concentrated in the retail grocery business, serving non-Korean and particularly low-income black customers. My survey conducted in 1988 showed that about one fourth of Korean businesses in New York City were green grocery, deli, and liquor stores. As of January 1992, there were nearly 1,800 Korean-owned green grocery stores in the New York metropolitan area, accounting for about 60% of the total green grocery stores in the metropolitan area.

Trade businesses dealing in wigs, handbags, jewelry, and other fashion items also make up a significant proportion of Korean-owned businesses in major Korean communities. Most of the merchandise for this type of business is imported from South Korea and other Asian countries. Korean immigrants' concentration in these businesses was originally possible because of the active trade relations between the United States and South Korea. Korean exports to the United States increased significantly in the early 1970s, when the massive influx of Koreans to the United States began. By virtue of their language and other ethnic advantages, it was easier for Korean immigrants to establish businesses dealing in Korean-imported merchandise. This type of business is very active, particularly in the New York Korean community, because of its convenient trade relations with South Korea. There are about 400 Korean-owned import and wholesale stores in the Broadway Korean business district in Manhattan. Although Broadway-based Korean importers currently import more merchandise from other Asian countries such as Taiwan, Hong Kong, and China, most of them were established in the 1970s, taking advantage of the expanding Korean exports to the United States. The Broadway Korean importers distribute manufactured goods imported from South Korea and other Asian countries mainly to Korean wholesalers, who in turn distribute them to Korean retailers. As a result, Korean immigrants have established a virtual monopoly over wigs and several other businesses, which are vertically integrated from importers to retailers.

Chinese immigrants monopolized the laundry business in the early 20th century. However, Korean immigrants, not Chinese, currently control the dry cleaning business in Los Angeles and other major cities. Korean immigrants have also penetrated garment manufacturing. There are approximately 700 Korean-owned garment businesses in Los Angeles and 350 in New York. Koreans in Los Angeles own a large number of gas stations and fast-food franchises, a direct connection between Korean

Table 8.5 Los Angeles Koreans' Household Income by Self-Employment
Status

Annual Household Income	Self-Employed N	%	Employed N	%	Total N	%
Below $25,000	47	19.4	108	36.7	155	28.9
$25,000-49,999	90	37.2	127	43.2	217	40.5
$50,000 or more	105	43.4	59	20.1	164	30.6

SOURCE: Min (1989c).

immigrant businesses and big U.S. corporations (Light & Bonacich, 1988).
Retail fish stores and manicure services are also important Korean businesses in New York (Ha, 1991).

Small Business and Economic Mobility

As noted in Chapter 2 (see Table 2.9), 1990 U.S. census data show that
Korean immigrants were behind white Americans and most other Asian
ethnic groups in median family income. However, census data may greatly
underestimate Korean immigrants' incomes, because self-employed workers, whether Korean immigrants or not, tend to severely underreport their
incomes (Routh, 1980; Scase & Goffe, 1980). Because Korean immigrants
have a higher self-employment rate than any other ethnic/immigrant group,
census data may underestimate their incomes to a greater extent.

Survey data collected by Korean researchers more accurately reflect
Korean immigrants' incomes. Table 8.5 presents family incomes for Korean immigrants in Los Angeles and Orange counties based on my 1986
survey. The median household income for all U.S. households in 1986 was
$24,897 (U.S. Bureau of the Census, 1988, p. 442), and over 70% of Korean
immigrant households in Los Angeles and Orange Counties reached that
income level. As expected, self-employed Koreans earned substantially
higher household incomes than employed Koreans. Only 19% of self-
employed workers, compared to 36% of employed workers, reported their
annual household income to be below $25,000. In contrast, 43% of en-
trepreneurial respondents chose $50,000 or more as their household in-
come, compared to only 20% of employed respondents.

Although self-employed and employed respondents significantly differed in income level, their families had similar numbers of workers. More

significantly, other indicators such as home ownership, number of bedrooms, and number of cars suggest that entrepreneurial Korean families maintain a higher standard of living than other families (Min, 1989c). Operation of a small business involves long hours of work and other social costs (see the last chapter of Light & Bonacich, 1988). Yet self-employment helps many Korean immigrants achieve economic mobility, which is difficult to attain through employment in the general labor market.

The Middleman Minority Role and Intergroup Conflicts

Middleman minority theory is a useful theoretical tool in understanding how intergroup relations are affected by Korean immigrants' concentration in small business. Theoretically, middleman minorities play an intermediate role between the ruling class and the masses by distributing products made by the former to the latter (Blalock, 1967; Bonacich, 1973; Hamilton, 1978; Rinder, 1959; Zenner, 1991). The original version of middleman minority theory postulates that the ruling group encourages an alien group to play a middleman minority role distributing goods and services to the masses because there is no intermediate group to bridge the status gap in a society.

As I argued before (Min, 1988a, 1990), there is no evidence that either the U.S. government or U.S. corporations encouraged Korean immigrants to start small businesses. Nevertheless, several researchers have indicated that Korean immigrant business owners in the United States play a role similar to the traditional middleman minority role (Bonacich & Jung, 1982; Kim, 1981; Min, 1990; Portes & Manning, 1986; Waldinger, 1989). There are two important reasons why Korean immigrant entrepreneurs have been compared to a middleman minority. First, they serve low-income minority customers in greater proportions than chance might suggest. For example, blacks accounted for most customers in 44% of Korean-owned businesses in Atlanta in 1982, although blacks made up only a quarter of the total population in the Atlanta metropolitan area (Min, 1988a).

Second, the description of Korean immigrants as a middleman minority is meaningful because Korean entrepreneurs engaged in business in minority areas largely distribute merchandise produced by U.S. corporations, rather than their own products. One major Korean business is the retail grocery, and most Korean-owned grocery stores are located in low-income, minority areas. Korean grocers in black neighborhoods in Los Angeles, New York, and other cities distribute products made by Coca-Cola and other large manufacturers to low-income minority customers.

Minority/immigrant groups concentrated in small business are commonly involved in conflicts with different interest groups in the host society. The middleman minority groups that take the intermediary role between the producers and minority consumers are subject to high levels of hostility and rejection, particularly from minority customers. Korean business owners in black ghetto areas have been targets of hostile and even violent reactions from customers. The Korean ethnic media are full of stories about strikes, boycotts, and other forms of rejection of Korean-owned stores by black customers, black community leaders, and the black media. These conflicts have occurred in all major Korean communities in the United States but have been most severe in New York and Los Angeles, the two largest. At least five black boycott movements have been staged against Korean merchants in New York City since 1981, each lasting 8 weeks or longer (Min, 1990). The most recent attracted national media attention for several months. The boycott started in January 1990 in a black neighborhood in Brooklyn and ended in May 1991 when one of the two boycotted stores was sold to another Korean (Min, 1991b, 1994).

During the 1980s, the Los Angeles Korean community maintained better relations with blacks than the New York Korean community; Korean merchants in Los Angeles did not encounter a long-term black boycott in that decade. However, intergroup relations quickly deteriorated in 1991 when two black persons were shot to death by Korean merchants in separate incidents. During most of 1991, blacks picketed one Korean store located in a South Central Los Angeles black neighborhood after the owner shot a black robber to death. Then, during the 1992 Los Angeles race riots, about 2,300 Korean-owned stores located in South Central Los Angeles and Koreatown were burned and/or looted by black and Hispanic rioters. Property damages incurred by Koreans during the riots are estimated at more than $350 million. Many Korean merchants in Los Angeles lost their businesses, established through several years of hard work.

It is not surprising that many Korean-owned stores in black neighborhoods were targets of destruction, vandalism, and looting. It is, however, surprising that black rioters targeted Korean stores in Koreatown, which is located 3 miles from black neighborhoods. The exaggerated and biased coverage of Korean-black conflicts by the mass media partly contributed to this. In addition, the police did not try to protect Koreatown from attack by rioters. Many Koreans in Los Angeles felt that Korean immigrants were used as scapegoats during the Los Angeles riots to downplay black-white racial conflicts. Unfortunately, this may be the fate of a middleman minority group in any society with a high level of racial stratification.

Ethnicity and Assimilation

High Level of Ethnic Attachment

The extent to which members of an ethnic/immigrant group maintain their native cultural tradition and participate in ethnic social networks is referred to as *ethnic attachment* or *ethnicity* (Hurh & Kim, 1984; Reitz, 1980; Yinger, 1980). Korean immigrants in the United States maintain a high level of ethnic attachment, higher than any Asian ethnic group. Most Korean immigrants speak the Korean language, eat mainly Korean food, and practice Korean customs most of the time. Most are affiliated with at least one ethnic organization and are involved in active informal ethnic networks. For example, Hurh and Kim (1988) report that 90% of Korean immigrants in Chicago speak mainly the Korean language at home and that 82% are affiliated with one or more ethnic organizations. A comparative study of three Asian ethnic groups indicates that a much larger proportion of Korean Americans (75%) than Filipino (50%) or Chinese Americans (19%) have joined one or more ethnic associations (Mangiafico, 1988, p. 174).

There are three major reasons Korean immigrants maintain a high level of ethnic attachment (see Min, 1991b, for an extended discussion). First, South Korea is a small and culturally homogeneous country, with only one racial group speaking one language. By contrast, Chinese, Indian, and Filipino immigrants include several language groups. Having one native language gives Koreans enormous advantages for maintaining Korean ethnic attachment. Currently, the ethnic media play a central role in integrating members of an ethnic group who live in a nonterritorial community. By virtue of their common language, all Korean immigrants can understand Korean language ethnic newspapers and Korean TV programs.

Second, Korean immigrants maintain strong ethnic attachment partly because most of them are affiliated with Korean ethnic churches. Some 55% of Korean adult immigrants attended Christian churches in Korea prior to immigration (Hurh & Kim, 1988; Park, Fawcett, Arnold, & Gardner, 1990), although Christians constitute little more than 20% of the Korean population (National Bureau of Statistics, 1988). Many Korean immigrants who were not Christians in Korea attend the Korean ethnic church here, probably for practical reasons. Thus more than 75% of Korean immigrants are affiliated with Korean immigrant churches, most of them Protestant denominations (Hurh & Kim, 1984, 1990; Min, 1989c, 1992b).

Korean immigrant churches help to maintain social interactions among Korean immigrants by serving as places for meeting co-ethnics. They also help to maintain the Korean cultural tradition through Korean language and other cultural programs. Thus Korean immigrant churches contribute to maintaining Korean ethnicity by helping to stimulate social interaction among Koreans on the one hand and by helping to preserve Korean culture on the other. Ethnic/immigrant churches have also contributed to maintaining ethnicity for other ethnic/immigrant groups, such as Jewish and Italian Americans (Rosenberg, 1985; Tomasi & Engel, 1970, p. 186) and current Indian immigrants (Fenton, 1988). Nevertheless, churches seem to be far more effective in sustaining the ethnicity of Korean immigrants, because Koreans have a much higher level of affiliation with their ethnic churches than other groups.

Third, Korean immigrants' concentration in small businesses also strengthens Korean ethnicity. As noted above, most Korean immigrants are segregated in the ethnic economy, either as small business owners or as employees of stores owned by co-ethnics. As indicated elsewhere (P. Min, 1989a, 1991b), this enhances ethnic attachment and ethnic ties in two different ways. First, it contributes to Korean ethnicity by tying Koreans together socially and culturally. Most Korean immigrants work for Korean businesses and therefore maintain social interactions with fellow Koreans at the workplace, speaking the Korean language and practicing Korean customs during work hours. Korean immigrants in the Korean ethnic economy have been found to maintain more frequent social interactions with fellow Koreans even during off-duty hours and to speak the Korean language more frequently at home than those in the general economy (Min, 1989c).

Korean immigrant entrepreneurship also enhances ethnic solidarity because the operation of small businesses involves conflicts with outside interest groups. As previously noted, Korean merchants in black ghetto areas have received a high level of hostility from ghetto residents. In addition, Korean immigrant proprietors have come into conflict with the following interest groups: (a) white suppliers, (b) white landlords, (c) local residents, (d) white labor unions, and (e) governmental agencies. A series of conflicts with black customers and other interest groups have made Korean store owners aware of their potential collective threat in this country. This has contributed to the fostering of Korean ethnic solidarity. Korean merchants in many Korean communities have established various trade associations to deal with intergroup conflicts effectively and have taken collective actions to protect their common interests. For example, Korean green grocery and fish retailers in New York have both staged demonstrations against white wholesalers to protest unfair treatment and have successfully boycotted wholesalers until they received written apologies (Min, 1991b, 1994).

Business-related conflicts with outside interest groups have led not only Korean business proprietors, but also other Koreans to be concerned about their common fate and marginal status in this country. This has led nonentrepreneurial Koreans to join Korean store owners in protecting Korean business interests against outside groups. These efforts were well-exemplified in the 1990 black boycott of two Korean stores in Brooklyn, New York. Sales volumes for each Korean store were reduced to almost nothing after the boycott started in January 1990. However, the two store owners were able to keep their businesses open for more than a year by virtue of community donations. Not only Korean business associations, but also many nonbusiness associations and nonentrepreneurial Koreans made donations to help. In September 1990, some 7,000 New York Korean immigrants, young and old, male and female, entrepreneurial and nonentrepreneurial, participated in a mass rally against the then-New York City mayor, David Dinkins, for not having taken positive actions to bring the black boycott to an earlier end.

The 1992 Los Angeles race riots, which were far more destructive to the Korean community, have had far greater effects on Korean ethnic solidarity. As previously noted, many Koreans believed that before and during the riots, the U.S. media intentionally focused on Korean-black conflicts in order to vent blacks' frustration on Korean merchants. Angry about the biased media coverage, a number of Koreans sent letters of protest to the U.S. media. On May 3, about 1,000 Korean students rallied at the ABC-TV station to protest the station's biased coverage (Hwangbo, 1992). Moreover, many Koreans considered the failure of the police to respond to Koreans' desperate calls for help to protect Koreatown another white conspiracy to use Koreans as scapegoats. Koreans in Los Angeles held a solidarity and peace rally at Ardmore Park in Koreatown on May 2, the day after rioting came to an end in Los Angeles. Some 30,000 Koreans from all over the Los Angeles area participated in the rally, making it the largest Korean meeting ever held in the United States (Sunoo, 1992).

In addition, the Los Angeles riots also heightened young Koreans' ethnic identity and ethnic solidarity. It was the first major event that provided Korean Americans who were born or raised in the United States with an opportunity to think about their common fate. They saw their parents targeted by blacks simply because they were Koreans. They realized that they can be targets of attack by another group simply because they are Korean Americans. Many young Koreans suspected that the police did not care about protecting Koreatown from attack by rioters mainly because Korean Americans are a powerless minority group. Immediately after the riots, many young Koreans showed their quick responses by writing articles in major English dailies in California, attacking the media bias and the police inactivity in protecting Koreatown and defending the position of the Korean community. A large number of young Koreans, born or raised in the United States, participated in the solidarity rally held at Ardmore Park, which made the rally truly multigenerational. They agreed that the riot exposed the political weakness of Koreans and that it is their obligation to protect the interests of the parent generation.

Low Level of Assimilation

Thus far, we have noted that Korean immigrants maintain a high level of ethnicity compared to other Asian immigrant groups. Their cultural homogeneity, high affiliation with Korean immigrant churches, and concentration in small businesses contribute to their strong ethnic attachment and ethnic solidarity. What about Korean immigrants' level of assimilation compared to other immigrant groups?

Assimilation and ethnicity are not mutually exclusive. Hurh and Kim (1984) have shown that Korean immigrants have achieved assimilation in proportion to their length of residence in the United States, but that their increased level of assimilation has not reduced the level of ethnic attachment. Nevertheless, it is also true that some components of ethnic attachment have negative effects on assimilation. For example, Koreans who more frequently speak Korean and eat Korean food depend on English and American food less frequently. Thus, as Korean immigrants maintain strong ethnic attachment, they are slower than other immigrant groups in achieving assimilation. Although they achieve assimilation in proportion to their length of residence, only a small proportion of Korean old-timers use English with their spouses at home and depend on English newspapers and magazines for news and information (Chang, 1991; Hurh & Kim, 1988).

Cultural homogeneity and economic segregation help Korean immigrants maintain strong ethnic attachment but hinder their assimilation into American society. Because Korean immigrants were not exposed to significant subcultural differences in their home country, most of them have a low level of tolerance for the cultural differences found in the United States; they are unwilling to learn English and American customs. Finding employment in Korean firms, new Korean immigrants have little motivation to learn English. Moreover, the confinement of the vast majority of Korean immigrants to the ethnic market provides them with little opportunity to learn English and American customs at the workplace. Korean immigrants are self-employed in small businesses mainly because of the language barrier and their lack of assimilation, but their concentration in small businesses further reduces their chances for assimilation.

Although Korean concentration in small businesses has hindered their assimilation, their business-related conflicts with outside interest groups have increased their political skills and political consciousness. The hostility from black customers and residents in particular has contributed to this political growth. During the 1990 black boycott of Korean stores in Brooklyn, New York, Korean community and business leaders visited the Brooklyn borough president, New York City mayor, federal government offices, and even the White House, pressing them to take effective measures to terminate the boycott.

The Los Angeles race riots have heightened Koreans' political consciousness more than any other incident. Los Angeles Koreans have made efforts to get government compensation for their property damages and to protect Koreans' overall interests. The Korean Lawyers' Association in Los Angeles has held several meetings to discuss the possibility of suing the government for neglecting to protect Koreatown during the riots. In July 1992, a group of Korean lawyers in Los Angeles organized the Korean American Legal Advocacy Foundation, a nonprofit organization, to protect Koreans' civil rights ("Korean-American," 1992). In the 1992 election, Jay Kim, a Korean immigrant, was elected to the House of Representatives, representing the 43rd congressional district in California. He was one of only four Asian American congressional members in 1993.

Intermarriage and International Inmarriage

For an effective look at Korean intermarriage, we need to treat three Korean groups separately: (a) Korean Americans in Hawaii, (b) Korean women married to U.S. servicemen, and (c) post-1965 immigrants and their descendants.

Intermarriage in Hawaii

The oldest U.S. Korean community was created in Hawaii, although as previously noted, that community is currently insignificant in population size. Research shows that Koreans in Hawaii are characterized by a high level of intermarriage, higher than any other ethnic group. For example, Harvey and Chung (1980) report that during the period between 1960 and

1968, 80% of Korean brides and grooms in Hawaii married members of non-Korean ethnic groups, compared to the 40% intermarriage rate for other ethnic groups. Based on marriage records in 1970, 1975, and 1980, research by Kitano, Yeung, Chai, and Hatanaka (1984) shows that nearly 90% of Korean marriages in Hawaii in those years were intermarriages. Although intermarriages are common in Hawaii, no other group reached a similar level. The absence of chain migrations in Hawaii, a small group size, no establishment of an ethnic enclave, and the high assimilation of the old Koreans in Hawaii all seem to have contributed to this exceptionally high intermarriage rate.

The study by Harvey and Chung (1980) indicates that intermarrying Korean females tended to prefer white grooms, whereas intermarrying Korean males chose Japanese women more often than whites. This pattern is primarily the result of a difference between Korean men and women in accepting traditional conjugal relations. American-born Korean women want more egalitarian conjugal relations and therefore prefer white men as their marital partners. The outmarrying Korean men, however, feel more comfortable with traditional conjugal relations and therefore prefer Japanese brides.

Intermarriage Between Korean Women and U.S. Servicemen

As previously noted, many U.S. servicemen stationed in South Korea during and since the Korean War have married Korean women. According to *Annual Reports* by the Immigration and Naturalization Service, 42,044 Korean female immigrants were admitted as wives of U.S. citizens in the 1970s, with an annual number of 4,204 (Shin, 1987); a similar number were admitted in the 1980s (Lee, 1991). The vast majority are married to U.S. servicemen. A report by the Korean Foreign Ministry indicates that intermarried emigrants constituted 15.4% of the Korean total to the United States between 1970 and 1989 (Lee, 1991). A study based on the 1980 census shows that 27% of married Korean women in California, compared to only 6% of their male counterparts, have spouses with non-Korean ethnic backgrounds (Jiobu, 1988, p. 161). The immigration of Korean women married to U.S. servicemen partly explains this gender differential in the intermarriage rate. However, even among Koreans who were born or raised in America, many more women than men engage in intermarriage.

Korean women who married U.S. servicemen generally had a low socioeconomic status, although there are many exceptions (Kim, 1972, 1978; Lee, 1989; Ratliff, Moon, & Bonacci, 1978). Many of them were born and raised in rural villages and migrated to Seoul and other large cities in search of urban employment. Their language barrier and lack of assimilation make marital adjustment very difficult (Jeong & Schumm, 1990). Moreover, many interracially married U.S. servicemen neglect and even abuse their Korean wives, deciding that the women who provided them with companionship in Korea are no longer valuable to them in this country. For these reasons, an unusually high proportion of intermarriages between Korean women and U.S. servicemen are known to have ended in divorce, although no hard data are available. Using the number of divorcees per 1,000 persons as a measure, Korean immigrant women show a divorce rate more than twice as high as their male counterparts (Min, 1988b, 1989b). This great sex differential in divorce seems to be due mainly to the high divorce rate of Korean women married to U.S. servicemen. Those Korean women who fail in this type of intermarriage usually have a severe language barrier and, therefore, do not have useful job skills. Thus they face great economic and adjustment difficulties.

Intermarriage and International Inmarriage for Koreans Born or Raised in the United States

Most Korean Americans who married during recent years are either U.S.-born Koreans or Koreans who were born in Korea but who accompanied their parents to the United States at early ages. A significant proportion of recently married Korean women married persons outside of the Korean group, mostly white males, whereas very few young Korean men are involved in intermarriages. For example, one survey in Los Angeles conducted in 1986 shows that approximately 13.7% of the Korean women married in the previous 5 years were involved in intermarriage, in comparison to only 2.5% of Korean men (Min, 1993b). Sixty-one percent of the intermarried Korean women were married to white spouses, whereas most of the few intermarried Korean men chose Asian women. Korean American males, even in the second generation, tend to accept a more traditional gender role orientation than native-born white males. It is therefore not surprising that Korean men avoid white spouses whereas Korean women see white men as desirable marital partners.

Thanks to the convenience of air transportation, many young Koreans bring their marital partners from Korea. Marriage between a Korean American and a partner from Korea might be referred to as *international inmarriage.* The 1986 Los Angeles survey indicates that 36.7% of Korean men and 30.7% of Korean women who had married in the previous 5 years brought their spouses over from Korea (Min, 1993b). This type of marriage involves adjustment problems similar to those involved in international outmarriage. First, a marriage between a Korean American partner and a partner from Korea has more sources of marital conflict because it involves more cultural differences than a marriage between two Korean American partners. A marriage between a Korean American woman and a man from Korea, in particular, is very problematic because the Americanized bride cannot accept the male chauvinism of the groom from Korea. Second, the marriage between a Korean American and a partner from Korea is likely to involve a higher level of personality or value incongruence because, unlike a marriage between two Korean Americans, an international inmarriage takes place without the usual processes of dating and courtship. Also, the international inmarriage is often characterized by adjustment difficulties, especially in the early years, because the partner from Korea has to adjust simultaneously to immigration and marriage.

Increase in Korean Women's Economic Role and Marital Conflicts

The Radical Increase in Korean Women's Economic Role

The Chinese Confucian cultural tradition has had a powerful influence on Korean culture, particularly the Korean family system. Confucianism's emphasis on a clear role differentiation between husband and wife has helped to establish an extreme form of patriarchy in Korea. In traditional Korean society, the husband was considered the primary breadwinner and decision maker in the family, exercising complete authority over his wife and children. The wife was expected to obey her husband, devotedly serve him and his family members, and perpetuate her husband's family lineage by bearing children.

Much of the traditional gender role differentiation has been preserved in South Korea. In spite of a high level of urbanization, industrialization, and economic development, only a small proportion of nonfarm married women (19%, according to the 1980 census) participate in the labor force in South Korea (Min, 1988b). Traditional gender role orientation, on the one hand, and employment/wage discrimination against women on the other, discourage married women from participating in the labor market in South Korea.

The immigration of Koreans to the United States has led to many changes in the traditional Korean family system, but the most noteworthy change is probably the radical increase in Korean women's labor force participation rate. The 1980 U.S. census shows that 56% of married Korean immigrant women were in the labor force, compared to 49% of married white women (U.S. Bureau of the Census 1983b, pp. 1-159). The census underestimates the rate of Korean women in the labor force, because many Korean immigrant women who work for their family businesses do not report their work to the census. My survey, conducted in 1988, indicates that 70% of Korean married women in New York City undertook an economic role (Min, 1992a). That compares to 57% for U.S. married women in general in 1988 (U.S. Bureau of the Census, 1989, p. 385). More significant is the fact that Korean immigrant women work exceptionally long hours. The New York City survey shows that those Korean married women who undertook an economic role (70% of the sample) worked an average of 51 hours per week, with 80% working full-time (Min, 1992a).

The high labor force participation rate of Korean immigrant women and their long work hours can be largely explained by the concentration of Korean immigrant families in small businesses. To operate a labor-intensive small business effectively, Korean male immigrants need their wives' help at the store. In fact, the coordination between husband and wife, along with long hours of work, was found to be the central factor that makes Korean small businesses successful (Min, 1988a). The New York City survey indicates that 38% of Korean married women who undertook the economic role worked in the family business with their husbands (Min, 1992a).

Double Burdens, Stress, and Marital Conflicts

Has the increase in the Korean immigrant wife's economic role led to a decrease in her domestic role? Several studies on this issue indicate that Korean immigrant wives, whether they work outside the home or not, bear the main responsibility for traditional domestic tasks; husbands' help is almost negligible (Kim & Hurh, 1988; Min, 1992a). Few Korean dual-worker families have a housemaid working part-time or full-time (Min, 1992a), although most career women in Seoul and other large cities in Korea depend on housemaids for cooking and other housework (Choe, 1985, p. 143). Korean immigrant working women can significantly reduce their housework only when they have elderly mothers or mothers-in-law cohabiting with them. Because most do not have that advantage, they suffer from double burdens. The New York City study indicates that Korean immigrant working wives spend 75.5 hours weekly between their job and their housework—12 hours more than their husbands (Min, 1992a).

Both Korean immigrant men and women tend to overwork compared to the U.S. adult population in general. However, overwork seems to be more stressful for Korean immigrant women than their husbands, because they suffer from role strain that their husbands usually do not experience. Of course, U.S. working women also suffer from stress, role strain, and other forms of depression due to their divided attention between paid and household work (Fox & Nichols, 1983). However, overwork seems to be much more stressful for Korean immigrant wives than for U.S. working wives, particularly because Korean working wives also experience stress relating to their language barrier and other adjustment problems.

Korean social workers and Korean ethnic newspaper articles suggest that many Korean immigrant families suffer from marital conflicts. One factor that might contribute to these marital conflicts is overwork and work-related stress. Second, the increase in Korean immigrant wives' economic role, combined with their husbands' unwillingness to give up power, seems to contribute to marital conflicts.

Although Korean immigrant wives' significant contribution to the family economy has increased their marital power, their husbands are unwilling to change traditional conjugal relations. Most Korean immigrant husbands want to cling to the traditional patriarchy common in their native country, but they have difficulty maintaining conjugal power because of their wives' increased economic independence. Finally, the downward mobility in social status experienced by most Korean adult immigrants might be another important source of marital conflicts. Although most Korean immigrants have improved their standard of living since immigration, they have lost the relatively high occupational positions they held in Korea. Their dissatisfaction with low social status has negative effects on their immigrant lives in general (Hurh & Kim, 1991) and their marital relations in particular (Min, 1992a).

Child Socialization and Children's Education

Achievement Orientation and Korean Children's Success in School

One important aspect of Confucianism is respect for educated people and emphasis on children's education. Under the influence of the Confucian cultural tradition, Koreans have historically had great faith in education as the main avenue for social mobility. In fact, emphasis on children's education is probably the most noteworthy feature of child socialization in

Korea. Parents in Korea tend to consider their children's education and their own careers equally important; many of them are willing to sacrifice their generation to offer their children a better education. In Seoul and other large cities, the typical family with a child in high school spends a significant amount of income on the child's extracurricular studies. To prepare for the competitive college entrance examination, most high school students in large Korean cities attend private institutions specializing in mathematics and English after school. A significant proportion also take lessons from private tutors. Thus parents in Korea bear a heavy financial burden for their children's extracurricular studies.

Korean immigrants to the United States have brought with them Korean values emphasizing the importance of children's education and the social practices exemplifying these values. Following the teaching by Mencius that "a good mother is ready to move three times to give children good education," most Korean immigrants with school-age children seem to decide where to live largely based on the academic quality of public schools in the neighborhood. Koreans' desire to buy houses in affluent suburban areas with good public schools is reflected in the 1990 census: Koreans, along with Indian Americans, show the highest rate of suburban residence among all ethnic groups (see Table 2.8 in Chapter 2). Korean immigrants have continued their practice of sending their children to private institutions after school to prepare them for admission to specialized high schools and prestigious universities. In Flushing (where about one fourth of New York City Koreans reside), there are about 20 Korean-run private institutions specializing in English and mathematics. My survey, conducted in 1988, indicates that about 20% of Korean junior and senior high school students in New York City take lessons after school, either in a private institution or with a private tutor. During summer vacation, many Korean students from Philadelphia, Atlanta, and other northeastern cities come to New York and stay for 2 months or so to attend private institutions for English and mathematics lessons.

Partly due to Korean parents' emphasis on children's education and partly due to their relatively high socioeconomic background, many Koreans born or raised in the United States have made remarkable achievements in their school work. There are many indicators of their success. For example, three specialized high schools in New York City base their admissions on competitive examinations in English and mathematics; Korean students make up more than 15% of the students accepted to these schools, although Koreans constitute less than 1% of the population in New York City. Two or three Korean students have annually received the presidential merit scholarship given to the two best high school seniors in each state based on school achievements and extracurricular activities.

Korean Children's Problems and Generational Conflicts

Although a large number of Korean students are highly successful in their school work, a significant proportion of them, particularly new immigrant children, have problems in school and are involved in a variety of delinquent acts. Most Korean adolescents seem to experience serious conflicts with their parents. To provide a more objective picture, we need to pay attention to the negative aspects of Korean children's adjustment in addition to their success in school.

Korean school counselors have told me that cutting class, skipping school without notice, fighting, and running away from home are common problems of Korean high school students. However, gang-related crimes have become the most serious juvenile problem in the Korean immigrant community. Youth gangs began to emerge in the Los Angeles Korean community in the late 1970s and in New York in the early 1980s. At present, both communities are fighting very hard against gang-related problems (Choi & Russell, 1989; Yu, 1987). Like gangs in Chinatown (Sung, 1987, p. 137), Korean gangs recruit immigrant children who have language barriers and difficulty with school work. These gangs start for recreational and self-defense purposes (Yu, 1987) but eventually engage in criminal activities such as group fighting, murder, armed robbery, burglary, kidnapping, and extortion of businesses. Korean ethnic newspapers recently published many articles reporting Korean gang-related robberies and burglaries of Korean restaurants and Korean homes.

According to Yu (1987, p. 34), about 150 Korean children in Los Angeles were affiliated with gangs in 1984, and another 150 who were not gang members were involved in juvenile delinquency. The number may be very small, considering the size of the Korean population in Los Angeles, yet Korean parents are gravely concerned about gang problems, because any child can join a gang and it is extremely difficult to get out once a member. Korean social workers in the New York area informed me that several Korean families permanently returned to Korea to get their children out of a gang. A 15-year-old Korean boy affiliated with a gang in New York City was stabbed to death by another Korean gang member in January 1988, just 10 hours before his expected return migration to Korea with family members (Choi & Russell, 1989, pp. 71-72).

Language barriers, cultural differences, and a sense of alienation and discrimination in school are just some sources of Korean children's problems, which explain why most of these problem children are immigrants rather than native born. In a survey of Korean junior and senior high school students in New York City, the respondents were asked whether they feel discriminated against by American students or teachers in school. Thirty percent of them reported that they felt personally discriminated against by American students, and 18% said that they had the feeling of being discriminated against by American teachers (Min, 1991a). Many respondents in the survey reported that Hispanic and black students gave them trouble more often than white students. Cultural differences very often cause American teachers to misunderstand Korean immigrant students, and there are too few Korean teachers and counselors in large Korean communities like Los Angeles and New York City to help.

However, Korean immigrant families seem to be more responsible for their children's problems than the school system. Although there are parent-child conflicts in all American families, the conflicts are more serious in Korean immigrant families due to the language barrier and value differences. Most Korean children, particularly those born in this country, cannot speak Korean fluently, whereas most adult Korean immigrants have difficulty speaking English. Therefore, in many Korean immigrant families, the parents speak Korean and the children speak English (Min & Min, 1992). Value conflicts, combined with this language barrier, build an unbridgeable distance between Korean parents and adolescent children. Korean immigrant parents embrace values emphasizing hard work, family ties, social status, and education, values which are far less important to their children (Min & Min, 1992). Most Korean parents put great pressure on their children to excel in school and to attend good colleges. Unsuccessful Korean students are not rewarded and are sometimes even neglected by parents, increasing the likelihood they will spend time on the street. Finally, Korean immigrant parents, who spend long hours at work, have little time to play with their children or supervise them at home. In a survey of Korean junior and senior high school students in New York City, 64% of the respondents reported that neither parent stays at home after school, and 46% said that no one stays at home after school (Min, 1991a). It is easy for Korean children uninterested in studying to go out, meet friends, and get caught up in delinquent activities when no one supervises them at home after school.

Conclusion

Although it has a century-long history, the Korean American community is largely composed of post-1965 Korean immigrants. Korean immigrants in the United States are concentrated in small businesses mainly because of the language barrier and other disadvantages in the general labor market. Korean immigrants in general are doing well economically by virtue of their long hours of work in small businesses. However, Koreans' concentration in small family businesses has led to an increase in immigrant women's economic role, an unfamiliar role to women in Korea. Although the gain in Korean women's economic independence has increased their power relative to their husbands, it has also led to role strain and an increase in marital conflict. Moreover, Korean parents' long hours of work give them little time to spend at home with their children, which contributes to a wider generational gap and more juvenile delinquency.

Korean immigrants maintain a higher level of ethnicity than other Asian immigrant groups, which can be explained by three factors. First, Korean immigrants' cultural homogeneity, characterized by one race, one language, and lack of subgroup differences, provides the cultural basis of Korean ethnicity. Second, the affiliation of the vast majority of Korean immigrants with Korean ethnic churches provides the physical and social basis of Korean ethnicity. Korean immigrants meet at the Korean church, where they interact with co-ethnics, maintaining the Korean cultural tradition. Finally, the concentration of Korean immigrants in a limited range of labor-intensive small businesses provides the economic basis of Korean ethnicity. Korean immigrants maintain strong ethnic attachment partly because more than 75% of them work in the segregated Korean ethnic subeconomy, either as business owners or as employees of businesses owned by co-ethnics. They also maintain strong solidarity mainly because of their business-related conflicts with outside interest groups.

Unfortunately, Koreans' cultural homogeneity, the affiliation of most Koreans with Korean churches, and their economic concentration in small businesses also hinder their assimilation. Most Korean immigrants resist learning English and American customs partly because they were not exposed to different languages and customs prior to their immigration to the United States. However, it is also true that most Korean immigrants have had little opportunity to learn English and American customs because they are physically segregated in religious services and economic activities here in the United States.

Although Koreans' economic segregation has hindered their assimilation, their business-related conflicts with outside interest groups have contributed to the development of their political savvy and political consciousness. The 1990 black boycott of Korean stores in New York and the material and psychological damage inflicted on Korean merchants by the 1992 Los Angeles race riots have enhanced their political consciousness. Korean immigrants now realize that they need to gain political power to protect their economic interests. In addition, the Los Angeles race riots have heightened younger Koreans' ethnic consciousness and ethnic identity. They also have given them the chance to speak up for the Korean community, increasing their obligations to and their power in the Korean community.

References

Blalock, H. M. (1967). *Toward a theory of minority group relations.* New York: John Wiley.

Bonacich, E. (1973). A theory of middleman minorities. *American Sociological Review, 37,* 547-559.

Bonacich, E., & Jung, T. H. (1982). A portrait of Korean small business in Los Angeles. In E. Y. Yu, E. Phillips, & E. S. Yang (Eds.), *Koreans in Los Angeles: Prospects and promises* (pp. 75-98). Los Angeles: Center for Korean-American and Korean Studies, California State University.

Chang, W. H. (1991). Korean Americans and Korean newspapers. In Pyong Gap Min (Ed.), *Koreans in the United States* [in Korean] (pp. 281-300). Seoul, Korea: Yurim.

Cheng, L., & Bonacich, E. (Eds.). (1984). *Labor migration under capitalism.* Berkeley: University of California Press.

Choe, J. S. (1985). *Studies of Korean contemporary families* [in Korean] (2nd ed.). Seoul: Illjisa.

Choi, S. W., & Russell, D. (1989). *I cannot believe my child can do it* [in Korean]. Seoul: Yurim.

Choy, B. Y. (1979). *Koreans in America.* Chicago: Nelson Hall.

Fein, D. J. (1990). Racial and ethnic differences in U.S. Census omission rates. *Demography, 27,* 285-301.

Fenton, J. Y. (1988). *Transplanting religious traditions: Asian Indians in America.* New York: Praeger.

Fox, K., & Nichols, S. (1983). The time crunch: Wife's employment and family work. *Journal of Family Issues, 4,* 61-82.

Ha, D. S. (1991). Business patterns in the New York Korean community. In P. G. Min (Ed.), *Koreans in the United States* [in Korean] (pp. 88-121). Seoul: Urim.

Hamilton, G. (1978). Pariah capitalism: Paradox of power and dependence. *Ethnic Groups, 1,* 1-15.

Harvey, Y. S., & Chung, S. H. (1980). The Koreans. In J. McDermott et al. (Eds.), *People and cultures of Hawaii* (pp. 135-154). Honolulu: University of Hawaii Press.

Hurh, W. M., & Kim, K. C. (1984). *Korean immigrants in America: A structural analysis of ethnic confinement and adhesive adaptation.* Madison, WI: Fairleigh Dickinson University Press.

Hurh, W. M., & Kim, K. C. (1988). *Uprooting and adjustment: A sociological study of Korean immigrants' mental health* (Final report submitted to National Institute of Mental Health). Washington, DC: U.S. Department of Health and Human Services.

Hurh, W. M., & Kim, K. C. (1990). Religious participation of Korean immigrants in the United States. *Journal of the Scientific Study of Religion, 19,* 19-34.

Hurh, W. M., & Kim, K. C. (1991). Adaptation stages and mental health of Korean male immigrants in the U.S. *International Migration Review, 24,* 456-479.

Hwangbo, K. (1992, May 11). Korean Americans organize and mobilize. *Korea Times Los Angeles* (English Edition), p. 3.

Immigration and Naturalization Service. (1950-1978). *Annual report.* Washington, DC: U.S. Government Printing Office.

Immigration and Naturalization Service. (1979-1992). *Statistical yearbook.* Washington, DC: U.S. Government Printing Office.

Jeong, G. J., & Schumm, W. (1990). Family satisfaction in Korean/American marriages: An exploratory study of the perceptions of Korean wives. *Journal of Comparative Family Studies, 21,* 325-335.

Jiobu, R. M. (1988). *Ethnicity and assimilation: Blacks, Chinese, Japanese, Koreans, Mexicans, Vietnamese, and Whites.* Albany: State University of New York Press.

Kim, B. L. (1972). Casework with Japanese and Korean wives of Americans. *Social Casework, 53,* 273-279.

Kim, B. L. (1978). Pioneers in intermarriage: Korean women in the United States. In H. H. Sunoo & D. S. Kim (Eds.), *Korean women in struggle for humanization* (pp. 229-245). Monteclair, NJ: The Association of Korean Christian Scholars in North America.

Kim, I. S. (1981). *New urban immigrants: The Korean community in New York.* Princeton, NJ: Princeton University Press.

Kim, K. C., & Hurh, W. M. (1985). Ethnic resources utilization of Korean immigrant entrepreneurs in the Chicago Minority Area. *International Migration Review, 19,* 82-111.

Kim, K. C., & Hurh, W. M. (1988). The burden of double roles: Korean wives in the U.S.A. *Ethnic and Racial Studies, 11,* 151-167.

Kitano, H., Yeung, W. T., Chai, L., & Hatanaka, H. (1984). Asian-American interracial marriage. *Journal of Marriage and the Family, 46,* 179-190.

Korean-American legal advocacy foundation to be established soon. (1992, July 25). *Korea Times Los Angeles,* p. 3

The Korean Statistical Association. (1991). *Korea statistical yearbook, 1991* (38th ed.). Seoul: The Korean Statistical Association.

Lee, D. (1989). Marital adjustment between Korean women and American servicemen. *Korean Observer, 20,* 321-352.

Lee, D. (1991). Contributions and adjustment problems of interracially married Korean women. In P. G. Min (Ed.), *Koreans in the United States* [in Korean] (pp. 317-350). Seoul: Urim.

Light, I., & Bonacich, E. (1988). *Immigrant entrepreneurs: Koreans in Los Angeles, 1965-1982.* Berkeley: University of California Press.

Lyu, K. (1977). Korean nationalist activities in Hawaii and the continental United States, 1900-1919. *Amerasia Journal, 1,* 23-90.

Mangiafico, L. (1988). *Contemporary Asian immigrants: Patterns of Pilipino, Korean, and Chinese settlement in the United States.* New York: Praeger.

Min, B. Y. (1986). *One hundred years of Korean immigration to the United States: Profiles of the early immigrants* [in Korean]. Los Angeles: *Korea Times Los Angeles.*

Min, J. Y., & Min. P. G. (1992). *The relationship between Korean immigrant parents and their children.* Paper presented at the Annual Meeting of the American Sociological Association, Pittsburgh.

Min, P. G. (1984). From white-collar occupations to small business: Korean immigrants' occupational adjustment. *Sociological Quarterly, 25,* 333-352.

Min, P. G. (1988a). *Ethnic business enterprise: Korean small business in Atlanta.* Staten Island, NY: Center for Migration Studies.

Min, P. G. (1988b). The Korean American family. In C. H. Mindel, R. W. Habenstein, & R. Wright, Jr. (Eds.), *Ethnic families in America: Patterns and variations* (pp. 199-229). New York: Elsevier.

Min, P. G. (1989a). Korean immigrant entrepreneurship: A multivariate analysis. *Journal of Urban Affairs, 10,* 197-212.

Min, P. G. (1989b). The social costs of immigrant entrepreneurship: A response to Edna Bonacich. *Amerasia Journal, 15*(2), 187-194.

Min, P. G. (1989c). *Some positive functions of ethnic business for an immigrant community: Koreans in Los Angeles.* Washington, DC: National Science Foundation.

Min, P. G. (1990). Problems of Korean immigrant entrepreneurs. *International Migration Review, 24,* 436-455.

Min, P. G. (1991a). Children's education and problems in the Korean immigrant community. In P. G. Min (Ed.), *Koreans in the United States* [in Korean] (pp. 217-248). Seoul: Yurim.

Min, P. G. (1991b). Cultural and economic boundaries of Korean ethnicity: A comparative analysis. *Ethnic and Racial Studies, 14,* 225-241.

Min, P. G. (1992a). Korean immigrant wives' overwork. *Korea Journal of Population and Development, 21,* 23-36.

Min, P. G. (1992b). The structure and social functions of Korean immigrant churches in the United States. *International Migration Review, 26,* 1370-1394.

Min, P. G. (1993a). Korean immigrants in Los Angeles. In I. Light & P. Bhachu (Eds.), *Immigration and entrepreneurship* (pp. 185-204). New York: Transaction.

Min, P. G. (1993b). Korean immigrants' marital patterns and marital adjustment: An exploratory study. In H. McAdoo (Ed.), *Family ethnicity: Strengths in diversity* (pp. 287-299). Newbury Park, CA: Sage.

Min, P. G. (1994). *Ethnic business and ethnic solidarity: Koreans in New York.* Unpublished manuscript, Department of Sociology, Queens College of the City University of New York.

National Bureau of Statistics. (1984). *Korea statistical yearbook, 1984* (31st ed.). Seoul: Economic Planning Board, Republic of Korea.

National Bureau of Statistics. (1988). *Korean statistical yearbook, 1988* (35th ed.). Seoul: Economic Planning Board, Republic of Korea.

Park, I. H., Fawcett, J., Arnold, F., & Gardner, R. (1990). *Korean immigrants and U.S.immigration policy: A predeparture perspective* (East-West Population Studies Series 114). Honolulu: East-West Center.

Patterson, W. (1988). *The Korean frontier in America: Immigration to Hawaii, 1896-1910.* Honolulu: University of Hawaii Press.

Portes, A., & Manning, R. (1986). The immigrant enclaves: Theory and empirical examples. In J. Nagel & S. Olzak (Eds.), *Competitive ethnic relations* (pp. 47-68). New York: Academic Press.

Ratliff, B. W., Moon, H. F., & Bonacci, G. H. (1978). Intercultural marriage: The Korean American experience. *The Social Casework, 59,* 221-226.

Reitz, J. (1980). *The survival of ethnic groups.* Toronto: McGraw Hill.

Rinder, I. D. (1959). Strangers in the land: Social relations in the status gap. *Social Problems, 8,* 253-261.

Rosenberg, S. (1985). *The new Jewish identity in America.* New York: Hippocrene.

Routh, G. (1980). *Occupation and pay in Great Britain, 1906-1979.* London: Macmillan.

Scase, R., & Goffe, R. (1980). *The real world of the small business owner.* London: Croom Helm.

Shin, E. H. (1987). Interracially married Korean women in the United States: An analysis based on hypergamy-exchange theory. In E. Y. Yu & E. Phillips (Eds.), *Korean women in transition: At home and abroad* (pp. 249-276). Los Angeles: Center for Korean-American and Korean Studies, California State University.

Sung, B. L. (1987). *The adjustment experience of Chinese immigrant children in New York City.* Staten Island, NY: Center for Migration Studies.

Sunoo, P. B. (1992, May 11). Out of ashes, solidarity. *Korea Times Los Angeles* (English Edition), pp. 1, 8.

Tomasi, S. M., & Engel, M. H. (1970). *The Italian experience in the United States.* Staten Island, NY: Center for Migration Studies.

U.S. Bureau of the Census. (1983a). *1980 census of population, general population characteristics, United States summary* (PC80-1-B1). Washington, DC: U.S. Government Printing Office.

U.S. Bureau of the Census. (1983b). *1980 census of population, general social and economic characteristics, United States summary* (PC80-1-1C). Washington, DC: U.S. Government Printing Office.

U.S. Bureau of the Census. (1988). *Statistical abstracts of the United States: 1988* (108th ed.). Washington, DC: U.S. Government Printing Office.

U.S. Bureau of the Census. (1989). *Statistical abstracts of the United States: 1989* (109th ed.). Washington, DC: U.S. Government Printing Office.

U.S. Bureau of the Census. (1993). *1990 census of population, general population characteristics, the United States* (CP-1-1). Washington, DC: U.S. Government Printing Office.

Waldinger, R. (1989). Structural opportunity or ethnic advantage? Immigrant business development in New York. *International Migration Review, 23,* 48-72.

Yinger, S. (1980). Toward a theory of assimilation and dissimilation. *Ethnic and Racial Studies, 4,* 249-264.

Yoon, I. J. (1991). The changing significance of ethnic and class resources in immigrant businesses: The case of Korean immigrant businesses in Chicago. *International Migration Review, 25,* 303-332.

Yoon, I. J. (1993). *The social origin of Korean immigration to the United States from 1965 to the present* (East-West Center Population Series No. 121). Honolulu: East-West Center.

Yu, E. Y. (1987). *Juvenile delinquency in the Korean community of Los Angeles.* Los Angeles: Korea Times, Los Angeles.

Yun, Y. (1977). Early history of Korean immigration to America. In H. C. Kim (Ed.), *The Korean Diaspora* (pp. 33-46). Santa Barbara, CA: ABC-CLIO.

Zenner, W. (1991). *Minorities in the middle: A cross-cultural analysis.* Albany: State of University of New York Press.

9

Vietnamese, Laotian, and Cambodian Americans

RUBÉN G. RUMBAUT

In the years following the end of the Indochina War in 1975, over 1 million refugees and immigrants from Vietnam, Cambodia, and Laos arrived in the United States. Together with their American-born children, by 1990 they already represented more than one out of every seven Asian Americans, adding significantly not only to the size but to the diversity of the Asian-origin population in the United States. They are the newest Asian Americans, and the story of their migration and incorporation in America differs fundamentally in various ways from that of other Asian-American ethnic groups reviewed in this volume.

To be sure, except for persons of Japanese descent, the overwhelming majority of Asian Americans today are foreign born, reflecting the central role of contemporary immigration in the formation of these ethnic groups. But unlike other Asians, most Indochinese[1] have come as *refugees* rather than as *immigrants*. Unlike post-1965 immigrants from the Philippines, South Korea, China, India, and elsewhere in Asia whose large-scale immigration was influenced by the abolition of racist quotas in U.S. immigration law, the Indochinese have entered outside of regular immigration channels as part of the largest refugee resettlement program in U.S. history, peaking in 1980 and continuing ever since. As refugees from three countries devastated by war and internecine conflicts, they have experienced contexts of exit far more traumatic than practically any other newcomers in recent times, and they have had no realistic prospect of return to their homelands. Moreover, their reception as refugees reflects a different legal-political entry status conferred by the U.S. government, a status that among other things facilitates access to a variety of public assistance programs to which other immigrants are not equally entitled. The American *welfare* state has shaped their incorporation far more than any other immigrant group in U.S. history, even as their exodus and resettlement were complex, unintended consequences of the intervention and ultimate failure of U.S. foreign policies and of the American *warfare* state. Indeed, the Indochinese case underscores the need to attend carefully to historical contexts, and particularly to the role of the state and of war itself, in explaining specific types of migrations and ethnic group formations.

Unlike the Chinese and Japanese, the Vietnamese, Laotians, and Cambodians do not share a history of several generations in America, a history marked early on by harsh discriminatory treatment and official exclusion. Unlike the Filipinos, they are not veterans of a half-century of direct U.S. colonization. At first the Indochinese could not be resettled into coethnic communities previously established by earlier immigration, because such communities were essentially nonexistent prior to 1975; in the resettlement process, they were more likely to be dispersed throughout the country than other large immigrant groups. Unlike recent Asian immigrant flows, most notably those from India, which have been characterized by large proportions of highly educated professionals and managers, the Indochinese flows, with the notable exception of the "first wave" of 1975 evacuees from South Vietnam, have been characterized by far larger proportions of rural, less educated people than any other Asian immigrant group in decades. There are also significant contrasts with other large refugee groups: For example, unlike refugees from Cuba and the former Soviet Union, who are among the oldest populations in the United States, the Indochinese are among the youngest, with median ages of less than 20 for all groups except the Vietnamese, partly a reflection of high levels of fertility. All of these particular sociodemographic characteristics and contexts of exit and reception have shaped their adaptation to the American economy and society.

As refugees of the Indochina War, they share a common history and experiences that distinguish them from other Asian American groups. However, the various Indochinese ethnic groups—Vietnamese, Khmer (Cambodian), lowland Lao, Hmong, Mien, and other Laotian and Vietnamese highlanders, and ethnic Chinese from all three countries—also differ from each other in fundamental ways. As we will see in this chapter, they have different social backgrounds, languages, cultures, and often adversarial histories, and they reflect different patterns of settlement and adaptation in America. They range from members of the elite of former U.S.-backed governments to Vietnamese and Chinese "boat people," survivors of the "killing fields" of Cambodia in the late 1970s, and preliterate swidden farmers from the highlands of northern Laos. And *within* each of these ethnic groups there are major differences, especially by social class, between different "waves" or cohorts of arrival and by gender and generation. Tens of thousands of Amerasians—children of Vietnamese mothers and American fathers who served in Vietnam during the war—have also been resettled in the United States under a special law enacted in 1987 (the Amerasian Homecoming Act); much discriminated against and stigmatized as *bui doi* (children of the "dust of life"), they too form yet another distinct and poignant legacy of the war.

Given its limitations, this chapter cannot consider each of these points in detail nor provide a comprehensive review of the large research literature that has accumulated on these topics over the past decade and a half; it will aim rather to provide an overview of the most salient patterns. The chapter will be organized in two main sections, moving from a review of the available data at the national level to more detailed survey and other comparative data collected in a major metropolitan area where Indochinese are concentrated. We begin, however, with a brief discussion of the war that led to the formation of Vietnamese, Cambodian, and Laotian communities in America. One of the ironies of the war that took America to Vietnam, and of the war's expansion into Cambodia and Laos, is that a sizable part of Vietnam, and also of Cambodia and Laos, has now come to America.

A Legacy of War: Indochinese Refugees in Historical Perspective

The Indochinese refugees are a product of the longest war in modern history—the 30-year Vietnam War (1945-1975) and its metastasis into Laos and Cambodia in the 1960s and early 1970s. An immensely complex conflict that still creates bitter controversy and whose full significance will continue to be assessed and debated for years to come, the war was a tragedy of staggering proportions for Americans, Vietnamese, Cambodians, and Laotians alike. With the exception of the American Civil War a century earlier, the Vietnam War became the most divisive event in U.S. history. By war's end about 2.2 million American soldiers had served in Vietnam: Their average age was 19, 5 to 7 years younger than in other American wars—and almost 58,000 died there or were missing in action, their names memorialized on a wall of polished black granite dedicated in 1982 in the nation's capital. The war also cost the United States over $120 billion during 1965 to 1973 alone, triggering a postwar inflation and an economic chain reaction that shook the world economy. The war defined an entire generation of young people in the 1960s, polarized the American electorate into "hawks" and "doves," and led to President Lyndon Johnson's early retirement from politics in 1968 and ultimately to the Watergate scandals of the Nixon Administration in the early 1970s (Baskir & Strauss, 1978; Hess, 1990; Kolko, 1985; Young, 1991). "The first war that the United States ever lost" produced a "Vietnam syndrome" whose political ramifications still affect the formulation of American foreign policy—for example, President George Bush promised "no more Vietnams" before launching Operation Desert Storm in 1991. It also influences the trajectory of national elections—for example, the controversies over the Vietnam-era draft status of former Vice President Dan Quayle in 1988 and of President Bill Clinton in 1992.

The war also produced a massive refugee population for whom the United States assumed a historic responsibility. Not coincidentally, Vietnam represents at once the worst defeat of U.S. foreign policy in the Cold War era and the leading example (with Cuba) of the functions of U.S. refugee policy; Vietnamese (and Cubans) admitted as political refugees into the United States have served as potent symbols of the legitimacy of American power and global policy (cf. Pedraza-Bailey, 1985; Portes & Rumbaut, 1990). The circumstances of the U.S. withdrawal from Vietnam, the dramatic fall of Saigon, and its aftermath—and indeed, the extent to which such refugee flows have been a dialectical consequence of U.S. foreign policy in an era of East-West superpower rivalry (Gibney, 1991; Hein, 1993; Zolberg, Suhrke, & Aguayo, 1989; Zucker & Zucker, 1987)— also provided added moral and political justification for significantly expanded domestic refugee programs, which totaled some $5 billion in cash, medical assistance, and social services to primarily Indochinese refugees during 1975 to 1986 alone (Rumbaut, 1989b).

If the war divided America, it devastated Vietnam, Laos, and Cambodia. During the period of U.S. involvement, starting with the defeat of the French at Dien Bien Phu in 1954, it is estimated that over 4 million Vietnamese soldiers and civilians on both sides were killed or wounded—a casualty rate of nearly 10% of the total population. The total firepower used by the United States in Vietnam exceeded the amount used by the United States in all its previous wars combined, including both world wars. In South Vietnam alone, about a third of the population was internally displaced during the war, and over half of the total forest area and some 10% of the agricultural land was partially destroyed by aerial bombardment, tractor clearing, and chemical defoliation. (Research on the long-term health effects on the local population of the dumping of more than 11 million gallons of the toxic defoliant Agent Orange is still fragmentary.) In Laos the war exacted its greatest toll on the Hmong, an ethnic minority from the rural highlands who fought on the U.S. side against the Pathet Lao; before the fall of Vientiane about a third of the Hmong population had been uprooted by combat, and their casualty rates were proportionately 10 times higher than those of American soldiers in Vietnam. In Cambodia, whose fate was sealed after the war expanded in 1970, as many as a quarter of its people may have died during the horror of the late 1970s. The war shattered the region's economy and traditional society. A tragedy of epic proportions, the "war that nobody won" left these three countries among the poorest in the world (Becker, 1986; Chanda, 1986; Isaacs, 1983; Karnow, 1991; Korn, 1991; Mason & Brown, 1983; Shawcross, 1984). By the mid-1980s, in an international economic ranking of 211 countries, Vietnam was ranked 202nd (with an estimated per capita national annual income of $130), Laos 208th ($100 per capita), and Cambodia 211th (the world's poorest at $50 per capita) (Rumbaut, 1991b, p. 522).

Since the war's end in 1975, over 2 million refugees are known to have fled Vietnam, Laos, and Cambodia. The refugee exodus was shaped by complex political and economic factors. As is true of refugee movements elsewhere, the first waves of Indochinese refugees were disproportionately composed of elites who left because of ideological and political opposition to the new regimes, whereas later flows included masses of people of more modest backgrounds fleeing continuing regional conflicts and deteriorating economic conditions (Portes & Rumbaut, 1990; Rumbaut, 1989b). Vietnamese professionals and former notables were greatly overrepresented among those who were evacuated to American bases in Guam and the Philippines under emergency conditions during the fall of Saigon. Lao and Cambodian elites, by contrast, were much more likely to go to France (the former colonial power in Indochina), where French-speaking Indochinese communities, particularly in Paris, had developed as a result of more than half a century of previous migration.

Among the first to flee on foot across the Mekong River into Thailand were the Hmong, but they were the least likely to be resettled by Western countries at the time. Most were to languish in Thai camps for years. In Vietnam and Laos, meanwhile, several hundred thousand persons with ties to the former regimes were interned in "re-education camps." Beginning in 1989, over 50,000 of those former Vietnamese political detainees would be resettled in the United States under special legislation. In Cambodia the cities were deurbanized as the population was forced into labor camps in the countryside; the capital of Phnom Penh became a ghost town practically overnight. But the exodus of the 1975 refugees was only the beginning of an emigration that has not yet run its course.

A massive increase of refugees beginning in late 1978 was triggered by a series of events:

> The Vietnamese invasion of Cambodia, which quickly ended 3 years of Khmer Rouge rule
>
> The subsequent border war between Vietnam and China in early 1979, which accelerated the expulsion of the ethnic Chinese petit bourgeoisie from Vietnam
>
> A new guerilla war in the Cambodian countryside, already wracked by famine and the destruction of the country's infrastructure
>
> The collapse of both the Chao Fa guerilla resistance against the Pathet Lao and the new system of collective agriculture in Laos, compounded by mismanagement and natural catastrophes

Hundreds of thousands of Cambodian survivors of the Pol Pot labor camps fled to the Thai border, along with increased flows of Hmong and other refugees from Laos; about 250,000 ethnic Chinese from North Vietnam moved across the border into China; and tens of thousands of Chinese and Vietnamese boat people attempted to cross the South China Sea packed in rickety crafts suitable only for river travel, many of whom drowned or were assaulted by Thai pirates preying on refugee boats in the Gulf of Thailand. By spring 1979 nearly 60,000 boat people were arriving monthly in the countries of the region.

These events led to an international resettlement crisis later that year, when those "first asylum" countries (principally Thailand, Malaysia, and Indonesia) refused to accept more refugees into their already swollen camps, often pushing boat refugees back out to sea (Malaysia alone pushed some 40,000 out) or forcing land refugees at gunpoint back across border mine fields (U.S. Committee for Refugees, 1985, 1986, 1987). In response, under agreements reached at the Geneva Conference in July 1979, Western countries began to absorb significant numbers of the refugee camp population in Southeast Asia.

In total, just over 1 million had been resettled in the United States by 1992 and 750,000 in other Western countries (principally Canada, Australia, and France); many others still languished in refugee camps from the

Thai-Cambodian border to Hong Kong. Harsh "humane deterrence" policies and occasional attempts at forced repatriation sought to brake the flow of refugees to first-asylum countries, with limited success. After 1979 the number of boat refugee arrivals declined, but it never dropped below 20,000 annually (until abruptly coming to a halt in 1992, when boat arrivals totaled a mere 41), exacting a horrific cost in human lives: It has been estimated that at least 100,000 boat people, and perhaps over twice that number, drowned in the South China Sea (U.S. Committee for Refugees, 1987).

Beginning in the 1980s, an Orderly Departure Program (ODP) allowed the controlled immigration of thousands of Vietnamese directly from Vietnam to the United States, most recently focusing on two groups with a unique tie to the war, Amerasians and former reeducation camp internees. By the end of 1992, over 300,000 Vietnamese had immigrated to the United States through the ODP, including 161,400 in the regular family reunification program, 81,500 Amerasians and their accompanying relatives, and 61,000 former political prisoners and their families (U.S. Committee for Refugees, 1993, p. 86; U.S. General Accounting Office, 1994). But the Amerasian program is scheduled to end in 1994, and refugee processing for former political prisoners may end in 1995. In Laos and Cambodia, meanwhile, refugee flows had virtually ended by the early 1990s, with the focus shifting to the voluntary repatriation of refugees still in camps in Thailand and elsewhere.

Indeed, an entire era was coming to a close, while a new phase of the Indochinese diaspora was opening. The end of the Cold War in 1989, the collapse of the former Soviet Union in 1991, U.N.-supervised elections in Cambodia in 1993 that sought to end its long-running civil war, and the end of the U.S. trade embargo against Vietnam in February 1994 were but the most remarkable events of a compressed period of extraordinarily rapid and fundamental changes in international relations that is transforming the nature of Indochinese refugee resettlement in the United States. In this post-Cold War context, the U.N. High Commissioner for Refugees proclaimed the 1990s the "decade of repatriation." Already most of the ODP family reunification cases in the 1990s have been leaving Vietnam as regular immigrants, not as refugees, a pattern likely to become more pronounced over time.

The flows from Laos and Cambodia to the United States have been, respectively, sharply reduced and virtually terminated. For some first-generation Indochinese adults exiled in America, the new developments in their homelands may open the possibility of return or of establishing business and other linkages between their native and adoptive countries (Kotkin, 1994a; Lam, 1994); but for a sizable and rapidly growing second generation of young Vietnamese, Laotian, and Cambodian Americans now rooted in communities throughout the United States and speaking accentless English, a new era was dawning in which the legacy of war will likely recede in practical importance. Theirs is an American future.

The Indochinese in America: A National Perspective

The research literature which has accumulated on Indochinese Americans over the past decade or so is surprisingly large, especially when compared to that of larger groups with much longer histories in the United States. As state-sponsored immigrants, the refugee status of this population has not only provided them with greater eligibility for various forms of government assistance, but in some respects it may have also made them an "overdocumented" population in comparison with other immigrants. Indeed, the 1975 refugees in particular may be the most closely studied arrival cohort in U.S. history.

In this section we summarize available information from a variety of national data sources to ascertain the size of the distinct Indochinese populations and to describe their patterns of immigration, settlement, and socioeconomic progress. In addition to the U.S. Bureau of the Census, these national data sources include the U.S. State Department, Immigration and Naturalization Service (INS), Internal Revenue Service, and the Office of Refugee Resettlement (ORR), established by the Refugee Act of 1980, and its predecessor the Indochinese Refugee Program. In a subsequent section we review a wide range of findings from local studies of Vietnamese, Chinese-Vietnamese, Cambodian, Lao, and Hmong ethnic groups, to examine in more depth their adaptation processes, including such topics as mental health, pregnancy outcomes, and the educational progress of their children. There are a number of advantages and disadvantages to both the national and local studies and available data sets, and these will be pointed out in the course of the discussion.

Immigration History and Population Size

Among Asian Americans, the Indochinese constitute the most recently formed ethnic groups. According to the INS, the first recorded Vietnamese immigration to the United States occurred in 1952, when eight immigrants were admitted; the first Cambodian immigrant arrived in 1953, and the first Laotian in 1959 (Immigration and Naturalization Service, 1991). As late as 1969, fewer than 200 Cambodians and Laotians combined had immigrated to the United States, and the total from Vietnam amounted to little more than 3,000—mostly university students from elite families, as well as diplomats and war brides who had come in the late 1960s in the wake of the rapid expansion of U.S. involvement in Vietnam. As Table 9.1 shows, in the early 1970s the number of these pioneer immigrants quintupled to nearly 15,000 from Vietnam, whereas it increased only slightly to nearly 300 each from Cambodia and Laos. Thus, when Saigon fell in April 1975, the Vietnamese in America numbered about 20,000, whereas the number of Cambodians and Laotians was still negligible.

About 130,000 refugees, nearly all from South Vietnam, were resettled in the United States during 1975. A small number arrived during 1976 to 1978, bottoming out in 1977, but a massive new inflow began in late 1978 in the context of the international refugee crisis described earlier. As Table 9.1 shows, about 450,000 Indochinese refugees arrived en masse during 1979 to 1982 alone, peaking in 1980 (the record year in U.S. refugee resettlement history) when 167,000 were admitted. Since 1982 Indochinese arrivals have oscillated between 40,000 and 80,000 annually. Vietnamese refugee admissions, totaling over 650,000 from 1975 to 1992, have been supplemented by a substantial, if little noticed, flow of over 170,000 nonrefugee Vietnamese immigrants who arrived in the United States during the same period—the latter including persons coming to the United States from other countries and from Vietnam through the ODP, among them the young Amerasians and accompanying relatives mentioned earlier. By 1992, total Indochinese arrivals numbered 1,223,699: 147,850 Cambodians (12%), 230,385 Laotians (19%), and 845,464 Vietnamese (69%). Of that total, 86% entered as refugees (the remainder as immigrants), and four out of five arrived in the United States since 1980. U.S. government agencies collect these data only by nationality, not ethnicity, so it is not possible to determine the proportion of ethnic Chinese and other minority groups among them; however, ORR estimates that of the 213,519 Laotian arrivals during 1975 to 1990, 92,700 were highlanders, primarily Hmong.

Immigration statistics do not include children born in the United States. A study of the newcomers' fertility patterns calculated this number at nearly 200,000 by 1985 (Rumbaut & Weeks, 1986). Allowing for natural increase, and adjusting for mortality (which is low because this is a very young population) and emigration (which is negligible), Bouvier and Agresta (1987) projected a 1990 Indochinese population of over 1.3 million

Table 9.1 Arrivals in the United States From Cambodia, Laos, and Vietnam, 1952-1992: Refugees, 1975-1992; Nonrefugee Vietnamese Immigrants, 1975-1992; and Pre-1975 Immigrants

Fiscal Year	Post-1975 Refugee Arrivals			Non-Refugee Immigrants Vietnam[a]	Total
	Cambodia	Laos	Vietnam		
1992	193	7,272	26,841	45,580	79,886
1991	199	9,232	28,450	33,764	71,645
1990	2,323	8,719	27,714	28,271	67,027
1989	1,916	12,432	22,664	15,880	52,892
1988	2,805	14,556	17,654	4,391	39,406
1987	1,539	15,564	23,012	3,635	43,750
1986	9,789	12,869	22,796	6,068	51,522
1985	19,097	5,416	25,457	5,134	55,104
1984	19,851	7,291	24,818	5,244	57,204
1983	13,114	2,835	23,459	3,290	42,698
1982	20,234	9,437	43,656	3,083	76,410
1981	27,100	19,300	86,100	2,180	134,680
1980	16,000	55,500	95,200	1,986	168,686
1979	6,000	30,200	44,500	2,065	82,765
1978	1,300	8,000	11,100	2,892	23,292
1977	300	400	1,900	3,194	5,794
1976[b]	1,100	10,200	3,200	4,201	18,701
1975	4,600	800	125,000	3,038	133,438
Subtotal:	147,460	230,023	653,521	173,896	1,204,900

Period	Pre-1975 Immigrant Arrivals			Total
	Cambodia	Laos	Vietnam	
1970-1974[c]	286	292	14,661	15,219
1960-1969	98	69	3,167	3,334
1952-1959	6	1	219	226
Subtotal	390	362	18,047	18,799
Total, 1952-1992	147,850	230,385	845,464	1,223,699

SOURCE: Compiled from records maintained by the Statistics Division, U.S. Immigration and Naturalization Service; U.S. State Department; and U.S. Office of Refugee Resettlement.
NOTE: Refugee arrivals from 1975 to 1981 are rounded to the nearest hundred.
a. Totals include 55,985 Amerasians from Vietnam admitted as immigrants in fiscal year 1989-1992.
b. The totals for 1976 include a transition quarter as a result of fiscal year changes.
c. Totals include 98 Cambodians and 96 Laotians who entered as immigrants in fiscal year 1975.

including 859,600 Vietnamese, 259,700 Laotians, and 185,300 Cambodians. But the 1990 U.S. census counted only 614,547 Vietnamese (well below even the number of actual arrivals from Vietnam since 1975—see

Table 9.1); a Laotian population of 239,096 (including 90,082 Hmong); and a Cambodian population of 147,411. Taken together, the 1990 census count of these Indochinese groups totaled just over 1 million, well below all available projections.

What accounts for such a significant disparity, especially among the Vietnamese? The gap is too large to be explained by a census undercount, which probably did not exceed 5% among the Vietnamese in particular. One clue is that the 1990 census also counted a Chinese population of 1,645,472—well above what had been expected (e.g., Bouvier and Agresta had projected a 1990 Chinese population of 1,259,038). It appears that sizable numbers of ethnic Chinese from Vietnam, Laos, and Cambodia indicated their ethnicity as Chinese in response to the appropriate census question. Earlier research had estimated that ethnic Chinese from Vietnam accounted for up to 25% of total Vietnamese arrivals and up to 15% of total Cambodian arrivals (Rumbaut & Weeks, 1986; cf. Whitmore, 1985). Applying these proportions to the 1990 census figures would yield an additional 200,000 from Vietnam and 20,000 from Cambodia, bringing the total Indochinese population in the United States more closely in line with both immigration and natural increase data. Future research on Indochinese Americans based on 1990 census data should be cognizant of the ambiguity surrounding ethnicity, birthplace, and country of last residence (all of which may differ), and of the apparent exclusion of sizable numbers of these ethnic Chinese groups. It is also not clear how Amerasians from Vietnam may have responded to census questions on race and ethnicity, although most Amerasians arrived in the United States after the 1990 census was taken.

Patterns of Settlement

The 130,000 (mostly Vietnamese) refugees who arrived in the United States during 1975 were first sent to four government reception centers—at Camp Pendleton, California; Fort Indiantown Gap, Pennsylvania; Fort Chaffee, Arkansas; and Eglin Air Force Base, Florida—where they were interviewed by voluntary agencies and matched with sponsors throughout the country, including individuals, church groups, and other organizations (for studies of the refugees sent to Fort Indiantown Gap and Camp Pendleton, respectively, see Kelly, 1977, and Liu, Lamanna, & Murata, 1979). U.S. refugee placement policy aimed to disperse the refugee population to all 50 states in order to minimize any negative impacts on receiving communities ("to avoid another Miami," as one planner put it, referring to the huge concentration of Cuban refugees there), and indeed the 1975

Indochinese refugees were more significantly dispersed than other immigrant or refugee populations (Forbes, 1984).

One study (Baker & North, 1984) found that the refugees were initially placed in 813 separate zip code areas in every state, including Alaska, with about two thirds settling in zip code areas that had fewer than 500 refugees and only 8.5% settling in places with more than 3,000 refugees. Less than half were sent to the state of their choice. Despite this general pattern of dispersal—shaped by government policy, the availability of sponsorships, and the relative absence of family ties and previously established ethnic communities in the United States—areas of Indochinese concentration nonetheless began to emerge, particularly in California, and to grow rapidly as a result of secondary migration from other states. Significantly, by 1980, 45% of the 1975 arrivals lived in a state other than the one where they had been originally sent; the proportion in zip code areas with fewer than 500 refugees had dropped to 40%, whereas those residing in places with more than 3,000 had more than doubled to 20%. The proportion of the refugee population living in California had doubled from about 20% to 40%; these were concentrated in Southern California metropolitan areas (Los Angeles, Orange, and San Diego counties) and, to the north, in the Silicon Valley city of San Jose.

As the much larger waves of Indochinese refugees began to arrive in the late 1970s and especially during the 1980s, their patterns of settlement continued to be shaped by the factors noted above, especially by the social networks that were becoming increasingly consolidated over time. Government policies and programs (such as the Khmer Guided Placement Project— dubbed the "Khmer Refrigerator Project" by Cambodians because of its Frostbelt locations—and the Favorable Alternative Sites Project) sought the dispersal of refugees without family ties away from high impact areas, whereas most others were reunited with family members already residing in areas of high concentration (Finnan & Cooperstein, 1983; Forbes, 1984, 1985). Remarkably, by the early 1980s about a third of arriving refugees already had close relatives in the United States who could serve as sponsors, and another third had more distant relatives, leaving only the remaining third without kinship ties subject to the dispersal policy (cf. Hein, 1993).

In addition, different localities of concentration emerged for the different ethnic groups, with the largest Cambodian community in the nation developing in the Long Beach area of Los Angeles County, the largest Lao enclave in San Diego, and the largest Hmong community around Fresno, in California's agricultural San Joaquin Valley (in the Fresno telephone directory, the Vangs—one of but two dozen Hmong clan names—are as numerous as the Joneses). By 1990 the largest Vietnamese concentration in the United States was found in Orange County, with its hub in the communities of Santa Ana and Westminster (Little Saigon); among recent Orange County home buyers, the Nguyens outnumbered the Smiths 2 to 1 (Kotkin, 1994b). Los Angeles, San Jose (where the Nguyens outnumbered the Joneses in the phone book 14 columns to 8), San Diego, and Houston followed in rank order. But Indochinese Americans continue to reside in every state of the nation, as the 1990 census makes clear, and their patterns of settlement differ in some significant ways from those of other Asian Americans.

With the earlier caveat in mind about missing data for ethnic Chinese from the Indochinese totals, Table 9.2 breaks down 1990 census data by selected states of settlement of Vietnamese, Cambodian, Lao, and Hmong groups. Although California is home for 12% of the total U.S. population, 39% of the Lao—and of all Asian Americans, for that matter—live there; the degree of concentration in California is even greater for the Vietnamese (46%), the Cambodians (46%), and the Hmong (52%). By contrast, whereas over 20% of Asian Americans reside in New York/New Jersey and Hawaii (compared to 10% of the U.S. population), less than 4% of all Indochinese have settled in those states.

After California, the Vietnamese are most concentrated in Texas (11%), with sizable communities in Houston and Dallas (which began to be formed by the 1975 cohort, attracted by employment opportunities), and along the Gulf coast (especially of shrimp fishers). Remarkably the Vietnamese are already the largest Asian-origin group in Texas and in the contiguous states of Louisiana, Mississippi, Arkansas, Kansas, and Oklahoma. After California, another 17% of all Cambodians are concentrated bicoastally in Massachusetts and Washington, and despite their comparatively small numbers they are the largest Asian-origin group in Rhode Island (see Martin, 1986). The Lao are the most dispersed among the Indochinese groups, and they do not predominate in any state; but the Hmong are the most concentrated, with another 37% located in the contiguous states of Minnesota and Wisconsin, where they are by far the largest Asian-origin group—an extraordinary development considering that prior to 1975 there had been virtually no immigration from Laos to America.

Social and Economic Characteristics

National data on social and economic characteristics of Vietnamese, Cambodian, and Laotian Americans are available from two main sources: the decennial census and annual government surveys of nationwide samples. Only the census reports data by ethnic groups (except, as noted, for

Table 9.2. Selected States of Settlement of Vietnamese, Cambodian, and Laotian Groups in the United States, Compared to the Total U.S. Population and the Total Asian-Origin Population, 1990[a]

		Total Population	Total Asian	Vietnamese	Cambodian	Lao	Hmong
Total U.S.	(N)	248,709,873	6,908,638	614,547	147,411	149,014	90,082
	(%)	100.0	100.0	100.0	100.0	100.0	100.0
Proportionately Above-Average States of Indochinese Settlement:							
California		29,760,021	2,735,060	280,223	68,190	58,058	46,892
		12.0	39.6	45.6	46.3	39.0	52.1
Texas		16,986,510	311,918	69,636	5,887	9,332	176
		6.8	4.5	11.3	4.0	6.3	0.2
Virginia		6,187,358	156,036	20,693	3,889	2,589	7
		2.5	2.3	3.4	2.6	1.7	0.0
Massachusetts		5,016,425	142,127	15,449	14,058	3,985	248
		2.4	2.1	2.5	9.5	2.7	0.3
Washington		4,866,692	195,918	18,696	11,096	6,191	741
		1.9	2.8	3.0	7.5	4.2	0.8
Wisconsin		4,891,769	52,782	2,494	521	3,622	16,373
		2.0	0.8	0.4	0.4	2.4	18.2
Minnesota		4,375,099	76,952	9,347	3,858	6,381	16,833
		1.8	1.1	1.5	2.6	4.3	18.7
Proportionately Below-Average States of Indochinese Settlement:							
New York		17,990,455	689,303	15,555	3,646	3,253	165
		7.2	10.0	2.5	2.5	2.2	0.2
Florida		12,937,926	149,856	16,346	1,617	2,423	7
		5.2	2.2	2.7	1.1	1.6	0.0
Pennsylvania		11,881,643	135,784	15,887	5,495	2,046	358
		4.8	2.0	2.6	3.7	1.4	0.4
Illinois		11,430,602	282,569	10,309	3,026	4,985	433
		4.6	4.1	1.7	2.1	3.3	0.5
Ohio		10,847,115	89,723	4,964	2,213	2,578	253
		4.4	1.3	0.8	1.5	1.7	0.3
Michigan		9,295,297	103,501	6,117	874	2,190	2,257
		3.7	1.5	1.0	0.6	1.5	2.5
New Jersey		7,730,188	270,839	7,330	475	478	25
		3.1	3.9	1.2	0.3	0.3	0.0

SOURCE: Adapted from U.S. Bureau of the Census (1993a, Table 253). These data report the official census counts (100% tabulations); by contrast, because the data in Table 9.3 are based on a sample, group sizes may differ.

a. These Indochinese population totals derive from the 1990 census question on race, which listed Vietnamese, Cambodian, Laos, Hmong, and Chinese among the available choices. As noted in the text, it appears that ethnic Chinese from Vietnam, Cambodia, and Laos indicated their ethnicity as Chinese in response to that census question, thereby significantly increasing the Chinese population counted by the 1990 census and decreasing that for the respective Indochinese groups. As many as 200,000 ethnic Chinese from Vietnam and 20,000 ethnic Chinese from Cambodia may be included among the 1,645,472 Chinese reported by the 1990 census.

the ethnic Chinese); data from the latter are reported only in aggregate form for the Indochinese as a whole. Here we discuss available information from both sources.

Table 9.3 presents a summary of socioeconomic characteristics from the 1990 census, comparing the main Indochinese ethnic groups to each other and to the total U.S. and Asian-origin populations. These data underscore the significant differences between the various Indochinese ethnic groups and between the Indochinese and other Asian Americans. All of the Indochinese groups are much younger than other Asians or the total U.S. population, reflecting their much higher levels of fertility. American and Asian American women average just under two children ever born per woman aged 35 to 44 (an approximate measure of completed fertility), compared to 2.5 for the Vietnamese, 3.5 for the Lao and Cambodians, and 6.1 per Hmong woman (possibly the highest in the country, confirming the results of earlier research; cf. Rumbaut & Weeks, 1986). Thus, despite the recency of their arrival, over a third of the Hmong (35%) were already U.S.-born in 1990; amazingly, their median age was under 13 years (compared to 33 for the American population), and that of U.S.-born Hmong Americans was just 5 years.

These indicators vividly demonstrate the dynamics of new ethnic group formation through immigration and rapid natural increase, and underscore the socioeconomic importance among the Indochinese of families with a high proportion of dependent children. Whereas less than half of American households have children under age 18, over two thirds of the Vietnamese, over four fifths of the Lao and Cambodian, and 90% of Hmong households consist of families with minor children. The structure of these families is a key social context shaping the adaptation of these recently resettled groups, including the tension over changing gender roles and intergenerational conflicts (cf. Kibria, 1993).

Indochinese groups and Asian Americans generally—who are preponderantly foreign born, as Table 9.3 shows—exhibit a smaller proportion of single-parent female-headed households than the U.S. norm; the main exception are Cambodian refugees, whose higher rate (25%) reflects in part the disproportionate presence of widows whose husbands were killed during the Pol Pot period of the late 1970s (one study in San Diego found that more than 20% of Cambodian women were widowed—see Rumbaut, 1989a). Among the Vietnamese, the proportion of children under 18 living at home with both parents is slightly above the U.S. norm of 73%, but well below that of Asian Americans generally (85%)—partly a reflection of the sizable number of unaccompanied refugee children from Vietnam and of

Table 9.3 Social and Economic Characteristics of Vietnamese, Cambodian, and Laotian Groups in the United States, Compared to the Total U.S. Population and the Total Asian-Origin Population, 1990

	Total U.S.	Total Asian	Vietnamese	Cambodian	Laos	Hmong
Total persons	248,709,873	6,876,394	593,213	149,047	147,375	94,439
Nativity and immigration						
% born in the U.S.	92.1	34.4	20.1	20.9	20.6	34.8
% immigrated pre-1980	4.5	27.9	30.5	9.4	16.3	15.7
% immigrated 1980-1990	3.5	37.8	49.3	69.6	63.1	49.5
Age						
Median age	33.0	29.2	25.6	19.7	20.5	12.7
Median age (U.S. born)	32.5	1.47	6.7	4.7	5.4	5.2
Family contexts[a]						
Fertility per woman 35-44	2.0	1.9	2.5	3.4	3.5	6.1
% female householder	16.0	11.5	15.9	25.4	11.3	13.6
% with own children						
<18 years	48.2	59.2	69.0	83.8	82.8	90.1
% children <18 with						
2 parents	73.0	84.6	76.6	71.0	82.6	86.2
English (persons over 5)[b]						
% speak English only	86.2	24.6	6.2	4.0	3.2	2.6
% does not speak "very well"	6.1	39.8	60.8	70.0	67.8	76.1
% linguistically isolated	3.5	25.1	42.1	54.7	51.5	59.8
Education (persons over 25)						
% less than 5th grade	2.7	7.1	11.4	40.7	33.9	54.9
% high school graduate	75.2	77.6	61.2	34.9	40.0	31.1
% college graduate	20.3	37.7	17.4	4.7	5.4	4.9
% postgraduate degree	7.2	14.4	4.4	1.6	1.5	1.5
Employment (persons over 16)[c]						
% in labor force	65.3	67.4	64.5	46.5	58.0	29.3
% unemployed	6.3	5.2	8.4	10.3	9.3	17.9
Of those employed						
% upper white-collar	26.4	31.2	17.6	9.8	5.0	12.8
% lower white-collar	31.7	33.3	29.5	23.3	15.2	18.9
% upper blue-collar	11.4	7.8	15.7	17.2	19.8	13.9
% lower blue-collar	14.9	11.9	20.9	30.0	43.9	32.1
Income						
Median family income ($)	35,225	41,583	30,550	18,126	23,101	14,327
Per capita income ($)	14,420	13,806	9,033	5,121	5,597	2,692
% below poverty	13.1	14.0	25.7	42.6	34.7	63.6
% receives public assistance	7.5	9.8	24.5	51.1	35.4	67.1
% own home	64.2	48.3	40.1	19.7	24.0	11.1

SOURCE: U.S. Bureau of the Census (1993b). These data are based on a sample (not the 100% tabulations) and are subject to sample variability; group sizes may differ from Table 9.2.

a. Fertility is measured by: children ever born per woman aged 35-44.

b. Linguistically isolated means a household in which no person age 14 or older speaks English only or very well.

c. Upper white-collar are professionals, executives, managers; lower white-collar are clerical, sales; upper blue-collar are repair, craft; lower blue-collar are operators, fabricators, laborers.

youths (disproportionately males) who escaped with other relatives or adult guardians.

As the most recently arrived Asian Americans, the substantial majority of the Vietnamese, Cambodians, and Laotians—not surprisingly—did not yet speak English "very well," as the 1990 census makes clear. In fact, about half of all Indochinese households were classified by the census as "linguistically isolated" (see Table 9.3 for a definition). Whereas 38% of all Asian American adults were college graduates and 14% also had postgraduate degrees—about double the respective levels of attainment of the U.S. population (20% and 7%)—all of the Indochinese groups were much less educated on average, particularly the non-Vietnamese groups, as detailed in Table 9.3. Only about a third of the refugees from Laos and Cambodia were high school graduates, and higher proportions had less than a fifth grade education, underscoring the rural origins and severe social class disadvantages of many refugees in these ethnic groups.

Relative to the U.S. population, Asian Americans as a whole also showed higher rates of labor force participation, lower unemployment, and a greater percentage of professionals and managers among those employed; but the profile for each of the Indochinese groups was precisely the opposite on each of these indicators. Employed Indochinese were twice as likely to have jobs as operators and laborers (significant levels of downward occupational mobility have been noted among the earlier arrivals; cf. Haines, 1985, p. 39), and their levels of self-employment were significantly below those for other Asian Americans and the U.S. population, as were family and per capita incomes and rates of home ownership.

Moreover, as specified in Table 9.3, poverty rates for the Indochinese groups were two to five times higher than for the U.S. population, and the disparity in welfare dependency rates was even greater. Approximately one fourth of the Vietnamese fell below the federal poverty line and received public assistance income, as did one third of the Lao, about half of the Cambodians, and two thirds of the Hmong (the latter are probably by far the highest rates in the country). By comparison, poverty rates for the U.S. and Asian American general populations were about the same (13-14%), with fewer than a tenth of households relying on public assistance. The diversity of these socioeconomic profiles underline the widely different social class origins, age and family structures, and modes of incorporation of Asian-origin immigrants and refugees and the senselessness of "model minority" stereotypes. These census data, however, tell us little about the equally significant differences *within* ethnic groups, especially between different waves or cohorts of arrival, and of the dynamics of their socio-

Table 9.4 Median Income of Indochinese Refugees (tax-filing units), 1982-1988, for Refugee Cohorts Arriving in the U.S. From 1975 to 1979

Tax Year	All Cohorts (1975-1979)	1975 Arrivals	1976-1979 Arrivals	Ratio of 1975/76-79	All U.S. Tax-Filing Units[a]
1982	12,192	14,232	8,803	1.62	14-15,000
1983	12,808	14,698	9,655	1.52	15-16,000
1984	14,377	16,377	11,105	1.47	16-17,000
1985	15,177	17,092	12,061	1.42	16-17,000
1986	16,021	17,861	12,907	1.38	17-18,000
1987	16,667	18,236	14,009	1.30	17-18,000
1988	17,560	18,963	15,261	1.24	18-19,000

SOURCE: Internal Revenue Service summary data on incomes and taxes paid by Indochinese refugees who arrived in the United States from 1975 through late 1979, as reported by the U.S. Office of Refugee Resettlement (1991, p. 99).
a. Comparative data provided by the Internal Revenue Service as a range.

economic progress over time. For that information we turn to available nationwide surveys.

Occupational and Economic Progress Over Time

One useful longitudinal data source on the economic progress of the 1975 to 1979 refugees comes from their federal income tax returns—a data source unique among all immigrant groups in the United States. Indochinese refugees who arrived between 1975 and late 1979 were issued social security numbers in blocks through a special program in effect at the time, and as a result it is possible to obtain annual aggregate data from the Internal Revenue Service on incomes received and taxes paid by these cohorts (U.S. Office of Refugee Resettlement, 1991, pp. 98-102). Table 9.4 shows the median adjusted gross income they received annually from 1982 through 1988, comparing the 1975 cohort (who, as noted above, numbered 130,000, including 125,000 Vietnamese) to the 1976 to 1979 arrivals (a much more heterogeneous group of 118,000 persons—including about 60,000 Vietnamese, 49,000 Lao and Hmong, and 9,000 Cambodians —most of whom arrived in 1979 and were thus about 4 years behind the 1975 cohort). The data show clearly the economic progress of these groups over time; worth noting is the fact that since 1985 the median income of the 1975 refugees has surpassed that of all U.S. tax-filing units. As would be expected, as of 1988 the incomes of the 1976 to 1979 cohort still lagged noticeably behind the incomes of the 1975 cohort, but the gap between them was closing rapidly: The income ratio of the 1975 cohort to the 1976 to 1979 cohort was 1.62 in 1982 but had dropped to 1.24 by 1988. Between 1982 and 1988, their income from wages more than doubled; still, as late as 1988 over a quarter (28.6%) of individual W-2 forms were under $5,000, whereas less than a fifth (19.6%) of W-2 forms were over $25,000. In 1988, more than 10,700 tax returns reported income from self-employment, totaling over $103 million. All together, these Indochinese Americans reported more than $2.2 billion in annual income in 1988 and paid $218 million in federal income taxes (U.S. Office of Refugee Resettlement, 1991).

From the beginning of the Indochinese refugee resettlement program in 1975, the federal government has funded annual surveys of representative national samples of this population (conducted through telephone interviews in the respondent's native language). Reported each year by Office of Refugee Resettlement, in its *Annual Report to the Congress,* these are the only national survey data available that provide a comprehensive picture of the Indochinese occupational and economic adaptation over time (Bach, 1984; Bach & Carroll-Seguin, 1986; Gordon, 1989; U.S. Office of Refugee Resettlement. 1991, 1992). The results, however, are not broken down by ethnicity but are reported for the Indochinese refugee population as a whole (except for the first few surveys, which were limited to the Vietnamese; see Montero, 1979). Until 1983 the surveys were cross-sectional and based on random samples of refugees who had arrived since 1975; after 1983 the survey was redesigned into a panel study, following new arrival cohorts over a period of 5 years and adding a sample of new arrivals every year. The new design has the advantage of a longitudinal study, but the disadvantage that it is restricted to refugees who have been in the United States 5 years or less; for example, the 1990 survey does not include any Indochinese refugees who arrived prior to 1986. In any case, Table 9.5 provides a summary of annual survey results on rates of labor force participation and unemployment during the 1980s for national samples of Indochinese who arrived in the United States between 1975 and 1989.

In general the data in Table 9.5 show increasing rates of labor force participation and, once in the labor force, decreasing unemployment rates over time in the United States. Arrival cohorts reflect very low rates of labor force participation and high rates of unemployment especially during their first year in the United States, when most refugees are enrolled in English as a Second Language (ESL) classes and job training programs

Table 9.5 Percentage Employment Status for Indochinese Refugees in the United States, 1981-1989 (Data for all household members age 16 and over in national samples of refugee households)

Year of Entry	Labor Force Participation				Unemployment Rate			
	1986	1987	1988	1989	1986	1987	1988	1989
1989				21				27
1988			20	30			21	24
1987		22	30	35		32	11	10
1986	31	32	33	38	25	11	7	7
1985	25	32	32	37	20	9	5	12
1984	34	34	35	36	18	16	15	10
U.S. rates[a]	65	66	66	66	7	6	5	5

Year of Entry	Labor Force Participation				Unemployment Rate			
	1981	1982	1983	1984	1981	1982	1983	1984
1984				30				41
1983			21	42			55	36
1982		25	41	45		63	30	13
1981	23	42	47	51	45	41	17	16
1980	53	51	55	55	27	32	21	12
1979	49	60	61	60	8	19	18	10
1978	49	68	68	66	5	19	20	3
1976-1977	71	74	80	76	4	9	17	5
1975	76	72	70	67	6	13	12	6
U.S. rates[a]	64	64	64	65	7.5	10	8	7

SOURCE: Annual surveys of national samples of Southeast Asian refugees reported by the U.S. Office of Refugee Resettlement (1982, p. 18; 1985, p. 91; 1991, p. 90). See also Gordon (1989, p. 30).
a. October unadjusted figures from the Bureau of Labor Statistics, U.S. Department of Labor, 1981-1989.

while receiving cash and medical assistance. However, more recent cohorts show only small increases in labor force participation rates over time, staying in the 30% to 38% range (about half the U.S. rate of 66%), unlike earlier cohorts who moved from first-year rates in the 20% to 30% range to 40% to 50% by their second and third year in the United States. In particular, the 1975 to 1978 cohorts have shown the highest rates of labor force participation, exceeding the rate for the U.S. population within their first 4 years in the country. They also had lower unemployment rates than the U.S. average as of 1981, but the recession of 1981 to 1983 hit them much harder, with their unemployment rates doubling to quadrupling during those years (see Table 9.5). By 1984, however, their recovery was rapid, and their unemployment rates again fell below the U.S. average. In part, these patterns reflect the relative socioeconomic and other handicaps of different arrival cohorts. For example, the annual surveys have documented a decline in the educational levels of adult refugees over time: 1975 arrivals averaged 9.4 years of education, those arriving during 1976 to 1979 averaged 7.4 years; 1980 to 1984 arrivals averaged 6.8 years, and 1985 to 1989 arrivals about 5 years (Haines, 1989, p. 7). The 1990 to 1992 cohorts (which included many former reeducation camp internees from Vietnam) reversed this trend, however, averaging 8 years of education (U.S. Office of Refugee Resettlement, 1985, 1991, 1992). Significantly an analysis of determinants of labor force participation based on the national data set (Bach & Carroll-Seguin, 1986) found that education was the strongest positive predictor.

The promotion of economic self-sufficiency is a principal goal of the U.S. refugee program, as enunciated by the Refugee Act of 1980; that is, to ensure early employment and minimal reliance on public assistance (such as Aid to Families with Dependent Children and Medicaid). Eligibility for the latter and levels of benefits vary widely among the states, however. For example, in 1982 monthly AFDC benefits for a family of four were $591 in California but $141 in Texas, the two largest states of Indochinese settlement; indigent two-parent families with dependent children were eligible for AFDC in California but not in Texas; and indigent adults without dependent children were eligible for local General Assistance in California but had no such "safety net" in Texas (Rumbaut, 1989b). A recent study of refugee use of public assistance based on the 1983 to 1988 national longitudinal survey data found that 18% of all Indochinese refugee households were economically self-sufficient after their first year in the United States, some of them never having used public assistance. Of those who did, 41% had left public assistance programs within their second year in the United States, as had 57% by their fifth year. However, there were significant differences between refugee households in California (home to over 40% of the total Indochinese population, as we saw earlier) and those in the rest of the country (the study grouped the other 49 states together, although there are major differences among them in their programs of public assistance). In California, only 7% of the Indochinese households were financially independent after their first year and only 18% had left public assistance by their second year, compared to 26% and 57%, respectively, outside California; by the end of 5 years, only one fourth (26%) of California refugee households had left public assistance, compared to three fourths (75%) outside California (Bach & Argiros, 1991).

If California residence is significantly associated with a higher level of reliance on public assistance, what are the determinants of such reliance among refugees within California? A major study of welfare dependency among Indochinese groups in Southern California found that the strongest determinant was the number of dependent children in the family; the proportion of family income coming from public assistance grew by about 10% for each dependent child. Welfare dependency significantly decreased over time in the United States and increased with age and poor health status (Rumbaut, 1989b). Indeed, concern over medical care coverage is often a decisive consideration for large refugee families who continue to remain on public assistance (including Medicaid), although it keeps them below the poverty line, rather than risk low-wage jobs that provide no health care insurance at all (Forbes, 1985; Rumbaut, Chávez, Moser, Pickwell, & Wishik, 1988). Cambodian refugees we interviewed in San Diego in the 1980s, for example, referred to their MediCal stickers (as Medicaid is called in California) as being "more valuable than gold."

The Indochinese in America: A Local Perspective

Since the late 1970s, a large number of community surveys, ethnographies, and epidemiological or clinical studies by sociologists, anthropologists, psychologists, psychiatrists, and other researchers have reported on many aspects of the Indochinese refugee experience in settings throughout the United States. Although they lack the generalizability of national survey data and use different samples and methodologies that often preclude comparisons across studies, they nonetheless have greatly added to the richness and depth of our available knowledge for specific ethnic groups. It is well beyond our scope here to review this literature, but we can refer the reader to a few selected sources.

A central focus of the research has been on the social and economic adaptation of Indochinese groups, from the national surveys of the first waves (Montero, 1979) and other ORR-sponsored research, to diverse studies such as those published in the 1981 and 1986 special issues of the *International Migration Review* on refugees, the 1982 special issue of *Anthropological Quarterly* on Southeast Asian refugees, and several major community surveys cited later (see also the recent review of research on socioeconomic mobility by Gold & Kibria, 1993). Another early focus, beginning with research done at Camp Pendleton and Seattle in 1975 (Lin, Tazuma, & Masuda, 1979; Liu et al., 1979; Rahe, Looney, Ward, Tung, &

Liu, 1978), concerned refugee mental health and the psychology of adaptation under conditions of severe stress; these have been followed by a wide range of research on this topic, from clinical studies to community mental health surveys (e.g., Meinhardt, Tom, Tse, & Yu, 1985-1986; Mollica & Lavelle, 1988; Owan, 1985; Rumbaut, 1985, 1991a, 1991b; Williams & Westermeyer, 1986). Ethnographic fieldwork includes research on Indochinese communities, neighborhoods, and families in California (Gold, 1992), Kansas (Benson, 1994), Chicago (Conquergood, 1992), and Philadelphia (Kibria, 1993, 1994); case histories of refugee adults (Freeman, 1989) and youth (Howard, 1990; Rumbaut & Ima, 1988); and edited collections of papers on each of the Indochinese ethnic groups (e.g., Haines, 1985; Hendricks, Downing, & Deinard, 1986).

The results of major community surveys have been collected by Haines (1989). They include:

A panel study of 1975 "first wave" Vietnamese in nine cities in Northern California, Louisiana, Alabama, and Florida (Roberts & Starr, 1989)

A survey of a sample of Vietnamese in Los Angeles, Houston, and New Orleans stratified by year of entry, 1975 to 1979 (Dunning, 1982, 1989)

A survey of 1975 to 1979 arrivals in Illinois, including samples of Vietnamese, Cambodian, Lao, and Hmong refugees (Kim, 1989; Kim & Nicassio, 1980)

A 1981 survey of Vietnamese, Cambodian, Lao, and Hmong refugees in San Diego (Strand, 1989; Strand & Jones, 1985)

A survey of Vietnamese, Chinese-Vietnamese, and Lao 1978 to 1982 arrivals residing in Boston, Chicago, Houston, Seattle, and Orange County, plus a follow-up survey of a subsample of their school-age children (Caplan, Whitmore, & Choy, 1989; Whitmore, Trautmann, & Caplan, 1989)

The Indochinese Health and Adaptation Research Project (IHARP), a longitudinal study of Vietnamese, Chinese-Vietnamese, Cambodian, Lao, and Hmong adults and children in San Diego based on representative samples of 1975 to 1983 arrivals (Rumbaut, 1989a)

The latter two are among the few to focus specifically on the ethnic Chinese from Vietnam; another is the study by Desbarats (1986) of Sino-Vietnamese and Vietnamese in Chicago, Orange County, and San Francisco.

Some illustrative findings from the IHARP study in the San Diego metropolitan area are presented below, focusing on aspects of the experience of Vietnamese, Laotian, and Cambodian refugees that are almost completely missing from census and other national data sources. First, we will look briefly at prearrival characteristics, migration motives and events, and mental health outcomes among Indochinese adults, and then touch on infant health outcomes and on the educational progress of their children. The respondents, ranging in age from 18 to 71, were interviewed at length in their native languages in 1983 and again a year later. Results are broken down by ethnic group and for three key cohorts of arrival (1975, 1976 to 1979, and 1980 to 1983, the latter being the most numerous).[2] We then conclude with a look at some intriguing comparative data for all racial-ethnic groups, including the Indochinese, drawn from the vital statistics for San Diego County (on infant health and mortality) and from the San Diego city schools (on the educational attainment of refugee children growing up in the United States).

Migration, Adaptation, and Mental Health

Who are they, why did they come, how did they leave? Table 9.6 summarizes information on the social background and migration process of the refugees. About 90% of the Hmong and 55% of the Cambodians came from rural areas, whereas the Chinese and Vietnamese were overwhelmingly from urban sectors in South Vietnam. These differences are reflected in their levels of premigration education: The Vietnamese were the most educated (9.8 years), followed by the Chinese (6.6), the Cambodians (4.9), and the Hmong (1.7). Two thirds of Hmong adults had never attended school and were preliterate, their language lacking an alphabet until the 1950s, when missionaries in Laos developed a written notation for what had been until then only an oral tradition.

There were also very significant social class differences by cohort of arrival. The 1975 refugees were much more likely to come from highly educated professional and managerial classes, whereas less educated farmers, fisherfolk, and manual laborers predominate among the more recently arrived. Vietnamese and Hmong men included high proportions of former military officers and soldiers. The ethnic Chinese—a largely segregated "middleman minority" of merchants from Saigon's *Cholon* (Large Market) area, which had been referred to as, "after Singapore, the largest Chinese city outside of China" (Whitmore, 1985, p. 65)—were least likely to have had any prior involvement with either the military (ARVN) or the South Vietnamese or American governments during the war. Indeed, very few Chinese-Vietnamese cited "past associations" in their motives to flee.

A distinction often made between refugees and other classes of immigrants revolves around their different motives for migration and the traumatic nature of their flight experiences (see Zolberg et al., 1989). Refugees

Table 9.6 Social Background Characteristics and Contexts of Exit of Indochinese Refugees in San Diego County, by Ethnic Group and Time of Arrival in the United States (IHARP longitudinal adult sample, *N* = 500)

	Ethnic Group				Time of Arrival		
	Viet-namese	*Chinese*	*Cam-bodian*	*Hmong*	*1975*	*1976-1979*	*1980-1983*
Educational background							
Number of years of education	9.9	6.6	4.9	1.8	11.9	6.5	5.2
% high school graduate	47.1	19.3	13.3	2.8	74.4	23.8	15.6
% knew some English	39.5	13.2	5.8	1.8	66.7	12.8	13.1
% never attended school	1.9	12.3	23.3	67.9	2.6	19.2	29.4
% rural background	5.1	4.4	55.0	89.9	5.1	36.0	39.1
Occupational background							
% professional/managerial	25.6	11.2	5.3	3.0	38.7	15.4	7.3
% military	25.6	6.1	15.9	31.3	35.5	20.8	17.9
% clerical	7.5	1.0	1.8	2.0	9.7	4.0	2.3
% sales	18.8	38.8	14.2	2.0	6.5	20.1	18.6
% blue collar	10.5	27.6	8.0	2.0	3.2	7.4	15.2
% farmers, fishers	10.5	14.3	54.0	59.6	3.2	32.2	37.6
Motives for exit[a]							
Number of political motives	3.3	2.9	5.1	4.2	2.7	3.9	4.0
TARGETS	2.6	2.3	4.5	3.9	2.1	3.3	3.5
REBELS	0.7	0.6	0.5	0.3	0.6	0.6	0.5
Number of economic motives	0.5	0.7	2.1	0.4	0.2	0.6	1.1
VICTIMS	0.1	0.2	1.7	0.2	0.1	0.2	0.7
SEEKERS	0.4	0.5	0.4	0.2	0.1	0.4	0.4
Migration events							
% fled without family	13.4	11.4	29.2	19.3	25.6	19.8	15.9
% gave bribes to exit	32.7	71.7	19.3	21.3	13.2	35.7	39.0
% feared would be killed	73.2	73.7	80.7	92.7	18.4	86.6	83.0
% assaulted in escape	30.6	36.8	25.2	25.7	0.0	24.4	36.7
Number of violent events during exit	2.1	1.9	3.1	2.5	0.9	2.2	2.7
Number of years in refugee camps	0.6	0.9	2.1	2.9	0.2	1.2	1.9
Mental health status, 1984							
% sleep problems	21.7	23.9	55.8	61.5	23.1	36.6	42.7
% appetite problems	14.6	11.4	42.5	22.0	5.1	18.0	27.0
% positive well-being	50.6	31.0	15.0	35.5	56.4	35.1	30.8
% demoralization, moderate	28.8	43.4	46.7	34.6	30.8	35.7	39.8
% demoralization, severe	20.5	25.7	38.3	29.9	12.8	29.2	29.4

a. Data refer to the number of migration motives reported by the respondent, classified as follows:

TARGETS: Forced relocation, to new economic zone, into reeducation camp; imprisoned prior to exit; fear of arrest or harm from new regime; past political involvement with old regime, armed forces; association with U.S. government, CIA or military; drafted to fight in Cambodia; loss or confiscation of personal property or wealth; general harassment.

REBELS: Protest communism, lack of freedom; refusal to join cooperative; other political-ideological reasons.

VICTIMS: Starvation, famine, lack of health care, harsh or poor economic conditions, inability to make a living.

SEEKERS: Seeking better future, education, prospects for children; family reunification; other miscellaneous reasons.

are said to be motivated to flee by fear of persecution (political motives), whereas immigrants are defined by their aspirations for better material opportunities and self-advancement (economic motives). IHARP respondents were asked to state all of their motives for leaving the homeland; over 50 different reasons were given, ranging from fear of repression or imprisonment in reeducation camps, to past associations with the former regime and ideological opposition to communism, to desires for family reunification, better education for their children, and an improved standard of living. Some of these reasons may be defined as political in nature, others as economic or social. Often both kinds of reasons were cited by the same respondent, making the usual distinction between refugees and nonrefugees simplistic and misleading.

Their exit motives were classified into four main types, as shown in Table 9.6. Two involved more clearly political motivations:

1. Specific perceptions and experiences of fear or force, past political associations, and related motives (TARGETS)
2. Explicit forms of protest and ideological reasons (REBELS)

The other two types involved more clearly socioeconomic considerations:

3. Harsh material conditions of famine and other dismal economic conditions (VICTIMS)
4. Miscellaneous "pull" motives, such as seeking a better education for the children or family reunification (SEEKERS)

Cambodians reported by far the most TARGET and VICTIM reasons for flight (reflecting their life-threatening experiences during the holocaust of the late 1970s) and hence both more political and economic exit motives. The Hmong also reported many TARGET motives, the Vietnamese the most REBEL motives, and the Chinese the most SEEKER or economic pull motives, as well as the fewest past associations with the former regime. Despite this diversity of motives in the refugees' decision to leave, by far more TARGET motives were reported overall (3.3 per person) than any of the other three motive types: REBELS (0.6), VICTIMS (0.5), and lastly SEEKERS (0.4). By this classification, far more political motives (3.8) than economic motives (0.9) were reported, underscoring the qualitative difference in modes of exit between refugees and conventional immigrants, but also the fact that economic and social as well as political factors were interwoven in the decision to flee. The effects of such different motives on subsequent psychological adjustment and mental health will be noted later.

Other aspects of the exit experiences of the refugee sample are broken down in Table 9.6 by ethnicity and cohort of arrival. Except for the 1975 refugees, most feared they would be killed during their escape. The Cambodians suffered the greatest number of family loss and violence events, followed by the Hmong and the Vietnamese. The Chinese—and more recent arrivals generally—were most likely to have left together as a family, to have given bribes to exit, and to have been assaulted during the escape (often by Thai pirates). Once they reached a country of first asylum, the Hmong stayed in refugee camps far longer than any other group before being resettled in the United States, followed by the Cambodians, the Chinese, and the Vietnamese. Taken together, such differences in the migration events experienced by these refugee groups may help explain why the Cambodians and the Hmong had a significantly higher number of chronic health problems (defined as existing physical symptoms or dysfunctions lasting 6 months or longer) whose onset occurred between their exit from their homeland and their arrival in the United States. By contrast, there were no significant differences by ethnicity or gender in chronic health problems whose onset occurred prior to migration.

Although not shown in Table 9.6, the refugees' social background characteristics were in turn reflected in their socioeconomic position in San Diego as they struggled to rebuild their lives. The same ethnic group rank order was mirrored in their levels of English literacy, employment and labor force participation in the local economy, income, and welfare dependency, although all groups were progressing gradually, if at different rates over time. English ability increases over time; it is primarily a function of level of prior education and secondarily of (younger) age and longer time of residence in the United States (Rumbaut, 1989a). The biggest differences in labor force participation and unemployment rates were seen between the 1975 first-wave refugees and later arrivals, reflecting the national survey data reviewed earlier. The most recently arrived refugee families reported very low annual incomes, and in 1984 about two thirds of the 1976 to 1979 arrivals and over four fifths of the 1980 to 1983 arrivals in the sample still had incomes that fell below the federal poverty line, compared to a poverty rate of about 15% for the general U.S. and local populations. One of the respondents in the IHARP study, a middle-aged Hmong refugee who had arrived in 1980 after spending 5 years in refugee camps in Thailand, had this to say about his situation, vividly and eloquently expressing the complexity of the economic and related psychosocial problems faced by these recently arrived groups:

> Any jobs they have require a literate person to get. We have the arms and legs but we can't see what they see, because everything is connected to letters and numbers. . . . When we were in our country we never ask anybody for help like this, [but] in this country everything is money first. You go to the hospital is money, you get medicine is money, you die is also money and even the plot to bury you also requires money. These days I only live day by day and share the $594 for the six of us for the whole month. Some months I have to borrow money from friends or relatives to buy food for the family. I'm very worried that maybe one day the welfare says you are no longer eligible for the program and at the same time the manager says that I need more money for the rent, then we will really starve. I've been trying very hard to learn English and at the same time looking for a job. No matter what kind of job, even the job to clean people's toilets; but still people don't even trust you or offer you such work. I'm looking at me that I'm not even worth as much as a dog's stool. Talking about this, I want to die right here so I won't see my future. . . . How am I going to make my life better? To get a job, you have to have a car; to have a car you have to have money; and to have money you have to have a job, so what can you do? Language, jobs, money, living, and so on are always big problems to me and I don't think they can be solved in my generation. So I really don't know what to tell you. My life is only to live day by day until the last day I live, and maybe that is the time when my problems will be solved. (as translated and quoted in Rumbaut 1985, pp. 471-472)

The measure of mental health status shown in the bottom panel of Table 9.6 was based on a screening scale used by the National Center for Health Statistics in a major national survey of the general American adult population (Link & Dohrenwend, 1980). The results showed that 74% of Americans scored in the *positive well-being* range, 16% in the *moderate demoralization* range, and only 9.6% in the *severe demoralization* range (indicative of "clinically significant distress"). By contrast, in 1984 the respective prevalence rates for the Indochinese refugees were 34% positive well-being, 38% moderate demoralization, and 28% severe demoralization. That latter figure was three times the level of severe distress found for the general American population; a year before, in 1983, the corresponding refugee rate had been four times higher than the U.S. norm. These demoralization rates were highest for the Cambodians—who had experienced the most traumatic contexts of exit—followed by the Hmong, Chinese, and Vietnamese.

The process of psychological adaptation appears to be temporally as well as socially patterned. The first several months after arrival in the United States tend to be a relatively hopeful and even euphoric period, but during the second year, a period of "exile shock," depressive symptoms reach their highest levels, followed by a process of psychological recovery after the third year (see Portes & Rumbaut, 1990; Rumbaut, 1989a; Vega & Rumbaut, 1991). The general pattern is described succinctly by an elderly Cambodian widow:

> I was feeling great the first few months. But then, after that, I started to face all kinds of worries and sadness. I started to see the real thing of the United States, and I missed home more and more. I missed everything about our country; people, family, relatives and friends, way of life, everything. Then, my spirit started to go down; I lost sleep; my physical health weakened; and there started the stressful and depressing times. But now [almost 3 years after arrival] I feel kind of better, a lot better! Knowing my sons are in school as their father would have wanted, and doing well, makes me feel more secure. (quoted in Rumbaut, 1985, pp. 469-470)

What, then, among all of the stressors reviewed above, affects refugee mental health the most? Briefly stated, controlling for physical health status and for a wide range of socioeconomic and demographic variables, an analysis of the psychological distress scores among the refugees in San Diego found that in 1983, the principal predictors of demoralization were prearrival factors: the number of TARGET motives reported, an index of family loss and separation, and a rural background. A year later, however, the effect of these prearrival stressors had receded and current difficulties, primarily being unemployed, emerged as stronger predictors of depressive symptoms. In addition, by 1984 a significant predictor of lower distress and greater satisfaction was an attitudinal measure of biculturalism; measures of monocultural styles (whether of traditionalism or of assimilationism) showed no effect on psychological outcomes. That is, refugees who adopt an additive acculturative strategy, adapting to American ways while retaining ethnic attachments and identity, appear to reduce psychological distress over time. This finding points to the importance of creativity and flexibility in the acculturative process (Rumbaut, 1991a).

Infant Health, Children's Educational Progress, and Some Paradoxes of Acculturation

Another health-related dimension of the Indochinese adaptation process may be gleaned from a follow-up study of the infant mortality rates (IMR)

Table 9.7 Infant Mortality Rates and Selected Risk Factors of Pregnancy by Ethnic Groups in San Diego County, 1978-1985

Ethnic Group	Total Live Births[a]	Infant Mortality Rate	Early Neonatal Death Rate	Post-early Neonatal Deaths	% Late or No Prenatal Care	% Teenage Mothers	% Un-married Mothers
Vietnamese	2,187	5.5	3.7	1.8	9.9	5.1	14.4
Cambodian	687	5.8	4.4	1.5	15.2	5.2	20.2
Laos	977	7.2	3.1	4.1	13.1	10.5	12.5
Hmong	990	9.1	3.0	6.1	20.3	16.5	11.4
All Indochinese	4,841	6.6	3.5	3.1	13.4	8.5	14.2
Japanese	2,253	6.2	3.1	3.1	2.4	8.7	11.5
Chinese	1,455	6.9	4.1	2.8	3.0	2.6	7.1
Filipino	12,445	7.2	4.2	3.0	3.4	5.6	7.9
Hispanic	71,641	7.3	4.1	3.2	6.6	15.4	23.5
White (non-Hispanic)	143,779	8.0	4.5	3.5	2.6	8.9	11.1
American Indian	5,714	9.6	4.4	5.3	4.2	16.4	28.3
Black (non-Hispanic)	22,080	16.3	8.9	7.4	4.6	19.0	45.8
Total county	269,252	8.5	4.7	3.7	4.2	11.6	18.0

NOTE: The number of live births = 269,252; the number of [linked] infant deaths = 2,281. Here is how the various factors were determined:

Infant Mortality Rate = number of (linked) deaths of infants under 1 year old, per 1,000 live births.

Early Neonatal Mortality Rate = number of deaths of infants under 7 days old, per 1,000 live births.

Postearly Neonatal Mortality Rate = number of deaths of infants 7 to 365 days old, per 1,000 live births.

Late Prenatal Care = cases where prenatal care was begun in the third trimester (7th to 9th month), or not at all.

Teenage Mothers = cases where mother was 19 years old or younger at the time of the baby's birth.

Unmarried Mothers = cases where mother was single, separated, divorced, widowed, or of unknown marital status.

a. N = number of live births in San Diego County during 1978-1985, on which the infant mortality rates are based.

of all ethnic groups in San Diego County, based on a linked data set of all live births and infant deaths recorded in the metropolitan area during 1978 to 1985 (Rumbaut & Weeks, 1989; Weeks & Rumbaut, 1991). The results are summarized in Table 9.7, along with selected risk factors of pregnancy. The various Indochinese ethnic groups appeared to be at high risk for poor infant health outcomes. After all, they had come from a background of high fertility and high infant mortality, often with preexisting health problems, and, as documented above, had levels of unemployment, poverty, welfare dependency, and depressive symptomatology that greatly exceeded U.S. norms. Lack of English proficiency limited their access to health care, and indeed Indochinese pregnant mothers exhibited the latest onset of prenatal care of all ethnic groups in San Diego.

Remarkably, however, the Indochinese overall were found to have much lower infant mortality rates (6.6 infant deaths per 1,000 live births) than the San Diego County average (8.5), and two refugee groups actually exhibited the lowest infant death rates: the Vietnamese (5.5) and the Cambodians (5.8). Only the Hmong (9.1) had a higher infant mortality rate than Hispanics (7.3) and non-Hispanic whites (8.0), although still much lower than blacks (16.3), and vastly lower than their own infant death rate prior to their arrival in the United States (104). The Lao and the Hmong, moreover, exhibited the unusual pattern of higher postearly neonatal death rates (deaths occurring to infants 7 days and older) than early neonatal death rates (occurring during the first week of life, usually in the hospital), suggesting that infant death rates for these two groups could be reduced by paying more attention to the overall home environment to which the infants are taken after birth. Several behavioral factors were associated with these positive outcomes, particularly the nearly universal absence of tobacco, alcohol, and drug use among pregnant Indochinese women—and among most immigrant women in the groups listed in Table 9.7—in contrast to U.S.-born groups. One implication of these findings is that subtractive acculturation—that is, a process of Americanization that involves the learning bad habits in the U.S. milieu—may have negative consequences for infant health.

Other evidence bearing on the future prospects of the coming generation of Indochinese Americans comes from a study of their educational attainment in San Diego schools (Portes & Rumbaut, 1990, pp. 189-198; Rumbaut, 1990, 1994). Table 9.8 presents data on academic grade point averages for all high school seniors, juniors, and sophomores in the district, including nearly 2,400 Indochinese students, broken down by ethnic groups and English language status. The latter involves a classification of all students who speak a primary language other than English at home into two categories: fluent English proficient (FEP) and limited English proficient (LEP). Among all groups in the school district, the Indochinese have by far the highest proportion of LEP students, reflecting the fact that they are the most recently arrived immigrants. Despite the language handicap, however, their academic grade point averages (GPAs) (2.47) significantly exceed the district average (2.11) and that of white Anglos (2.24).

Indeed, the latter is surpassed by most Asian and European language minorities; falling below the district norm are African Americans, Mexican Americans, and Pacific Islanders. At the top are Chinese, Asian Indian, and

Table 9.8 Academic Grade Point Average (GPA)[a] of San Diego High School Students, in Rank Order, by Ethnolinguistic Groups and English Language Status, 1986

Ethnolinguistic Groups[b]	English[c]		Non-English[d] FEP		Non-English[d] LEP		Total	
	N	GPA	N	GPA	N	GPA	N	GPA
East Asians	493	2.38	220	3.05	113	2.83	826	2.62
Chinese			98	3.40	68	2.94	166	3.21
Korean			33	3.00	23	2.76	56	2.90
Japanese			89	2.70	22	2.56	111	2.67
Southwest Asians	NA		127	2.67	106	2.42	233	2.56
Indian			16	3.11	3	2.62	19	3.04
Hebrew			20	3.18	17	2.50	37	2.85
Persian			49	2.70	68	2.46	117	2.56
Arab			42	2.21	18	2.21	60	2.21
Indochinese	140	2.66	607	2.88	1,641	2.30	2,388	2.47
Vietnamese			451	2.96	733	2.38	1,184	2.60
Cambodian			32	2.77	359	2.30	391	2.34
Hmong			30	2.66	83	2.27	113	2.37
Laos			94	2.63	466	2.18	560	2.26
Filipinos	794	2.33	1,034	2.53	236	2.02	2,064	2.39
Europeans	NA		308	2.39	103	2.24	411	2.36
German			58	2.73	16	2.54	74	2.69
French			28	2.70	13	1.71	41	2.39
Portuguese			74	2.17	32	2.23	106	2.19
Italian			66	2.11	16	1.83	82	2.05
Other Europe			82	2.48	26	2.59	108	2.51
White Anglos	19,796	2.24	NA		NA		19,796	2.24
Pacific Islanders	123	1.84	101	1.96	47	1.78	271	1.87
Guamanian			44	2.05	11	1.74	55	1.99
Samoan			51	1.80	13	1.51	64	1.74
Hispanics	2,296	1.81	2,631	1.85	2,080	1.71	7,007	1.79
Blacks	5,720	1.69	69	1.82	32	1.89	5,821	1.70
Totals	29,362	2.10	5,099	2.22	4,359	2.01	38,820	2.11

NOTE: $N = 38,820$ high school seniors, juniors, and sophomores in the San Diego Unified School District.
a. GPA = Cumulative grade point average, excluding physical education courses; A = 4, B = 3, C = 2, D = 1, F = 0.
b. Groups classified by ethnicity and (for mainly immigrant students) primary language spoken at home if other than English.
c. Primary home language is English; speaks English only.
d. Primary home language other than English; students' English proficiency is fluent (FEP) or limited (LEP).

Korean students, with GPAs exceeding the norm by almost a full point. The highest GPAs among the Indochinese are found for the Vietnamese

(2.60), Hmong (2.37), Cambodian (2.34), and Lao (2.26); within these groups they are significantly higher for FEP students. Remarkably, the GPAs of Cambodian and Hmong LEP students surpass the white Anglo average. Another noteworthy result is that for all ethnic groups without exception, English monolinguals (who tend to be U.S.-born) exhibit lower GPAs than their bilingual FEP coethnics (who tend to be foreign born); this is particularly clear among East Asians, Filipinos, and the Indochinese. One important implication of these findings is that educational achievement appears to decline from the first to the second and third generations. Another implication of these data is that they lend strong support to previous research noting a significant positive association between "true" bilingualism (most closely approximated by FEP students in Table 9.8) and educational achievement, in contrast to the lower GPAs registered by either of the essentially monolingual types (LEPs and English-only).

In a follow-up study using the 1983 IHARP sample of refugee parents (including the Lao), we identified all school-age children enrolled in the San Diego Unified School District (Rumbaut & Ima, 1988). Complete academic histories for this subsample of Indochinese students (including GPAs and standardized achievement test scores) were then obtained from the school district in 1986 and again in 1989 and matched with our 1983 data on their parents and households, producing an exceptionally in-depth data base on 340 secondary school students. Thus the design permitted, in a causally unambiguous way, the analysis of the effects of parental and family characteristics measured in 1983 on their children's academic achievement measured 3 and 6 years later. An analysis of the students' GPAs found that several student characteristics besides gender showed significant positive effects: the younger the students and the longer in U.S. schools, the higher their GPA; and FEP students (fluent bilinguals) clearly had an advantage over those classified as LEP (limited bilinguals). Objective family characteristics did not affect GPA directly, but two subjective variables did: (a) the level of psychological distress of the mother (the higher this score, the lower the student's GPA) and (b) the parents' score on an index measuring their sense of ethnic resilience and cultural reaffirmation (the higher this score, the higher the GPA of their children). The latter finding confirms similar results reported by Caplan, Whitmore, and Choy (1989) for Indochinese students in five other cities, but it runs counter to the conventional assumption that the more acculturated and Americanized immigrants become, the greater will be their success in the competitive worlds of school and work. Instead, it suggests an opposite proposition, parallel to the findings noted above with respect both to mental health and infant health: Namely, that Americanization processes—all other things being equal and to the extent that they involve subtractive rather than additive forms of acculturation—may be counterproductive for educational attainment.

But all other things are never equal, except in mathematical models, and acculturative processes always unfold within concrete structural and historical contexts. Exactly why and how the immigrant ethic—which appears to yield the positive outcomes reviewed earlier, often despite significant disadvantages—erodes over time in the United States, remain at present unanswered questions. It is also unclear (if not unlikely) whether additive adaptations, such as fluent bilingualism, can be sustained beyond one generation in the United States. In the end, however, the complex processes of assimilation to different sectors of American society will vary for different types of second-generation Indochinese Americans located in different types of familial, school, and community contexts—from the inner cities to the suburbs to diverse ethnic enclaves—and exposed to different types of role models and forms of racial discrimination. Bilateral relations between the United States and the countries of origin are also likely to affect not only future immigration flows but also entrepreneurial opportunities and the very nature of institutional life within established refugee communities in areas of concentration. Many outcomes are possible: from a "lost generation" of Amerasian youth in Boston (Terris, 1987), to the reactive formation of Southeast Asian gangs in San Diego (Rumbaut & Ima, 1988), to Vietnamese "valedictorians and delinquents" in Philadelphia (Kibria, 1993), to the predominance in the electronics field of young Vietnamese technicians in Orange County (Kotkin, 1994b). The future of Vietnamese, Laotian, and Cambodian Americans will likely be as diverse as their past, and will be reached by multiple paths.

Conclusion

Vietnamese, Laotian, and Cambodian Americans now form a sizable and diverse component of the Asian-origin population in the United States. They are the newest Asian Americans, most having arrived only after 1980; they are also among the fastest-growing populations in the country as a result of both the largest refugee resettlement program in American history—a legacy of the nation's bitterest and most divisive war—and of fertility rates that are among the highest of any ethnic group in the United States. They differ from other Asian Americans in significant ways, especially in the contexts of exit and reception that have shaped their refugee experience. They differ from each other in equally significant ways, and, if the research studies reviewed here are any indication, the Vietnamese, Cambodian, Lao, Hmong, and ethnic Chinese generations now coming of age in America will differ again from their parents. In their diversity they are writing yet another chapter in the history of the American population and society, and in the process they are becoming, quintessentially, Americans.

Notes

1. *Southeast Asian* is sometimes preferred over *Indochinese,* mainly to avoid any connection to the usage of the latter term during the period of French colonial rule. Southeast Asian, however, is a broad and imprecise term both geographically and historically, covering as it does a vast region and countries as diverse as Thailand, Burma, Malaysia, Indonesia, Brunei, Papua New Guinea, and the Philippines, none of whom share the fateful history of U.S. involvement during the Indochina War, nor of special U.S. sponsorship of refugees who fled after the collapse in 1975 of U.S.-backed governments in Saigon, Vientiane, and Phnom Penh. To avoid the cumbersome repetition of each of the nationalities and ethnic groups being considered here while retaining those more precise geographic and historical meanings, Indo- chinese will be used in this chapter to refer collectively to refugees from the three countries of Vietnam, Laos, and Cambodia. In any case, it should be noted that persons from those countries do *not* identify ethnically either as Indochinese or Southeast Asian.

2. Because only cross-sectional data are available for the Lao, they are not included in Table 9.6; however, IHARP data on the Lao have been reported elsewhere (Rumbaut, 1985; Rumbaut et al., 1988; Rumbaut & Ima, 1988; Rumbaut & Weeks, 1986).

References

Bach, R. L. (1984). *Labor force participation and employment of Southeast Asian refugees in the United States.* Washington, DC: U.S. Office of Refugee Resettlement.

Bach, R. L., & Argiros, R. (1991). Economic progress among Southeast Asian refugees in the United States. In H. Adelman (Ed.), *Refugee policy: Canada and the United States* (pp. 322-343). Toronto: York Lanes.

Bach, R. L., & Carroll-Seguin, R. (1986). Labor force participation, household composition, and sponsorship among Southeast Asian refugees. *International Migration Review, 20*(2), 381-404.

Baker, R. P., & North, D. S. (1984). *The 1975 refugees: Their first five years in America.* Washington, DC: New TransCentury Foundation.

Baskir, L. M., & Strauss, W. A. (1978). *Chance and circumstance: The draft, the war, and the Vietnam generation.* New York: Knopf.

Becker, E. (1986). *When the war was over: Cambodia's revolution and the voices of its people.* New York: Simon & Schuster.

Benson, J. (1994). The effects of packinghouse work on Southeast Asian refugee families. In L. Lamphere, A. Stepick, & G. Grenier (Eds.), *Newcomers in the sorkplace: Immigrants and the restructuring of the U.S. economy* (pp. 99-126). Philadelphia: Temple University Press.

Bouvier, L. F., & Agresta, A. J. (1987). The future Asian population of the United States. In J. T. Fawcett & B. V. Cariño (Eds.), *Pacific bridges: The new immigration from Asia and the Pacific Islands* (pp. 285-301). Staten Island, NY: Center for Migration Studies.

Caplan, N., Whitmore, J. K., & Choy, M. H. (1989). *The boat people and achievement in America: A study of family life, hard work and cultural values.* Ann Arbor: University of Michigan Press.

Chanda, N. (1986). *Brother enemy: The war after the war—A history of Indochina since the fall of Saigon.* New York: Macmillan.

Conquergood, D. (1992). Life in the Big Red: Struggles and accommodations in a Chicago polyethnic tenement. In L. Lamphere (Ed.), *Structuring diversity: Ethnographic perspectives on the new immigration* (pp. 95-144). Chicago: University of Chicago Press.

Desbarats, J. (1986). Ethnic differences in adaptation: Sino-Vietnamese refugees in the United States. *International Migration Review, 20*(2), 405-427.

Dunning, B. B. (1982). *A systematic survey of the social, psychological and economic adaptation of Vietnamese refugees representing five entry cohorts, 1975-1979.* Washington, DC: Bureau of Social Science Research, Inc.

Dunning, B. B. (1989). Vietnamese in America: The adaptation of the 1975-1979 arrivals. In D. W. Haines (Ed.), *Refugees as immigrants: Cambodians, Laotians and Vietnamese in America* (pp. 55-84). Totowa, NJ: Rowman & Littlefield.

Finnan, C. R., & Cooperstein, R. A. (1983). *Southeast Asian refugee resettlement at the local level: The role of the ethnic community and the nature of refugee impact.* Menlo Park, CA: SRI International.

Forbes, S. S. (1984). *Residency patterns and secondary migration of refugees.* Washington, DC: Refugee Policy Group.

Forbes, S. S. (1985). *Adaptation and integration of recent refugees to the United States.* Washington, DC: Refugee Policy Group.

Freeman, J. M. (1989). *Hearts of sorrow: Vietnamese-American lives.* Stanford, CA: Stanford University Press.

Gibney, M. (1991). U.S. foreign policy and the creation of refugee flows. In H. Adelman (Ed.), *Refugee policy: Canada and the United States* (pp. 81-111). Toronto: York Lanes.

Gold, S. J. (1992). Refugee communities: A comparative field study. Newbury Park, CA: Sage.

Gold, S. J., & Kibria, N. (1993). Vietnamese refugees and blocked mobility. *Asian and Pacific Migration Journal, 2*(1), 27-56.

Gordon, L. W. (1989). National surveys of Southeast Asian refugees. In D. W. Haines (Ed.), *Refugees as immigrants: Cambodians, Laotians and Vietnamese in America* (pp. 24-39). Totowa, NJ: Rowman & Littlefield.

Haines, D. W. (Ed.). (1985). *Refugees in the United States: A reference handbook.* Westport, CT: Greenwood Press.

Haines, D. W. (Ed.). (1989). *Refugees as immigrants: Cambodians, Laotians and Vietnamese in America.* Totowa, NJ: Rowman & Littlefield.

Hein, J. (1993). *States and international migrants: The incorporation of Indochinese refugees in the United States and France.* Boulder, CO: Westview Press.

Hendricks, G. L., Downing, B. T., & Deinard, A. S. (Eds.). (1986). *The Hmong in transition.* Staten Island, NY: Center for Migration Studies.

Hess, Gary R. (1990). *Vietnam and the United States: Origins and legacy of war.* Boston: Twayne.

Howard, K. K. (Ed.). (1990). *Passages: An anthology of the Southeast Asian refugee experience.* Fresno, CA: Southeast Asian Student Services, California State University.

Immigration and Naturalization Service. (1991). Immigrants admitted by country or region of birth, fiscal years 1925-1990 (unpublished data tables). Washington, DC: Author.

Isaacs, A. R. (1983). *Without honor: Defeat in Vietnam and Cambodia.* Baltimore: Johns Hopkins University Press.

Karnow, S. (1991). *Vietnam: A history* (rev. ed.). New York: Penguin Books.

Kelly, G. P. (1977). *From Vietnam to America: A chronicle of the Vietnamese immigration to the United States.* Boulder, CO: Westview Press.

Kibria, N. (1993). *Family tightrope: The changing lives of Vietnamese Americans.* Princeton, NJ: Princeton University Press.

Kibria, N. (1994). Household structure and family ideologies: The dynamics of immigrant economic adaptation among Vietnamese Americans. *Social Problems, 41*(1), 81-96.

Kim, Y. Y. (1989). Personal, social, and economic adaptation: 1975-1979 arrivals in Illinois. In D. W. Haines (Ed.), *Refugees as immigrants: Cambodians, Laotians and Vietnamese in America* (pp. 86-104). Totowa, NJ: Rowman & Littlefield.

Kim, Y. Y., & Nicassio, P. M. (1980). *Psychological, social and cultural adjustment of Indochinese refugees.* Chicago: Travelers Aid Society of Metropolitan Chicago.

Kolko, G. (1985). *Anatomy of a war: Vietnam, the United States, and the modern historical experience.* New York: Pantheon.

Korn, P. (1991, April 8). Agent Orange in Vietnam: The persisting poison. *The Nation,* pp. 440-446.

Kotkin, J. (1994a, April 24). An emerging Asian tiger: The Vietnamese connection. *Los Angeles Times,* p. M1-6.

Kotkin, J. (1994b, April 22). Immigrants lead a recovery. *Wall Street Journal,* p. A10.

Lam, A. (1994, February 6). Vietnamese: Should we laugh or cry? *San Jose Mercury News,* pp. 1-3C.

Lin, K., Tazuma, L., & Masuda, M. (1979). Adaptational problems of Vietnamese refugees: 1. Health and Mental Health Status. *Archives of General Psychiatry, 36,* 955-961.

Link, B., & Dohrenwend, B. P. (1980). Formulation of hypotheses about the true prevalence of demoralization. In B. P. Dohrenwend (Ed.), *Mental illness in the United States: Epidemiological estimates* (pp. 114-132). New York: Praeger.

Liu, W. T., Lamanna, M., & Murata, A. (1979). *Transition to nowhere: Vietnamese refugees in America.* Nashville: Charter House.

Martin, G. (1986, October). Phnom Penh, Rhode Island. *New England Monthly,* pp. 40-47, 105-111.

Mason, L., & Brown, R. (1983). *Rice, rivalry, and politics: Managing Cambodian relief.* Notre Dame, IN: University of Notre Dame Press.

Meinhardt, K., Tom, S., Tse, P., & Yu, C. Y. (1985-1986). Southeast Asian refugees in the "Silicon Valley:" The Asian Health Assessment Project. *Amerasia, 12*(2), 43-65.

Mollica, R. F., & Lavelle, J. P. (1988). Southeast Asian refugees. In L. Comas-Díaz & E. E. H. Griffith (Eds.), *Clinical guidelines in cross-cultural mental health* (pp. 262-302). New York: John Wiley.

Montero, D. (1979). *Vietnamese-Americans: Patterns of resettlement and socioeconomic adaptation in the United States.* Boulder, CO: Westview Press.

Owan, T. C. (Ed.). (1985). *Southeast Asian mental health: Treatment, prevention, services, training, and research.* Rockville, MD: National Institute of Mental Health.

Pedraza-Bailey, S. (1985). *Political and economic migrants in America: Cubans and Mexicans.* Austin: University of Texas Press.

Portes, A., & Rumbaut, R. G. (1990). *Immigrant America: A portrait.* Berkeley: University of California Press.

Rahe, R. H., Looney, J., Ward, H. W., Tung, T. M., & Liu, W. T. (1978). Psychiatric consultation in a Vietnamese refugee camp. *American Journal of Psychiatry, 135,* 185-190.

Roberts, A. E., & Starr, P. D. (1989). Differential reference group assimilation among Vietnamese refugees. In D. W. Haines (Ed.), *Refugees as immigrants: Cambodians, Laotians and Vietnamese in America* (pp. 40-54). Totowa, NJ: Rowman & Littlefield.

Rumbaut, R. G. (1985). Mental health and the refugee experience: A comparative study of Southeast Asian refugees. In T. C. Owan (Ed.), *Southeast Asian mental health* (pp. 433-486). Rockville, MD: National Institute of Mental Health.

Rumbaut, R. G. (1989a). Portraits, patterns and predictors of the refugee adaptation process. In D. W. Haines (Ed.), *Refugees as immigrants: Cambodians, Laotians and Vietnamese in America* (pp. 138-182). Totowa, NJ: Rowman & Littlefield.

Rumbaut, R. G. (1989b). The structure of refuge: Southeast Asian refugees in the United States, 1975-1985. *International Review of Comparative Public Policy, 1,* 97-129.

Rumbaut, R. G. (1990). *Immigrant students in California public schools: A summary of current knowledge* (CDS Report No. 11). Baltimore: Center for Research on Effective Schooling for Disadvantaged Students, The Johns Hopkins University.

Rumbaut, R. G. (1991a). Migration, adaptation, and mental health. In H. Adelman (Ed.), *Refugee policy: Canada and the United States* (pp. 383-427). Toronto: York Lanes Press.

Rumbaut, R. G. (1991b). Passages to America: Perspectives on the new immigration. In A. Wolfe (Ed.), *America at century's end* (pp. 208-244). Berkeley: University of California Press.

Rumbaut, R. G. (1994). The new Californians: Comparative research findings on the educational progress of immigrant children. In R. G. Rumbaut & W. A. Cornelius (Eds.), *California's immigrant children: Theory, research, and implications for educational policy.* San Diego: Center for U.S.-Mexican Studies, University of California.

Rumbaut, R. G., Chávez, L. R., Moser, R. J., Pickwell, S. M., & Wishik, S. M. (1988). The politics of migrant health care: A comparative study of Mexican immigrants and Indochinese refugees. *Research in the Sociology of Health Care, 7,* 143-202.

Rumbaut, R. G., & Ima, K. (1988). *The adaptation of Southeast Asian refugee youth: A comparative study.* Washington, DC: U.S. Office of Refugee Resettlement.

Rumbaut, R. G., & Weeks, J. R. (1986). Fertility and adaptation: Indochinese refugees in the United States. *International Migration Review, 20*(2), 428-466.

Rumbaut, R. G., & Weeks, J. R. (1989). Infant health among Indochinese refugees: Patterns of infant mortality, birthweight, and prenatal care in comparative perspective. *Research in the Sociology of Health Care, 8,* 137-196.

Shawcross, W. (1984). *The quality of mercy: Cambodia, holocaust and modern conscience.* New York: Simon & Schuster.

Strand, P. J. (1989). The Indochinese refugee experience: The case of San Diego. In D. W. Haines (Ed.),*Refugees as immigrants: Cambodians, Laotians and Vietnamese in America* (pp. 105-120). Totowa, NJ: Rowman & Littlefield.

Strand, P. J., & Jones, W., Jr. (1985). *Indochinese refugees in America.* Durham, NC: Duke University Press.

Terris, D. (1987, June 14). Kids in the middle: The lost generation of Southeast Asians. *The Boston Globe Magazine,* pp. 2-11.

U.S. Bureau of the Census. (1993a). *1990 census of the population, general population characteristics, the United States* (CP-1-1), Washington, DC: Government Printing Office.

U.S. Bureau of the Census. (1993b). *1990 census of the population, Asians and Pacific Islanders in the United States* (CP-3-5), Washington, DC: Government Printing Office.

U.S. Committee for Refugees. (1985). *Cambodians in Thailand: People on the edge.* Washington, DC: Author.

U.S. Committee for Refugees. (1986). *Refugees from Laos: In harm's way.* Washington, DC: Author.

U.S. Committee for Refugees. (1987). *Uncertain harbors: The plight of Vietnamese boat people.* Washington, DC: Author.

U.S. Committee for Refugees. (1993). *World refugee survey: 1993 in review.* Washington, DC: Author.

U.S. General Accounting Office. (1994). *Vietnamese Amerasian Resettlement: Education, employment, and family outcomes in the United States* (GAO/PEll4D-94-15). Washington, DC: Author.

U.S. Office of Refugee Resettlement. (1982). *Annual report.* Washington, DC: U.S. Department of Health and Human Services.

U.S. Office of Refugee Resettlement. (1985). *Annual report.* Washington, DC: U.S. Department of Health and Human Services.

U.S. Office of Refugee Resettlement. (1991). *Annual report.* Washington, DC: U.S. Department of Health and Human Services.

U.S. Office of Refugee Resettlement. (1992). *Annual report.* Washington, DC: U.S. Department of Health and Human Services.

Vega, W. A., & Rumbaut, R. G. (1991). Ethnic minorities and mental health. *Annual Review of Sociology, 17,* 351-383.

Weeks, J. R., & Rumbaut, R. G. (1991). Infant mortality among ethnic immigrant groups. *Social Science and Medicine, 33*(3), 327-334.

Whitmore, J. K. (1985). Chinese from Southeast Asia. In D. W. Haines (Ed.), *Refugees in the United States: A reference handbook* (pp. 59-76). Westport, CT: Greenwood Press.

Whitmore, J. K., Trautmann, M., & Caplan, N. (1989). The socio-cultural basis for the economic and educational success of Southeast Asian refugees (1978-1982 arrivals). In D. W. Haines (Ed.), *Refugees as immigrants: Cambodians, Laotians and Vietnamese in America* (pp. 121-137. Totowa, NJ: Rowman & Littlefield.

Williams, C. L., & Westermeyer, J. (Ed.). &6. *Refugee mental health in resettlement countries.* New York: Hemisphere.

Young, M. B. (1991). *The Vietnam wars, 1945-1990.* New York: HarperCollins.

Zolberg, A. R., Suhrke, A., & Aguayo, S. (1989). *Escape from violence: Conflict and the refugee crisis in the developing world.* New York: Oxford University Press.

Zucker, N. L., & Zucker, N. F. (1987). *The guarded gate: The reality of American refugee policy.* New York: Harcourt Brace Jovanovitch.

10

Future Prospects of Asian Americans

PYONG GAP MIN

In the previous chapters we examined the past and present experiences of Asian Americans as a whole and of six Asian ethnic groups individually. This chapter, the final of the book, speculates on the future prospects of Asian Americans. What will be the implications of the further growth of the Asian American population in the next decades? Will Americans accept Asian Americans better in the future? How will descendants of post-1965 Asian immigrants fare in their socioeconomic adjustment? To what extent will they maintain their native cultural traditions? Will second-generation Asian Americans achieve stronger Pan-Asian identity and unity than their immigrant parents? This chapter will try to answer these questions, using educated speculations.

The Impact of Asian Population Growth on American Society

As noted in the previous chapters, the influx of immigrants from Asian countries over the last 2 decades has led to a great increase in the Asian American population. Provided the U.S. government does not drastically change the immigration law, the current scale of Asian immigration will continue in the next 2 decades. Thus the Asian American population will continue to grow rapidly in the 21st century. The Asian Pacific population grew from 1.5 million in 1970 to 7.3 million in 1990. Population projections indicate that it will reach 20.2 million in the year 2020 (Ong & Hee, 1993).

271

We noted in Chapter 2 that Asian Americans are concentrated in several states, particularly in California, New York, and Hawaii. As a result of chain migration, Asian immigrants will continue to move to states with large Asian American populations. Consequently, the Asian American population in these three states will continue to increase sharply. According to population projections, the Asian American population in California will increase from 2.9 million in 1990 to 8.5 million in 2020 (Ong & Hee, 1993). Asian Americans will account for a large proportion of the population in Los Angeles, San Francisco, San Diego, New York City, and several other cities. These cities will surely influence the lives of Asian Americans, particularly new Asian immigrants. But Asian Americans will also have an impact on major institutions in these cities—education, politics, business, welfare programs, art, and other cultural life.

In the beginning of the next century, public schools in Los Angeles and other major Asian American cities will make significant changes in response to the tremendous increase in Asian American students. Public schools will hire more Asian American administrators, teachers, and counselors. Moreover, they will incorporate Asian languages and cultures in their curricular and extracurricular programs. American corporations are also likely to make necessary adjustments to the rapid increase in the Asian American population, as Asian Americans have greater consuming power than their share of the total population. AT&T, Coca-Cola, and other companies have already established Asian American marketing departments and have tried to reach Asian American communities with donations and advertisements. More corporations are expected to establish Asian American marketing departments to target the rapidly increasing Asian American clientele. At present, there are a few Asian American models appearing in TV commercials; we are likely to see more and more Asian American faces in the future.

The radical increase in the Asian American population in Los Angeles, San Francisco, and other cities will affect politics as well. It will help Asian Americans move into electoral politics as members of school boards, city councils, state legislatures, and even Congress. Asian Americans' large population will also give them bargaining power as a voting block. In the year 2020, mayoral and city council candidates in Los Angeles, San Francisco, and San Jose may not be able to win election without support from the Asian American community. Thus they will have to respond favorably to Asian American issues and agendas. Mayors of several cities with major Asian American populations will be pressured to appoint Asian Americans as high-ranking officials. On the national level, the President will be pressured to appoint Asian Americans to high-ranking positions in the federal government. Both Democratic and Republican parties are likely to be more active in their efforts to create links with Asian American communities.

The impact of Asian Americans on American culture will be no less significant. The recent wave of immigrants from Third World countries has already changed the Eurocentric American culture—art, music, dance, clothing designs, movies, food, and so on. Asian Americans have played an important role in the recent surge of the "cultural carnival." The popularity of the movie *The Joy Luck Club,* directed by a Chinese American, reflects the magnitude of Asian Americans' impact on American art, music, and movies during recent years. The increase in the Asian American population will result in a tremendous Asian cultural impact in 10 to 20 years. Asian immigrant artists, musicians, dancers, and film makers will introduce their cultural repertoires to the American audience, as well as to Asian Americans. The number and proportion of American-born Asian Americans will dramatically increase 20 years from now. Whereas Asian immigrants now struggle for economic security, many second-generation Asian Americans will pursue their careers in art. By amalgamating the cultural traditions of the mother country and America, native-born Asian Americans will develop uniquely Chinese American, Korean American, Indian American, and other multicultural American art, music, movies, and other cultural genres.

The increase in the Asian American population is likely to change American higher education institutions, particularly elite universities, most significantly. As noted in the introductory chapter, the influx of Asian immigrants has already changed the ethnic composition of students in the University of California system. Asian American students emerged as the largest or the second-largest racial group in several California universities. To meet Asian American students' demands, UCLA and other universities in California recently established Asian American studies centers or programs or expanded already existing programs, increasing the Asian American faculty and Asian American courses. Ten years from now, Asian American students will emerge as the largest group, outnumbering white students, in such elite universities as Harvard, Yale, Cornell, and the University of Chicago. These elite universities in the Northeast and Midwest will then make similar adjustments by establishing Asian American programs and increasing the numbers of Asian American faculty members. Thus Asian Americans will have a much greater political and cultural impact in major American universities than in American society in general.

Increasing Acceptance of Asian Americans and Their Cultures

As Hurh and Kim (1989) have shown, most Americans' images of Asian Americans have fluctuated over time, reflecting changes in international relations and socioeconomic and political conditions in the United States. When large numbers of Chinese laborers migrated to California in the latter half of the 19th century, Californians stereotyped them as unassimilable, immoral, or heathens. During World War II, Americans stereotyped Japanese Americans as disloyal or enemy aliens. However, Americans' images of Asian Americans have changed from negative to positive since World War II. They now stereotype Asian Americans as industrious, law-abiding, hard-working, intelligent, and successful. Most Americans now consider Asian Americans a successful "model minority," different from other disadvantaged minority groups.

Although most Americans' images of Asian Americans are positive, many Americans still stereotype Asian Americans negatively. Americans generally have positive views about Asian Americans' socioeconomic adjustment, yet many Americans consider Asian Americans culturally unassimilable. That is, many Americans still view Asian Americans as "strangers from a different shore." The influx of Asian immigrants with language barriers may have reinforced the image of Asian Americans as unassimilable. Many white Americans often ask native-born Asian Americans what country they were born in. This reflects the image of Asian Americans as strangers or aliens. Some white Americans cannot believe Asian Americans were born in the United States. Several years ago, I went to a farmers' market in Atlanta, Georgia. When I tried to bargain on the price of vegetables I selected, the white male owner of the vegetable stand screamed: "Go back to your country! Here, you cannot haggle prices." I responded: "This country belongs to American Indians. You go back to Europe." Certainly, many other Asian Americans have received the same "Go back to your country" rejection by Americans.

I speculate that Asian Americans and Asian American subcultures will be accepted more favorably in the future with a concomitant decline in anti-Asian prejudice. This speculation is based on observations of three major factors. First, as their number increases in the future, Asian Americans will look less strange than they do now. Even at present, the large number of Asian Americans in many California cities makes them more familiar to Americans. In 10 years, many white Americans in San Francisco, Los Angeles, and other cities will have Asian American neighbors. The increasing intergroup contact will make white Americans view Asian Americans less as outsiders or newcomers. The next decade or two will witness a drastic increase in the number and proportion of native-born Asian Americans. The increase in well-assimilated native-born Asian Americans is likely to alter Americans' images of Asian Americans as newcomers or strangers.

Second, partly as a result of the increasing emphasis on multiculturalism, Asian Americans and their subcultures will be accepted more positively in the future. Since the early 1970s, the increase in nonwhite minority populations, among other factors, has led to a change in government policy from Anglo conformity to cultural pluralism. Federal and local governments have encouraged multiculturalism in public schools through ethnic festivals, bilingual education, and multicultural curriculums. Many colleges and universities recently volunteered to adopt multicultural educational programs, significantly revising the traditional Eurocentric curriculum. As a result of both demographic and policy changes, nonwhite minority subcultures are now more positively accepted than 20 years ago. American governments, public schools, colleges and universities, and local communities will further emphasize multiculturalism in the 21st century. Various multicultural programs and a social environment tolerating subcultural differences are expected to enhance non-European minority members' ethnic pride and facilitate retention of their native cultural traditions. Asian ethnic groups, along with other minority groups, will enjoy the newly emerging multicultural environment.

Third, the increasing importance of Asian countries as economic and political powers will positively affect Americans' images of Asian Americans. In 1946, just after World War II, Japanese Americans were almost at the bottom of the social distance scale. But research conducted in 1956 and after indicates that Japanese Americans' rank improved significantly as Japan emerged as a world economic power (Bogardus, 1968; Owen, Eisner, & McFaul, 1981). Singapore, Taiwan, Hong Kong, and South Korea recently emerged as Asian economic tigers. In addition, South Korea and the Philippines recently established civilian governments, putting an end to dictatorship. Economic and political improvements in Asian countries and the establishment of diplomatic relations between the U.S. and mainland China during recent years have given Americans positive views both of Asian countries and people of Asian ancestry in the United States. At present, many Americans show great interest in Asian cultures, as evidenced by Asian language courses offered in many colleges and universities and various cultural programs offered by Asia Society. Asian countries are expected to play a more important role as American economic partners and political allies in the 21st century. This will lead Americans to view Asian Americans and their cultures more positively.

Asian Americans' Socioeconomic Adjustment

In Chapter 3 and in chapters focusing on particular Asian ethnic groups, we noted several problems in Asian immigrants' socioeconomic adjustment: underemployment and unequal reward, occupational segregation, underrepresentation in important positions, and class polarization. Asian immigrants will continue to encounter these problems in socioeconomic adjustment. However, native-born Asian American adults—whose number will increase rapidly—will do better than Asian immigrants in socioeconomic adjustment, moderating these problems.

The vast majority of Japanese Americans are native born. Their socioeconomic adjustment patterns are similar to those of white Americans in terms of rewards for their investments, representation in executive and managerial occupations, and more equal distribution in incomes. If native-born Japanese Americans' socioeconomic adjustment patterns provide clues to what will happen to other native-born Asian Americans in the future, descendants of post-1965 Asian immigrants will fare better socioeconomically than their immigrant parents. Let us see how native-born Asian Americans will compare to white Americans in rewards for their investments, representation in executive and managerial occupations, and income distribution in the population.

Although generally well educated, recent Asian immigrants, Asian male immigrants in particular, do not hold occupations commensurate with their educational levels. They are generally underemployed and underrewarded. Employers' refusal to recognize certificates and diplomas earned in Asian countries, Asian immigrants' job information deprivation, their language barriers, and discrimination against them all contribute to their underemployment and underreward. By contrast, native-born Asian Americans are better rewarded for their education and other human capital investments. Their earnings from human capital investments are close to white Americans' earnings. For example, a study by Hurh and Kim (1989) shows that when background variables were controlled, native-born Asian American men's earnings ratios to white American men' earnings were 95%, 93%, and 95% for Japanese, Chinese, and Filipinos, whereas two of the three native-born Asian female groups earned more than white women. In as little as 2 decades, descendants of post-1965 Asian immigrants may encounter even fewer barriers in the labor market than native-born Asian Americans at present. Therefore, in the future native-born Asian Americans are likely to gain rewards for their human capital investments almost equal to white Americans.

Asian Americans' severe underrepresentation in managerial and executive positions will also be mitigated in the future. An actual lack of leadership skills among Asian Americans, stereotypical views about their leadership skills, and failure to apply affirmative action to Asian Americans are the major factors for Asian Americans' underrepresentation in executive and managerial positions. We expect all three factors to change in the future. Asian Americans' lack of leadership skills has much to do with their immigrant status, particularly language barriers. As assimilated native-born Asian Americans move into the labor market in large numbers, they will overcome not only the language barrier, but also other disadvantages that partly stem from their Asian cultures. Moreover, the increase in the Asian American population in general and the growth in the native-born Asian American population in particular are likely to change stereotypical views of Asian Americans as passive, docile, and lacking communication skills. Finally, as the number of Asian Americans increases, governments, public schools, colleges and universities, and corporate firms will be under pressure to hire Asian Americans for high-ranking leadership positions. In response to the rapidly growing Asian American student body, many colleges and universities have recently hired Asian Americans as provosts, deans, admissions directors, and counselors. Governments, school districts, and private corporations will make similar adjustments in the future.

Another major problem in Asian Americans' economic adjustment is their class polarization. A larger proportion of Asian Americans are on the poverty line than white Americans, although for most Asian ethnic groups the median individual income is higher than or equal to the white median individual income. This problem too will be mitigated in the future. At present, Indochinese refugees, immigrants from mainland China, women divorced from U.S. servicemen, and a significant proportion of new immigrants from any Asian country generally suffer from poverty. The number of poor Asian immigrants will be reduced in the future. The influx of Indochinese refugees has already ended, although they will continue to bring family members to join them. The U.S. military bases in the Philippines were the major factor contributing to intermarriages between Filipino women and American servicemen. When the U.S. military bases were closed in 1992, the intermarriages significantly decreased and will continue to do so. Moreover, native-born Asian Americans, who will make up a larger proportion of the Asian American population, will be socioeconomically more homogeneous than the Asian immigrant population.

Assimilation, Ethnicity, and Pan-Asian Ethnicity

To what extent will descendants of post-1965 Asian immigrants assimilate into the mainstream? To what extent will they maintain their ethnic attachment? Is Pan-Asian ethnicity possible? The final section of this chapter speculates on these issues.

One of my colleagues at the UCLA Sociology Department told me that he was surprised to find that most of his Asian American students were culturally Americanized and had lost their native languages. Little research has been conducted on descendants of post-1965 Asian immigrants. However, my colleague's casual observation of UCLA Asian American students seems to indicate the level of second-generation Asian Americans' cultural assimilation. We measured Korean high school students' ethnic attachment, using a sample of Korean high school students in New York City (Min & Choi, 1993). Korean high school students showed a high level of acculturation in terms of using English and watching American TV programs. We found that only a small proportion of native-born Korean high school students speak Korean fluently. Because Koreans have only one language, it is easier for them to teach second-generation Koreans their native language than other Asian ethnic groups. Yet only a small proportion of second-generation Koreans have learned the Korean language in a satisfactory manner. Even smaller proportions of second-generation Chinese, Indian, and Filipino Americans are likely to have mastered their mother tongues. This high acculturation will continue to characterize second-generation Asian Americans in the future.

Gordon (1964, pp. 70-71) distinguished between cultural and social assimilation: He suggested that a minority group can achieve a high level of cultural assimilation, but that such cultural assimilation does not guarantee a high level of social assimilation. This social phenomenon—great cultural assimilation but lack of significant social assimilation—was observed in earlier Jewish and Japanese American immigrant groups (Kitano, 1976; Rosenthal, 1960). The findings from our survey of Korean high school students in New York City (Min & and Choi, 1993) generally support Gordon's theoretical view. Although Korean adolescents show a high level of cultural assimilation, their cultural assimilation and loss of an ethnic subculture have not significantly reduced their involvement in ethnic networks. Most Korean high school students prefer other Koreans as close friends and dating partners. Moreover, the vast majority show strong psychological ethnic attachments by identifying themselves as Korean or Korean American rather than as American. Young Koreans' strong ethnic identity and preference for Korean friendship networks are likely to increase as they grow older and encounter social barriers at college and at the workplace. The findings from our study provide important clues about the assimilation and ethnic attachment patterns that other second-generation Asian Americans might take in the future. Although the vast majority of second-generation Asian Americans will lose their native language and cultural tradition, they are likely to maintain a strong ethnic identity and to interact mainly with co-ethnics.

Finally, let us speculate on the degree of Pan-Asian ethnicity in the future. As noted in Chapter 2, Asian Americans consist of physically and culturally diverse groups. Their physical, cultural, and historical differences in experience make it difficult for Asian immigrants to develop Pan-Asian identity and unity. However, as analyzed in Chapter 2, Asian Americans' common values, the combining of all Asian Americans into the same racial group, and their practical need to protect their common interest in politics, education, social services, and other areas tie them together. As old timers and second-generation Asian Americans increase in the future, we expect them to develop stronger Pan-Asian identity and unity. Native-born Asian Americans can overcome barriers to Pan-Asian solidarity that stem from cultural differences and differences in historical experiences. Asian American programs recently established in many elite universities and various Asian American courses offered in colleges and universities will enhance Asian American students' Pan-Asian identity and solidarity.

In winter 1993, Japanese American students in Boston organized a demonstration protesting against the Japan-bashing movement in the area. Many Korean American students participated in the demonstration. When I visited Wellesley College in spring 1993 to give a talk for the Korean club, I asked Korean students why they believed Japan bashing was an important issue for them. They told me that there would be Korean bashing after Japan bashing. This reasoning would be impossible for Korean immigrants who vividly remember Japanese colonization. In fact, I found many Korean immigrants who reasoned that boycotting Japanese cars would help to sell more Korean cars.

Conclusion

This chapter speculates on future prospects of Asian Americans. Unless the U.S. government drastically changes the immigration law, the influx of Asian immigrants will continue, leading to a phenomenal increase in the

Asian American population in the next 2 decades. First, the significant growth of the Asian American population and its concentration in several cities will enable Asian Americans to have a greater impact on social institutions. They will have significant effects on public schools, private corporations, politics, culture, and most important, colleges and universities.

Second, Americans will come to view Asian Americans and their cultural traditions more positively. The increase in the Asian American population, particularly in the native-born population, the increasing emphasis on multiculturalism, and the increasing importance of Asian countries as economic and political powers will contribute to this change.

Third, Asian Americans' socioeconomic adjustment will be much smoother in the future. Asian immigrants will continue to encounter several problems in their socioeconomic adjustment—unequal rewards for their human capital investments, occupational segregation, underrepresentation in managerial and executive positions, and class polarization. However, native-born Asian American adults, whose number will increase at a faster rate than the total Asian American population, are likely to find these problems less significant.

Fourth, descendants of post-1965 Asian immigrants will be characterized by a high level of cultural assimilation but at the same time by a high level of social ethnic attachment. Most second-generation Asian Americans may lose their native language and customs, but they are likely to maintain strong ethnic identity and interact mainly with co-ethnics. In addition, second-generation Asian Americans will maintain stronger Pan-Asian identity and solidarity than their immigrant parents.

References

Bogardus, E. (1968). Comparing racial distance in Ethiopia, South Africa, and the United States. *Sociology and Social Research, 52,* 149-156.

Gordon, M. (1964). *Assimilation in American life: The role of race, religion, and national origin.* New York: Oxford University Press.

Hurh, W. M., & Kim, K. C. (1989). The "success" image of Asian Americans: Its validity, and its practical and theoretical implications. *Ethnic and Racial Studies, 12,* 512-537.

Kitano, H. (1976). *Japanese Americans: The evolution of a subculture* (3rd ed.). Englewood Cliffs, NJ: Prentice Hall.

Min, P. G., & Choi, Y. (1993). Ethnic attachment among Korean-American high school students. *Korea Journal of Population and Development, 22,* 167-179.

Ong, P., & Hee, S. (1993). The growth of the Asian Pacific population: Twenty million in 2020. In LEAP Asian Pacific American Public Policy Institute and UCLA Asian American Studies Center (Eds.), *The state of Asian America: Policy issues to the year 2020* (pp. 11-24), Los Angeles: LEAP Asian Pacific American Public Policy Institute and UCLA Asian American Studies Center.

Owen, C. A., Eisner, H. C., & McFaul, T. R. (1981). A half-century of social distance research: National replication of the Bogardus studies. *Sociology and Social Research, 66,* 80-97.

Rosenthal, E. (1960). Acculturation without assimilation? The Jewish community of Chicago, Ill. *American Journal of Sociology, 66,* 275-288.

Author Index

Subject Index

About the Contributors

Pauline Agbayani-Siewert is Assistant Professor at the University of California, Los Angeles (UCLA) with a joint appointment in the School of Public Policy and Social Research, Department of Social Welfare, and Asian American Studies. Prior to her position at UCLA, she was an Assistant Professor at the School of Social Work at the University of Washington. Her areas of research include cross-cultural mental health and the delivery of social services to Filipino Americans and other minority populations. She received her bachelor's degree in sociology and her master's and Ph.D. degrees in social welfare at UCLA.

Pyong Gap Min is Associate Professor of Sociology, Queens College and the Graduate School of the City University of New York. He is the author of *Ethnic Enterprise: Korean Small Business in Atlanta* (Center for Migration Studies, 1988) and numerous articles on Korean and Asian Americans. He is also author of a forthcoming book, *Korean Small Business and Reactive Solidarity.* Currently he is conducting research on ethnic attachment for native-born Chinese, Korean, and Asian Indian college students.

Setsuko Matsunaga Nishi is Professor of Sociology, Brooklyn College and the Graduate School, City University of New York. She received her Ph.D. from the University of Chicago and has done research on Japanese Americans during World War II in the Santa Anita Assembly Center, in early resettlement in Saint Louis, and in the postwar reestablishment of their ethnic community in Chicago. As consultant to the Commission on Wartime Relocation and Internment of Civilians on "social and psychological effects of exclusion and detention," she organized a research conference, testified before Congress, and co-authored, with John A. Clausen, the preface to the conference proceedings. Her main work has been on American race relations, focusing on institutionalized discrimination in complex organizations. Her current research is on life course effects of wartime incarceration.

Linda A. Revilla, a 2.5 generation Filipina American, is a Visiting Assistant Professor in Ethnic Studies at the University of Hawaii and a Research Health Specialist at the Pacific Center for the Study of Post-Traumatic Stress Disorder. She received her Ph.D. in developmental psychology. Her research interests are Filipino American identity and family, Asian American mental health, and Asian American veterans.

Rubén G. Rumbaut is Professor of Sociology at Michigan State University. He received his Ph.D. from Brandeis University in 1978 and has taught at San Diego State University and the University of California, San Diego. He is the co-author of *Immigrant America: A Portrait* (1990), with Alejandro Portes, with whom he is conducting a large-scale longitudinal study of over 5,000 second-generation immigrant youth in the Miami and San Diego metropolitan areas. He has published widely on Asian and Latin American immigrants in the United States, particularly on refugees from Vietnam, Laos, and Cambodia, and is finishing a book, *Between Two Worlds: Southeast Asian Refugee Youth in America,* with Kenji Ima. He is the co-editor, with Wayne Cornelius, of *California's Immigrant Children: Theory, Research, and Implications for Educational Policy* (1994). He has recently traveled throughout Vietnam and Cambodia, and to refugee camps in Hong Kong.

Manju Sheth, Department of Sociology, Rowan College, was born in India. She received her B.A. and law degree from Bombay University, and her M.A. and Ph.D. in Sociology from Temple University and University of Pennsylvania, respectively. She is the author of several articles on Asian Indians in America, especially those who live in Philadelphia and the southern part of New Jersey. A book on India and Asian Indians in the United States is in process. She serves as editorial consultant to publishers and professional journals on new and subsequent editions of textbooks on topics such as international relations, corporate crime, sociology of law, and criminology. She has been a founder and president of several regional and national professional organizations for international, multicultural and Asian American studies since 1988; she is now president of South Asian Sociologists. She is a consultant to higher educational institutions, businesses, communities, and the U.S. Census, Philadelphia office; as an officer and a leader, she has volunteered her services to community organizations for the last 20 years.

Morrison G. Wong is Associate Professor of Sociology at Texas Christian University. His research interests are Asian immigration, socioeconomic stratification, and social inequality. His publications have focused primarily on the Asian experience in America, examining such aspects as socioeconomic status and achievement, model student stereotypes, discrimination against Asians, female labor force participation, the elderly, Chinese sweatshops, and Asian immigration.